# *Bhakti-Yoga: The Easy Path of Devotional Yoga*

## From the Depths of Illusion
## To Making Contact with God

## The Practice and
## Philosophy of Bhakti-Yoga

### By
### Stephen Knapp

Dedicated to
My own spiritual master
His Divine Grace Srila A. C. Bhaktivedanta Swami Prabhupada
who gave the world, including me, this extraordinary spiritual knowledge, for which I am eternally grateful and trying to share with all those who are searching for the means to attain and experience the truth and bliss of the Supreme.

Copyright © 2017, by Stephen Knapp
All rights reserved. No part of this book may be reproduced without written permission from the copyright owner and publisher, except for brief quotations for review or educational purposes.

COVER PHOTO: This shows the joyful boat festival wherein the devotees give the Deities of Radha and Krishna a ride on a small boat in the pond next to the *pushpa samadhi* shrine of Srila Prabhupada in Mayapur, India. This shows one of the many kinds of blissful activities that are included in the path of bhakti-yoga, done for the pleasure of Lord Krishna, but which automatically makes all the devotees very happy.

    Numerous color prints and photographs of the various Vedic temples, divinities and artifacts can be seen, downloaded or printed for your perusal, meditation or use from the author's website at: www.stephen-knapp.com and www.stephenknapp.info.

ISBN-10: 1977610196
ISBN-13: 978-1977610195

Published by
The World Relief Network,
Detroit, Michigan

    You can find out more about Stephen Knapp and his books, free ebooks, research, and numerous articles and photos, along with many other spiritual resources at:

**www.Stephen-Knapp.com**
**http://stephenknapp.info**
**http://stephenknapp.wordpress.com**

# Other books by the author:
1. The Secret Teachings of the Vedas: The Eastern Answers to the Mysteries of Life
2. The Universal Path to Enlightenment
3. The Vedic Prophecies: A New Look into the Future
4. How the Universe was Created and Our Purpose In It
5. Toward World Peace: Seeing the Unity Between Us All
6. Facing Death: Welcoming the Afterlife
7. The Key to Real Happiness
8. Proof of Vedic Culture's Global Existence
9. The Heart of Hinduism: The Eastern Path to Freedom, Enlightenment and Illumination
10. The Power of the Dharma: An Introduction to Hinduism and Vedic Culture
11. Vedic Culture: The Difference it can Make in Your Life
12. Reincarnation & Karma: How They Really Affect Us
13. The Eleventh Commandment: The Next Step for Social Spiritual Development
14. Seeing Spiritual India: A Guide to Temples, Holy Sites, Festivals and Traditions
15. Crimes Against India: And the Need to Protect its Ancient Vedic Tradition
16. Destined for Infinity, a spiritual adventure in the Himalayas
17. Yoga and Meditation: Their Real Purpose and How to Get Started
18. Avatars, Gods and Goddesses of Vedic Culture: Understanding the Characteristics, Powers and Positions of the Hindu Divinities
19. The Soul: Understanding Our Real Identity
20. Prayers, Mantras and Gayatris: A Collection for Insights, Protection, Spiritual Growth, and Many Other Blessings
21. Krishna Deities and Their Miracles: How the Images of Lord Krishna Interact with Their Devotees.
22. Defending Vedic Dharma: Tackling the Issues to Make a Difference.
23. Advancements of Ancient India's Vedic Culture.
24. Spreading Vedic Traditions Through Temples.
25. The Bhakti-yoga Handbook: A Guide to Beginning the Essentials of Devotional Yoga
26. Lord Krishna and His Essential Teachings
27. Mysteries of the Ancient Vedic Empire.
28. Casteism in India
29. Ancient History of Vedic Culture
30. A Complete Review of Vedic Literature

# CONTENTS

INTRODUCTION     x
     Why so Many Quotes in This Book * Use of the Srimad-Bhagavatam

CHAPTER ONE     1
RECOGNIZING LIFE IN THE ILLUSION

CHAPTER TWO:     9
BHAKTI IN ALL RELIGIONS
     Bhakti: The Universal Religion

CHAPTER THREE:     14
WHY KRISHNA?
     Krishna as Bhagavan * The Attractive Qualities of Krishna * The Loving Nature of the Living Being * The Advantage of Devotion to Krishna * Srimati Radharani: The Feminine Aspect of Krishna

CHAPTER FOUR:     35
WHY BHAKTI-YOGA?
     The Easy and Joyful Path of Bhakti-Yoga * The Easy Release From Karma * Reaching the Goal of Bhakti-Yoga * An Overview of Bhakti-Yoga * Other Important Factors About Bhakti-Yoga * The Stages of Bhakti-Yoga

CHAPTER FIVE:     60
STARTING WITH FAITH

CHAPTER SIX:     64
SADHANA-BHAKTI: THE REGULATIVE STAGE
     Thinking of the Form of Krishna * Molding One's Life for Spiritual Advancement * Climbing the Ladder of Success * Attaining the Higher Levels of Bhakti

CHAPTER SEVEN: 78
ADOPTING THE PRINCIPLES
　　The Lord Accepts Our Devotional Mentality * Approaching a Spiritual Master * Association With Devotees * The Food We Eat

CHAPTER EIGHT: 96
RISING ABOVE MATERIAL DESIRES AND OBSTACLES AND ATTAINING THE SUPREME PEACE
　　The Main Factors That Ruin One's Spiritual Advancement * How the Immature Devotee Can Be Successful

CHAPTER NINE: 104
THE HIGHEST PRINCIPLE FOR THIS AGE–CHANTING THE HOLY NAMES
　　Chanting the Holy Names is the Recommended Process for this Age of Kali-Yuga * Some Important Benefits of Chanting the Holy Names * Chanting the Maha-Mantra Purifies the Consciousness * The Advanced Position of One Who Chants Hare Krishna * The Bliss in Chanting the Holy Names * Self-Realization Through Chanting * The Significance and Meaning of the Holy Names of the Lord * How the Maha-Mantra can Deliver All Living Beings * The Most Worshipful Object is the Holy Name * The Most Important Principle in Bhakti-Yoga * How to Chant the Holy Names

CHAPTER TEN: 142
GETTING THE RIGHT INSTRUCTIONS FROM A PROPER GURU
　　What is a Spiritual Master * Recognizing a Qualified Guru * The Rare Good Fortune of Meeting a Pure Devotee * Is It Necessary to Have a Spiritual Master? * The Importance of Approaching a Spiritual Master * Stages of Association with Pure Devotees * Transmitting Spiritual Sound * Taking Initiation of a Qualified Guru * The Significance of the Parampara or Disciplic Lineage * The Significance of Initiation * How the Spiritual Master Teaches * The Duty of a Disciple * If One Rejects His

Contents                                           vii

Spiritual Master * When to Reject a Guru * Conclusion

CHAPTER ELEVEN:                                    180
STARTING TO GET THE TASTE FOR BHAKTI-YOGA

CHAPTER TWELVE:                                    187
FEELING RECIPROCATION FROM LORD KRISHNA
      How the Lord is Ready to Protect His Pure Devotees *
Special Attention From Lord Krishna

CHAPTER THIRTEEN:                                  197
BEGINNING TO UNDERSTAND THE LORD

CHAPTER FOURTEEN:                                  203
ATTAINING LOVE OF GOD
      How to Attain the Stage of Love of God

CHAPTER FIFTEEN:                                   214
DIFFERENT TYPES OF LOVE FOR GOD

CHAPTER SIXTEEN:                                   219
THE TYPES OF DEVOTEES AND DEVOTIONAL SERVICE
AND RISING TO THE TOPMOST POSITION
      The Types of Devotees Practicing Bhakti-Yoga * Kinds of
Devotional Activity * Varieties of Activities After Liberation *
Rising to Pure Bhakti

CHAPTER SEVENTEEN:                                 236
THE OUTLOOK AND BEHAVIOR OF A DEVOTEE

CHAPTER EIGHTEEN:                                  243
HOW THE LORD REVEALS HIMSELF TO HIS DEVOTEE

CHAPTER NINETEEN:                                  252
ATTAINING THE EXPERIENCE OF GOD

**CHAPTER TWENTY:** 259
**BEING ABSORBED IN GOD**
    Reaching Trance or Samadhi in Bhakti-Yoga * Attaining Oneness with God on the Path of Bhakti-Yoga * Absorption in God is the Goal of Life

**CHAPTER TWENTY-ONE:** 268
**REALIZING THE HIGHEST LEVELS OF SPIRITUAL KNOWLEDGE**

**CHAPTER TWENTY-TWO:** 275
**ATTAINING YOUR BLISS: THE HIGHEST HAPPINESS IS IN SPIRITUAL ACTIVITIES**
    Symptoms of Ecstatic Emotions * Why the Early Vedic Texts Often Do Not Describe This Bliss

**CHAPTER TWENTY-THREE:** 291
**ATTAINING REALIZATION OF ONE'S SPIRITUAL IDENTITY**

**CHAPTER TWENTY-FOUR:** 298
**ENTERING RAGANUGA BHAKTI: SPONTANEOUS DEVOTIONAL ATTRACTION**
    How to Attain Raganuga Bhakti * Raganuga Bhakti Brings the Devotee to Krishna * Devotion in the Feeling of Separation

**CHAPTER TWENTY-FIVE:** 316
**ATTAINING LIBERATION AND ENTERING THE SPIRITUAL WORLD**
    How We Reach the Spiritual World * How a Devotee Attains a Spiritual Body * Attaining a Spiritual Body in the Mood of Your Devotion * Entering Krishna's Pastimes in Another Universe * Entering the Spiritual Realm * Additional Descriptions of Vaikuntha * Descriptions of the Lord's Supreme Abode * More Descriptions of Goloka Vrindavana * Entering Krishna's Confidential Pastimes * Conclusion

Contents

**CHAPTER TWENTY-SIX:** 352
HOW DEVOTIONAL YOGA BENEFITS OTHERS

**CHAPTER TWENTY-SEVEN:** 358
TELLING OTHERS ABOUT BHAKTI-YOGA

**CHAPTER TWENTY-EIGHT:** 364
HOW GOD CAME TO GIVE LOVE
  The Story of Sri Caitanya Mahaprabhu * Sri Caitanya
Bhagavat (Adi-Lila, Chapter Three)

READING LIST 378

GLOSSARY 380

REFERENCES 397

INDEX 408

ABOUT THE AUTHOR 419

BOOKS BY STEPHEN KNAPP 422

# INTRODUCTION

This book is a companion study to my previous book on bhakti-yoga called *The Bhakti-Yoga Handbook, A Guide for Beginning the Essentials of Devotional Yoga*. That was a description of the practice of bhakti-yoga, how to follow a morning program, how to set up an altar and do the worship, and how to follow basic etiquette and do the main kind of meditation for adhering to this path. This present book, *Bhakti-yoga: The Easy Path of Devotional Yoga*, is a much deeper study of the philosophy of bhakti-yoga with more elaborate explanations, based on Vedic *shastra*, on the reasons why we do things and how bhakti-yoga works, the spiritual benefits of doing it, and why it is the most recommended process in this age for rapid spiritual development. I try to use a conversational style of writing so that anyone can understand it, remember it, and easily apply it to their lives.

So both books should be used and studied together for a more complete understanding. Plus, at the end of this book, I have provided a list of additional books for further study and reference for those who are more interested.

One of the reasons why I wanted to write this book was because when it came to understanding and following a definite progressive spiritual path, there is none easier than that of devotional or bhakti-yoga.

I have studied so many kinds of religions, philosophies, yogas and cultures, and many of them are either too elementary, or they are expressed in a way that easily goes way over the heads and intellect of most people. So how can we expect that people will understand it if it is too nebulous, unclear, too lofty, or simply impractical? How can we expect anyone to take such a philosophy serious if they cannot comprehend it, or apply it to their lives if it is so vague that they cannot understand exactly what is to be done and how to practice it? In this age especially, when everyone is in a hurry and often want "instant enlightenment," it is not possible.

So we have to present things in a way wherein everyone can understand the path simply, clearly, and so they can remember it, and then easily apply it. And we also need to present that path which is known for being the most recommended for this age because of those reasons. This does not mean that the path of bhakti-yoga is the most watered-down, or the least effective, with the least amount of potency. No. But it is offered in the age, our present *yuga*, in which it is the most potent, most effective, and most easily understood and applied.

So that points to the path of bhakti-yoga, the path of least resistance and the most easily adaptable for people of this age. Of course, this does not mean that other forms of yoga are not important, or do not have as much to offer. They all have their value. But other forms of yoga, at least in taking them to the highest level of their intended development to reach the perfectional stage, are not as easy as we might think. Actually, in some forms of yoga, it is difficult to take them beyond even the most elementary levels of practice. But according to the descriptions in the Vedic literature, that is expected because of this age we are in, which is an age with so many distractions, difficulties, quarrels, and so on. Plus, humanity does not have the level of intellectual capacity as they used to compared to the Vedic age, nor do we have all of the basic resources, such as clean air, pure water, non-contaminated food, and so on that are important on the yogic path to provide us with clear-minded perception for meditation and gaining a focused insight into our spiritual identity. So we have to take these into consideration and use the path that is most appropriate in light of our present limitations.

For example, I have had talks with Westerners and Indians alike in regards to the language that the early Vedic texts use and the descriptions of things that are offered, and it is very difficult for most people to fathom the deeper meanings of what is being described therein. And, like I said, if they cannot understand it, they often will not pursue it. Therefore, many of the verses we find in the early Vedic *samhitas* need much explanation for us to see the deeper meaning held within, which often is not so easy to find and often results in indulging in mere speculation. Few are those who can intuitively see and explain the inner meanings accurately. They must be spiritual experienced to do so. And even if we are fortunate enough to know the inner meaning of such Vedic and Sanskrit verses, the next challenge is to know how to apply it to our spiritual practice.

These days people love yoga and spirituality, over and above fanatical religion. However, if it is too difficult to understand, or if there are so may other distractions, once there is a delay in being able to follow along with it, or some difficulty or some bump in the road in seeing how it can benefit us, people may put the book down and not pick it up again. Then you have lost them, and rather than being able to penetrate into the deeper understanding of what is being offered, they simply go on to something else or forget about it. So this book is an attempt to give people an easy way to engage in this form of yoga, which is especially recommended for this age of Kali-yuga, while still providing explanations of the complete path.

If God created this world, do not think He did not give us the means to get out, or at least to reach higher realms. But it does not require the use of anything material. It simply requires the change of our consciousness, when done in the right way. And the path of bhakti-yoga is the means to uplift our consciousness, to spiritualize it, so we can enter that supreme destination known as the spiritual world.

## WHY SO MANY QUOTES IN THIS BOOK

Some people ask why I use so many quotes, as if I have nothing to say on my own. There are a few reasons why I do this.

1. First of all, I want to show what the various Vedic texts have to say, and let them speak for themselves.

2. I also want to authorize everything I present. I do not want to just say something and expect the readers to accept it based merely on trust. I want to show where this knowledge comes from, and that this is verified in the Vedic texts or authorized commentaries. That offers more confidence in the reader in what I am saying, and is the way I would prefer a book to be if I was reading it.

3. Furthermore, this is the way the previous *acharyas* have presented the information in their books. This is the way Srila Krishnadasa Kaviraja wrote his *Caitanya-caritamrita*. And how Srila Rupa Gosvami wrote his *Bhakti-rasamrita-sindhu*. And how Srila

Introduction

Bhaktivinoda Thakur wrote his *Sri Caitanya-Sikshamrita* and other books. Many spiritual saints have written their books in the same way, using numerous quotes from *shastra* to verify it, and illustrate the message they are giving by examples taken from the various Vedic literature.

Also, it has taken much research and much introspection to organize this information in a way that I would hope will provide the reader a progressive understanding of all the information that is offered. Not everyone has the time to do so much research. In this way, they can see where the information is coming from and how it is developed into explaining the systematic process that can be applied in a practical step-by-step manner for the practice of bhakti-yoga.

Obviously, I admit, I do not write for everyone. But I try to write for those who want a summary study, using numerous sources of information, so they do not need to read every volume that is used as a reference, and so they can get to the conclusion of the topic quickly, but authoritatively. Then if they want to proceed more deeply, there is the list of references that can allow them to get the books to study for themselves. At least the majority of my readers seem to appreciate this. It is the way that I would want to acquire this spiritual knowledge if I was the reader. So that is why I do it this way.

## USE OF THE SRIMAD-BHAGAVATAM

I have researched all of the main Vedic literature, and use many references from an assortment of sources. But there are many reasons why you will find numerous quotes from the text of *Srimad-Bhagavatam*. First of all, it is described as the sound incarnation of God, and is also Vyasadeva's own commentary of his previous Vedic works that he compiled. This is described in the *Garuda Purana* like so:

*grantho 'shtasasha-sahasrah shrimad-bhagavatabhidhaha*
   *sarva-vedetihasanam saram saram samuddhritam*

*sarva-vedanta-saram hi shri-bhagavatam ishyate*
*tad-rasamrita-triptasya nanyatra syad ratihi kvachit*

"The work composed of 18,000 slokas, which explains the meaning of the *Mahabharata* and the *Brahma-sutras*, being full of the import of the *Vedas*, is the natural commentary on the *gayatri-mantra* and is called *Srimad-Bhagavatam*. It is the essence of all the *Vedas*, histories, and the *Vedanta*. Satisfied with the sweet taste of this work, one will have no attraction for anything else."

It also shows that beyond spiritual realization there is a level of perception which is the participation in the eternal, spiritual pastimes of the Lord, namely in Goloka Vrindavana, the supreme abode. Therefore, though the *Bhagavatam* contains many, many of the teachings of Vedic Dharma from beginning to end, it also includes in its Tenth Canto the descriptions of many of the transcendental pastimes of Lord Krishna.

The process of bhakti-yoga leads the yogi into various levels of self-realization and enlightenment. But it can also lead the yogi into entering the very pastimes which are described, providing that the yogi can attain the spiritual love that the residents of that abode have in their own transcendental relations with Krishna. And this is the objective of bhakti-yoga, which is what the *Srimad-Bhagavatam* ultimately encourages.

# CHAPTER ONE

# *Recognizing Life in the Illusion*

So what does it mean to be in the illusion? It essentially means to think that your real identity is your body, mind and senses, and forgetting your identity as the spirit soul within the body. This is called the bodily conception of life. And from this conception comes the motivation to do whatever it takes to make the mind and body happy and comfortable, and to try to reduce anything that causes misery or discontent and unhappiness. This simple misconception then expands to so many other areas of life, and why we do what we do, all for trying to become fulfilled on the physical, mental, emotional, or intellectual platforms of our existence. But since the body is temporary, and the mind is ever so fleeting in what it wants from one moment to the next, and because this concept has little to do with the eternal soul within the body, this is called the illusory existence.

The illusory energy in this world primarily means "that which is temporary," which can mean the results for which we work, our rewards, the objects of our desires, and the very body in which we exist. We may work so hard for what we want, but then it is soon gone or fades away, or our mind decides it was not good enough, or we want something else. So, working hard for that which is temporary is like working so hard for nothing at all. Because even if we get everything we want, ultimately time takes it away, or we lose it, and then we become disappointed. Or we forget that we die, wherein we lose everything anyway. But that means losing everything material. However, since we are actually spiritual in nature, whatever spiritual development we make stays with the soul. It is eternal and stays with us wherever we go. And that is the importance of spiritual progress.

While we are in the illusory energy and in the bodily concept of life, there are so many things we will think we have to do or want to do in order to be happy. One of the first things, which we can see with any baby, for example, is the need to eat, sleep and defend its existence. That is the most basic level of happiness. If we can get enough to eat, then we think we are happy and content. So one of our biggest motivations is to get enough to eat. With a full stomach, then we sleep in comfort. But, as we get older, we do not simply want enough to satisfy our hunger or fill our stomach, but we want specific food items to satisfy our sense of taste through our tongue. So then, in order to be happy, we want particular kinds of food, and then we are happy. But satisfying the tongue is compared to the pleasure of drinking tingling soda pop. As long as we have tingle for the tongue, we feel some pleasure. But it is very temporary and once the tingle is gone, then we have to find something else to occupy our sense of pleasure, or we need to get more soda to keep the tingling sensation going. That can lead to so many other attractions for satisfying the senses.

    The next form of happiness is the means to defend our existence. A baby may feel comfort and protection in the arms of its mother. So, with enough to eat and getting proper sleep, and now being protected, it is happy. So that continues in life with the sense that if I can protect my existence from threats, from natural disasters, from criminals, from being unemployed, and so on, then I feel somewhat happy with my situation. So there can be so many endeavors we undergo to make sure our existence is not threatened. In this endeavor we may try to get the right kind of education so that we can acquire the best career possible to make sure we have a good income. So we may have to spend so much time, money and energy to attain a certain college degree. Sometimes we also see when people have grown up in poverty, one of the most important things in their life is to become free from being poor. So they may become preoccupied with making more and more money, and in that way they feel successful and happy.

    However, this can also reach to the desire to control others, because if you are in control, then others cannot be a threat to you. So a person may go on to seek the ways of gaining more money or control by engaging in crime, or gaining a better position, a more influential career, or enter politics to attain more prestige. Politics may be something people enter at first to help others, but often politics is a system in which everyone must appease the desires of other politicians in order to get their support for what you want to do. Then it becomes a whole game of scratching each others back in order to get even the simplest things accomplished. Or backroom agreements go on so that everyone can gain more money, which is often one of the perks of being in politics. Otherwise, most politicians could not live on their own salaries. But it is all these perks that make politics a motivation for someone, often times at the expense of the people who pay taxes for whom the politicians are supposed to be working.

There may be the desire for physical happiness in the way we engage our bodies. On this level we may find happiness in different sporting activities, both in participating in them or watching others engage in various games. Or in keeping our bodies in good shape. Or in gardening, farming, or landscaping, construction, or other things like this.

Then there is mental and intellectual happiness, or the ways to make our minds feel happy and stimulate the intelligence. We may find some pleasure in the arts, or in poetry and literature, or in music which also satisfies the ears, or in other forms of entertainment. Some people may find pleasure by learning about the sciences, such mathematics, or history, or astronomy, or studying the mysteries of the universe, and so on.

Sometimes people resort to intoxication of some kind, which is like visiting the river of forgetfulness. Through drugs or alcohol, or even prescription drugs, we can forget our troubles, life's pains, our loneliness, or numb ourselves of the feeling of worthlessness, and other problems. But if we are not careful, we lose control over it and it becomes an addiction. This creates more trouble instead of solving our problems. Because then we have to get more money to keep the intoxication habit going so we can acquire our addiction, or there are damages from being drunk, either in our driving, the lack of proper social behavior, and so on. And if we come to our senses and realize how much trouble this is causing, then it often takes so much endeavor to get off drugs or alcohol. Then we may realize it would have been better never to have gotten started with such habits in the first place.

Then with most people, there is the need to find love, a deep exchange that we want to share with another person. After all, no matter how much we accomplish in life, it is hardly complete, in most cases, if we do not have someone to share it with. So, besides career and position, we want a loving relationship with someone. Then, even if we do not have a prominent situation or great success in something, we may still feel on top of the world if we know someone loves us, and we can love that person in return. However, many times it also takes a lot of effort to make a relationship work, many sacrifices of various kinds. And when they do not work and there is a divorce, then again there is much trouble and financial arrangements that need to be made.

Finally, if we are not completely satisfied with one or more of these levels of supplying happiness to the mind and senses, we may then seek out spiritual happiness. We may focus on following a religion to believe in, or look for a spiritual process to practice that helps us feel more complete, or to understand how we are not just this material body, but something beyond that. Then we may find a higher level of happiness above merely trying to satisfy the body, mind and senses.

Unfortunately, some people approach religion in order to satisfy their material needs, such as praying for bread, or house and home, and other facilities. Naturally, we need these things, and it is appropriate that we pray to God for His assistance, but real religion or spirituality is to attain a release from the material predicament in which we find ourselves. Not just pray for an easier way through life.

However, one thing to understand is that on the material platform of existence, everything goes through six basic changes, which includes birth, growth, sustenance, producing some by-products, then old age or decay, and then death. All of us go through these changes, but even ordinary ideas and action plans also go through these same changes. Nothing material lasts forever. Only that which is spiritual and is beyond the material influences will have any permanence. Therefore, everything must have a spiritual foundation for it to truly mean something or be of importance and have any serious duration. We can have everything else, but without spirituality we remain incomplete.

We have often seen particular people who seem to have everything, with great wealth, big houses, fancy cars, beautiful wife, or who even manage big companies, and so on, but who were nonetheless far from happy, and had to resort to alcoholism or drug abuse and other bad habits or addictions in their attempt to find wholeness, or dull the pain of feeling unfulfilled or inadequate. This simply means that most people need something more than material facility to feel complete and happy.

However, even if a person has reached happiness in some or all of these levels, there are still problems we cannot escape, and that make us realize the temporary nature of this material life anyway. These include disease, old age and death. Disease can strike at any time and in many forms. They may be short-term diseases, and others that are much more serious and can cause death. But they still must be dealt with for the discomfort that they cause.

Then there is the problem of old age, which not only causes the slow deterioration of the body, but certainly reminds us that our time here is limited. We can see the decline of the body in so many ways, whether it is the decrease in eyesight and hearing, or the loss of strength or memory, or the inability to do what we often took for granted in our younger years. Or, what is worse for some people, the increase in wrinkles and the loss of our familiar youthful bodily identity to which we had become so accustomed. This can cause quite an identity crisis for some people, when they are forced to adjust to the changes of the body caused by old age. This is also why the endeavor to look younger is such a widespread and profitable industry. People identify so much with the way they look, especially if they are attractive. They never want to lose that and it is so problematic when they do.

However, we should now realize that simply having the temporary body is the reason why we have many of these problems or difficulties. Three types of constant difficulties are because of the body itself, or because of other bodies or entities, and because of nature. The body itself requires so much care, and is not guaranteed to be everything you would like. Sometimes the body does things that we do not want it to do, or at the most inopportune times. Or we have troubles caused to the body by nature, whether it is dealing with the weather, like hot summers, cold winters, floods, hurricanes, tornadoes, and things like this that can take away our homes and ruin our existence. So we have to prepare for these possible situations as well. Then there are problems from other beings, like biting insects, barking dogs, or irritating neighbors, or the demand for taxes from governments, and on and on. These occur simply because we are here in this material world.

Then there is death, which can be viewed as the final loss of everything we have acquired, whether they be material assets, money, land, houses, or the loss of relations and anything else connected with the body. Then the body turns into earth if it is buried, ashes if it is burnt, or stool if it is eaten by other living beings. As the saying goes, for earth, stool or ashes we are taking so much care. The point is that it is all part of the temporary material existence for which we work so hard to take care of the body, mind and senses, when we are none of these things anyway. We are the soul within.

However, in this light of being the soul, death can be viewed as the final door to that journey from which we never return, and the means by which we can move closer to reaching a higher destiny. But again, this view requires spiritual understanding so that we can approach such changes with balance, equipoise, and a higher purpose than merely trying to work out the ups and downs of our material existence. This is the advantage of acquiring and developing a spiritual perspective on life.

Trying to satisfy the mind and senses is like trying to satisfy a fish out of water. It is only longing for its natural environment of being back in the lake or ocean. The soul is the same way, in that it, meaning you, will never be really happy or satisfied until it attains its natural environment of the spiritual atmosphere. Only then can you be truly content, happy and fulfilled.

The thing is that we may ask why does God allow all of these problems to exist. But there is a point to them: they provide the impetus to ask ourselves "Why am I suffering?" This leads to the question, "why am I here?" Then next is, how can I find relief, not just temporary release from anxiety and distress, but permanent relief and happiness? And as we realize the temporary nature of the material body, or even our house and home, the next question is: where is my real home? Where do I really belong? This is what we should be asking. In fact, the Vedic literature says that you are hardly even a human being until you reach the stage of asking these questions. Otherwise, you are like any other animal that works to find the means to eat, sleep, mate, and defend yourself.

Seeking the answers to these questions provides the motivation for looking at life from a deeper and more spiritual perspective. And if we do that, we will also realize the great opportunity of human existence, and that this body is a great portal through which we can not only acquire spiritual knowledge, but also realize our real spiritual identity. Then we can also begin to realize that as we have been looking for happiness, as we have been looking for love, we realize we have been looking for love in all the wrong places. If we want real and forever-lasting love, which often does not work out in the material world, we have to connect with the source. We have to connect with the Supreme Lover, which is God.

In this way, the human body is a fantastic vehicle, and life on earth is a great opportunity for spiritual progress. It is a great portal through which we can attain higher levels of existence. No other form of life, at least on this planet, gives this opportunity for developing ourselves in this way. It is the doorway for attaining the spiritual realm. So, we should rejoice that somehow and finally we have attained this human form of life. Therefore, now is the time for spiritual advancement. So let us not misuse or spoil this life by spending all of our time in material or trivial pursuits, or too much news, gossip, television, movies, or interests to appease the mind and senses, which always want more. The time we have is precious, and once it is gone we can never get it back. Therefore we must use our time wisely by allocating a certain amount for our continued spiritual progress.

The more we understand this, the more we rise above the problems of this world, and the less effect they have on us. As we engage in a proper spiritual process, the more our consciousness becomes spiritualized and the more we can actually begin to enter into a higher and more refined level of reality, and stronger connection with God. This is what can actually satisfy the soul, which automatically pacifies the mind. When we become content in this way, then we can find happiness wherever we go because it is within us. But this is our own internal and self-sufficient happiness which does not depend on the desires of the mind and senses. Actually, such desires then become very trivial and even meaningless. And then we long for the deeper happiness and bliss that comes from our contact with the spiritual atmosphere and with God.

This is the purpose of bhakti-yoga. It is a step by step process that takes you beyond mere faith and dedication to experience by direct perception your own spiritual identity, and a relationship with God. And this can be accomplished, as other gurus and acharyas have shown and guided us, as long as you take it to its full conclusion. But even a little progress can do wonders. Out of all the yoga processes, this is the easiest and most natural, which is explained as we move forward in this book.

# CHAPTER TWO

# *Bhakti in All Religions*

Bhakti or devotion can be recognized in all religions. It is not exclusive to only one path. However, someone may be very dedicated to their religion, but devotion is more than merely being dedicated. Dedication may be seriously following the rules and regulations, but devotion is when there are feelings of the heart in what you do, feelings of love toward your object of worship, which is God.

You can see such devotion in Christianity and the teachings of Jesus. This was, essentially, relating to God with love and seeing everyone as parts of God. You can also see this in the devotional habits and rituals of Judaism. You can see it in the prayers of Islam. You can recognize devotion in most of the indigenous tribal traditions around the world, whether it be in the way they acknowledge a great spirit that can be found in all living beings, or the respect they have for nature.

The essence of religion, as found in the Vedic, the Judaic, the Christian, the Islamic, and other cultures, instructs us to surrender to God. But that surrender is based on our devotional love, not merely a fanatical adherence to the rules and regulations. For example, when the Pharisees asked Jesus which was the great commandment in the law, he told them: "Thou shalt love the Lord thy God with all thy heart and with all thy soul, and with all thy mind. This is the first and great commandment." (*Matthew* 22.37-38)

Lord Krishna also taught the same thing in *Bhagavad-gita*: "Always think of Me and become My devotee. Worship Me and offer your homage unto Me. Thus you will come to Me without fail. Abandon all varieties of religion and just surrender unto Me. I shall protect you from all sinful reaction. Do not fear." (*Bg*.18.65-66)

Similarly, in the *Koran* (9.112) we find it said that those who turn to God in repentance and serve and praise Him, and engage in devotion to God, who bow down and pray, who do good and avoid evil, will rejoice. So proclaim these glad tidings to the believers. Also (in 19.65) we find it said that everyone should worship the Lord of the heavens and the earth and be patient in constant worship. For who is worthy of the same name as God?

In Zoroastrianism it is also believed that a person must live according to the religious tenets if one hopes to joyfully go before the Creator in the next world. The best of all such practices is the worship of God, for all are servants of God. So, one must lead a righteous life since it is one's thoughts, words and deeds that determine one's next life after death. Also, in Sikhism we find the precept that a true follower serves the Supreme Soul alone.

Even in the Vedic systems we find devotion in Vaishnavism in the worship of Lord Vishnu and Krishna, or in Shaivism in the worship of Lord Shiva, or in Trantrism in the worship of Devi or the Divine Feminine, and so on. So this devotion is advocated everywhere. In this way, you can find bhakti at all kinds of levels of intensity and in all kinds of religions. One must have such devotion to continue whatever line of spiritual development one chooses.

However, when we speak of bhakti, we are speaking of heartfelt devotion, not mere dedication and determination to follow the path. Bhakti is when you feel your heart's longing to engage in worship through love and devotion, which develops into a loving attachment to God. But the deepest level of bhakti, as outlined in the Vedic literature, can be found in the love of devotion that can be expressed to Lord Krishna, who is often called the God of love. God has many forms, but it has been recognized that Lord Krishna is the form of God who engages in the most and deepest loving pastimes with His worshipers, His devotees.

## BHAKTI: THE UNIVERSAL RELIGION

The word *religion* comes from the Latin word *religio*, which also means to bring back or bind ourselves to God. The Sanskrit root of the word *yoga* is *yuj*, which also means to bind, link, or unite with the object of our meditation. Thus, it is to unite the mind, intellect, the will, body, and soul to God, or the *jivatma* to the *Paramatma*, the individual soul to the Supersoul, through the discipline of yoga. Thus, there is no difference between the goal of yoga and the ultimate goal of religion. But it is the process of bhakti or devotional yoga which describes the system more deeply than what most religions offer, up to and including making contact with God, even in this lifetime.

Usually we find rules or moral standards offered in religions, such as in the ten commandments of Christianity. However, in bhakti-yoga we find the development of deeper and deeper levels of love for God that provide the means for more intense and intimate heights of connecting with God. This is far different than merely developing faith or devotion, but enters into tasting genuine loving sentiments to God in which there is a reciprocation between ourselves and the Supreme.

Since bhakti-yoga is the process of offering our love and devotion to God, bhakti-yoga is the means to attain our loving relationship with God, or uniting with God through our love. Therefore, bhakti is the universal element in most religions. This devotion is what expresses the essence of what religion is all about, and teaches us how to dovetail our loving propensity toward God. Yet, it is developed to varying degrees in various religions. This means that in some cases it is the worship of God in awe and respect, or even fear, while in other religions, like the Vedic system, God can be worshiped with heartfelt love, with a longing to be closer to God, not just on Sundays or other particular days when we dedicate our time, but all the time.

When we study the Vedic literature, we find that Lord Krishna's pastimes are most deeply described in the *Puranas*, especially in the *Vishnu Purana* and the *Bhagavata Purana*. Therein it also describes the kind of devotional relationships that a person can have with the Lord, such as in acting as His friend, or loving Him as a parent loves his or her child, or even engaging in pastimes as His lover. There is no other form of God, or in any other form of literature, in which such intense levels of bhakti are described. Most religions do not have such a conception of this kind of love for God. But these are the deep expressions of bhakti that a person can attain. And this can be attained through the process of bhakti-yoga.

This is why we explore the teachings of bhakti-yoga in the Vedic or Vaishnava traditions, specifically as related in the *Bhagavad-gita* and *Bhagavata Purana* and other associated texts. And when this is followed properly, a person can attain these emotions, or heartfelt feelings for love of God not merely in a future life, but in this life, right here, right now, in this body. Of course, we cannot take this cheaply, and this may not be possible for many people. But the point is, that if we take this process seriously, there is much progress we can make in spiritualizing our consciousness and the means we have to attain a loving reciprocation with God.

By uplifting our consciousness, one will realize his or her spiritual identity and know that the immaterial realm pervades everything within as well as outside this material creation. Therefore, one who has become evolved and detached from the material focus of life knows that he is a spiritual being and a part of the divine strata, which he recognizes everywhere. In this sense, wherever he goes, he is already home. A person who lives in this consciousness knows that there are only three things that are eternal: (1) the Supreme Being, (2) all the individual spiritual entities, and (3) the relationship between them, which is based on divine love. This is all that is eternal. And this spiritual love is all that has to be reawakened. This is the real goal of life. The spiritual strata, or fully enlightened consciousness, is where that love can manifest to the fullest degree. That is our real home and where we are meant to be.

If somehow or other the people of the world could give up their superficial differences and join together in genuine spiritual activity, the consciousness of society in general could change to such a degree that this very planet could become spiritually surcharged. It is not that we have to work for a specific change to bring about solutions to the world's problems, but when the consciousness of the people becomes purified, the solutions to the problems will become obvious and the necessary changes will automatically begin to manifest. Therefore, entering the spiritual realm, or changing the world in which we presently live, is simply a matter of reawakening our dormant divine consciousness. It is not a matter of outward observation or arrangements, but it is an inward process of transformation and development. Everything else will follow.

If the people of the world would be more inclined to recognize that spiritual advancement is a process of inner transformation and participate in this process, and share with each other the different levels of higher knowledge from other cultures rather than merely accepting one particular religious dogma while rejecting or even persecuting all other forms of spiritual growth, then it becomes possible for all of humanity to be a united people. After all, a true religion or spiritual process respects whatever level of universal truth is found in any other culture and religion. Everyone could band together with a common cause of helping each other become enlightened: A universal religion based on hearing about and glorifying the Supreme. Every religion does this, so why not do it together? The only difference then would be whether people were theists or atheists, and atheists are simply those who have no spiritual experience or cannot fathom the depths of divine knowledge.

Spiritually, we are all one family. The Vedic texts say in Sanskrit: *Vasudhaiva Kutumbakam,* "the universe is one family." And when we are on this level of consciousness it becomes obvious that all temporary material differences are superficialities. It is only people's own immature prejudice, caused by their spiritual ignorance, that stop people of the world from being united and cooperating together. Remembering that God is in everyone, and everyone is here by the will of God, and that God cares for all beings, you can respect anyone. It is simply a matter of everyone reaching that stage of perception. And bhakti-yoga can do that for us. So that is what we will be describing in the following chapters.

# CHAPTER THREE

# *Why Krishna?*

So when it comes to bhakti-yoga, and offering love and devotion to God, one question may be: To which God or form of God is the most reciprocal in our loving relations? Some people may even say there is a difference between the gods of the different religions, wherein one God is an angry and jealous God, or another has no tolerance for nonbelievers, and so on. And even in Hinduism there are so many *devatas*, or divinities that are worshipable, and so many forms accepted as Divine. So where do we focus our bhakti-yoga? The fact of the matter is that we can focus our devotion toward anyone we want. But with a comparative study, there is a Supreme Being that displays unconditional love toward all beings, all of His parts and parcels, but especially His devotees. That form of God is for whom we should search.

## KRISHNA AS BHAGAVAN

One of the first things to understand is that transcendentalists agree that there are three aspects of the Absolute Truth that we should understand, and these are the Brahman, Paramatma, and Bhagavan. Without understanding all three of these characteristics, our understanding of the Absolute Truth remains incomplete. However, once we understand and have reviewed all three of these aspects, we may then prefer to focus on one over another. Different types of yoga will focus on merging into the Brahman, while other forms of yoga will concentrate on realizing the Paramatma, the Supersoul in the heart of all individuals. And other types of yoga, like bhakti-yoga, will focus on attaining and reawakening our love for the Supreme, in His form as Bhagavan. Lord Krishna is accepted as Bhagavan, the

Supreme Personality.

As explained in the *Srimad-Bhagavatam* (1.3.28): "All of the incarnations of God are either plenary portions or parts of the plenary portions of the *purusha-avataras* [expansions of the Purusha, or the Supreme Being, Krishna]. But Krishna is the Supreme Personality of Godhead Himself. In every age He protects the world through His different features when the world is disturbed by the enemies of Indra."

"There are three kinds of spiritual processes for understanding the Absolute Truth–the processes of speculative knowledge [jnana-yoga], mystic yoga and bhakti-yoga. According to these three processes, the Absolute Truth is manifested as Brahman, Paramatma or Bhagavan."

"The manifestation of the impersonal Brahman effulgence [the great white light], which is without variety, is the rays of Krishna's bodily effulgence. It is exactly like the sun. When the sun is seen by our ordinary eyes, it simply appears to consist of effulgence." [1]

This means that the Brahman has a source, but unless we can see beyond its brilliance, like the sun, we cannot clearly see its source, which is described as the form of Krishna. So how do we see the source of the Brahman? Herein it is explained that there are different kinds of yoga that bring one to different levels of realization and perception. Through the path of jnana-yoga, or spiritual and speculative knowledge, you can reach a stage of understanding the Brahman. By engaging in mystic yoga, such as raja-yoga or astanga-yoga, you can reach the realization of the Paramatma or Supersoul within the heart of everyone, which is the localized expansion of the Supreme. But through bhakti-yoga, or devotional service, one can understand the Supreme as Krishna. [2]

Therefore it is recommended that the Brahman is only a part of the Supreme. You need to go farther in order to view the Supreme Personality and the spiritual pastimes that go on in the spiritual world. In this way, Krishna is the source of everything. But this must be realized, not merely theorized. And bhakti-yoga is the process in which we can do that.

Even in the *Bhagavad-gita*, Lord Krishna clearly says, "There is no Truth superior to Me. Everything rests upon Me, as pearls are strung on a thread ³... I am the source of all spiritual and material worlds. Everything emanates from Me. The wise who know this perfectly engage in My devotional service and worship Me with all their hearts." ⁴ ... I am the father of the universe, the mother, the support, and the grandsire. I am the object of knowledge, the purifier and the syllable om. I am also the Rig, the Sama, and the Yajur [*Vedas*]. I am the goal, the sustainer, the master, the witness, the abode, the refuge, and the most dear friend. I am the creation and the annihilation, the basis of everything, the resting place, and the eternal seed." ⁵

It is further explained: "Both the material and spiritual worlds are transformations of Krishna's external and internal potencies. Therefore, Krishna is the original source of both material and spiritual manifestations... Krishna is the source of everything and the sum total of everything. He appears as the supreme youth, and His whole body is composed of spiritual bliss. He is the shelter of everything and master of everyone." ⁶

Krishna is also called *sat-chit-ananda vigraha*, which means, as mentioned above, the complete form (*vigraha*) of eternal (*sat*) knowledge (*chit*) and spiritual bliss (*ananda*). Therefore, if we want to experience the highest joy and happiness, we need to connect with Lord Krishna.

## THE ATTRACTIVE QUALITIES OF KRISHNA

The attractive nature of the Supreme is further described in the *Caitanya-caritamrita* (Madhya-lila, 17.139-140): "The transcendental qualities of Sri Krishna are completely blissful and relishable. Consequently Lord Krishna's qualities attract even the minds of self-realized persons from the bliss of self-realization. Those who are self-satisfied and unattracted by external material desires are also attracted to the loving service of Sri Krishna, whose qualities are transcendental and whose activities are wonderful. Hari, the Personality of Godhead, is called Krishna because He has such transcendentally attractive features."

# Chapter Three

*Krishna playing His flute, a classic pose.*

Krishna is also called the ocean of mercy, endowed with inconceivable energies. Who is worshipped by all perfected beings, who is the source of all *avataras*, who is the Lord of lords, the most worshipable, the most forgiving, the protector of those surrendered to Him, the most graceful, the embodiment of truth, the most powerful, the friend of the devotees, the generous, the most influential, possessing all strength, the most grateful, and controlled by love. [7]

In the thirty-first chapter of the *Jaiva Dharma* by Srila Bhaktivinoda Thakur, Lord Krishna is described as follows: "Krishna is the color of a new monsoon cloud, pleasant, sweet, endowed with all good qualities, strongly built, adolescent, a good speaker, powerful, pleasing to hear, intelligent, a genius, mild, crafty, happy, grateful, skillful, controlled by love, grave, excellent, glorious, attractive to women, eternally fresh, performer of wonderful activities, most dear, and player of the flute... His sidelong glances bewitches the hearts of all. He is the transcendental ocean of wonderful pastimes, which inundates the hearts of young maidens with unlimited good fortune. Krishna, the repository of all transcendental divine qualities and of splendorous form, is the sole object of love of this mysterious *madhurya-rasa* [loving mood]. This divine Krishna will become increasingly visible in the heart purified by bhakti."

Many of the Gosvamis of Vrindavana who had personally realized the attractive features of the Supreme wrote many books about the transcendental personality of God. One of the greatest of these saints was Rupa Gosvami (1489-1564 CE) who wrote a list of Krishna's characteristics in his book, *Bhakti rasamrita-sindhu*. This list describes 64 different qualities of God that are mentioned in the Vedic literature. This again confirms that the Lord is not merely an impersonal force, but a person who interacts in every way with the creation and the living entities that are within the creation that manifests from Him.

The list includes the following qualities: 1) beautiful features of the entire body; 2) marked with all auspicious characteristics; 3) extremely pleasing; 4) effulgent; 5) strong; 6) ever youthful; 7) wonderful linguist; 8) truthful; 9) talks pleasingly; 10) fluent; 11) highly learned; 12) highly intelligent; 13) a genius; 14) artistic; 15) extremely clever; 16) expert; 17) grateful; 18) firmly determined; 19) an expert judge of time and circumstances; 20) sees and speaks on the authority of the scriptures--the *Veda*; 21) pure; 22) self-controlled; 23) steadfast; 24) forbearing; 25) forgiving; 26) grave; 27) self-satisfied; 28) possessing equilibrium; 29) magnanimous; 30) religious; 31) heroic; 32) compassionate; 33) respectful; 34) gentle; 35) liberal; 36) shy; 37) protector of surrendered souls; 38) happy; 39) well-wisher of devotees; 40) controlled by love; 41) all-auspicious; 42) most powerful; 43) all-famous; 44) popular; 45) partial to devotees; 46) very attractive to all women; 47) all-worshipable; 48) all-opulent; 49) all-honorable; and 50) the Supreme controller.

These fifty qualities, however, may also be found in varying degrees in some of the *jivas* or common living entities in this universe. But they are found in Lord Krishna to an unlimited degree. But besides these 50 qualities, there are five more which may also be manifested at times in the forms of Lord Brahma and Shiva. These are: 51) changeless; 52) all-cognizant; 53) ever-fresh; 54) *sat-cid-ananda-vigraha*--possessing a transcendental form of eternity, full of knowledge and absolute bliss; and 55) possessing all mystic perfection.

Beyond the above mentioned qualities, which may be seen in other forms of Divinity such as the *devatas* and demigods, Lord Krishna has the following exceptional qualities which are also manifested in the form of Narayana or Vishnu, which is His form as the Lord of the spiritual Vaikuntha planets. These, which cannot be applied to anyone else, are: 56) inconceivable potency; 57) uncountable universes are generated from His body; 58) the original source of all incarnations; 59) the giver of salvation to the enemies He kills; and 60) the attractor of liberated souls.

Besides the above-mentioned traits, Lord Krishna has four more qualities that are found only in Him, and not even in His forms of Vishnu, not to mention any of the demigods. These are: 61) the performer of wonderful pastimes (especially his childhood pastimes); 62) surrounded by devotees endowed with unsurpassed love of Godhead; 63) the attractor of all living entities in all universes through the expert playing of His flute; and 64) possessor of unexcelled beauty without rival. All of these qualities are those of someone who has a highly developed form and personality. Ultimately, these qualities are those of the form of the Supreme Being, Krishna, who can reciprocate in loving exchanges in a way that no other form of God or any of the demigods can manifest. You do not find such a loving reciprocation in the personality of Brahma or Shiva. This is why Sri Krishna is the God of love like none other. He is the actual basis and standard of loving affection.

"Of all the conceptions of God existing in the world, the form of Krishna is the most suitable for developing pure love. The conception of Allah in the Koran is not suitable for developing pure love. Even the dear prophet of the Lord could not see the form of Allah, for, although the Lord is friendly, He remains at a distance from the worshipper because of the conception of God as the 'Master' [which stifles the mood of loving reciprocation since it is outweighed by respect, fear, awe, and reverence]. God as perceived in the Christian faith is also a distant entity, what to speak of the impersonalists' concept of the quality-less Brahman. Even Narayana, certainly a personal form, is not the form by which the soul can most easily obtain pure love. Krishna alone, who resides in the spiritual abode of Vraja [Vrindavana], is the object of pure love." [8]

In this way, Krishna is the form of God that embodies spiritual loving mellows or loving relational moods, also called *rasa*, to the highest degree. This is also described in the *Taittiriya Upanishad* (2.7), "The Absolute Truth is the reservoir for all kinds of reciprocal exchanges of loving sentiments."

## THE LOVING NATURE OF THE LIVING BEING

The living being is spiritually a part and parcel of the lord, even though the living entities may become entrapped by material attractions and contamination, and then experiences whatever joys or suffers all the miseries of material existence, compared to its fully spiritual and blissful position when purified. The material energy is called the inferior energy of the Supreme, while the living beings are considered the marginal potency, the *tatastha-shakti*. This means that though the living being is a completely spiritual parcel of God, it can identify as being a part of the material energy when it identifies itself as the material body. But when purified of material contamination, it can be part of the spiritual realm.

However, because the living being is a natural part and expansion of God, it is naturally connected with the Lord and has a inherent tendency to love God. As it is explained: "Pure love for Krishna is eternally established in the hearts of the living entities. It is not something to be gained from another source. When the heart is purified by hearing and chanting [about Krishna], the living entity naturally awakens [to its normal constitutional position as a pure spirit soul in a loving relationship with the Lord]." [9]

In this way, love is a natural condition of the soul. This is why, while in the material world, the living being becomes attracted to many forms of the energy of God, and is also looking for a loving relationship. If the person cannot find love with another person, then he or she may get a pet in which there is some object for the soul's love, when actually we are looking for the supreme most lovable object, which is Krishna, the god of loving reciprocation. In fact, Krishna is said to be the perfect master, and best friend. [10]

## THE ADVANTAGE OF DEVOTION TO KRISHNA

There is a natural inherent inclination to love in the soul, and we are either expressing love for someone or something, or our actions are a calling for love or crying for love, or a show and feeling of frustration because we cannot find love. And the epitome of that love is to reawaken one's love for God. That is the purpose of bhakti-yoga. Within the process of bhakti-yoga, there are three basic sources that are used to empower the individual to reawaken that love, and that is the experienced guru who can teach us the way, the Vedic texts and their explanations, and the other devotees who can share their advice and guide a person along the way in attaining that love.

In the material atmosphere, there are four types of people who become motivated to search out the means for peace of mind, or the purpose of life, and then go forward to seek or offer their love and service to Krishna. This is described in the *Bhagavad-gita* (7.16-17) where Krishna explains that four kinds of pious men render devotional service to Him: 1) those who are distressed, or those looking for solutions to their material problems; 2) the desirer of wealth, or those who want to overcome their problems by gaining money or influence; 3) the inquisitive, or those who are looking for answers to the mysteries of the universe and the purpose of life; and 4) those searching for knowledge, or those who want to know more about how to attain the goal of life. However, the wise one who is already in knowledge about Krishna and is in union with Krishna through devotional service is the best. For Krishna is very dear to him and he is very dear to Krishna.

Lord Krishna says that, "After many births and deaths, he who is actually in knowledge surrenders unto Me, knowing Me to be the cause of all causes and all that is. Such a great soul is very rare."[11]

There are also those who gain the favor of Lord Krishna by their bhakti or devotion and become very, very dear to Him. As Lord Krishna describes in *Bhagavad-gita* (9.22): "For those who worship Me with devotion, meditating on My transcendental form–to them I carry what they lack and preserve what they have."

This means that whatever abilities, qualities and devotion a person has developed, or not yet acquired, Krishna will assist that person in the ways to return to Him. Then Krishna goes on to say: "I envy no one, nor am I partial to anyone. I am equal to all. But whoever renders service unto Me in devotion is a friend, is in Me, and I am also a friend to him... He quickly becomes righteous and attains lasting peace. O son of Kunti [Arjuna], declare it boldly that My devotee never perishes.[12]

For anyone who becomes Krishna's friend through such devotion, He assures that person of being delivered to the spiritual world. "For one who worships Me, giving up all activities unto Me and being devoted to Me without deviation, engaged in devotional service [bhakti-yoga] and always meditating upon Me, who has fixed his mind upon Me, O son of Pritha, for him I am the swift deliverer from the ocean of birth and death."[13]

"Always think of Me and become My devotee. Worship Me

and offer your homage unto Me. Thus you will come to Me without fail. I promise you this because you are My very dear friend. Abandon all varieties of religion and just surrender unto Me [through the process of bhakti-yoga]. I shall deliver you from all sinful reaction. Do not fear." [14]

By reaching Krishna, or simply by reaching the stage of life after many lifetimes wherein we accept the process of bhakti-yoga to Lord Krishna, means that we have attained an extraordinary accomplishment in our evolutionary development. In fact, it accomplishes all other duties of life, and achieves the goal of all other spiritual processes. The *Srimad-Bhagavatam* (4.31.14) begins to explain, "By pouring water on the root of a tree, one automatically satisfies the trunk, branches and twigs. Similarly, by supplying food to the stomach, where it nourishes the life air, one satisfies all the senses. In the same way, by worshiping Krishna and rendering Him service, one automatically satisfies all the *devatas* [or demigods]."

This indicates that all the duties of life are accomplished by approaching the Supreme Lord through this process. Furthermore, under the shelter of Lord Krishna, a person is relieved of the greatest kind of fear and danger. That is the fear of descending into the lower species of life after death. What have we done if we still have not attained this? Even a small amount of spiritual advancement in bhakti-yoga assures a person that he or she will certainly continue in their progress by no less than attaining a human birth in their next existence.

Lord Krishna further explains to Uddhava in the *Srimad-Bhagavatam* (11.20.32-33), "Everything that can be achieved by fruitive activities, penance, knowledge, detachment, mystic yoga, charity, religious duties, and all other means for perfecting life is easily achieved by My devotee through loving service unto Me. If somehow or other My devotee desires promotion to heaven, liberation, or residence in My abode, he easily achieves such benedictions."

In this way, worshiping Lord Krishna accomplishes the results of any other process of spiritual development. As also said in *Srimad-Bhagavatam* (8.16.21) in a conversation between Kashyapa Muni and Aditi, "The Supreme Personality of Godhead, who is very merciful to the poor, will fulfill all of your desires, for devotional service to Him is infallible. Any method other than devotional service is useless. That is my opinion."

When Lord Krishna, the center of all happiness, becomes the center of one's life, all activities can become blissful. This is why even the sages who are established in the Brahman realization become attracted to Lord Krishna. The pleasure of contact with and service to Krishna outweighs whatever bliss comes from the Brahman experience.

Bilvamangala Thakur wrote in his book, *Krishna-karnamrita*, "Let the impersonalists be engaged in the process of transcendental realization by worshiping the impersonal Brahman. Although I was also initiated into that path of Brahman realization, I have now become misled by a naughty boy [Krishna], who is very cunning, and who has made me His maidservant. So I have now forgotten the process of Brahman realization." [15]

This is also why Adi Shankaracharya, the great teacher of the *advaita* or impersonalist philosophy for realizing the Brahman effulgence, has advised in the first verse of his prayer called *Bhaja Govindam* that everyone should worship Govinda [Krishna]:

*bhajagovindam bhajagovindam*
*govindam bhajamuudhamate*
*sampraapte sannihite kaale*
*nahi nahi rakshati dukrijnkarane*

"Worship Govinda, Worship Govinda, Worship Govinda. Oh fool! Rules of Grammar will not save you at the time of your death."

Even in verse thirty-four of this prayer, Adi Shankaracharya again emphasizes this point:

*bhajagovindam bhajagovindam*
*govindam bhajamuudhamate*
*naamasmaranaadanyamupaayam*
*nahi pashyaamo bhavatarane*

"Worship Govinda, worship Govinda, worship Govinda, Oh fool! Other than chanting the Lord's names, there is no other way to cross the life's ocean."

There is a story attached to the composition of this Hymn. It is said that Shankara was walking along a street in Varanasi one day, accompanied by his disciples. He heard an old scholar teaching his grammatical rules. Taking pity on him, he went up and advised him not to waste his time on grammar at his age but to turn his mind to God in worship and adoration. The *Hymn to Govinda* was composed on this occasion. Besides the refrain of the song beginning with the words *Bhaja Govindam*, Shankara is said to have sung twelve verses, hence the hymn bears the title *Dvadasamanjarika-Stotra* (A hymn which is a bunch of twelve verse-blossoms). The fourteen disciples who were with the Master then are believed to have added one verse each. These fourteen verses are together called *Chaturdasa-manjarika-Stotra* (A hymn which is a bunch of fourteen verse-blossoms).

It is in this prayer that he emphasizes above all else the importance for developing devotion for Lord Krishna, which is the principle means for attaining the grace for the Supreme, and the freedom from further rounds of reincarnating in material existence. It is this prayer that leaves us no doubt that his final instruction was to give up our egotistical differences and surrender to Lord Krishna. It also encapsulates the sum and substance of all Vedantic thought in whatever other works that he had written. [16]

Also, you can visit the birthplace of Adi Shankaracharya in Kaladi, a small town north of Vaikom, just east of Angamaly by 10 kilometers along the banks of the Periyar River. The main attraction in town is the Shankara Janmasthan, or Shankara birthplace. This is enclosed in a complex with several shrines. As you approach it and look toward the front gate of the pavilion, directly to your right is the temple of Lord Krishna that has a deity of Krishna that was installed by Shankara himself, proving that in spite of his impersonalistic preaching he was actually a devotee of Krishna. It is said that Shankara established this deity especially for his mother, so his mother could worship Lord Krishna. So even Shankara was aware of the advantages of worshiping Lord Krishna and engaging in bhakti-yoga. Otherwise, why did he not teach his own mother the impersonal philosophy and the means to realize the great Brahman instead of worshiping Lord Krishna?

More about the characteristics and qualities of Lord Krishna can be found in my book, *Lord Krishna and His Essential Teachings*.

## SRIMATI RADHARANI: THE FEMININE ASPECT OF KRISHNA

Krishna also has a feminine aspect that for some devotees is even more attractive than Lord Krishna Himself, simply because of the mercy and compassion She shows toward all devotees. So they have great attraction in engaging in service to Her.

Srimati Radharani is the Supreme Goddess. She is most always seen with Lord Krishna. It is described that She is the Chief Associate and devotee of Lord Krishna, and topmost of all Goddesses. Her name means the She is the most excellent worshiper of Lord Krishna. However, She is also an expansion of the Lord's energy. Since She is also an extension of Krishna, She is the feminine aspect of God. Thus, in the Gaudiya Vaishnava tradition, God is both male and female. They are One, but Krishna expands into two, Himself and Radharani, for the sake of divine loving pastimes. If They remained as One, then there is no relationship, there are no pastimes, and there can be no dynamic exchange of love. [17]

Actually, if we all remained merged or amalgamated into one single force or light, then there is no further need of anything else. There certainly would be no need for the material manifestation to provide the innumerable conditioned souls with the means to seek out the way to satisfy their senses, minds, emotions, desires for self-expression, intellectual pursuits, and on and on. They could all remain floating in an ocean of eternal light. But not everyone wants that, and there is a reason why.

So, the spiritual world is the manifestation wherein all souls have the opportunity to engage in a multitude of pastimes in loving relationships in full spiritual variety, without the many hindrances we find in this material world. The only difference is that the spiritual world is centered around the Supreme Being. And that Supreme Personality has expanded Himself into Radharani for exhibiting the supreme loving relationship, in which so many others assist Them.

In the *Brihad-Gautamiya Tantra*, Radharani is described as follows:

> *devi krishna-mayi prokta*
> *radhika para-devata*
> *sarva-lakshmi-mayi sarva*
> *kantih sammohini para*

"The transcendental goddess Srimati Radharani is the direct counterpart of Lord Sri Krishna. She is the central figure for all the goddesses of fortune. She possesses all the attractiveness to attract the all-attractive Personality of Godhead. She is the primeval internal potency of the Lord."

To explain further, Srimati Radharani is also the source of the other goddesses, who are expansions of Her. Just as Lord Krishna is the source of all other expansions and incarnations of God, Radharani is the source of all other expansions of the energies of God, the *shaktis*, or other goddesses. Thus, Vishnu, Rama, even Shiva are all expansions of the one Supreme Being, and similarly Lakshmi, Sita, and even Durga are all expansions of this Supreme Feminine form of God, Radharani.

It is explained that the beloved consorts of Lord Krishna are of three kinds, namely the goddesses of fortune or Lakshmis, His queens in Vaikuntha, and the milkmaids of Vraja called the *gopis*. All of them proceed from Radharani. The Lakshmis are partial manifestations, or plenary portions of Srimati Radharani, while the queens in Vaikuntha and in Dvaraka are reflections of Her image. The Vraja-devis or *gopis* are Her expansions and assist in the increase of *rasa*, or the mood and taste of divine loving pastimes. Among them there are many groups that have various sentiments and moods, which help Lord Krishna taste the sweetness of the *rasa* dance and other pastimes.[18]

"Among the *gopis* of Vrindavana, Srimati Radharani and

another *gopi* are considered chief. However, when we compare the *gopis*, it appears that Srimati Radharani is most important because Her real feature expresses the highest ecstasy of love. The ecstasy of love experienced by the other *gopis* cannot be compared to that of Srimati Radharani." [19]

Radharani has many names according to Her qualities and characteristics. Some of the names that Radharani is known by include Govinda-anandini--She who gives pleasure to Govinda [Krishna]; Govinda-mohini--She who mystifies Govinda; Govinda-sarvasa--the all-in-all of Lord Govinda; Shiromani Sarva-kanta--the crown jewel of all the Lord's consorts; and Krishnamayi--the one who sees Krishna both within and without. She is also called Radhika in the *Puranas* because Her worship [*aradhana*] of the Lord consists of fulfilling His desires. *Aradhana* is the root of the name Radharani, which indicates one who excels in worshiping the Lord. She is also called Sarva-lakshmi, the original source of all the goddesses of fortune. This also means that She is the supreme energy of Lord Krishna, and represents His six opulences, which include fame, fortune, strength, wealth, knowledge, and detachment. She is also known as Sarva-kanti, which indicates that all beauty and luster rest in Her spiritual body, and all the Lakshmis derive their beauty from Her. It also means that all the desires of Lord Krishna rest in Srimati Radharani. As Lord Krishna enchants the world with His beauty and charm, Sri Radha enchants Him. Therefore She is the Supreme Goddess. Sri Radha is the full power, and Lord Krishna is the possessor of full power. [20] Thus, the two are non-different, as the sunshine is nondifferent from the sun, or as the energy is non-different from the energetic or source of energy.

In this way, without Radha there is no meaning to Krishna and without Krishna there is no meaning to Radha. Because of this, in the Vaishnava tradition we always pay respects first to the Lord's internal energy in the form of Radha, and then to the Lord. Thus They are referred to as Radha-Krishna, or in other names as Sita-Rama, Lakshmi-Narayana, and so on. In this way, Radha and Krishna are one, but when Lord Krishna wants to enjoy, He manifests Himself as Radharani. Otherwise, there is no energy in which Krishna can attain pleasure outside Himself.

## Chapter Three

*Srimati Radharani, the feminine aspect of God, Sri Krishna.*

To understand Himself through the agency of Radha, or the *hladini-shakti*, the Lord manifests Himself as Lord Sri Caitanya Mahaprabhu, who is Lord Krishna but with the super-excellent emotions of Radharani's love toward Lord Krishna. This is because the Lord accepts a position and the emotions of a devotee in order to fully taste His own sweetness.

It is also described that the potency of love of God is called *hladini*, the Lord's pleasure potency. Whenever the Lord wants to enjoy pleasure, He exhibits His own spiritual potency known as *hladini*. And the essence of that love is in the emotion called *bhava*. The ultimate development of that emotion is *mahabhava*, or great *bhava*. Mahabhava is the mood that is full of the pleasure potency, and it is an exhibition of the highest love for Lord Krishna. Sri Radharani is the embodiment of that transcendental consciousness found in *mahabhava*. Her mind, senses and body are steeped in that highest sort of love for Krishna. She is as spiritual as the Lord Himself. In fact, being the personification of the *hladini-shakti*, the pleasure giving energy of the Lord, She is the only source of enjoyment for the Lord. This pleasure potency manifests spiritually as Radharani in a way that attracts even Lord Krishna. He takes no pleasure in anything material.

The Lord could never enjoy anything that is less spiritual than Himself. Therefore Radha and Krishna are identical. Then She expands Herself into different forms, known as Lalita, Visakha, and Her other confidential associates that increase the mood of divine love. However, being the Lord's *hladini* feature, She is also the ultimate source of all happiness for all the living beings. In other words, everything that gives pleasure and happiness within the spiritual or the material worlds is because of Her and the energy that emanates from Her. [21]

That same pleasure potency expands and spreads throughout the spiritual worlds, and then descends into the material creation into the many forms of happiness that is experienced by the conditioned soul, though it may be called by different names and perceived in assorted ways. Since we are all parts and parcels of the Lord, we also have that pleasure potency within us to a minute degree. But we are trying to enjoy it in the material world. Therefore we are like sparks that are dying out because we have left our place which is in the blazing fire of Lord Krishna's association.

The Hare Krishna mantra also directs one's attention and devotion to Radha as well as Krishna. Radha is also known as Mother Hara, which is the name Hare in the vocative form within the mantra. So in chanting Hare Krishna, we are first approaching the Lord's internal potency and asking Radha to please engage us in the service of Lord Krishna. Concentrating on Krishna through His names is one form of that service. In other words, it is through Radha that one more easily attains Krishna and service to Krishna. This is the advantage of approaching Lord Krishna through Radharani as in the Hare Krishna mantra.

The descriptions of the beauty of Radharani are wonderfully poetic and descriptive. Actually, the residents of Vrindavana care more for Radharani than they do for Lord Krishna. They know that Krishna can be influenced through Radharani. They know that Radha can bring one to Krishna. She is also the compassionate nature of the Lord, and thus more easily approached than trying to reach Lord Krishna directly. And when we read these descriptions of Radha, it is no wonder why they are devoted to Her. For example, it is explained that Srimati Radharani has unlimited transcendental qualities, of which twenty-five are principal. These include: 1) She is very sweet. 2) She is always freshly youthful. 3) Her eyes are restless. 4) She smiles brightly. 5) She has beautiful, auspicious lines. 6) She makes Krishna happy with Her bodily aroma. 7) She is very expert in singing. 8) Her speech is charming. 9) She is very expert in joking and speaking pleasantly. 10) She is very humble and meek. 11) She is always full of mercy. 12) She is cunning. 13) She is expert in executing Her duties. 14) She is shy. 15) She is always respectful. 16) She is always calm. 17) She is always grave. 18) She is expert in enjoying life. 19) She is situated in the topmost level of ecstatic love. 20) She is the reservoir of loving affairs in Gokula. 21) She is the most famous of submissive devotees. 22) She is very affectionate to elderly people. 23) She is very submissive to the love of Her friends. 24) She is the chief gopi. 25) She always keeps Krishna under Her control. In short, She possesses unlimited transcendental qualities, just as Lord Krishna does. [22]

*Radha and Krishna together in the groves of Vrindavana.*

In describing Srimati Radharani, it is also said in the *Vidagdha-madhava* (1.32) by Rupa Gosvami, "The beauty of Srimati Radharani's eyes forcibly devours the beauty of newly grown blue lotus flowers, and the beauty of Her face surpasses that of an entire forest of fully blossomed lotuses. Her bodily luster seems to place even gold in a painful situation. Thus the wonderful, unprecedented beauty of Srimati Radharani is awakening Vrindavana."

"Although the effulgence of the moon is brilliant initially at night, in the daytime it fades away. Similarly, although the lotus is beautiful during the daytime, at night it closes. But, O My friend, the face of My most dear Srimati Radharani is always bright and beautiful, both day and night. Therefore, to what can Her face be compared?" [23]

"When Srimati Radharani smiles, waves of joy overtake Her cheeks, and Her arched eyebrows dance like the bow of Cupid. Her glance is so enchanting that it is like a dancing bumblebee, moving unsteadily due to intoxication. That bee has bitten the whorl of My heart." [24]

There is much more to be known about Srimati Radharani, but this should suffice for now. Thus, the spiritual exchange of divine love between Radha and Krishna is the display of the internal energy of the Lord, and is very confidential and difficult to understand. No materialist can begin to comprehend this topic of the relationship between Radharani and Lord Krishna. But the more we awaken our dormant love for God, which is natural state of being for a fully awakened soul, then the more we can comprehend and actually enter into such spiritual loving exchanges.

**CHAPTER NOTES**
1. Caitanya-caritamrita, Madhya-lila, 20.157-8
2. Ibid., 24. 83-84
3. Bhagavad-gita 7.7
4. Ibid., 10.8
5. Ibid., 9.17-18
6. Caaitanya-caritamrita, Madhya-lila, 20.150, 153
7. Bhakti-rasamrita-sindhu 3.2.11-15
8. Sri Caitanya Shikshamrita, p. 13

9. Caitanya-caritamrita, Madhya-lila, 22.107
10. Srimad-Bhagavatam 11.7.18
11. Bhagavad-gita 7.19
12. Ibid., 9.29, 31
13. Ibid., 12.6-7
14. Ibid., 18.65-66
15. Nectar of Devotion, pp. 296-7
16. www.stephen-knapp.com/bhaja_govindam.htm
17. Caitanya-caritamrita, Adi-lila, 4.55-56
18. Ibid., Adi-lila. 4.75-81
19. *Ujjvala-nilamani* 4.3 of Srila Rupa Gosvami
20. Caitanya-caritamrita, Adi-lila, 4.82, 84, 87-96
21. Ibid., Adi-lila.4.68-72
22. *Ujjvala-nilamani*, Sri-radha-prakarana 11-15
23. *Vidagdha-madhava* 5.20
24. Ibid., 2.51

# CHAPTER FOUR

## *Why Bhakti-yoga?*

So why bhakti-yoga? We have already explained some of its importance in a previous chapter. But this chapter will explain its special nature and advantages.

To comprehend the significance of bhakti-yoga, one of the first things we need to understand is the purpose of life. Why are we here? What am I supposed to do? Where am I going?

The whole purpose of the Vedic Dharma and the lifestyle it recommends is to reach the highest potential that we can, in every way, including mentally, emotionally, intellectually, healthfully, and so on, including spiritually. There are so many aspects of the Vedic studies that focus on these potentials. But, ultimately, it is meant to uplift all of humanity to the point where we can rise above material existence, and finally reach the spiritual realm. Otherwise, we are still like animals, eating, sleeping, defending ourselves, engaging in sex, and finally dying. For what? In fact, as everyone in the world engages in materialistic and fruitive activities [actions that are attempts at enjoying the fruits or results] in their search to find happiness, one generally finds neither complete satisfaction or the mitigation of all distress.

Unless we attain the platform of understanding our spiritual identity, we remain on the platform of ignorance, motivated simply toward satisfying our mind and senses, and thus going nowhere but remaining in maya, the illusion that we are these temporary material bodies. In that way we remain absorbed in karma, the reactions to the things we do, which keeps us bound to the cycle of repeated birth and death, or reincarnation. Actually, we are meant for something far more advanced than that.

A hint at what more we are meant to accomplish comes from the inherent propensity to love. We all look for love. As the saying goes, love makes the world go 'round. So we all ultimately seek love, a deep loving relationship. That is what everyone is searching for. This deep love depends on communication. How deep that communication with another can go will also make a difference in how deep the loving relationship will be. Look around and see how much everyone is trying to express love for another, whether through songs, poetry, writings, giving of gifts, loving actions, and so on. It is a continual attempt, unless of course someone is simply so psychologically deranged that they do not want to express love but feel they have to take it by force, which is simply another way of crying for love. But the fact of the matter is that the kind of deep love we wish to attain is not actually possible on this physical, three dimensional level of existence. What we really want is so much more, so much higher, so much deeper, which is only available beyond this plane of existence, on the more spiritual level.

The missing point, therefore, is where to direct our love for the ultimate happiness. We may love our family, our neighbors, our country, or our own selves. But there is little information on how to direct our love so that we can all be truly happy.

Nonetheless, the second hint at the purpose of human life as given in the Vedic literature is how to direct our love for that ultimate happiness. One reference is in the *Srimad-Bhagavatam* (1.2.6, 22), which explains that the supreme occupation [*dharma*] for all of humanity is that by which people can attain to ecstatic loving devotional service unto the transcendent Lord. Such unmotivated and uninterrupted devotional service is all that can completely satisfy the self [soul].

This is a great instruction on how to become fully satisfied. Certainly, therefore, since time immemorial, all transcendentalists have been rendering devotional service to Lord Krishna, the Supreme Being, with great delight, because such devotional service [bhakti-yoga] is enlivening to the self.

Another reference in this regard is when Rishabhadeva tells his sons that out of all the innumerable living beings scattered across this universe, those who have become human beings should not work hard day and night simply to make arrangements to satisfy the mind and senses, which is possible even for the dogs and hogs that eat stool. One should engage in the penance to attain the position of devotional service (bhakti-yoga). By such activity, one's heart is purified, and when one attains this position, he attains the eternal, blissful life, which is transcendental to material happiness and which continues forever. [1]

People may say that penance sounds like an inconvenience. Who wants to do that? But you are doing penance every day, such as in going to work, working with people you often do not care for, trying to please your boss so you can keep your job, driving home from work and putting up with traffic, going shopping to put food on the table, paying your taxes, paying your rent, cleaning the house, keeping your yard looking nice so neighbors will not complain about you, and so on. And you do not want to do a little penance for spiritual development? But this is the way to attain a blissful life.

In this way, we start to see how to arrive at the natural pleasure of the soul. The soul is naturally loving, but when we love an object of our senses for the pleasure of the mind and senses, it is called *moha*, or lust. We love it for our own satisfaction and the fulfillment of our own desires. But when such affinity to love is directed toward pleasing God, it is called bhakti, and gives direct pleasure to the soul, not merely to our mind and senses which is temporary anyway. Such bhakti is the constitutional devotion from the soul for our Divine object of love, the Supreme Lover, Krishna.

Therefore, we must reach the stage of life wherein we act in the ways that actually touch the reality of the soul, or who and what we really are. Otherwise we are merely trying to satisfy ourselves by pleasing only the container in which we are situated. For example, we may cover ourselves with a paper bag, with holes so that we can see through it, hear through it, smell and taste through it. But in reality, no matter how much we try to please the paper bag, it is only superficial and does not touch the real person inside. No matter how much we try to pamper our paper bag covering, we remain unfulfilled. That is what it is like to merely work to please the mind and senses without touching the soul inside, which is the real person. How do we do this, how we make a loving connection between the soul and Supersoul, the *atma* and Paramatma, is the process of bhakti-yoga.

## THE EASY AND JOYFUL PATH OF BHAKTI-YOGA

So what is so special about bhakti-yoga? Aren't there more scientific or even mystical forms of yoga that a person can learn?

There are certainly various forms of yoga that focus on different levels of realization and accomplishment. But the means to attain spiritual realization and to rise above material existence, and to make contact with the Supreme, can all be accomplished with one process, and that is bhakti-yoga.

One reference that helps explain this is: "The human form of life affords one a chance to return home, back to the Godhead, the spiritual domain. Therefore, every living entity especially in the human form of life, must engage in devotional service to the lotus feet of Lord Vishnu [or Krishna]. This devotional service is natural because the Lord, the Supreme Personality, is the most beloved, the master of the soul, and well-wisher of all other living beings." [2]

It is natural for the soul to love God because the soul is a manifestation of the energy of God. Just as a spark is a molecular part of the sun, the soul is an eternal, loving servant of God. So, as we explained, the soul has an inherent nature to love, and the process of bhakti-yoga is to not only invoke our loving propensity but direct it toward the Supreme, which is natural to the soul. Therefore, when we connect that love to Krishna, the God of love, it becomes easy and spontaneous, since bhakti springs from the eternal nature of the soul. It is the natural *dharma* or proclivity of the soul. We simply have to uncover ourselves from all the material conditioning that has clouded our consciousness for many lifetimes.

The basic activities of devotional service, which are hearing about Krishna, talking about Him, chanting His holy names, remembering and meditating on Him in such a way, and so on, are the natural characteristics of bhakti-yoga. This simply awakens our dormant love for Krishna, and as we practice it, it increases that natural attraction. This pure love is established in the hearts and consciousness of all living beings, and it simply has to be revived, though for now it may be deeply hidden or forgotten due to many lifetimes of material activities. But when the heart is purified from deep material attachments by such hearing and chanting, the dormant love of the living being naturally awakens. [3]

Through bhakti-yoga, a person can find a superior level of happiness that far supercedes any pleasure that comes from the work it takes to gratify the senses. After all, it does take work, it takes time, and it takes money to satisfy the mind and senses. And after all that, sometimes we are still not completely fulfilled. But as Lord Krishna relates, "Those who fix their consciousness on Me, giving up all material desires, share with Me a happiness that cannot possibly be experienced by those engaged in sense gratification. One who does not desire anything within this world, who has achieved peace by controlling his senses, whose consciousness is equal in all conditions, and whose mind is completely satisfied in Me, finds only happiness wherever he goes." [4] In this way, there is no other form of happiness and bliss that can be compared to that which is received through the service of the Divine, namely in the form of Radha and Krishna.

The *Srimad-Bhagavatam* (10.84.36) further explains, "Learned authorities who see through the eye of scripture have demonstrated that this is the easiest method of subduing the agitated mind and attaining liberation, and that it is a sacred duty which brings joy to the heart."

In this way, bhakti-yoga bestows inherent eternal peace and bliss to the soul. It is the way of life for the human being. Bhakti gives to the soul in this material world the sentiment, love and activities that are found in the spiritual domain of Lord Krishna. Thus, the goal justifies the means. It paves the way to attain deep love for God. "Remembrance of Lord Krishna's lotus feet destroys everything inauspicious and awards the greatest good fortune. It purifies the heart and bestows devotion for the Supreme Soul, along with knowledge enriched with spiritual realization and material renunciation." [5] In other words, it accomplishes all the requirements of any spiritual path all at once. This is one reason why bhakti-yoga is such an easy path.

Another factor why bhakti-yoga is the easiest of all spiritual paths is explained in the *Narada Bhakti Sutras* (59): "The reason devotional service is the easiest of all spiritual processes is that it does not depend on any other authority for its validity, being itself the standard of authority." This means that it does not depend on any other process to complete its purpose, and that it is the easiest path because it gives the direct experience of spiritual pleasure to both the individual and the Supreme Being, which is what fulfills the individual in his or her search for a loving experience and the realization of the Absolute Truth. Both are accomplished simultaneously.

Bhakti-yoga is not only considered the easiest, but also the best by Lord Krishna Himself, as He says in *Bhagavad-gita* (6.47): "And of all yogis, he who always abides in Me with great faith, worshiping Me in transcendental loving service, is most intimately united with Me in yoga and is the highest of all." In this way, anyone can engage in bhakti-yoga without difficulty and progress toward the highest goal of human existence. Even an old person who is nearing death can focus and lovingly meditate on Lord Krishna and in this way free him or herself from any further rounds of birth and death and attain the spiritual domain, as Lord Krishna again describes in *Bhagavad-gita* (8.5): "And whoever, at the time of death, quits his body, remembering Me alone, at once attains My nature. Of this there is no doubt."

Even one who is not fully realized in knowledge still has every opportunity to attain the spiritual world. Krishna explains this as such, "To those who are constantly devoted and worship Me with love, I give the understanding by which they can come to Me. Out of compassion for them, I dwelling in their hearts, destroy with the shining lamp of knowledge the darkness born of ignorance." [6]

This all indicates that whatever position a person may have, high or low, rich or poor, good or bad, or from any part of the universe, it is still very easy for a person to progress spiritually in this path of bhakti-yoga and approach the supreme destination. [7] Even Rupa Gosvami, another spiritual master in our line, mentions that every person has the birthright to accept devotional service and to become a devotee of Krishna. No one is barred from doing so. [8]

It is also explained that even dull creatures can be situated in Krishna's devotional service. [9] Even fourth-class men, hill tribes, and even birds and beasts can engage in the service of the Supreme Person, and follow the path of the devotees and take instructions from them. Although the ocean of nescience is vast, they can still cross over it. [10]

Krishna further explains in the *Bhagavatam* (11.20.31), "For one who is fully engaged in my devotional service, whose mind is fixed on Me in bhakti-yoga, the path of speculative knowledge [such as jnana-yoga] and dry renunciation is not very beneficial."

"The path of speculative knowledge and renunciation is not very essential for devotional service. Indeed, good qualities such as nonviolence and mind and sense control automatically accompany a devotee of Lord Krishna." (Caitanya-caritamrita, Madhya-lila, 22.145)

In this way, we do not need to engage in the long hours of meditation as in raja-yoga, or the long hours of studying and debate as in jnana-yoga. Love for and faith in God are the two qualifications that a person needs in bhakti-yoga, which are not difficult to attain. If anyone has these two qualifications, he or she can easily and quickly advance toward Krishna by the virtue of their devotion. We do not find any other path to deliver a person as easily and swiftly as bhakti-yoga. We can even see this with the example of Maharaja Pariksit. He was destined to die in seven days and asked how best to spend the remainder of his time. Then it was Shukadeva Goswami who showed up at the assembly of sages, and they had him recite the *Srimad-Bhagavatam* to fully enlighten Pariksit in just seven days.

The greatness of bhakti-yoga is that it is an eternal process that can be found and performed anywhere in any of the universes. The process never changes in any time in history, whether it be Satya-yuga or Kali-yuga. It is always directly related to the eternal nature of the soul and the ever-present relationship between God and the living being. It can be adopted by any person in the world, or incorporated into any person's religion. It is gifted and instructed by the Lord Himself for the benefit of all living beings, and does not require any physical hardship, no special meditation postures or training, nor any strain on the brain with too much heavy thinking, nor is there any age requirement. It does not require that a person needs to be healthy, nor be performed at any particular time of the day. It is an easy path that anyone can do. Bhakti-yoga is essentially the path to awaken the pure love in your heart that hankers for meeting or directing itself toward the Divine beloved of your soul. Plus, depending on how sincere you are, or how greedy you are to reach your spiritual fulfillment, this can be attained in this very lifetime. There are no limitations except that which is given by your own mind. Once you can overcome that, you can know a bliss that has no bounds.

This gives assurance that the Supreme and the spiritual world can be attained in a comparatively short time. It merely depends on your sincerity and dedication. Plus, it is not a matter of trying to see God, but it is a matter of acting in a way that God sees us. Then He will reveal Himself to us, and pave the way for us to attain Him.

The *Mundaka Upanishad* (3.2.3) also relates how the Supreme can be revealed: "The Supreme Lord is not obtained by means of expert explanations, vast intelligence or even much hearing. He is obtained only by one whom He Himself chooses. To such a person, He manifests His own form." In other words, only after the Supreme is pleased with someone by their devotional attitude does the Supreme reveal His own ultimate form, and thus the highest of spiritual truths.

Therefore, it is confirmed that the process of bhakti-yoga is a universal spiritual principle and process, which is applicable in any country, for any person, and at all times in history, and in all circumstances.[11] The point is that the relationship between the living entities and the Supreme is eternally established. Therefore, no impediment exists in pleasing the Lord, whether one is an old man or a young child.[12] Only for those who are outrightly evil, wicked, or demonic does bhakti to the Supreme become difficult to understand or appreciate or practice.

Furthermore, it is not a matter that we direct our attention to Him only, but we can also work to attain Her, the feminine aspect of God, which is Krishna's expansion of Radharani, His feminine potency. So devotees often pray not just to Krishna, but to Radha-Krishna together.

Chapter Four 43

*Sri Radha and Sri Krishna together, the complete form of the most ecstatic, loving and spiritual bliss.*

## THE EASY RELEASE FROM KARMA

Karma is a big topic, so we will not explain it all here. But karma includes both good reactions to pious activities as well as negative reactions to selfish or wicked activities. And either kind of karma will cause future rounds of lifetimes in this material existence. Plus, it is also one's karma from past actions that cause our continued attraction to activities based on satisfying the mind and senses. And it has been described that living an average life of typical material activities creates enough karma for another seven lifetimes. In other words, it takes seven lifetimes to work out the karma we have accumulated in a single life. That is how karma increases. So in our attempt to make spiritual progress, we need to somehow become relieved of our karma.

Naturally, as we advance spiritually, or engage in other processes of yoga, etc., we will slow down the accumulation of karma. But the real point is how do we become free of it. We cannot enter the spiritual world until we are free from our karma and the materialistic attractions for pleasing the mind and senses.

The good news is that as we act on our natural spiritual level, such as in bhakti-yoga, we do not have to undergo special endeavors to free ourselves of our karma. Acting on the spiritual platform and taking up the natural engagement of the soul in service to the Supreme Being automatically frees us from our karma, and also evaporates the subtle body, which is what carries our karma from one life to another. This makes bhakti-yoga an easy way to help free ourselves from karma. As it is said in the *Srimad-Bhagavatam* (3.25.33), "Bhakti, devotional service, dissolves the subtle body of the living entity without separate effort, just as fire in the stomach digests all that we eat." And with the dissolution of the subtle body comes the purification or freedom from of our karma.

Lord Krishna clearly explains the potency of performing bhakti-yoga in His service in *Srimad-Bhagavatam* (11.14.19): "As all fuel is burned to ashes by a full-fledged fire, all sinful activities are totally erased when one engages in devotional service to Me."

Furthermore, the *Bhagavatam* (1.9.23) explains, "The Personality of Godhead, who appears in the mind of the devotee by attentive devotion and meditation and by chanting of the holy names, releases the devotee from the bondage of fruitive activities [or karma] at the time of his quitting the material body."

In *Bhagavad-gita* (4.36) Krishna further says, "Even if you are considered the most sinful of all sinners, when you are situated in the boat of transcendental knowledge, you will be able to cross over the ocean of miseries [meaning material existence]."

Transcendental knowledge means the knowledge acquired by studying these spiritual texts, as well as through the performance of bhakti-yoga which purifies the mind and gives deeper realizations, and awakens our love for God. This is the constitutional position of the soul, which is the platform in which all material entanglement dissipates, including our karma. So as we develop ourselves spiritually through bhakti-yoga, the freer we become from what Lord Krishna calls "the ocean of miseries," and further rounds of reincarnation in this temporary material existence. [More information on karma and how to be free from it can be read in my book *Reincarnation and Karma: How They Really Affect Us*.]

## REACHING THE GOAL OF BHAKTI-YOGA

Many yogis and Hindus feel that the primary goal of yoga is to reach *moksha*, which is liberation from material existence, and from the repetition of the rounds of birth and death, and to merge into the Brahman effulgence. But this will depend on which school of philosophy you study, and which process of yoga you practice. However, in *Srimad-Bhagavatam* (5.5.16), Lord Rishabhadeva instructs his sons to give up their attachment to the process of liberation or their desire for *moksha*, because that is not the ultimate goal of yoga.

The point of this is to understand that jnana-yoga and raja-yoga do not take one to God, Krishna. The function of jnana-yoga, the yoga through knowledge, is to remove ignorance and understand our spiritual identity. It is often said that one who knows or realizes his or her spiritual identity is a *jivan-mukta*, a liberated soul. But this is only part of the way there. While in yoga, such as raja or astanga-yoga, the goal is to reach *nirvikalpa samadhi*, the thoughtless trance on the Brahman. If a person is a devotee, the goal of Yoga may be to reach a meditative trance on the Paramatma, or Supersoul. Either way, they do not take him or her all the way to understand God. Moreover, such practice is extremely difficult, especially in this age of quarrel and confusion and constant distractions, for which Kali-yuga is known.

As explained by Sri Caitanya Mahaprabhu, there are different methods for the liberation of the conditioned soul–karma, jnana, yoga, and bhakti–but all are dependent on bhakti for its completion. But for devotional service, bhakti-yoga, all other methods for spiritual realization are weak and incomplete. Unless one comes to the devotional service of Lord Krishna, jnana and yoga cannot give the desired results or complete the process to its ultimate perfection... Speculative knowledge [jnana-yoga] alone, without devotional service, is not able to give liberation. On the other hand, even without knowledge one can obtain liberation if one engages in the Lord's devotional service. [13]

"The other processes cannot yield [the desired] results unless they are associated with devotional service. Devotional service, however, is so strong and independent that it can give one all the desired results." [14]

Even Lord Krishna says the same thing in the *Bhagavad-gita* (8.28), "A person who accepts the path of devotional service is not bereft of the results derived from studying the *Vedas*, performing austere sacrifices, giving charity or pursuing philosophical and fruitive activities. At the end he reaches the supreme abode."

As Prahlada Maharaja explains to his friends, all other processes of spiritual and moral development are the means to reach or evolve to the position wherein we can engage in bhakti-yoga. He says, "My dear friends, O sons of the demons, you cannot please the Supreme Personality of Godhead [meaning the source of all forms of God] by becoming perfect brahmanas, demigods or great saints, or by becoming perfectly good in etiquette or vast learning. None of these qualifications can awaken the pleasure of the Lord. Nor by charity, austerity, sacrifice, cleanliness, or vows can one satisfy the Lord. The Lord is pleased only if one has unflinching, unalloyed devotion to

Him. Without sincere devotional service, everything is simply a show." [15]

"Prahlada Maharaja continued: One may possess wealth, an aristocratic family, beauty, austerity, education, sensory expertise, luster, influence, physical strength, diligence, intelligence, and mystic yoga power, but I think that even by all these qualifications one cannot satisfy the Supreme Personality of Godhead. However, one can satisfy the Lord simply by devotional service. Gajendra did this, and thus the Lord was satisfied with him." [16]

So, without this, one's spiritual progress remains incomplete. "Those who are not faithful on the path of devotional service cannot attain Me, O conqueror of foes [Arjuna], but return to birth and death in this material world." [17]

To those who do not show any interest for this spiritual path, which is anyone's personal freedom to choose, they remain bound in the repeated cycles of birth and death. As they become increasingly infected with materialism, or in evil and wicked ways, they may also enter into the lower species of life. However, this is for their own good to work out their animalistic desires and tendencies, and so they will reduce whatever harm they may cause to other members of the human race. If they are too wicked, better that they not remain within the human species. But if they perform pious activities, they may still one day have the opportunity to again have the chance to engage in bhakti-yoga.

It is only by devotional service that one can reach Krishna and His spiritual abode. As Lord Krishna discusses with His friend Uddhava, "My dear Uddhava, I am personally the ultimate shelter and way of life for saintly liberated persons, and thus if one does not engage in My loving devotional service, which is made possible by associating with my devotees, then for all practical purposes, one possesses no effective means for escaping from material existence."[18]

"As one can derive fire from wood, milk from the milk bag of a cow, food grains and water from the land, and prosperity in one's livelihood from industrial enterprises, so, by the practice of bhakti-yoga, even within this material world, one can achieve Your favor or intelligently approach You. Those who are pious all affirm this." [19]

In this way, we can understand that for anyone to realize

Ishvara, the Lord, it is up to the Supreme to directly bless the person and reveal Himself. It is not possible to know the Lord simply through the instruction of others or by some mechanical yoga system or by the above-mentioned qualities. And such grace is attained only by the loving service to the Supreme. It is only this grace which subdues the affects of *maya* and reduces our material attachments. This allows us to get closer to the Lord. As this increases, Krishna reveals Himself to the devotee, and with this, the divine spiritual knowledge. Then love for God builds up, which increasingly unites the devotee with the grace of God, and frees the devotee from the forces of the material world, paving the way for his or her liberation from the material world and entry into the spiritual realm. As Krishna explains, "This divine [material] energy of Mine, consisting of the three modes of material nature, is difficult to overcome. But those who have surrendered unto Me can easily cross beyond it." [20]

Therefore, devotion to the Supreme is the highest process to realize the Absolute Truth. Once Krishna is pleased with someone, the Lord reveals everything to Him. As Sri Krishna says in the *Srimad-Bhagavatam* (9.4.63), "I am completely under the control of My devotees. Indeed, I am not at all independent. Because My devotees are completely devoid of material desires, I sit only within the cores of their hearts. What to speak of My devotee, even those who are devotees of My devotee are very dear to Me."

Lord Krishna goes on to say, "Everything that can be achieved by fruitive activities, penance, knowledge, detachment, mystic yoga, charity, religious duties, and all other means of perfecting life is easily achieved by My devotee through loving service unto Me. If somehow or other My devotee desires promotion to heaven, liberation, or residence in My abode, he easily achieves such benedictions." [21]

This is the beauty of performing bhakti-yoga, or loving devotional service to the Lord, it makes the Infinite submissive to the infinitesimal. This is one of the secrets of bhakti-yoga, as it is explained, "The Supreme Lord, who is greater than the greatest, becomes submissive to even a very insignificant devotee because of his devotional service. It is the beautiful and exalted nature of devotional service that the infinite Lord becomes submissive to the infinitesimal living entity because of it..." [22]

By now it should be obvious how we can attain to the highest spiritual strata and attain Krishna: "By following the paths of speculative knowledge [jnana-yoga], fruitive activity, or mystic yoga to control the senses, one cannot satisfy Krishna, the Supreme Lord. Unalloyed devotional love for Krishna is the only cause for the Lord's satisfaction." [23]

It is even explained that in this age of Kali-yuga, wherein we no longer have the mental stability or capability to reach the complete perfection of raja- yoga or astanga-yoga, what to speak of other religions, though they may still provide some benefits, without bhakti-yoga, especially in this age of Kali-yuga, there is no means of attaining liberation from the repeated cycle of birth and death in this material existence. This is explained herein: "In this age of Kali, one cannot attain liberation without taking to the devotional service of the Lord [bhakti-yoga]. In this age, even if one does not chant the holy names of Krishna perfectly, he or she still attains liberation very easily." [24]

"My dear Lord, devotional service unto You is the only auspicious path. If one gives it up simply for speculative knowledge or the understanding that these living beings are spirit soul and the material world is false, he undergoes a great deal of trouble. He only gains troublesome and inauspicious activities. His actions are like beating a husk that is already devoid of rice. One's labor becomes fruitless." [25]

"O lotus-eyed one, those who think they are liberated in this life but who are devoid of devotional service to You are of impure intelligence. Although they accept severe austerities and penances and rise to the spiritual position, to the impersonal Brahman realization, they fall down again because they neglect to worship Your lotus feet." [26]

This means that even if a person enters the great Brahman effulgence by their endeavors of yoga practice, wherein one simply floats as one spirit soul amongst innumerable others in a continuous spiritually blissful but unconscious state of being, like one drop of water in an ocean amongst so many other drops, if they ever have an inclination for engaging in activity, which is the natural state of the soul, they must return to the material worlds for such engagement. Why? Because they have not learned what it means to have spiritual engagement, which is the pure loving, variegated activities that are performed with the spiritual body in the devotional service to the Supreme Being. Therefore, it is advised that in order to learn all the different aspects of the Absolute Truth, one should not only understand the Brahman, Paramatma and Bhagavan, but one should learn how to engage in bhakti-yoga to Bhagavan, that Supreme Person.

Therefore, it is only by devotional service, beginning with hearing about the Supreme Lord Sri Krishna, that one can approach Him. [27] As the *Bhagavad-gita* (18.55) further explains, "One can understand the Supreme Personality as He is only by devotional service. And when one is in full consciousness of the Supreme Lord by such devotion, he can enter into the kingdom of God."

"... Once having taken shelter at the root of the lotus feet of the Lord, a devotee never comes back to this material existence, which is full of the threefold miseries." [28]

We should be able to understand by now that out of all the different kinds of religion and worship that are available, devotional service unto Krishna is the supreme form of worship, and offers us all that we need to understand who and what is God, and how to understand Him, and become free from the difficulties of this material world and enter into the spiritual realm.

As explained by Lord Kapiladeva, "Bhakti-yoga, as described above, is the ultimate goal of life. By rendering devotional service to the Supreme Personality of Godhead, one transcends the modes of material nature and attains the spiritual position on the platform of direct devotional service." [29]

"The yogis, equipped with transcendental knowledge and renunciation, and engaged in devotional service for their eternal benefit, take shelter of My lotus feet, and since I am the Lord, they are thus eligible to enter into the kingdom of God without fear." [30]

The reason why this is important is that bhakti-yoga is said to open our real eternal senses to being activated on the spiritual platform, even while existing in this material world. Then even before leaving the present material body, we can start relating to and being aware of the spiritual level of reality as it exists all around us. However, outside of the material cosmic creation there is the Brahman effulgence, and deep within this great white light are the spiritual Vaikuntha planets, and Krishna's highest abode, Goloka Vrindavana. On any of these planets the residents all have spiritual bodies in which their spiritual senses are fully activated to engage in varieties of loving activities and exchanges in service to the Supreme Lord in any of His many forms, such as Lord Narayana and Krishna. In the spiritual world, no one has any concern for the material energy. There is only the blissful loving service of the servants to the served, meaning the Supreme Being. It is the process of bhakti-yoga that delivers the means to reach that destination.

## AN OVERVIEW OF BHAKTI-YOGA

So, to simplify things, the point is that we are all spiritual, that is our constitutional position as transcendent beings that are beyond the constraints of this temporary material body. The purpose of all yoga and all religions is to raise our consciousness from materialistic to spiritualistic, to reach that state of transcendence.

The way this material cosmic manifestation was created, according to the Vedic texts, is that the Carana or causal ocean formed in a corner of the spiritual sky. It is said that it is like a cloud in the Brahman effulgence. In this description we will leave out all the details of this creative process, which you can read about in my book *How the Universe was Created and Our Purpose in It: The Vedic Answers to the Mysteries of Life*. But in that causal ocean, the spiritual atmosphere develops from extremely subtle to increasingly dense to the point wherein it manifests the ingredients for the material elements. Some people call this the process of devolution rather than evolution, going from the highly refined spiritual energy to the increasingly dense material energy. These ingredients gradually form the physical elements of earth, air, fire, water, ether, and the subtle elements of mind, intelligence and false ego. These were then organized to create all the forms of life necessary to accommodate the different levels of consciousness, which was the basis for all of the species of life. These species of life are scattered across the heavenly and subtle planets, and the earthly and intermediary planets, and the most dense or hellish planets. And here we are now in the human species on planet earth.

So it is as if the world of light projects the three-dimensional creation. Beings of light can enter into the material creation, but beings from the three-dimensional worlds cannot enter the world of light without major modifications of love, light and peace to oppose darkness, hate and envy that exists in the worlds of darkness. We must all rise above these lower attributes. And this is one of the purposes of bhakti-yoga, to manifest these modifications so that people can enter the world of light, the spiritual atmosphere.

The point of human life is to use it in a way that allows us to become free of this cosmic material creation and attain the spiritual realm, which is our natural home that is filled with loving activities. This is what we are naturally attracted to and what makes us search for this even while in this material manifestation. We just do not know where to look. Vedic culture and especially bhakti-yoga is meant to direct us in this way. It is meant to lift our consciousness up and reawaken and manifest that spiritual love that is natural to our soul, and which is the foundation of the spiritual world.

Ordinary religion can help us by advocating a moralistic and pious lifestyle in worshiping God and treating all others with respect. This can help us reach heaven, but the heavenly planets are still part of the cosmic material creation. We need more than that to reach the spiritual realm. We need something that uplifts our consciousness so that it vibrates and operates on the same frequency as the spiritual domain. When that begins to happen, with steady practice, the doors, so to speak, begin to open and can reveal to us the spiritual level of reality that exists all around us. Then we can attain personal perception and experience of it. Remember, the spiritual vibration is all pervasive, while the material frequency exists only within the Carana Ocean. The more we begin to perceive that transcendent reality, or get a taste for the devotional service for the Supreme, and work in that same vibration, the more we begin to prepare ourselves for entering that dimension of existence. This is the real goal of bhakti-yoga.

This is why we worship and meditate on Lord Krishna, or discuss and remember His pastimes, or chant and sing His holy names, and engage in devotional service to Him in the form of the Deity in the temple, and so on–it all raises our consciousness and brings us closer to Him. It helps us purify ourselves of our material attachments and contamination so that we begin to function on the same frequency level as the spiritual world, in the atmosphere of pure spiritual love. This is how we become qualified to enter it that world.

This is also why it is recommended that we live in one of the holy places, like Vrindavana, where Krishna's pastimes took place, or where the spiritual vibration is naturally very high, and actually manifests there, which we can personally witness when we are qualified. This helps our own vibrational level to rise to that state of being. But if we cannot live there, then we should think of loving there, or live near a temple that we can visit and participate in the service, or even make our own home into a temple where the frequency, based on our activities, thoughts, words, and consciousness, is naturally very high or spiritual.

By this kind of activity and meditation, we develop a level of consciousness of love for the Supreme by which we can attract Krishna to us, who will then help us return home to His abode. We need that assistance, like trying to see a country's president without his approval is next to impossible. But with his approval it is easy. Similarly, we need the grace of God to enter the kingdom of God, which is why any other process remains incomplete without bhakti.

By the end of our lives in this kind of Krishna consciousness, we can return at the time of death to the spiritual realm where everything is in harmony, centered around the one Supreme Being. Yet, it does not require that we give up these bodies to enter the transcendental world. We can do that whenever we are qualified. But at the time of death, at least for those who are successful, they will no longer require continued rounds of birth and death in this material existence, but will return to the spiritual world. That is the goal of human life and the process of bhakti-yoga.

## THE RARE OPPORTUNITY TO ENGAGE IN BHAKTI-YOGA

Even though the process of bhakti-yoga is the easiest to engage in, and a most powerful process from which no one is barred, it is still rare to see anyone take it seriously. The reason for that is there are two primary ways that allow us to reach the stage of life wherein we engage in bhakti-yoga. That is from pious activities from our previous lives, or simply from the mercy of another devotee who gives us the chance to know about and instructs us in the way of engaging in bhakti-yoga. Devotional service is a continuous process from one lifetime to another. This is how even a little advancement on this path is never lost. It is directly connected with the soul and follows you wherever you go. In your next life you begin from wherever you left it in your previous existence. [31]

As Lord Krishna explains, "By virtue of the divine consciousness of his or her previous life, a person automatically becomes attracted to the yogic principles–even without seeking them. Such an inquisitive transcendentalist, striving for yoga, stands always above the ritualistic principles of the scriptures... Persons who have acted piously in previous lives and in this life, whose sinful actions are completely eradicated and who are freed from the duality of delusion, engage themselves in My service with determination." [32]

Even if one is greatly materially attached to sense enjoyment, but is still genuinely attracted to Krishna, such a person is eligible to begin the process of bhakti-yoga and engage in devotional activities to Lord Krishna. This attraction to engage in service in the association of other devotees is a sign of great fortune. A person can build on that and become increasingly purified and spiritualized through such practice. Then that person's taste for Krishna will increase, and his material attachments will fade. As Lord Krishna says, "My dear Uddhava, only by great fortune does someone become attracted to Me." [33]

Krishna also explains in *Bhagavad-gita* (7.19, 25) that, "After many births and deaths, he who is actually in knowledge surrenders unto Me, knowing Me to be the cause of all causes and all that is. Such a great soul is very rare... I am never manifest to the foolish and unintelligent. For them I am covered by My eternal creative potency [*yoga-maya*]; and so the deluded world knows Me not, who am unborn and infallible." So herein we can again recognize how rare it is for someone to understand Krishna and engage in service to Him, while anyone who remains unintelligent or more attached to satisfying the mind and senses will never understand Krishna or the importance of bhakti-yoga.

This is further elaborated in the *Srimad-Bhagavatam* (6.14.3-5): "In this material world there are as many living entities as there are atoms. Among these living entities, a very few are human beings, and among them, few are interested in following religious principles. O best of the brahmanas, Shukadeva Gosvami, out of many persons who follow religious principles, only a few desire liberation from the material world. Among many thousands who desire liberation, one may actually achieve liberation, giving up material attachment to society, friendship, love, country, home, wife, and children. And among many thousands of such liberated persons, one who can understand the true meaning of liberation is very rare. O great sage, among many millions who are liberated and perfect in knowledge of liberation, one may be a devotee of Lord Narayana, Krishna. Such devotees, who are fully peaceful, are extremely rare."

## OTHER IMPORTANT FACTORS ABOUT BHAKTI-YOGA

One point we should understand is that the human form is attained only with great fortune and after much circulation through the different species in the universe. It is the proper vehicle for spiritual development and should not be wasted but used for the highest purpose. In fact, as pointed out in the Vedic texts, nothing can provide the means for the spiritual progress we need, anywhere in the universe, than this process of bhakti-yoga in this human form of life on this planet earth. This is explained in this verse, "The residents of both heaven and hell desire human birth on the earth planet because human life facilitates the achievement of transcendental knowledge and love of Godhead, whereas neither heavenly nor hellish bodies efficiently provide such opportunities." [34]

In this way, we can understand that it is human life on planet earth which provides the portal to practically any level of reality we want to attain. It all depends on how we live our life and the type of consciousness we develop by the end of our life. This opportunity is found to be on no other planet in this universe.

Not only is human life on planet earth a key portal to attaining the spiritual realm, but being here during the age of Kali-yuga, an age of constant quarrel and confusion, nonetheless has further benefits. In the *Skanda Purana* (Brahmakhanda, Setu-Mahatmya XLIII.3-4), it explains the advantage of spiritual pursuits in Kali-yuga: "The merit which was earned in Satya-yuga by prosecuting *sadhana* (the spiritual practices for God-realization) for ten years could be earned in the course of a year in Treta-yuga, and in a month in Dvapara-yuga. The same can be acquired in a single day in Kali-yuga (if one strives for God realization) with the same zeal... This age of Kali is replete with vices, but it has one great virtue, that humanity can realize God in a very short time through spiritual endeavor." [35]

Furthermore, there are other acharyas or spiritual masters who have also perfected their spiritual lives through the process of bhakti-yoga. Some have apparently entered into the spiritual domain while still living here on this earthly realm, and then have left instructions for us to follow so that we can do the same. We can look at Adi Shankaracharya, Ramanujacharya, Madhvacharya, Vallabhacharya, Nimbarkacharya, Tulasidas, the famous *Bhagavatam* commentator Shridhar Swami, Haridas Thakura, Namadeva, Sri Caitanya Mahaprabhu, the devotional poet Tukaram, the Alwars of South India, Meera Bai, the Six Gosvamis of Vrindavana, Vishvanatha Thakur, Srila Bhaktivinoda Thakur, Srila Bhaktisiddhanta Sarasvati Thakur, our own Srila A. C. Bhaktivedanta Swami, and many others, who have all practiced or advised everyone else to engage in bhakti-yoga for the highest levels of spiritual realization and bliss. They did not teach the importance of rituals for attaining material benefits, or how to practice yoga exercises, but taught the soul's natural affinity for Govinda, Krishna, and how to awaken that.

Plus, it is because of the potency of bhakti-yoga that it is applicable for anyone in any position. It is even said that people engaged in householder life can remain completely transcendental by

Chapter Four                                                    57

adjusting their life for the performance of bhakti-yoga. That is how easy it is. It is not a question of going into the mountains for a life of solitude, but it is only a matter of adjusting your motivation and purpose in what you do. "Those who are engaged in auspicious activities in devotional service certainly understand that the ultimate enjoyer or beneficiary of all activities is the Supreme Personality of Godhead. Thus when one acts, he offers the results to that Supreme Personality of Godhead and passes life always engaged in topics of the Lord. Even though such a person may be participating in family life, he is not affected by the results of his actions." [36]

"Always engaging in the activities of devotional service, devotees feel ever-increasingly fresh and new in all their activities. The all-knower, the Supersoul within the heart of the devotee, makes everything increasingly fresh. This is known as the Brahman position by the advocates of the Absolute Truth..." [37]

This is the ease and happiness that accompanies the process of bhakti-yoga.

## THE STAGES OF BHAKTI-YOGA

One last thing to point out is that the practice of bhakti-yoga is a progressive process, whereby a person starts by practicing the basic principles, but with advancement and purification from materialistic tendencies, a person can attain increasingly deeper sentiments, realizations and reciprocation from the Supreme. This is also explained in the *Caitanya-caritamrita* (Madhya-lila, 24.30, 32-34) as follows:

"There are ten meanings to the word *bhakti*, devotional service. One is execution of devotional service according to the regulative [rules and] principles, and the other, called *prema-bhakti* [ecstatic love] has nine varieties. [These grow from attraction–*rati*, love–*prema*, affection–*sneha*, adverse feelings–*mana*, intimacy–*pranaya*, attachment–*raga*, subattachment–*anuraga*, ecstatic love–*bhava*, and to sublime ecstatic love–*mahabhava*.] The attraction to Krishna of devotees on the platform of neutrality increases up to love of Godhead [*prema*], and the attraction of devotees on the platform of servitorship can increase to spontaneous attachment [*raga*]. Devotees in Vrindavana [or in that particular mood] who are friends of the Lord can increase their ecstatic love to the point of *anuraga*. Paternal affectionate lovers, such as Krishna's father and mother [or those in that mood], can increase their love of Godhead up to the *anuraga* point [subattachment in ecstatic love]. The *gopis* [cowherd girls] of Vrindavana who are attached to Krishna in conjugal love can increase their ecstatic love up to the point of *mahabhava* [the greatest ecstatic love]. These are some of the glorious meanings of the word *bhakti*, devotional service." This is what we will uncover as we proceed through this book.

Therefore, just as the *Vedanta Sutras* begin with the phrase, *athato brahma-jijnasa*, which means "Now [that we have reached this human form of life] is the time for spiritual inquiry," similarly now that we have understood the ease, importance, and the rarity of its achievement, let us begin to understand the process of bhakti-yoga as described in the Vedic literature and commentaries. As the *Narada-Bhakti Sutras* (1) states: "Now, therefore, I will try to explain the process of devotional service."

**CHAPTER NOTES**
1. Srimad-Bhagavatam 5.5.1
2. Ibid., 7.6.5 & 8.24.48
3. Caitanya-caritamrita. Madhya-lila 22.104-107
4. Srimad-Bhagavatam 11.14.12-13
5. Ibid., 12.12.55
6. Bhagavad-gita 10.10-11
7. Ibid., 9.32
8. Nectar of Devotion, p.47
9. Caitanya-caritamrita, Madya-lila 24.185
10. Ibid., 24.190
11. Ibid., 25.120
12. Srimad-Bhagavatam 7.6.19
13. Caitanya-caritamrita, Madhya-lila, 22.17-18, 21
14. Ibid., 24.92
15. Srimad-Bhagavatam 7.7.51-52
16. Ibid., 7.9.9

17. Bhagavad-gita 9.3
18. Srimad-Bhagavatam 11.11.48
19. Ibid., 8.6.12
20. Bhagavad-gita 7.14
21. Srimad-Bhagavatam 11.20.32-33
22. Caitanya-caritamrita, Adi-lila 7.145
23. Ibid., 17.75
24. Caitanya-caritamrita, Madhya-lila, 25.30
25. Srimad-Bhagavatam 10.14.4 & Caitanya-caritamrita, Madhya-lila 25.31
26. Ibid., 10.2.32 & Ibid., 25.32
27. Caitanya-caritamrita, Adi-lila, 7.141
28. Srimad-Bhagavatam 4.21.32
29. Ibid., 3.29.14
30. Ibid., 3.25.43
31. Nectar of Devotion, p.18
32. Bhagavad-gita 6.44 & 7.28
33. Srimad-Bhagavatam 11.20.8 & Nectar of Devotion, p.28
34. Srimad-Bhagavatam 11.20.12
35. *Skanda Purana,* Maheshwarakhanda, Kumarikakhanda, xxxv.115 & 117
36. Srimad-Bhagavatam 4.30.19
37. Ibid., 4.30.20

# CHAPTER FIVE

# *Starting With Faith*

So how do we begin the process of bhakti-yoga? If we have no experience with it, we may not be sure if it will work or not, or what may happen. After all, it takes confidence for us to begin anything, whether it be a process of education to get a university degree, or to get a higher paying job, or even in renovating a home that when finished will be improved and more livable, or in learning how to play guitar so that we can eventually play with other musicians or even join a musical group and maybe become successful in the entertainment world. No matter what we do, to begin we have to have faith that we will succeed, or that we will reach a certain goal.

However, in this spiritual endeavor, we do have the descriptions of it and directions for following the path in the Vedic literature, along with the advice and stories about it from the previous *acharyas* and gurus, and experiences as told by the older devotees who have been practicing it for a while. So this should at least give us the confidence that if we begin and follow the instructions properly, there is a good chance of success.

The fact of the matter is that we are always serving somebody, no matter what we do. As we grow up, we have to serve our parents by following their instructions. Then we have to serve our teachers and do what they expect us to do if we are going to get good grades. Then we serve our bosses or company supervisors if we expect to keep our job. Then we have to serve the government by paying our taxes. Then, in our search for love, we have to serve our beloved, and if we get married then we serve our wife or husband in particular ways, at least if we want a good marriage. And then if we have children, we have to serve our children by taking care of them nicely. We also have to abide by the laws of the country, or we may end up in jail where we are forced into particular labor to serve the government whether we like it or not. And all the while, we have been serving the demands of our own minds and senses, and also making sure we can feed and give shelter, etc., to our own body. This is a never-ending endeavor.

The point is, in this way we are forced to be servants, either willingly or unwillingly. But all of the above situations is service to the various energies of the Supreme. So why not learn to engage in service that is directly toward the Supreme, as described and taught in the process of bhakti-yoga? We may be happy in family life or in a good career for a time, but after a while there is always a need for a change, or for something new. Something deeper, something more fulfilling, something to fill the void within us that material pursuits do not seem to reach. This is where bhakti-yoga can fill that deeper longing, even if we simply add it to what we are already doing.

As the *Bhagavad-gita* (6.45) explains, as a person engages with sincere intentions, for further progress, being increasingly freed from material motivations or contamination, ultimately, even if it takes many births, a person can attain the supreme spiritual goal of life.

Reaching the supreme goal means a few different things, depending on what stage of spiritual development we have attained. The first stage of success is simply reaching the level of engaging in bhakti-yoga, or loving service to the Supreme. As our consciousness becomes spiritualized, such a service attitude and constant awareness of the Supreme, which is the purpose of yoga, prepares us for leaving this body with God or Krishna in the center of our attention. When that happens, as Lord Krishna explains, and then, as we show in later chapters of this book, we enter directly into Krishna's domain in the spiritual atmosphere. "Engage your mind always in thinking of Me, offer obeisances and worship Me. Being completely absorbed in Me, surely you will come to Me. (*Bg*.9.34) That is the way of the spiritual and godly life, after attaining which a man is not bewildered. Being so situated, even at the hour of death, one can enter the spiritual world." (*Bg*.2.72) Then we reach our real home of eternal bliss in spiritual loving activities.

In the meantime, we have to start with faith that as this has happened to others, it can also work for us. An example of this is described in the *Srimad-Bhagavatam* (6.2.36-38): "Because of identifying oneself with the body, one is subjected to desires for sense gratification, and thus one engages in many different types of pious and impious activities. This is what constitutes material bondage. [But] now I shall disentangle myself from my material bondage, which has been caused by the Supreme Personality of Godhead's energy [which in this case is] in the form of a woman [but can be any object desired by the mind and senses]. Being a most fallen soul, I was victimized by the illusory energy and have become like a dancing dog led around by a woman's hand. Now I shall give up all lusty desires and free myself from this illusion. I shall become a merciful, well-wishing friend to all living entities and always absorb myself in Krishna consciousness.

"Simply because I chanted the holy names of the Lord in the association of devotees, my heart is now becoming purified. Therefore, I shall not fall victim again to the false lures of material sense gratification. Now that I have become fixed in the Absolute Truth, henceforward I shall not identify myself with the body. I shall give up false conceptions of 'I' and 'mine' and fix my mind on the lotus feet of Krishna."

So faith, also known as *shraddha*, refers to a firm and confident belief that by engaging in bhakti-yoga, or service to Krishna, we will certainly make spiritual progress. In this way, the main duties for attaining the purpose of life will be fulfilled. Or, as explained in the *Srimad-Bhagavatam* (4.31.14): "As a tree's trunk, branches, twigs, and leaves are nourished by watering its roots, and as all the senses are satisfied by giving food to the stomach, so similarly, all living beings are served [and fulfilled] by worshiping the infallible Supreme Being."

At first, before we have a real taste for engaging in service to the Supreme, or if our faith is weak, we may have to simply act out of duty, dedication to the path, following the regulative principles under the proper guidance of a qualified guru. However, as we perform devotional activities and feel the happiness of associating with devotees, even unconsciously, the soul becomes satisfied. Then by engaging in the eternal function of the soul, which naturally wants to connect with God, the inherent *shraddha* or faith appears. Then material attachments and desires, and those things that used to be so significant to us, gradually decrease and become meaningless. Then, with continued practice of bhakti-yoga, our connection with the Supreme becomes increasingly important and enjoyable to us.

Then as our faith increases due to continued uplifting experiences in our devotional service, the devotee develops *raga*, or *raga-marga*. This is when the devotee actually begins to acquire a taste or a reciprocation from the service to Lord Krishna that is being performed. The devotee develops an attachment, especially for hearing about Krishna and His qualities and pastimes, and for talking about Him and chanting His holy names. Then one's faith develops into steadiness or *nishta*, which is a constant state of remembrance. Then it develops into a serious taste and attachment for one's service, called *ruchi*, and then to *bhava* or love for Krishna, and then to *prema*, which is an intense reciprocal love for Krishna. (*Cc.* Madhya-lila, 23.9-13 & *Sri Caitanya-Siksamrta*, 18-19)

In this way, when a person reaches the stage of *ruchi* or *bhava*, the spiritual taste that one has for their service to the Lord overtakes the need for simply following the rules and regulations. Then it becomes a spiritual life of experiencing the bliss and reciprocation between the devotee and the Lord, which becomes the prime motivation for the devotee's continued engagement in bhakti-yoga.

This is further described like so: "The *vaidha-bhaktas* [devotees engaged in the regulative principles] are practitioners. They are of three types: those with *shraddha* (faith); those with *nishtha* (steadiness); and those with *ruchi* (taste). Those with *shraddha* take shelter of a guru, take initiation and perform the devotional activities. By performing devotional activities in association with devotees, the *anarthas* (unwanted material desires) disappear. When the *anarthas* disappear, *shraddha* becomes *nishtha* [being steady in always remembering and never forgetting Krishna]; this, intensified with spiritual desire, becomes *ruchi*. This is the limit of *sadhana-bhakti* [bhakti based on faith and regulative activities]. *Ruchi* then becomes *asakti* (attachment), which then progresses to *bhava* (ecstatic emotion). These stages will be discussed later." (*Sri Caitanya-Siksamrta*, 136)

# CHAPTER SIX

# *Sadhana-Bhakti*
# *The Regulated Stage*

To begin bhakti-yoga, we naturally start at the first stage, which is taking up the regulated practices to begin purifying our consciousness. But first we should ask ourselves, why should we undergo a spiritual process? Why should we take up any discipline to develop ourselves spiritually? The reason, as it is said in the *Kena Upanishad* (2.5): "If a man is able to realize God in this life, his purpose will have been achieved; if, however, he fails to do so in the course of this life, it would spell a terrible ruin (for him)."

Therefore, while we have this unique opportunity that remains incomprehensible for many people, let us make progress, whether great or minimal, to accomplish the purpose of this human life. So, as it says in the *Kathopanishad* (1.3.14) "Rise, awake, and approaching the great [wise ones], learn the truth [from them]."

When we are engaged in the *sadhana* or practice of bhakti-yoga, which is the practical application of our mind and senses in the devotional service to the Lord, we first follow the regulative principles, which is called *vaidhi-bhakti*, or *sadhana-bhakti*. It is performing our service out of obedience to the instructions in the Vedic literature for spiritual advancement, under the guidance of a spiritual master. As Krishna says in *Bhagavad-gita* (5.11), "The yogis, abandoning attachment, act with body, mind, intelligence, and even with the senses, only for the purpose of purification."

In this process, at first we may hear about and discuss the glories and pastimes of the Lord from a sense of duty, but as we become purified, our taste for our service increases until we feel great attachment to our activities dedicated to the Lord, which is called *raganuga*, or devotional service in natural love. This is more spontaneous. So in the beginning, we may follow out of duty, but later we engage in our service out of love. [1]

The living entities naturally want freedom to be happy, which means, ultimately, they want to be free from the limitations imposed upon them by this life in the ocean of material existence, which is a constant source of waves of various forms of material happiness interrupted by various kinds of miseries, anxiety and trouble. However, every so often we begin to ask ourselves if this life is all there is, if this is as good as it gets. Or if there could be something better. And out of all of the living beings scattered across this material universe, some few fortunate souls in their search for answers may receive the seed, the *bhakti-lata-bija*, of the creeper of devotional service, *bhakti-yoga*, by the grace of Krishna or a wandering pure devotee.[2] If someone accepts this seed, then it can develop into this vine of devotional progress, the *bhakti-lata*, that begins to grow from the soul of the materially conditioned living being, up through the material creation and into the spiritual realm until it reaches the lotus feet of Lord Krishna. But this takes steady practice and great care. And this all begins with *sadhana-bhakti*, the regulated devotional activities.

The *Srimad-Bhagavatam* (1.2.17-19) explains it like this, "Sri Krishna, the Personality of Godhead, who is the Paramatma [Supersoul] in everyone's heart and the benefactor of the truthful devotee, cleanses the desires for material enjoyment from the heart of the devotee who has developed the urge to hear His messages, which are in themselves virtuous when properly heard and chanted.

"By regular attendance in the classes on the *Bhagavatam*, and by rendering of service to the pure devotee, all that is troublesome to the heart is almost completely destroyed, and loving service unto the Personality of Godhead, who is praised with transcendental songs, is established as an irrevocable fact.

"As soon as irrevocable loving service is established in the heart, the effects of nature's modes of passion and ignorance, such as lust, desire and hankering, disappear from the heart. Then the devotee is established in [the mode of] goodness, and he becomes completely happy."

Therefore, the premise of engaging in bhakti-yoga,

performing loving devotional service to the Lord, is to engage our mind and senses in thinking about and practicing activities meant for aligning our desire for love and meaningful actions into thinking about and serving the Supreme. When the senses and mind are satisfied in the Supersoul, and merge into [thoughts of] Him, all miseries are completely vanquished, as after a sound sleep. [3]

There are so many easy ways to use this body and our senses in bhakti-yoga. We can attend the temple functions like the *arati* ceremony and see the Deities, hear the singing of devotional songs, smell the incense and flowers that have been offered to the Deity, watch dramatic performances and dances that depict Krishna's pastimes, or see the paintings of the Supreme, etc. We can also travel and go on pilgrimages to see the holy places, and realize that all aspects of material nature can be related to the power of the Supreme. We can also use the tongue to taste the delicious food items that are offered to the Deity. If we want to render other services, we can use our bodies to clean the temple, or wash the pots that have been used in the temple kitchen, or help grow a garden to offer vegetables and flowers to the Deities. In these and many more ways we can use our body in bhakti-yoga. In this way, it becomes fun and enlivening to engage in this process.

The important point is to keep in mind that what we do is an offering to the Lord. This is the meditation that makes it service in bhakti-yoga. As Lord Krishna says in the *Bhagavatam* (11.29.9), "Always remembering Me, one should perform all his duties for Me without being impetuous. With mind and intelligence offered to Me, one should fix his mind in attraction to My devotional service."

In accordance with the particular nature or proclivities one has acquired in conditional life, whatever one does with body, mind, words, senses, intelligence, or purified consciousness, one should offer to the Supreme, thinking, "This is for the pleasure of Lord Nayarana [Vishnu or Krishna]." [4]

Such simple remembrance of God destroys inauspiciousness and awards the greatest of all good fortune. It purifies the heart and bestows devotion for the Supreme Soul, along with spiritual knowledge enriched with realization and renunciation. [5]

In the *Bhagavad-gita* (8.7), Lord Krishna also tells Arjuna,

"Therefore, Arjuna, you should always think of Me in the form of Krishna, and at the same time carry out your prescribed duties... With your activities dedicated to Me, and your mind and intelligence fixed on Me, you will attain Me without doubt."

So the point is that you go on with your duties, but keep your mind fixed on Krishna and try to dedicate your activities as offerings to the Lord. Then you will attain Krishna and reach His eternal spiritual domain. In this way, *sadhana-bhakti* is a purely spiritual process. One sincerely engaged in such devotional service is practically already in the spiritual world. He or she only needs to be steady in this process. [6]

## THINKING OF THE FORM OF KRISHNA

As mentioned, remembering Lord Krishna is an importance principle. That itself is a form of meditation on the Absolute Truth. Furthermore, Krishna accepts things that are offered to Him in meditation. In this way, meditation means to engage the mind in thinking of the form of Lord Krishna, His activities, qualities, and in the ways we can continue our service to Him. This is real bhakti-yoga.

This is also the importance of the Deity of Krishna in the temple. No matter whether the Deity is made of paint, wood, marble, metal, or whatever, the Lord and His form are absolute, completely spiritual. In other words, He can turn what is material into spiritual, or what is spiritual into material. When we do the *prana-pratishta* ceremony, we call the Lord to take up residence in the form of the Deity in order to easily accept our service. So the Deity is non-different from the Lord in this way. Besides, metal, wood, marble etc., are all energies of the Lord, and His energies are never completely separate from Him anyway, just as the sunshine is still a part of the sun's energies. However, with Krishna, He is always in control of all of His energies.

It is not like us who are different from our names, or the body we inhabit. You may call my name all day, but it will have no effect on me or you. Whereas when you call the name of Krishna, His energy is His name, they are non-different. So, even though it may take some time for you to perceive this, there is no difference between the Deity in the temple and Lord Krishna when we worship Him. Such worship takes our consciousness directly to Krishna. [7]

This is also the way we can see something spiritual with our material eyes. The Deity is formed according to the descriptions in Vedic *shastra*, and is installed per the same instructions. Thereafter, when called properly and with devotion, the Lord takes up residence in the Deity form. Thus, the authorized Deity is not imaginary or concocted. It is the reason why so many devotees derive great bliss when approaching the Deity in the temple. There can be a direct reciprocal exchange between ourselves and the Deity in this way, which is the meaning of the word *darshan*. Through *darshan* we see the Deity in the temple, but are also seen by the Deity in a reciprocal loving exchange. Thus, devotees are not idol worshipers. Unfortunately, those who are devoid of bhakti, or who think that God has no form, cannot understand the Deity and then think He is just an idol.

Nonetheless, there are lots of stories of how the Deities of Lord Krishna interact with His devotees. [You can read my book *Krishna Deities and Their Miracles: How the Images of Lord Krishna Interact with Their Devotees*, which contains numerous stories of how the Deities come alive to engage in pastimes with Their devotees.] Therefore, the Deity is the causeless mercy of the Lord. Otherwise, we cannot see the form of the Lord directly with our materialistic minds and senses.

In this way, meditating or simply thinking about Lord Sri Krishna or His instructions is as good as trance meditation. "... One should therefore meditate on the Supreme Personality of Godhead and upon His devotees. One should meditate on the eternal form of the Lord until the mind becomes fixed." [8]

# Chapter Six

*Krishna playing His flute in the Vrindavana forests in the moonlight with devotees like his cow and peacock next to Him.*

## MOLDING ONE'S LIFE FOR SPIRITUAL ADVANCEMENT

As we develop ourselves spiritually, we can see that it is advantageous to arrange our lives for continued progress in all avenues of life so we can develop the habits and characteristics that mold our consciousness. This is also described as follows, "A candidate for spiritual advancement must be nonviolent, must follow in the footsteps of the great *acharyas*, must always remember the nectar of the pastimes of the Supreme Personality of Godhead, must follow the regulative principles without material desire, and, while following the regulative principles, should not blaspheme others. A devotee should lead a very simple life and not be disturbed by the duality of opposing elements [the ups and downs of life]. He should learn to tolerate them.

"The devotee should gradually increase the culture of devotional service by constant hearing of the transcendental qualities of the Supreme Personality of Godhead. These pastimes are like ornamental decorations on the ears of devotees. By rendering devotional service and transcending the material qualities, one can easily be fixed in transcendence in the Supreme Personality of Godhead." [9]

These instructions show how a person can easily advance in bhakti-yoga while at the same time developing the characteristics to become a better human being.

In this way, our success in bhakti-yoga, Krishna consciousness, is also proportional to our material detachment. If one's material attractions are not becoming minimized, then it is a sign that he or she is not advancing spiritually very much. It is natural that as a person increasingly realizes their spiritual identity within the material body, the inclination to pursue bodily pleasures loses its meaning. You become indifferent to it. It becomes a waste of time. Why? Because you realize there is a higher taste and a more intense level of bliss to be attained.

This is also described to some degree by the Supreme Lord as Kapila in the *Bhagavatam* (3.27.28-9), "My devotee actually becomes self-realized by My unlimited causeless mercy, and, thus, when freed from all doubts, he steadily progresses toward his destined abode, which is directly under the protection of My spiritual energy of unadulterated bliss. This is the ultimate perfectional goal of the living entity. After giving up the present material body, the mystic devotee goes to that transcendental abode and never comes back."

However, one must engage in bhakti-yoga with great patience and with confidence. You must not give up prematurely, nor expect great changes or experiences before you are qualified. I have personally seen devotees give up just before they were starting to make great strides in their advancement. Sometimes they leave for good, but most of the time they return to start again in some way, or at least maintain their connection, because they cannot forget the taste that they had while engaged in devotional service with other devotees. So it would have been best if they could have simply endured and continued with their spiritual development.

However, in the beginning, when a person may still be in the immature stage of bhakti-yoga, they may still fall away from following the principles, either accidently or purposefully because of weakness to the illusory energy. In either case, Lord Krishna explains in the *Bhagavad-gita* (3.39) that one may fall down from the proper standards, but may still continue to advance if the person continues in the process of bhakti-yoga. Krishna further explains (*Bg.* 9.30) that devotional service itself rectifies occasional fall downs since the person is still properly situated in spiritual progress.

The *Srimad-Bhagavatam* (1.5.17) also clearly explains, "One who has forsaken his material occupation to engage in the devotional service of the Lord may sometimes fall down while in an immature stage, yet there is no danger of his being unsuccessful. On the other hand, a nondevotee, though fully engaged in occupational duties, does not gain anything."

Therefore, if a devotee keeps working on his spiritual progress through the path of bhakti-yoga, he will still become purified and will advance. But a person who pursues all of his occupational duties successfully will still lose everything simply because of the temporary nature of all material activities and possessions.

In this way, one must be patient and steady, or *nishta*, which means to remain focused on the goal with faith and without distraction. In fact, patience is one of the six basic principles that guarantee success on the path of bhakti-yoga, as explained in the *Upadeshamrita* (Text 3) of Srila Rupa Gosvami, "There are six principles favorable to the execution of pure devotional service, 1) being enthusiastic, 2) endeavoring with confidence, 3) being patient, 4) acting according to regulative principles [such as hearing, chanting and remembering Krishna], 5) abandoning the association of nondevotees, and 6) following in the footsteps of the previous *acharyas*. These six principles undoubtedly assure the complete success of pure devotional service."

## CLIMBING THE LADDER OF SUCCESS

The effect of *sadhana-bhakti* is like climbing the ladder of success, steadily working our way upwards. We may start with little feeling, as in merely following the regulations, but it can lead to the highest bliss. It is stated in the *Brahma-samhita* (58-60): "When the pure spiritual experience by means of cognition and service [bhakti], superexcellent unalloyed devotion characterized by love of Godhead is awakened towards Krishna, the beloved of all souls. The highest devotion is attained by slow degrees by the method of constant endeavor for self-realization with the help of scriptural evidence, theistic conduct and perseverance in practice. These preliminary practices [*sadhana-bhakti*] are conducive to the realization of loving devotion, which goes hand in hand in attaining the exclusive state of supreme bliss, which leads to Myself [Krishna]."

The *Caitanya-caritamrita* (Madhya-lila, 19.177) summarizes it like this: by regularly rendering devotional service, one gradually becomes attached to the Supreme Being. When that attachment is intensified, it becomes love for God. And that loving exchange brings the highest bliss.

# Chapter Six

## ATTAINING THE HIGHER LEVELS OF BHAKTI

As we progress, we will experience the different levels of bhakti. First we engage in *sadhana-bhakti*, but when we get a taste for our service to the Lord, it gradually becomes *raga*. This means to engage in such service without merely doing our duty, without fear of punishment, and without motivation or desire for personal gain. It means a natural attraction.

*Raga* means the tendency of the mind to be spontaneously attracted to an object immediately upon seeing it. There is no intellectual analysis involved. "Devotional service with ecstatic attachment for that service, which becomes natural for the devotee, is called *raga*, or transcendental attachment." [10]

Those who become naturally attracted in their hearts as soon as they think of Krishna are worshiping the Lord in the mood of *raga*. Those who worship from fear, desire or duty are not on such a pure level, even though bhakti can begin with these feelings. Those who worship according to *raga*, a natural inclination, are the real worshipers. This is the goal of bhakti-yoga.

The loving nature of the soul, especially towards the Supreme, is very deep. When *raga* appears, this loving relationship increasingly manifests. It is only hidden for the materially conditioned and attached souls. However, when given the right environment and instructions, this relationship can fully manifest. By continued *sadhana* or practice, the living being can feel an increasingly loving relation with the Lord. [11]

If this were not possible, how could the Lord reciprocate with the infinitesimal soul of the living being? The Supreme Lord is filled with the highest love and eager to exchange love with the living beings. Yet, being the Unlimited Lord, how can He be willing to accept the meager offerings and sentiment of us humans? Or become genuinely happy with the simple offerings of love we have to present? Yet, He also feels His own bliss by exchanging such loving pastimes with the qualified and purified devoted souls in the transcendental abode of Vrindavana. This is the secret of how God is not attracted by anything we do, unless it is covered with love. This is what can attract Him. This is why He is the ultimate object of love and the ultimate person to reciprocate our love.

So we maintain our practice of *sadhana-bhakti*, but when the natural attraction of *raga* appears, the path of *vaidhi-bhakti* loses its effectiveness. Why? Because the natural attraction outweighs the need to simply follow the rules and regulations. But as long as *raga* has not been developed, a person must continue their path of *vaidhi* or *sadhana-bhakti*. Only those who are most advanced and fortunate can practice the path of *raga-bhakti*. [12]

Nonetheless, we can be successful in this way if we are sincere and patient. *Sadhana-bhakti* can lead to *bhava-bhakti*, which is the level of loving ecstasy. This can lead to the level of pure love, which is *prema-bhakti*. *Bhava-bhakti* is attained when the devotional service in practice has become mature, and when intensified it becomes *prema-bhakti*.

Love and devotion are the eternal characteristics of the soul. But that devotion toward God only needs to be reawakened. It is not that *sadhana-bhakti* or following regulated rules will produce *bhava-bhakti*. *Sadhana-bhakti* simply purifies the heart of the devotee so that *bhava* or love for Krishna is revealed in the heart, like when the muddy water clears in a pond or a puddle to reveal what lies on the bottom. This natural love is part of the eternally perfect nature of the soul, called *nitya-siddha*. Though it is rare, we all can reach the stage of *nitya-siddha* through the practice of *sadhana*, regulated devotional service. [13] Then we are called *sadhana-siddhas*, or those who have become perfected through the practice of our *sadhana*.

As further explained in the *Caitanya-caritamrita* (Madhya-lila, 24.289), "By executing regulative devotional service, one is elevated to the platform of an eternally perfect associate [of Lord Krishna]–such as a servant, friend, superior [like a father, mother, uncle, etc.] or a beloved [like the gopis, the cowherd girls of Vrindavana]. These are the four varieties." In this way, one who is engaged in sincere bhakti-yoga is practically already in the spiritual domain. The bhakti yogi only has to continue the process in a steady manner and every necessary quality eventually will be revealed. Or as Lord Krishna Himself explains in *Bhagavad-gita* (9.22), "Those who worship Me with devotion, meditating on My transcendental form–to them I carry what they lack and preserve what they have."

So here Krishna provides the means for the devotee to continue their progress up to and including entering the spiritual world. Or as Lord Krishna says elsewhere in *Bhagavad-gita* (12.6-7), "For one who worships Me, giving up all his activities unto Me and being devoted to Me without deviation, engaged in devotional service and always meditating upon Me, who has fixed his mind upon Me, O son of Partha, for him I am the swift deliverer from the ocean of birth and death."

So when a person receives the seed of devotional service, he or she should take care of it by becoming a gardener [a perfect practitioner of bhakti-yoga] and sowing the seed in his or her heart. If the seed is watered properly with the process of *shravana* and *kirtana* [hearing and chanting about Krishna], gradually the seed will begin to sprout. [14] Then it will continue to grow to the abode of Lord Krishna.

Therefore, while being engaged in the rules of *vaidhi-bhakti*, we should keep in mind that what we want to attain is *bhava-bhakti*, engaging in our devotional service with strong loving sentiments for Krishna. This is further cultivated by strong attention to reach the level of *prema-bhakti*, the ultimate pure loving bliss. [15] This pure love is the nature of the spiritual world. The more we attain this loving nature, and operate on this frequency level, the more we become qualified to enter into that spiritual atmosphere.

*Prema* or true love for God, appears in a marginal form when the living being is under the illusion of the material energy. That is when he falls in love with all kinds of energies of the Lord within this material creation, like wife, husband, friends, and other things he or she finds attractive, but not directing it towards God. So this level of *prema* is not in its *svarupa* or natural and fully manifested form. It is only a reflection or shadow of reality. But by performing *sadhana-bhakti*, gradually *prema* is revealed like a hidden fire, and love for Krishna begins to be revealed. In this way, a person can continue to develop until they feel the blissful ecstasy of a loving reciprocation between themselves and the Supreme. Then, when such devotees finally cast off their physical and subtle body and attain spiritual bodies, *prema* appears in its pure *svarupa*, or fully manifested form without any physical or mental limitations. In this way, Krishna *prema* is the perfect object and goal, which is not born from practice, but rather it is revealed in the pure heart of the successful devotee by the process of hearing, chanting, and other devotional activities.

Thus, there are two kinds of bodies to consider; one is the *sadhana-rupa*, or the body we possess while we engage in our *sadhana*. The second is the *siddha-rupa*, our spiritual body, the real form without any material limitations that is the most suitable for executing our service to Krishna. We may follow in the footsteps of a great devotee or servant of Krishna whose mood is very attractive to us. As we engage in this way, we develop that mood in our own loving service. We do not imitate, but we try to develop the loving mood of the devotee we most appreciate. Then that mood helps develop our *raga-bhakti*, or natural taste and attachment for doing our service. This helps carry us to the destination of intense, ecstatic love for Krishna, and helps deliver us to our spiritual body. This is what attracts Krishna, which then helps bring Krishna's blessings to us for our continued progress and attainment of the spiritual abode.[16]

There are two ways to execute such devotional service with attachment; internally and externally. Externally the devotee continues to follow all of the regulative principles, beginning with hearing and chanting, while internally he or she thinks of the attachment or devotional mood in which they are most attracted to serve the Lord.[17]

Those who become fully engaged in such bhakti-yoga, under the guidance and in the footsteps of the Lord's beloved devotees, can attain such perfection of being transferred to the spiritual world.[18] Though we may not be able to do that in the beginning, but as we progress and our taste for such service increases, then the heart finds a way. It is also this kind of dedication which purifies the mind from all material attachments and memories that keep us bound to this material world. Gradually we can become free and attain steady joy and happiness in our connection with Krishna.

**CHAPTER NOTES**
1. *Nectar of Devotion*, p. 21 & *Cc.* Madhya-lila, 22.108-9.
2. *Caitanya-caritamrita,* Madhya-lila, 19.151.
3. *Srimad-Bhagavatam,* 3.7.13.

4. Ibid., 11.2.36.
5. Ibid., 12.12.55.
6. *Sri Caitanya-Siksamrta*, p.103 & *Caitanya-caritamrita,* Madhya-lila, 4.134.
7. *Caitanya-caritamrita,* Adi-lila, 5.226.
8. *Bhagavatam* 3.28.18.
9. Ibid., 4.22.24-5.
10. *Bhakti-rasamrita-sindhu* 1.2.270.
11. *Sri Caitanya-Siksamrta*, p.5-6.
12. Ibid., p.14.
13. *Art of Sadhana*, p. 22.
14. *Caitanya-caritamrita,* Madhya-lila, 19.152.
15. *Sri Caitanya-Siksamrta*, p. 65.
16. *Art of Sadhana,* p. 225.
17. *Teachings of Lord Caitanya*, p. 135.
18. *Narada-Bhakti-Sutra*, p.11 & *Nectar of Instruction*, text 8.

# CHAPTER SEVEN

# *Adopting the Principles*

When we begin to adopt the principles, we have to remember, as previously explained, that at first we may engage in them out of faith, or out of duty to the instructions of the Vedic *shastra* or the guru. But as we progress, we can notice that our consciousness is getting materially purified, or spiritualized. Our material attractions or addictions begin to subside. Then we get a taste for these spiritual activities, a reciprocation for what we do in trying to please the Lord. When that begins to happen, our purpose in accepting such rules out of duty turns to doing them out of love. Then we acquire an attachment for progressing in this way, and for our devotional activities that are for pleasing the Supreme, Lord Sri Krishna, the God of love.

So to begin with, there are a number of rules that a bhakta (devotee) should try to follow. The more important rules are fairly simple, which include: 1. To accept everything that is favorable for devotional service, 2. To reject everything which is unfavorable, 3. To believe that Lord Krishna will always give protection, 4. To identify oneself as one of Krishna's devotees, 5. To always feel inability without the help of Krishna, 6. And to always think of oneself as inferior to Krishna, even though one may have full capacity to do something on his or her own. These rules will help create a mood of reverential devotion. [1]

These rules are the foundation of everything else we may do. Additional basic rules are listed for advancing in bhakti-yoga that we should also try to follow as best we can. Depending on our situation, we may be more or less successful in following these. But the more we can do so, and the more we have help from other devotees or bhakti-yogis, the easier it gets. These additional rules are as follows, of which the first five are very important, and the first three are most important: 1) accepting the shelter or guidance of a genuine spiritual master, 2) becoming initiated by the spiritual master and learning the process of bhakti-yoga from him, 3) obeying the orders of the spiritual master with faith and devotion, 4) following in the footsteps of great *acharyas*, spiritual teachers, under the direction of your spiritual master, 5) inquiring from the spiritual master how to advance in Krishna consciousness, 6) being prepared to give up any materialistic activity for the satisfaction of the Supreme Being, Sri Krishna, 7) residing in a sacred place of pilgrimage or holy place like Vrindavana or Dvaraka, 8) dealing with the material world only as much as necessary, which may be difficult if we have a job or career, but we do that as professionally as possible, while retreating to our spiritual engagement as much as possible, 9) observing the fasting day of *Ekadashi*, and 10) worshiping or respecting the sacred trees like the banyan or *tulasi* trees, shown by offering water to such trees.

As one grows in devotional advancement, he or she can also apply these additional rules, as best one can, which are to assist us in developing our spiritual consciousness. 1) One should give up the company of nondevotees, which will certainly bring a person down to materialistic thought patterns and activities, 2) One should not instruct a person who is not desirous of accepting devotional service, 3) One should not be very enthusiastic about constructing huge, costly temples, 4) One should not try to read too many books (which may increase one's confusion about what to do since there are so many different schools of thought), nor should one try to make a profession out of speaking on *Bhagavad-gita* or *Srimad-Bhagavatam*, 5) One should not be neglectful in ordinary dealings, 6) One should not be under the spell of lamentation in loss or tribulation in gain, 7) One should not disrespect the *devatas* or demigods, 8) One should not give unnecessary trouble to any living entity, or any species, 9) One should carefully avoid the various offenses in chanting the holy name of the Lord, or in worshiping the Deity in the temple, 10) One should be intolerant towards the blasphemy of the Supreme Personality of Godhead, or His devotees [which can quickly reduce one's spiritual merit].

All of these rules or regulations are meant to assist you in engaging all of your activities of body, mind and speech in various ways of bhakti-yoga, devotional service. These come to a total of 64 items when we include the following 44:

This is the next list of items to observe, some of which may be repeated for their importance, and some of which are more easily performed while living in India. These include: 1) One should decorate the body with *tilaka*, which is the sign of a serious Vaishnava devotee, 2) this may also include writing the name of Hare Krishna on the body, 3) One should accept and wear flowers and garlands that have been offered to the Deity or spiritual master (which is known to reduce one's karma), 4) One should learn to dance before the Deity, 5) One should bow down immediately upon seeing the Deity in the temple or the spiritual master, 6) While visiting a temple of Krishna, one should stand in respect of the Deity, after paying obeisances [bowing to the Deity when first seen], 7) A devotee should follow the procession of the Deity, such as when the Deity is brought out of the temple on a cart or palanquin, which is an old custom followed in India, 8) It is best to visit a Krishna or Vishnu temple once or twice a day, 9) You can also circumambulate the temple, which is another old custom in India, when devotees visit a temple they walk around it three times or more, according to their vows, 10) When visiting Vrindavana, circumambulate the whole town is very auspicious, 11) One should worship the Deity in the temple according the regulative principles, such as offering or observing the *arati* ceremony, honoring *prasadam* (the food that has been offered to the Deity), dressing the Deity, etc. 12) Render personal service to the Deities, 13) Singing the holy songs or mantras before the Deities, 14) Engage in *sankirtana*, the congregational singing of the holy names that happens in most Krishna temples, 15) Chanting of the holy names, 16) Offer prayers, 17) Recite notable prayers, especially those of the previous *acharyas* and pure devotees, 18) taste the *maha-prasadan*, the food that has been directly offered to the Deities, 19) Drink a few drops of *charanamritam*, which is the water that was used to bathe the Deities that is offered to guests at the temple. (There is often a little cup or bowl near the alter with this water which guests can use the spoon to pour a few drops into their hand to sip.), 20) Smell the incense and flowers that have been offered to the Deities, usually done while observing the *arati* ceremony, 21) One can touch the holy feet of the Deity (only at certain temples, otherwise no one but the priests are allowed on the altar), 22) One should see the Deity with great devotion, 23) One must offer *arati* (*aratrika*) to the Deity at times, 24) One must hear about the Lord and His pastimes from books like the *Srimad-Bhagavatam* and *Bhagavad-gita*, 25) One must pray to the Deity for His mercy, 26) One should remember the Deity throughout the day, 27) In this way one should meditate on the Deity, 28) One should render voluntary service, 29) One should think of the Lord as your friend, 30) One should offer everything to the Lord, 31) One should offer to the Lord your favorite article, like food or garment, when prepared specifically for the Deity, 32) A person should take all kinds of risks for Krishna's benefit, 33) In every condition, a person should be surrendered to Krishna, 34) One should water the *tulasi* plant, 35) Regularly hear *Srimad-Bhagavatam* and similar literature, 36) Live in a sacred place (or at least near a temple or make a temple in your house), 37) Offer service to other devotees, 38) Arrange your devotional service according to your means and ability, 39) Make special arrangements for the month of Kartika (October and November), which is considered a time when you can make rapid advancement, 40) Observe some special service during Janmashthami, the day celebrated as Krishna's appearance day, 41) Do whatever you can do with great care and devotion for the Deity, 42) Relish the pleasure of reading and discussing *Bhagavatam* amongst the devotees, 43) Associate with devotees who are considered more advanced, and 44) Live near the jurisdiction of places like Mathura (Krishna's birthplace) if possible.

    These rules are listed in the *Nectar of Devotion* (pp. 53-54) by A. C. Bhaktivedanta Swami Prabhupada, which is a summary study of the *Bhakti-rasamrita-sindhu* by Srila Rupa Gosvami. Further elaborations on these can be found in the *Caitanya-caritamrita* (Madhya-lila. 22.115-146). Basically, they are ways and guidelines simply to help absorb yourself in activities that can enhance your spiritual development on the path of bhakti-yoga. How well we can follow these rules not only depends on our sincerity, but also on the living facilities we have, or where in the world we are located. One example is that if we live in the northern climates, we may not see or have the weather where *tulasi* trees can proliferate. You may be able to see them at some Krishna temples, but that is often after they have made elaborate arrangements with grow lights and a warm room for their development. The same applies if we would want to grow them in our house. So we may have to make adjustments if possible.

Reading so many rules may also seem confusing, but they can all be narrowed down to the first five, and the following nine ways of engaging in devotion. These are explained in the *Srimad-Bhagavatam* (7.5.23-24) when Prahlada Maharaja is talking with his father, Hiranyakashipu, when he told him, "(1) Hearing and (2) chanting about the transcendental holy name, form, qualities, paraphernalia, and pastimes of Lord Vishnu [or Krishna], (3) remembering them, (4) serving the lotus feet of the Lord, (5) offering the Lord respectful worship with sixteen types of paraphernalia, (6) offering prayers to the Lord, (7) becoming His servant, (8) considering the Lord one's best friend, (9) and surrendering everything unto Him (in other words with the body, mind and words)–these nine processes are accepted as pure devotional service. One who has dedicated his life to the service of Krishna through these nine methods should be understood to be the most learned person, for he has acquired complete knowledge."

As further explained in the *Caitanya-caritamrita* (Antya-lila.4.70-71): "Among the ways of executing devotional service, the nine prescribed methods are the best, for these processes have great potency to deliver Krishna and ecstatic love for Him. Of the nine processes of devotional service, the most important is to always chant the holy name of the Lord. If one does so, avoiding the ten kinds of offenses [to the holy name], one very easily obtains the most valuable love of Godhead." [These ten offenses are listed in Chapter Nine.]

Furthermore, all rules and regulations can be boiled down to two basic principles, as described herein from the *Padma Purana*: "Krishna is the origin of Lord Vishnu. He should always be remembered and never forgotten at any time. All the rules and prohibitions mentioned in the *shastras*, should be considered the servants of these two principles."

One point to remember is that it may not be possible to execute each and every principle, or even do all nine of these processes. But it is explained that even if you are able to be successful in one of these nine processes and do it sufficiently, that is enough for one's full success in bhakti-yoga and attaining the spiritual abode.

Also, to enjoy life on the path of bhakti-yoga, Lord Krishna Himself advises His friend Uddhava how a person should engage him or herself in devotional activities. This shows that bhakti-yoga is not limited to only meditation and physical exercises or research, but offers a wide range of variegated engagements that can propel a devotee to taste different types of happiness. This is described in the *Srimad-Bhagavatam* (11.11.34-41):

"My dear Uddhava, one can give up false pride and prestige by engaging in the following devotional activities. One may purify oneself by seeing, touching, worshiping, serving, and offering prayers of glorification and obeisances to My form as the Deity and to My pure devotees. One should also glorify My transcendental qualities and activities, hear with love and faith the narration of My glories and constantly meditate on Me [in this way]. One should offer to Me whatever one acquires, and accepting oneself as My eternal servant, one should give oneself completely to Me. One should always discuss My birth and activities and enjoy life by participating in festivals, such as Janmashtami [Lord Krishna's birth celebration], which glorify My pastimes. In My temple, one should also participate in festivals and ceremonies by singing, dancing, playing musical instruments, and discussing Me with other Vaishnavas. One should observe all the regularly celebrated annual festivals by attending ceremonies, pilgrimages [to temples and holy places] and making offerings. One should observe religious vows such as Ekadashi and take initiation by the procedures mentioned in the *Vedas*, *Pancaratra* and other, similar literatures. One should faithfully and lovingly support the installation of My Deity, and individually or in cooperation with others one should work for the construction of Krishna conscious temples and cities as well as flower gardens, fruit gardens and special areas to celebrate My pastimes.

"One should consider oneself to be My humble servant, without duplicity, and thus should help to clean the temple, which is My home. First one should sweep and dust thoroughly, and then one should further cleanse with water and cow dung [a known antiseptic].

Having dried the temple, one should sprinkle scented water and decorate the temple with mandalas. One should thus act just like My servant. A devotee should never advertise his devotional activities; therefore his service will not be the cause of false pride.

"One should never use lamps that are offered to Me for other purposes simply because there is a need of illumination, and, similarly, one should never offer to Me anything that has been offered to or used by others. Whatever is most desired by one within this material world, and whatever is most dear to oneself–one should offer that very thing to Me. Such an offering qualifies one for eternal life."

The way these devotional principles are divided and the inner effects they have on us also depends on the level of spiritual development a person has acquired. Naturally, some people are more advanced than others. This may simply be a matter of how much a person had developed themselves in a previous life, or how sincerely they take the process now, or both. In any case, if a person wants to make rapid advancement, they can take to heart the instructions as given by Sri Caitanya Mahaprabhu when He was speaking to Sri Sanatana Gosvami, as found in the *Caitanya-caritamrita* (Madhya-lila, 22.104-110, 113), to understand how engaging in regulative bhakti-yoga will help one advance to the spontaneous stage:

"My dear Sanatana, please now hear about the regulative principles for the execution of devotional service. By this process, one can attain the highest perfection of love of Godhead, which is the most desirable treasure.

"When transcendental devotional service by which love for Krishna is attained is executed by the senses, it is called *sadhana-bhakti*, or the regulative discharge of devotional service. Such devotion eternally exists within the heart of every living being. The awakening of this eternal devotion is the potentiality of devotional service in practice." [2]

"The spiritual activities of hearing, chanting, remembering, and so forth are the natural characteristics of devotional service. The marginal characteristic is that it awakens pure love for Krishna. Pure love for Krishna is eternally established in the hearts of living entities, it is not something to be gained from another source. When the heart is purified by hearing and chanting, the living entity naturally awakens.

"There are two processes of practical devotional service. One is regulative devotional service, and the other is spontaneous devotional service. Those who have not attained the platform of spontaneous attachment in devotional service render devotional service under the guidance of a bona fide spiritual master according to the regulative principles mentioned in the revealed scriptures. According to the revealed scriptures, this kind of devotional service is called *vaidhi-bhakti*."

The importance of regulative service, also called *vaidhi-bhakti* or *sadhana-bhakti*, was explained in the previous chapter. It is the means by which a person becomes spiritually purified to the level in which he or she experiences spontaneous bhakti, which we will discuss later.

## THE LORD ACCEPTS OUR DEVOTIONAL MENTALITY

The grace of the Lord is that even though we may not perfectly engage in or fulfill all of the devotional rules and regulations as listed above, the Lord accepts the love with which the activities are offered. For example, if we cook something to offer to the Deity, we may successfully prepare it, or maybe we put too much salt in it, or something else may go wrong. But what Lord Krishna accepts is the love with which it is offered. Otherwise, Lord Krishna explains that even if elaborate arrangements are made to offer something to Him, if there is no love involved, then why should He accept it? So it is what is in the heart, or the devotional mentality or intent of the activity that is really accepted by the Lord. It is also said that the Lord feeds on the love that is offered. Whereas the demonic, ghostly or lower subtle beings feed off the fear, envy, anger, or addictive tendencies that our mind dwells on. But the higher beings accept the more advanced feelings like love. It is actually the love that is offered which determines how successful our devotional activities are.

Even a simple offering will be accepted by the Lord if it is offered with love. As Lord Krishna Himself explains, "If one offers Me with love and devotion a leaf, a flower, fruit, or water, I will accept it." [3]

"Bali Maharaja said [to Lord Vishnu], What a wonderful effect there is in even attempting to offer respectful obeisances to You! I merely endeavored to offer You obeisances, but nonetheless the attempt was as successful as those of pure devotees. The causeless mercy You have shown me, a fallen demon, was never achieved even by the demigods or the leaders of various planets." [4]

In this way, it is not necessary to engage in separate endeavors to start climbing the ladder of success in devotional service. In whatever one's situation may be, you can start the path of bhakti-yoga. Even if a devotee remains in household life, or is very old, if he is engaged in bhakti-yoga, he is still considered sober and progressing in what really matters in human life. [5]

Even if a person is surrounded by wife, husband, children, job, etc., he or she can still engage in bhakti-yoga, either at home or by going to the temple and learning the art of Deity worship or by participating in the temple programs. Even spending a small amount of time at a temple of Krishna is enough for one to make great strides in spiritual advancement. It is not necessary to completely free oneself from household life. In fact, to prematurely do so can be counter productive if a person tries to renounce all of one's responsibilities for full engagement in spiritual activities. If a person is not mature enough, he or she may still have a taste for such activities and go back to them, or still maintain such desires. As Lord Krishna explains in *Bhagavad-gita* (3.7), "One who restrains the senses of action but whose mind dwells on sense objects certainly deludes himself and is called a pretender."

Also, if a person still has material or familial responsibilities, it can produce bad karma to prematurely give up such responsibilities or use spiritual life as an excuse to give them up.

As explained in the *Narada-Bhakti-Sutra* (37, 62), "One achieves bhakti by hearing and chanting about the Supreme Lord's special qualities, even while engaged in the ordinary activities of life in this world... Even after one has achieved devotional service, one should not abandon one's responsibilities in this world but should rather continue surrendering the results of one's work to the Lord. And while still trying to reach the stage of pure devotion, one must certainly continue executing prescribed duties."

"In this endeavor there is no loss or diminution, and a little advancement on this path can protect one from the most dangerous type of fear." [6]

Therefore, one's success in bhakti-yoga is as simple as cultivating a respectful but humble service attitude in all we do. Therefore, the highest perfection is simply learning how to please the Lord by one's love and service.

## APPROACHING A SPIRITUAL MASTER

One of the important principles that was mentioned for advancing in devotional service is to seek the guidance of a realized spiritual master. This way you can approach him with questions for further instructions, advice, and for making sure you correctly follow the path.

The first approach to such a guru or spiritual master may be simply reading his books or articles. Or by listening to his lectures, either in person, or through the internet, tapes, CDs, or other ways. Eventually, by such association, if you feel properly inspired by such a master, you can then approach him as an aspiring disciple, and take initiation from him to become a full fledged initiated disciple. This paves the way for even further progress and dedication to the path of bhakti-yoga. The most important point is that the disciple must be very inquisitive in understanding spiritual knowledge. No one should try to become a disciple of a guru for their own ego, to increase their fame, or to boost themselves as spiritually advanced, or for some sort of material success.

A proper disciple should also be qualified by following the most basic of principles, namely no meat eating, no intoxication, no gambling, and no illicit sex. He or she should also be chanting the Hare Krishna mantra the required number of times for at least six months to a year to be qualified for initiation.

The first initiation is often called Harinama initiation, which is when the spiritual master gives you your spiritual name (*nama*) which is generally connected to the Lord (Hari), and indicates that you are a servant of the Lord (*dasa* or *dasi*). Later, if you keep advancing according to the approval of the spiritual master, you may then also qualify for receiving brahmana initiation, which is when you get the sacred thread and receive the gayatri mantra. This order of events will depend on which school or sect you may be a part of, but this is how it is done in the Gaudiya Vaishnava tradition of bhakti-yoga.

The principle of approaching a spiritual master is first enunciated in the *Bhagavad-gita* (4.34), wherein Lord Krishna explains to Arjuna, "Just try to learn the truth by approaching a spiritual master. Inquire from him submissively and render service unto him. The self-realized soul can impart knowledge unto you because he has seen the truth."

Furthermore, we, as potential disciples, must also be qualified. So how does a disciple become qualified? We need to understand that any neophyte devotee has no qualification or ability to approach the Absolute Truth directly merely by the strength of his or her own limited mind and senses. He or she must proceed along the path under the guidance of someone who knows how to do so. Therefore, only under the instruction of the spiritual master can a person be trained in the transcendental service of the Lord. Even a few days worth of training can propel the qualified disciple to continue the path to eventually be promoted to the spiritual world to become a liberated associate of the Supreme. [7]

Even studying the books like *Bhagavad-gita*, the essence of Upanishadic knowledge, and the *Bhagavata Purana*, the postgraduate course of transcendental knowledge, should be done with the assistance of the spiritual master. This helps remove any confusion or difficulties in understanding the deeper meanings of such texts. Just as a person cannot become a doctor merely by reading medical journals at home, we also need to have the guidance of the guru to become qualified to take the proper turns on the path to the spiritual world. Just as Sukadeva Gosvami was a liberated soul from the moment of his birth, he still took lessons on the *Srimad-Bhagavatam* from his father, Srila Vyasadeva, who was the great sage who composed the *Srimad-Bhagavatam* and other Vedic texts. [8]

As explained, the knowledge of the *Bhagavatam* can be understood by respect, faith, sincerity, and paying full attention to the subject matter. "The very *Srimad-Bhagavatam* I shall recite before you because you are the most sincere devotee of Lord Krishna. One who gives full attention and respect to hearing *Srimad-Bhagavatam* achieves unflinching faith in the Supreme Lord, the giver of liberation." [9]

However, it is also important to understand how to recognize a true guru. The first sign of a pure devotee is a person who is unflinchingly engaged in the service of the Supreme, primarily in the regulative principles that were previously described.

The guru must be situated in the topmost platform of devotional service. A guru is a *gosvami*, meaning one who can control his mind and senses.

There are many so-called "gurus," which some people like to call themselves. But you need to observe their qualifications. The guru must be one who understands the spiritual science and all the steps in the process of bhakti-yoga, not only in theory but also in experience and perception. Then he can also be called an *acharya*, or one who teaches by example.

As the *Bhagavad-gita* (18.42) relates, "Peacefulness, self-control, austerity, purity, tolerance, honesty, wisdom, knowledge, and religiousness–these are the qualities by which the brahmanas work."

Without these qualities, one cannot be known as a brahmana, a spiritual teacher who knows the difference between Brahman or spiritual substance, and the material energy. Being born in a brahmana family does not give an automatic designation without proper training. Such a person must be properly trained by another genuine guru.

This means that the guru should also be initiated by an authorized spiritual master in an authentic lineage or line of spiritual masters, called a *sampradaya*. In this way, a potential disciple should not accept a cheap guru, or one who poses as something he is not. You must ask him what is his *sampradaya* or lineage, and he must be able to explain.

We need to understand how rare it is to achieve the

association of devotees, especially a pure devotee of the Lord. Out of all the species of life there are throughout this universe, the rarity of attaining the association of a pure devotee is like being somewhere on the bottom of the Pacific Ocean, and coming up to the surface, and by chance putting your head through the hole in a piece of wood that just happens to be floating above you. It is practically an impossible occurrence. In this way, "The association of great souls is rarely obtained, difficult to understand, and infallible. The association of great souls can be attained–but only by the Lord's mercy." [10]

As the king of Videha, Nimi, expressed to nine great devotees known as the Yogindras, "Birth in a human body is a very rare achievement for the embodied soul, but I hold that for one having such a short-lived human body, it is even a rarer fortune to see a devotee who is dear to the Lord of Vaikuntha. In this world, even a moment's association with saintly persons like yourselves is the greatest treasure in human life..." [11]

As the *Narada-Bhakti-Sutra* (38) also relates, "Primarily, one develops bhakti by the mercy of great souls, or by a small drop of the Lord's mercy." This means that even the seed of knowledge about bhakti is received only by the mercy of another, who is a devotee. And the drop of mercy from the Lord comes to you in the form of such a devotee who gives you this transcendental knowledge. This knowledge may be in the form of personal lectures that you hear, or in the form of books that such a devotee writes, or these days in the form of internet articles, videos, and so on. In any case, it is by superior arrangement of the Supreme that any materially conditioned soul gets this kind of association. Therefore, it is the direct help from the Lord Himself, and we should be highly grateful and respectful to whatever form that mercy comes into our life. We must recognize that whatever devotional experience we receive and advancement we make is because of the grace and kindness of our spiritual master.

## ASSOCIATION WITH DEVOTEES

Along with guidance from a spiritual master, associating with other like-minded people, especially other devotees, is very important. It can be difficult if your main association involves materialistic people. You tend to take on the same topics of discussion and characteristics as those with whom you associate. So you have to be careful about this if you are serious to make genuine spiritual progress.

The best association is, of course, those who are also following the path of bhakti-yoga, and discuss the principles of how to best take to this process, and who also discuss the characteristics and pastimes of Lord Krishna. Without such association it can be very difficult to make real advancement. As the *Srimad-Bhagavatam* (11.26.26) explains, "An intelligent person should therefore abandon all bad association and hold fast to the company of devotees. Such saints are the only ones who, through their instructions, can cut through our unhealthy mental attachments."

"One achieves bhakti by giving up sense gratification and mundane association... One should give up all kinds of degrading association." [12]

One thing to understand is that materialistic or even degrading association will never give us happiness, though it may stimulate the mind. However, since such association is often based on mere mutual behavior, which often centers around intoxication, lewd music, or other types of useless activity, once that mutual behavior ends, the friendship also often disappears. Then we have to ask ourselves how deep or how superficial was that friendship. And if it was so superficial, then what value in it was there? Furthermore, such activity and association is a sure way to continue in the cycles of birth and death, forever reincarnating in these material bodies in this temporary cosmic creation. In other words, no matter how famous, rich, or unique your life and association may be, or how bad, desperate or difficult it is, until you can free yourself from this temporary material existence, you have not solved anything. That again leads us to understand how important is proper and spiritual association.

"Material association is the cause of lust, anger, confusion, forgetfulness, loss of intelligence, and total calamity. Rising like waves from material association, these bad effects mass into a great ocean of misery. Who can cross beyond illusion? One who abandons material association, serves the sages, and becomes selfless." [13]

Therefore, "Persons who are peaceful, equipoised, cleansed and purified, and who know the art of pleasing all other living entities, keep friendship only with devotees of the Lord; they alone can very easily achieve the perfection of going home, back to Godhead." (*Bhag.* 4.12.37)

How that loving exchange between devotees is exhibited is exemplified like this: "Offering gifts in charity, accepting charitable gifts, revealing one's mind in confidence, inquiring confidentially, accepting *prasada* and offering *prasada* are the six symptoms of love shared by one devotee and another." [14] These and inviting devotees to our home and offering them *prasada* (sanctified food first offered to Krishna) is another way of having pleasant exchanges amongst devotees.

## THE FOOD WE EAT

This brings us to another thing to consider, which is the type of food you eat, because what you put inside you will certainly affect your consciousness. Food and drink can even affect your attitude, and your state of mind. Therefore, it is important to control what you consume in satisfying the belly and tongue. The tongue is only a small muscle in your mouth, but it still has so much influence over us. If you cannot control the tongue, you will never be able to control your mind. And the mind is the biggest slave master with which we deal. We are slaves of the mind and senses if we cannot control them, which turns into a vicious circle with the tongue telling us what it wants. Then we try to satisfy that urge from the tongue, and then the mind goes into hyper mode telling us the kinds of new things that it wants. And good luck with that, especially when we do not even recognize how we are being influenced in such a way.

Therefore, if we are going to be real yogis, even in bhakti-yoga, we must control and discriminate what we eat, what is good for us, or will help create mental tranquility, or what will create further mental agitation or more bad karma. Since we eat only vegetarian food, we do not participate in the cruel process of animal slaughter simply to satisfy the tongue. This greatly reduces the karma that we acquire that must be dealt with at some time in our future. In this way, we should be aware to make sure we are not adversely affected by what we eat. Even if we eat food cooked by sensuously influenced people, that defect or tendency is transferred into the food by the cooking process. Then when we eat food cooked by such people, it will also affect our thinking process. By eating food prepared by worldly men, one's mind becomes wicked. [15] So we also have to be cautious about where we eat and who cooks it.

To keep our consciousness up, we also should not eat in restaurants, and we eat only vegetarian food, and better than that is that we eat food that has been prepared by devotees and first offered to Krishna. We follow this as best we can. Or we cook wholesome vegetarian food ourselves and offer it to Krishna in the form of His picture or on our home altar, and then we honor it. We do not simply eat it, but we eat it with respect.

Also, once the food is offered to Krishna, which He accepts by glancing at it with His eyes and accepting the love with which it is offered, then we take the remnants as *prasadam*. *Prasadam* means the Lord's mercy. Then it is highly spiritually charged and actually makes our eating a part of the yoga process. Honoring such food will help raise our consciousness, plus we think of Krishna as we are eating. This purifies and spiritually surcharges our minds and bodies. This is why we try to eat such food as often as possible when we are hungry.

Simply eating such *prasadam* affects us so much that it guarantees us from slipping back into the lower species if we must reincarnate again after death. Even offering such *prasada* to animals will also help them reach a human existence in their next life. That is how powerful it can be.

As Lord Krishna explains in *Bhagavad-gita* (3.13), "The devotees of the Lord are released from all kinds of sins because they eat food which is offered first for sacrifice [being offered to Krishna first]. Others, who prepare food for personal sense enjoyment, verily eat only sin."

Furthermore, *Srimad-Bhagavatam* (11.25.28) explains how food effects us, "Food that is wholesome, pure and obtained without difficulty is in the mode of goodness, food that gives immediate pleasure to the senses is in the mode of passion, and food that is unclean and causes distress is in the mode of ignorance."

Also, *Bhagavad-gita* says, "Foods in the mode of goodness increase the duration of life, purify one's existence and give strength, health, happiness, and satisfaction. Such nourishing foods are sweet, juicy, fattening, and palatable. Foods that are too bitter, too sour, salty, pungent, dry, and hot, are liked by people in the modes of passion. Such foods cause pain, distress and disease. Food cooked more than three hours before being eaten, which is tasteless, stale, putrid, decomposed, and unclean, is food liked by people in the mode of ignorance." [16]

The *Mahabharata* also describes the karmic implications of eating meat, "He who desires to augment his own flesh by eating the flesh of other creatures, lives in misery in whatever species he may take his birth. [17] . . . The purchaser of flesh performs violence by his wealth; he who eats flesh does so by enjoying its taste; the killer does violence by actually tying and killing the animal. Thus, there are three forms of killing. He who brings flesh or sends for it, he who cuts off the limbs of an animal, and he who purchases, sells, or cooks flesh and eats it--all these are to be considered meat-eaters. [18] . . . The sins generated by violence curtail the life of the perpetrator. Therefore, even those who are anxious for their own welfare should abstain from meat-eating." [19]

Also, Krishna explains in *Srimad-Bhagavatam* (11.21.30), "Those who are addicted to satisfying their senses cannot understand the confidential conclusion of Vedic knowledge, as explained by Me. Taking pleasure in violence [killing], they cruelly slaughter innocent animals in sacrifice for their own sense gratification and thus worship demigods, forefathers and leaders among ghostly creatures. Such passion for violence, however, is never encouraged within the process of Vedic tradition."

Herein we can understand that whenever the Vedic literature gives license for sacrificing animals in rituals, it is only meant to curb the tendency that the more uncivilized people may have. It is never to give free permission to kill animals for satisfying the tongue and belly, nor is such violence to be condoned for worshiping various demigods or ghostly beings.

Therefore, bhakti-yoga is very easy for the simple, but difficult for the crooked, and we simply eat vegetarian food, especially that which is first offered to Krishna who leaves the remnants so that we can still nourish the material body, mind, and senses, along with spiritualizing our consciousness. In this way, both our cooking and our eating are part of the yoga process.

More information about these topics and the process for offering our food to Krishna is given in *The Bhakti-Yoga Handbook*, which is the companion to this book.

**CHAPTER NOTES**
1. *Nectar of Devotion*, p. 320 & *Caitanya-caritamrita*, Madhya-lila 22.100.
2. *Bhakti-rasamrita-sindhu* 1.2.2.
3. *Bhagavad-gita*, 9.26.
4. *Srimad-Bhagavatam*, 8.23.2.
5. Ibid., 8.19.2.
6. *Bhagavad-gita*, 2.40.
7. *Srimad-Bhagavatam*, 1.6.23.
8. Ibid., 2.1.8 pur. & 2.1.10.
9. Ibid., 2.1.10.
10. *Narada-Bhakti-Sutra*, 39-40.
11. *Srimad-Bhagavatam*, 11.2.29-30.
12. *Narada-Bhakti-Sutra*, 35, 43.
13. Ibid., 44-46.
14. *Nectar of Instruction*, Text 4.
15. Ibid., p.45.
16. *Bhagavad-gita*, 17.8-10.
17. *Mahabharata, Anu Parva*, 47.116.
18. Ibid., *Anu*.115.40.
19. Ibid., *Anu*.115.33.

# CHAPTER EIGHT

# *Rising Above Material Desires and Obstacles and Attaining the Supreme Peace*

Once we start engaging ourselves in bhakti-yoga, we can begin to feel our hearts and consciousness change. Many of the desires for material or sensual happiness that we once thought were so important begin to subside. The worries or concerns that we had also begin to be small stuff, things that are not as significant as they once were. And as we continue to realize that our real identity is beyond the body, then we also gain a feeling of fearlessness, a sense of not being worried about so many threats to our life. We also begin to attain a peace of mind and contentment in our situation, regardless of how simple it may be. We no longer need the grander things in life as most materialists seem to want. This is a blessing that few people attain. It gives us the freedom from so many desires that would, otherwise, motivate us or even force us to act in certain ways, or fulfill certain habits that are merely unnecessary distractions, which is called being the slave to our mind and senses. The mind and senses tell us what we want, and the intelligence kicks in to make a plan to fulfill those desires. And freedom from such compulsions and activities is only part of what bhakti-yoga can give us.

Generally, a person worries about how to acquire what he wants, and then if he gets it, he worries about how to protect and keep it. But if he loses it, he laments for its loss. Or if he gets it, it may not be as nice as he thought it would be. Then he is disappointed. This is like a vicious circle of activity that a person accepts when he or she is influenced by the mind and senses. But with a little spiritual understanding, we can begin to rise above this. In this way, we begin to lose our hankerings for material possessions, and all the anxiety and endeavors that go with the attempts to fulfill such desires. Why? Because we begin to feel a higher taste from spiritual activities which transcends the influence of the mind and senses and directly affects the soul with peace. Only when the soul is content can the mind truly be at peace.

"One who actually satisfies the Supreme Personality of Godhead during one's lifetime becomes liberated from the gross and subtle material conditions. Thus being freed from all material modes of nature, he achieves unlimited spiritual peace." [1]

This is repeated later to emphasize its importance in the conversation when Sri Kavi said to Maharaja Nimi, "My dear King, the devotee who worships the lotus feet of the infallible Personality of Godhead with constant endeavor thus achieves unflinching devotion, detachment and experienced knowledge of the Personality of Godhead. In this way, the successful devotee of the Lord achieves supreme spiritual peace." [2]

Lord Krishna explains to Uddhava in *Srimad-Bhagavatam* (11.15.18) that anyone who places His form within his or her heart can surpass the pangs of the six material tribulations: namely hunger, thirst, birth, death, lamentation, and illusion. This is a way one can attain their transcendental form.

"Simply by chanting and hearing of the transcendental name, form, etc., of the Personality of Godhead, Sri Krishna, one can achieve cessation of unlimited miserable conditions. What to speak of those who have attained attraction for serving the flavor of the dust of the Lord's lotus feet." [3]

In that position of self-realization, by the practice of knowledge in devotional service, one sees everything in the right perspective. Instead, he becomes indifferent to material complications, which act less powerfully upon him. (*Bhag.* 3.25.18) In this way, meditating on the Lord creates a cooling feeling like moonshine that relieves the suffering in the heart of a pure devotee.[4]

Through the process of bhakti-yoga we can feel that all of our desires are fulfilled by plugging into that higher spiritual taste. After all, once we begin to make a connection with the Supreme Being, what further benediction would we want? Therefore, when a *jiva* soul becomes a devotee, sorrow disappears.

This is because the devotee transfers his or her consciousness to the spiritual world, and thus achieves his or her constitutional position of immortality beyond the affects of this material world, and becomes completely peaceful, all of which is the highest perfection of life. This perfection means to attain one's original spiritual form and engage in the loving service of the Supreme. [5]

This means if the materially conditioned soul engages in bhakti-yoga and carries out the instructions of the spiritual master, he or she gets free from the illusion and becomes eligible for the shelter of Lord Krishna. [6] It is said that Krishna is like sunshine and the illusory energy, *maya*, is compared to darkness. Wherever there is sunshine, there can be no darkness. As soon as one takes shelter of Krishna consciousness, the darkness of illusion and the influence of the external energy will immediately vanish. [7]

It is only bhakti-yoga, the devotional activities for the pleasure of the Lord, that can not only uproot the seeds of material desires in a way they can no longer survive or grow back, but can also stop the reactions to such deeds. It is like when the sun dissipates the morning fog by the heat of its rays. [8] Just as a blazing fire turns firewood into ashes, similarly devotion to Krishna completely burns to ashes the sins committed by Krishna's devotees. [9] In this way, "The taste for loving service is like the water of the River Ganges, which flows from the feet of Lord Krishna. Every day that taste diminishes the results of sinful activities acquired over a period of many births by those who perform austerities [such as following the principles of bhakti-yoga]." [10]

Therefore, activities of devotional service cut the hard knot of karma that keeps a person bound up in material existence, and the repeated cycles of birth and death in order to work out that karma. Karma must become dissolved in order to be free of having to take another birth in material existence. It is not enough to merely reduce one's karma, but it must be extinguished, both good and bad karma, so that no more reactions need to be endured in this world. Then a person can actually enter into the spiritual realm, and also fully taste the nectar of spiritual existence while still in this material body. This is an automatic result of engaging in bhakti-yoga.

"With sword in hand, intelligent men cut through the binding knot of reactionary work [karma] by remembering the Personality of Godhead. Therefore, who will not pay attention to His message?" [11]

Not only does bhakti-yoga burn up one's karma, but it will also burn up the subtle body, which is where the material desires and mental misconceptions reside. Then there is no separation between the engagement of the body, which becomes spiritually surcharged, and the soul in the devotional service to the Lord. "Upon becoming fixed in his attachment to the Supreme Personality of Godhead by the grace of the spiritual master and by awakening [spiritual] knowledge and detachment [from material life], the living entity, situated within the heart of the body and covered by the five elements, burns up his material coverings [both subtle and physical] exactly as fire, arising from wood, burns the wood itself." [12]

"One who engages in full devotional service, who does not fall down in any circumstance, at once transcends the modes of material nature and thus comes to the level of Brahman [and tastes spiritual bliss]." [13]

## THE MAIN FACTORS THAT RUIN ONE'S SPIRITUAL ADVANCEMENT

However, there is a warning. Even though spiritual advancement in bhakti-yoga can relieve a person from all kinds of miseries, which are mostly based on misconceptions of our real identity which then produces false aims of life, material desires can also keep one from relishing the higher taste of devotional service to the Supreme. If anyone has any desires for satisfying the senses, to that degree it will keep a person from entering the higher taste of bhakti-yoga. [14]

We must understand that the desire for gratifying the demands of the senses is the root cause of material existence. And you cannot satisfy your material desires without a material body. Which is why in any process of yoga one of the main points is to rise above the temporary demands of the mind and senses. Only then can your spiritual advancement go into high gear. Otherwise, trying to make spiritual progress while still feeding the mind and senses with the material pleasures they crave is like rowing a boat while still having the anchor in the water–you may work ever so heard, but will not be going anywhere. You will only be going through the motions, like practicing for the day when you can actually follow the process. But this is your opportunity to put it into motion, so it is best not to create any more delays.

As explained in the *Upadeshamrita* (text 2), the main factors that can ruin one's engagement in bhakti-yoga to the Supreme Lord are outlined, "One's devotional service is spoiled when he becomes too entangled in the following six activities: (1) eating more than necessary or collecting more funds than required; (2) overendeavoring for mundane things that are difficult to obtain; (3) talking unnecessarily about mundane topics; (4) practicing the scriptural rules and regulations only for the sake of following them and not for the sake of spiritual advancement, or rejecting the rules and regulations of the scriptures and working independently or whimsically; (5) associating with worldly-minded persons who are not interested in Krishna consciousness; and (6) being greedy for mundane achievements."

So this clearly indicates that it is best to keep our lives simple, and not to overendeavor for things that are not important or helpful towards our spiritual progress, and practice what is helpful by the order of the spiritual master. If we can follow these basic principles, we can stay on the path toward spiritual progress. Therefore we must pray to keep from being materially attracted, and stay on course on the path of bhakti-yoga.

## HOW THE IMMATURE DEVOTEE CAN BE SUCCESSFUL

Nonetheless, *maya*, the illusory energy, and our attraction to it is very strong. We have to understand that we have been circulating around this cosmic creation for many lifetimes. So we are conditioned to thinking that the body is our real identity, and our mind and senses is what needs to be happy and pleased. So our whole concept of life is to work to satisfy the demands of the mind and senses. To change that to understanding that the physical body and mind are only temporary coverings of our real self will take time, practice, the acquirement of spiritual knowledge, and the realization of our predicament and the suffering that goes with being in such a temporary form. Then we may reach the stage of asking ourselves if this is all there is, and what more can life provide, and who am I and how did I get here. Only the most mature of wanderers begins to ask themselves how do I get out of here.

Therefore, as we start to make progress in our spiritual practice, we may not be successful overnight, nor should we expect to be so. We have to work at it. But with sincerity, and by taking instructions of the spiritual master, advancement will come, and we will feel peace of mind and overcome any obstacles on the path to spiritual development, though we may still hold some attachment to material attractions.

Lord Krishna explains it in this way: "My dear Uddhava, if My devotee has not fully conquered his senses, he may be harassed by material desires, but because of his unflinching devotion to Me, he will not be defeated by [*maya*, or the desire for] sense gratification." [15]

So, even if a devotee has material desires, by approaching the Lord directly shows the intelligence of such a person, knowing that everything ultimately comes from the Lord anyway. Then the Supreme Being Himself will take care of such a devotee in just the right way so that all his desires are fulfilled, yet he still makes spiritual progress. This is explained in the following verse: "The Supreme Personality of Godhead fulfills the material desires of a devotee who approaches Him with such motives, but He does not bestow benedictions upon the devotee that will cause him to demand more benedictions again. However, the Lord willingly gives the devotee shelter at His own lotus feet, even though such a person does not aspire for it, and that shelter satisfies all his desires. That is the Supreme Personality's special mercy." [16]

In this way, we cannot even imagine how special is this direct mercy of the Lord Himself to any person who genuinely approaches Him. And if this kind of mercy is not effective enough, sometimes the Lord will simply take away all of the distracting assets the devotee may have. Then the devotee will be left with no other shelter than Krishna so that he will then progress even more than before. It is said that if the Lord likes someone, He can give him everything. But if the Lord loves someone, He may take away everything that distracts him from Krishna. [17]

So, even a devotee who is immature in his or her practice, but is sincerely trying, can still move forward on the road of spiritual progress in bhakti-yoga. As Lord Krishna Himself goes on to explain further to Uddhava in the *Srimad-Bhagavatam* (11.20.29), "When an intelligent person engages constantly in worshiping Me through loving devotional service as described by Me, his heart becomes firmly situated in Me. Thus all material desires within the heart are destroyed."

Or like Lord Krishna also explains in *Bhagavad-gita* (2.59). "The embodied soul may be restricted from sense enjoyment, though the taste for sense objects remains. But, ceasing such engagements by experiencing a higher taste, he is [or becomes] fixed in consciousness."

In such a transcendental state there is no need for artificial control of the mind, mental speculation or meditation as performed by the jnanis and yogis. One gives up such processes just as the heavenly King, Indra, forgoes the trouble to dig a well. [18] In other words, just as Indra, the King of heaven, is surrounded by so many opulences that undergoing the trouble to dig a well for water is mere folly, similarly, the higher taste, the spontaneous attraction to Krishna takes over and outweighs the need for any other forms of yoga, or rules and regulations to keep one on the right track. Because of *bhava*, the love in the heart of the devotee for the Lord that has been awakened, he or she experiences a higher taste that motivates him or her to continue going deeper and deeper into the path of bhakti, devotion.

Finally, when one's material bondage is broken, the obstacles on the road to spiritual advancement are removed. Then such a yogi can advance and eventually enter into the divine love, *prema*, for Radha and Krishna.

To conclude, the *Srimad-Bhagavatam* (6.2.46) explains,

"Therefore, one who desires freedom from material bondage should adopt the process of chanting and glorifying the name, fame, form and pastimes of the Supreme Personality of Godhead, at whose feet all the holy places stand. One cannot derive the proper benefit from other methods, such as pious atonement, speculative knowledge and meditation in mystic yoga, because even after following such methods one takes to fruitive activities again, unable to control his mind, which is contaminated by the qualities of nature, namely passion [*raja-guna*] and ignorance [*tama-guna*]."

In this way, the ultimate goal and purpose of this human life, which is an opportunity attained only after numerous lives in both heavenly or hellish conditions, is to attain unalloyed devotion to the Supreme Being. Once we start this path, if we are sincere and do not give up or become too distracted, arrangements will be made so that we can ultimately become successful and reach our real home in the spiritual realm.

**CHAPTER NOTES**
1. *Srimad-Bhagavatam*, 4.11.14.
2. Ibid., 11.2.43.
3. Ibid., 3.7.14.
4. Ibid., 11.2.54.
5. *Narada-Bhakti-Sutra*, p.11.
6. *Caitanya-caritamrita, Madhya-lila,* 22.25.
7. Ibid., 22.31 & *Bhagavatam* 2.9.34.
8. *Bhagavatam,* 6.1.15.
9. Ibid., 11.14.19.
10. Ibid., 4.21.31.
11. Ibid., 1.2.15.
12. Ibid., 4.22.26.
13. *Bhagavad-gita*, 14.26.
14. *Nectar of Devotion*, p.32.
15. *Bhagavatam*, 11.14.18.
16. Ibid., 5.19.27.
17. *Caitanya-caritamrita,* Madhya-lila, 22.38-42.
18. *Bhagavatam,* 2.7.48.

# CHAPTER NINE

# *The Highest Principle for this Age: Chanting the Holy Names*

One of the most important principles in the process of bhakti-yoga is the chanting of the holy names of the Lord, especially in the form of the Hare Krishna *maha-mantra*. The word *maha* means "great," as in the greatest mantra for deliverance. This means delivering the mind from unnecessary thoughts, agitation, worries, and concerns, and to bring the spiritual vibration into our consciousness. In this way, this is also the use of mantra-yoga as part of the bhakti-yoga process. Furthermore, this mantra can be chanted quietly for personal development as in *japa* meditation, as when we chant it a certain number of times on beads, or it can be sung in a group as in congregational chanting or singing. It also has numerous melodies that can be used along with instruments to inspire and enthuse everyone who wants to chant or sing along. Plus, the mantra consists of only three words, and is chanted as: Hare Krishna, Hare Krishna, Krishna Krishna, Hare Hare / Hare Rama, Hare Rama, Rama Rama, Hare Hare. You can't get much easier than that. So, let's explain some of the points about this mantra and why it is so important.

### CHANTING THE HOLY NAMES OF GOD IS THE RECOMMENDED PROCESS FOR THIS AGE OF KALI-YUGA

It is found in the Vedic literature that chanting the holy names of God is recommended as the most effective and easiest process for becoming spiritually realized in this age of Kali-yuga. This is why it is called the *yuga-dharma*, which means the main spiritual process for this age of Kali. And as we can plainly see by a simple survey, almost every religion and spiritual path in this age recommends the chanting or singing of the Lord's names and glories, no matter whether it is Christianity, Judaism, Islam, Hinduism, or so many others. All accept the idea of glorifying God by calling and singing His names.

Out of so many processes of spiritual development that can be found within the Vedic tradition, and which still can be done if a person wants to do them, it is said that, "In this age of Kali there is no other religious principle than the chanting of the holy name, which is the essence of all Vedic hymns. This is the purport of all scriptures."[1]

So no matter what else you may include in your spiritual development, you should also include the chanting of the holy names of Krishna to reach spiritual success. Furthermore, the *Kalisantarana Upanishad* explains the importance of chanting Hare Krishna in this age of Kali-yuga, "Hare Krishna, Hare Krishna, Krishna Krishna, Hare Hare / Hare Rama, Hare Rama, Rama Rama, Hare Hare–these sixteen names composed of thirty-two syllables are the only means to counteract the evil effects of Kali-yuga. In all the *Vedas* it is seen that to cross the ocean of nescience there is no alternative to the chanting of the holy name."

The *Narada-pancharatra* also describes in the *trayo vedah shad-angani* verse: "The essence of all Vedic knowledge–comprehending the three kinds of Vedic activity [*karma-kanda*, *jnana-kanda* and *upasana-kanda*], the *chandah* or Vedic hymns, and the processes for satisfying the demigods–is included in the eight syllables Hare Krishna, Hare Krishna. This is the reality of all Vedanta. The chanting of the holy name is the only means to cross the ocean of nescience."

The *Narayana-samhita* verse, as confirmed by Madhvacharya in his commentary on the *Mundaka Upanishad*, also states:

*dvapariyair janair vishnuh pancharatrais tu kevalaiha*
*kalua tu nama-matrena pujyate bhagavan harihi*

Which means, "In the Dvapara-yuga people should worship Lord Vishnu only by the regulative principles of the *Narada-pancharatra* and other such authorized books. In the age of Kali, however, people should simply chant the holy names of the Supreme Personality of Godhead, Bhagavan."

This is similar to the verse in the *Brahan-naradiya Purana* (38.97), which says:

> *dhyayan krite yajan yajnais*
> *tretayam dvapare 'rcayan*
> *yad apnoti tad apnoti*
> *kalua sankirtya keshavam*

"Whatever is achieved in Satya-yuga by meditation, in Treta-yuga by offering ritual sacrifices, and in Dvapara-yuga by temple worship, is achieved in Kali-yuga by chanting the names of Lord Keshava [Krishna] congregationally."

This point is so important that it is also mentioned in the *Vishnu Purana* (6.2.17), the *Padma Purana* (Uttara-khanda 72.25), and in the *Srimad-Bhagavatam* (12.3.51-2), which says, "My dear King, although Kali-yuga is an ocean of faults, there is still one good quality about this age; Simply by chanting the Hare Krishna *maha-mantra*, one can become free from material bondage and be promoted to the transcendental kingdom. Whatever result was obtained in Satya-yuga by meditating on Vishnu, in Treta-yuga by performing ritual sacrifices, and in Dvapara-yuga by serving the Lord's lotus feet [as in temple worship] can be obtained in Kali-yuga simply by chanting the Hare Krishna *maha-mantra*."

Another verse in the *Bhagavatam* (8.23.16) explains this further, "There may be discrepancies in chanting the mantras and observing regulative principles, and, moreover, there may be discrepancies in regard to time, place, person, and paraphernalia. But when Your Lordship's holy name is chanted, everything becomes faultless."

In other words, each *yuga* or age has its recommended process for spiritual success. In Satya-yuga it was the long process of meditation when people lived for many years and could practice such a method. In Treta-yuga it was by elaborate rituals. In Dvapara-yuga the recommended process was by extensive worship to the Deities in the temples. But in Kali-yuga, humanity hardly has the wealth, stamina, long life, mental equilibrium, or general facility to do all that. Therefore, it is recommended that you simply and easily chant the holy names of the Hare Krishna mantra because no other religious process is as powerful or illuminating, or as joyfully performed for the fallen souls. This is why it is the *yuga-dharma*.

This is why the *Brihan-naradiya Purana* (38.126) also explains:

> *harer nama harer nama*
> *harer namaiva kevalam*
> *kalau nasty eve nastya eve*
> *nastya eva gatir anyatha*

"Chant the holy names, chant the holy names, chant the holy names of the Lord, for in this age of quarrel and confusion, there is no other way, there is no other way, there is no other way."

The *Srimad-Bhagavatam* (11.5.32), in its reference to worshiping Sri Caitanya Mahaprabhu who was recognized as the most recent *avatara* of the Lord, and who started the movement to propagate the chanting of the holy name of Krishna just 500 years ago, is very clear when it says, "In the age of Kali, intelligent persons perform congregational chanting to worship the incarnation of Godhead who constantly sings the name of Krishna. Although His complexion is not blackish, He is Krishna Himself. He is accompanied by His associates, servants, weapons, and confidential companions."

This chanting is the sublime and easy way to attain spiritual realization, so easy in fact that it is one of the advantages of being born in this difficult age of Kali-yuga. Even beings from the higher planetary systems wish to take birth on earth at this time simply to utilize the favorable conditions for engaging in this process. As the *Srimad-Bhagavatam* (11.5.36-40) describes, "Those who are actually advanced in knowledge are able to appreciate the essential value of this age of Kali. Such enlightened persons worship Kali-yuga because in this fallen age, all perfection of life can easily be achieved by the performance of *sankirtana* [the congregational chanting of the Lord's holy names.]

"Indeed, there is no higher possible gain for embodied souls forced to wander throughout the material world than the Supreme Lord's *sankirtana* movement, by which one can attain the supreme peace and free oneself from the cycle of repeated birth and death.

"My dear King, the inhabitants of Satya-yuga and other ages eagerly desire to take birth in this age of Kali, since in this age there will be many devotees of the Supreme Lord, Narayana. These devotees will appear in various places, but will be especially numerous in South India. O master of men, in the age of Kali those persons who drink the waters of the holy rivers of Dravida-desha, such as the Tamraparni, Kritamala, Payasvini, the extremely pious Kaveri, and the Pratichi Mahanadi, will almost all be pure-hearted devotees of the Supreme Personality of Godhead, Vasudeva."

In this way, Kali-yuga, wherein quarrel and confusion abound, can become like the golden age of Satya-yuga by bringing the spiritual vibration into our midst through the chanting of the holy names of Krishna. The *Vishnu-dharma* describes:

> *kalau krita-yugam tasya*
> *kalis tasya krite yuge*
> *yasya chetasi govindo*
> *hridaye yasya nachyutaha*

"For one who has Lord Govinda in his heart, Satya-yuga becomes manifest in the midst of Kali-yuga, whereas conversely even Satya-yuga becomes Kali-yuga for one who does not have the infallible Lord in his heart."

The *Srimad-Bhagavatam* (6.2.11-12) further explains how chanting the holy names of Krishna is more effective than many of the other processes of spiritual purification, which is a benefit for this age: "By following the Vedic ritualistic ceremonies or undergoing atonement, sinful men do not become as purified as by chanting once the holy name of Lord Hari. Although ritualistic atonement may free one from sinful reactions, it does not awaken devotional service, unlike the chanting of the Lord's names, which reminds one of the Lord's fame, qualities, attributes, pastimes, and paraphernalia.

"The ritualistic ceremonies of atonement recommended in the religious scriptures are insufficient to cleanse the heart absolutely because after atonement one's mind again runs toward material activities. Consequently, for one who wants liberation from the fruitive reactions of material activities, the chanting of the Hare Krishna mantra, or glorification of the name, fame and pastimes of the Lord, it is recommended as the most perfect process of atonement because such chanting eradicates the dirt from one's heart completely."

This is the difference in associating with the names of God and other Vedic processes of spiritual purification. The names enter the heart and eradicates the material desire seeds. Other process may decrease one's karma, or give some enlightenment, but the material or sensual desires in the heart are not fully extinguished. Thus, a person may engage in so many spiritual pursuits and still turn around and continue their own materialistic activities which reduce one's spiritual merit or higher consciousness.

The point is that everyone is looking for happiness of some kind. That is the natural condition of the soul. But it is a matter of attaining a higher state of spiritual happiness from the chanting of the names of God that can alleviate the taste for the sporadic states of sensual or mental happiness that come and go, or are always interrupted by different kinds of distress or misery.

Therefore, in Kali-yuga, one of the highest forms of welfare work that can be done for humanity is to help broadcast the glories of the Lord and to help spread the chanting of His holy names. As described, "My dear Lord, those pious and saintly persons who in this age of Kali hear about Your transcendental activities and also glorify them will easily cross over the darkness of the age of Kali-yuga." [2]

## SOME IMPORTANT BENEFITS OF CHANTING THE HOLY NAMES

The main benefit of chanting the holy names is that it

immediately fixes the mind on the Absolute Truth without the need for clearing the mind of all thoughts as is necessary with other forms of meditation. In that way it is very easy. Plus, anyone can do it. "One does not have to undergo initiation or execute the activities required before initiation. One simply has to vibrate the holy name on the lips. Thus even a man of the lowest class [*chandala*] can be delivered." [3]

To emphasize this point, Srila Rupa Goswami also says in his *Padyavali* (29), "The holy name of Lord Krishna is an attractive feature for many saintly, liberal people. It is the annihilator of all sinful reactions and is so powerful that save for the dumb who cannot chant it, it is readily available to everyone, including the lowest type of man, the *chandala*. The holy name of Krishna is the controller of the opulence of liberation, and it is identical with Krishna. Simply by touching the holy name with one's tongue, immediate effects are produced. Chanting the holy name does not depend on initiation, pious activities or the *purashcharya* regulative principles generally observed before initiation. The holy name does not wait for all these activities. It is self-sufficient."

This is the glory of the chanting process, it is clearly open to anyone. In the previous *yugas*, there were so many prerequisites that had to be accomplished before a person could properly engage in the various forms of spiritual development. But it is like Krishna is saying that since the age of Kali-yuga is so bad, like you are My worst son, so I will give you the easiest process. Nonetheless, being initiated by a pure devotee spiritual master will certainly help one's chanting, and propel him or her forward in spiritual development. Still, whether initiated or not, a person can follow the instructions of such a guru for his or her ultimate benefit, and chant the Hare Krishna mantra.

Even when one chants the holy name in a joking way, it still has its effect. Or even when a person chants it to mean something else, some potency is still there. For example, when we say something about the Ramada Inn, which is a popular hotel chain, the name *Rama* is there. As the *acharya* or authority on the chanting of the holy name Haridasa Thakur said "The chanting of the Lord's holy name to indicate something other than the Lord is an instance of *namabhasa*. Even when the holy name is chanted in this way, its transcendental power is not destroyed." [4]

*Namabhasa* is the stage above offensive chanting when a person still gets a dim reflection of the power of the holy name. It is not pure chanting, yet some effect is still there, though it may not produce the full result. Nonetheless, when we begin to chant without offenses, being sincere and alert to our chanting, then the power of the holy name and its effect on us becomes much stronger. But as it is said in the *Caitanya-caritamrita* (Antya 3.60), if a devotee once utters the holy name of the Lord, and it enters the ear, which is the channel of aural reception, and then penetrates the mind, that holy name will certainly deliver him from material bondage, whether vibrated properly or improperly, with correct or incorrect grammar. The potency of the holy name is certainly great.

This is also repeated in the *Srimad-Bhagavatam* (6.16.44), "My Lord, it is not impossible for one to be immediately freed from all material contamination by seeing You. Not to speak of seeing You personally, merely by hearing the holy name of Your Lordship only once, even *chandalas*, men of the lowest class, are free from all material contamination. Under the circumstances, who will not be freed from material contamination simply by seeing You?"

So here the potency of the holy name becomes clear. Furthermore, it is most purifying spiritually while we chant the holy name during our life, but if we can chant it just before or while we are leaving this body at the time of death, it will certainly transfer us into a higher dimension in our next existence. This is why we must practice chanting the holy names throughout our lives, and especially during times of danger when we may be forced to leave this body, and that way we will be more likely to remember to chant the holy names while we leave this body. It is not always possible to leave this world in a smooth transition, but we may leave through some sudden and unexpected incident. Therefore we must be ready to chant the holy name of Krishna at the time of death so we can be transferred to the next best situation possible. This is also explained in the *Srimad-Bhagavatam* (3.9.15), "Let me take shelter of the lotus feet of Him whose incarnations, qualities and activities are mysterious imitations of worldly affairs [which means they are not of this world at all]. One who invokes His transcendental names, even unconsciously, at the time he quits this life, is certainly washed immediately of the sins of many, many births and attains Him without fail."

It is this way that the holy name propels a person into higher realms of existence if he or she chants the holy names at the time of death, as explained herein, "If one chants the holy name of Hari and then dies because of an accidental misfortune, such as falling from the top of a house, slipping and suffering broken bones while traveling on the road, being bitten by a serpent, being afflicted with pain and high fever, or being injured by a weapon, one is immediately absolved from having to enter hellish life, even though he is sinful.

"Authorities who are learned scholars and sages have carefully ascertained that one should atone for the heaviest sins by undergoing a heavy process of atonement, and one should atone for lighter sins by undergoing lighter atonement. Chanting the Hare Krishna mantra, however, vanquishes all the effects of sinful activities, regardless of whether heavy or light." [5]

In the *Skanda Purana* it also says:

> *sakrid uccharitam yena*
> *harir ity akshara-dvayam*
> *baddha-parikaras tena*
> *mokshaya gamanam prati*

"By one chanting the holy name of the Lord, which consists of the two syllables *ha-ri*, one guarantees his path to liberation."

Chanting the holy names is so easy but powerful, it is recommended that even householders, or those who are married and with children, can achieve success by this chanting process. Usually householders are completely preoccupied with materialistic pursuits, such as trying to make money, maintaining a job, taking care of one's health, overseeing the progress and growth of the children, taking care of the house, and so many other things. They hardly have time for anything truly spiritual. Nonetheless, the chanting of the holy names is so powerful that even householders can reach spiritual success if they simply engage in this process. In fact they can reach the same spiritual success as the renounced sages. This is explained by the great sage Narada Muni to Maharaja Yudhishthira when he was outlining the instruction for a civilized human society, "The process of chanting the holy name of the Lord is so powerful that by this chanting even householders [*grihasthas*] can very easily gain the ultimate result achieved by persons in the renounced order. Maharaja Yudhishthira, I have now explained to you that process of religion."[6]

However, to attain all of these benefits means that we have to chant with faith, sincerity and devotion. We have to have some respect for the holy name or our chanting will not produce the fullest effects that we may wish. It is still potent under any circumstance, but due regard while chanting the holy names will produce deeper benefits.

When we understand that the Lord and His name are identical, we can see the personality of the name the more we give it proper respect. It also has divine qualities like forgiveness, serenity, compassion, kindness, love, wisdom, etc., and all of these qualities will also rub off on us as we associate with the name through chanting or singing it.

## CHANTING THE MAHA-MANTRA PURIFIES THE CONSCIOUSNESS

As mentioned, it is this chanting of the names of Krishna which purifies the consciousness to open the individual, the bhakti-yogi, to experience the spiritual frequency or transcendental dimension. Of course, there is the immediate joy and pleasure in congregational chanting to sing and dance to the musical sound and melodies of the holy names being chanted. But as one goes deeper, the spiritual vibration begins to clear away the darkness of past karma, bad habits, habitual thought patterns, or old attachments, and brings one to experience the real happiness on the spiritual platform. This is another reason why it is said to be the easiest spiritual process for this age.

In this way, the chanting cleanses the dust from the heart, after which the person can realize the importance of the holy name.

Of course, if a person is not interested in changing his habits or consciousness, then it is not possible for a person to fully experience the positive and spiritual effects of the name of Krishna. But if a person takes it sincerely, the association of the holy name of Krishna will purify one from the effects of his bad karma.

How the holy name effects us is that it is eternally situated in pure goodness. It is the transcendental name of the Lord and is non-different from the Lord. It actually descends from the spiritual world. So it has the same transcendental frequency when it is chanted properly. Associating with the name through chanting removes the unwanted things from the heart, which softens the heart and evokes compassion for all souls and the desire to remove the cause of suffering for all living beings. It also makes the propensity to engage in impious activities subside. [7] In this way, the chanting purifies the heart and consciousness of anyone who takes it seriously, and brings one's spiritual awareness to a progressively higher level. As the chanting becomes more serious, the effects become deeper. Then the bhakti-yogi can perceive the personality of the holy name and continues to perceive increasingly higher levels of the spiritual dimension all around him.

Srivas Thakur, as noted in the *Caitanya-caritamrita* (Adi.17.96), said, "Anyone who takes to Your holy name vanquishes ten million of his offenses immediately."

The very last verse in the *Srimad-Bhagavatam* (12.13.23) also explains, "I offer my respectful obeisances unto the Supreme Lord, Hari, the congregational chanting of whose holy names destroys all sinful reactions, and the offering of obeisances unto whom relieves all material suffering."

Therefore, the chanting of the holy names burns away the sinful reactions of the foolish things we have done in our lives, as further described: "As fire burns dry grass to ashes, so the holy name of the Lord, whether chanted knowingly or unknowingly, burns to ashes, without fail, all the reactions of one's sinful activities. If a person unaware of the effective potency of a certain medicine takes that medicine or is forced to take it, it will act even without his knowledge because its potency does not depend on the patient's understanding. Similarly, even though one does not know the value of chanting the holy name of the Lord, if one chants knowingly or unknowingly, the chanting will be very effective." [8]

In the *Brihad-vishnu Purana* it says:

> *namno hi yavati shaktihi*
> *papa-nirharane hareh*
> *tavat kartum na shaknoti*
> *patakam pataki naraha*

"Simply by chanting one name of Hari, a sinful man can counteract the reactions to more sins than he is able to commit."

In the *Garuda Purana* it is also described:

> *avashenapi yan-namni*
> *kirtite sarva-patakaihai*
> *puman vimuchyate sadyaha*
> *simha-trastair mrigair iva*

"If one chants the holy name of the Lord, even in a helpless condition or without desiring to do so, all the reactions of his sinful life depart, just as when a lion roars, all the small animals flee in fear."

There is also the story of Ajamila in the sixth Canto of the *Bhagavatam*. Ajamila was known as an extremely sinful person, but fortunately he named his son Narayana. And because he would chant the name so often when calling his son, it was as if he was practicing the chanting of it so that even at the time of death he would call it out. So when he was leaving his body, he became very afraid and in earnest he called for his son, Narayana. By doing so, as the Vishnudutas [soldiers of Lord Vishnu] explained, "Ajamila has already atoned for all of his sinful actions. Indeed, he has atoned not only for sins performed in one life, but for those performed in millions of lives, for in a helpless condition he chanted the holy name of Narayana. Even though he did not chant purely, he chanted without offense, and therefore he is now pure and eligible for liberation." [9]

"Even previously, while eating and at other times, this

Ajamila would call his son, saying 'My dear Narayana, please come here.' Although calling the name of his son, he nevertheless uttered the four syllables na-ra-ya-na. Simply by chanting the name of Narayana in this way, he sufficiently atoned for the sinful reactions of millions of lives." [10]

This is how effective the chanting the Lord's names can be if we chant sincerely. It is even described, "One who has killed a brahmana, one who has killed a cow or who has killed his father, mother or spiritual master can be immediately freed from all sinful reactions simply by chanting the holy name of Lord Narayana. Other sinful persons, such as dog-eaters and *chandalas*, who are less than shudras, can also be freed in this way." [11]

Of course, this does not mean we can purposefully engage in such activities and think we can merely chant the holy names and be free from all karmic results. That is called engaging in sinful activities on the strength of chanting the holy names, which is greatly offensive to the holy names. That means the effect of such sinful activities will not go away at all. It is like the elephant who may bathe in the water but then again throws sand over itself when it comes out of the water. However, if we genuinely realize the wrong we have done and begin to chant the holy names in sincere remorse for our previous activities, with the intention to not do such things again, the name will certainly have its positive effects. "Thus worship the Lord, whose name is like the sun, for just as a slight appearance of the sun dissipates the darkness of night, so a slight appearance of the holy name of Krishna can drive away all the darkness of ignorance that arises in the heart due to greatly sinful activities performed in previous lives." [12]

"Even a faint light of the holy name of the Lord can eradicate all the reactions of sinful life." [13] It is this way in which it raises our consciousness and extinguishes our bad habits and attachments to materialism.

## THE ADVANCED POSITION OF ONE WHO CHANTS HARE KRISHNA

The persons who can engage in the chanting of the Lord's holy names are not ordinary. It is considered that they have already been engaged in spiritual development for some time, even lifetimes, and can now engage in what many of the spiritual texts call the epitome of spiritual progress.

For example, when Sri Caitanya Mahaprabhu was talking with Prakashananda Sarasvati, He explained that His guru told Him, "You are a fool. You are not qualified to study Vedanta philosophy, and therefore You must always chant the holy name of Krishna. This is the essence of all mantras or Vedic hymns. Simply by chanting the holy name of Krishna, one can obtain freedom from material existence. Indeed, simply by chanting the Hare Krishna mantra one will be able to see the lotus feet of the Lord." [14]

Of course, it is not that Sri Caitanya was a fool, but to exhibit an example that anyone these days is hardly qualified to extensively study Vedanta philosophy, even if they are interested. However, regardless of one's qualifications, anyone can engage in the chanting of the holy names. It goes beyond the need for qualifications. But, if someone does engage in such chanting, it shows how extremely fortunate they are. They had to have engaged in numerous pious activities over the course of their past lives, and now can simply follow the easiest and most effective path for this age.

An example of this is found in the *Srimad-Bhagavatam* (3.33.7) where Srimati Devahuti describes to her son, Lord Kapiladeva, "Oh, how glorious are they whose tongues are chanting Your holy name! Even if born in the family of dog-eaters, such persons are worshipable. Persons who chant the holy name of Your Lordship must have executed all kinds of austerities and fire rituals and achieved all the good manners of the Aryans. To be chanting the holy name of Your Lordship, they must have bathed at holy places of pilgrimage, studied the *Vedas*, and fulfilled everything required."

In this way, even for those who have done everything necessary for spiritual advancement, chanting the holy names will also complete their endeavors for spiritual success. But even if a person has not made any such progress, the chanting will still bring them to the highest levels of spiritual development. This was also expressed by Sri Shukadeva Goswami to the King, "O King, constant chanting of the holy name of the Lord after the ways of the great authorities is the doubtless and fearless way of success for all, including those who are free from all material desires, those who are desirous of material enjoyment, and also those who are self-satisfied by dint of transcendental knowledge." [15]

Therefore, it is through this hearing and chanting of the Hare Krishna mantra, and also hearing about and discussing the spiritual qualities of the Supreme Being, that the conditioned souls become most fortunate to have found the path that will bring them to spiritual reality. As Lord Krishna Himself says in the *Srimad-Bhagavatam* (11.20.8), "If somehow or other by good fortune one develops faith in hearing and chanting My glories, such a person, being neither very disgusted with nor attached to material life, should achieve perfection through the path of loving devotion to Me [bhakti-yoga]."

## THE BLISS IN CHANTING THE HOLY NAMES

By now we should begin to see how the holy name of Krishna, when we absorb it into our hearts and consciousness, and when it connects to our soul, can bring us into a higher stage of awareness, happiness and bliss. Of course, if we are absorbed in materialism and our consciousness is focused on bad habits and sensual delights, then we may not be able to taste the joy that can be attained through the holy names. It is like when we are diseased with jaundice. At that time sugar, which is naturally sweet, becomes terribly distasteful. But that is because of our diseased condition. When we are cured of jaundice, then sugar again tastes very sweet. In the same way, in a diseased condition of life, while focused on the materialistic aims and goals, we cannot taste the sweetness of spiritual life, nor the bliss in the chanting of the holy names. But it is the chanting itself that can help relieve us of this diseased condition and give us the cure. Then, what was once bitter becomes like nectar.

This is described in the *Upadeshamrita* (Text 7), "The holy name, character, pastimes, and activities of Krishna are all transcendentally sweet like sugar candy. Although the tongue of one afflicted by the jaundice of *avidya* [ignorance] cannot taste anything sweet, it is wonderful that simply by carefully chanting these sweet names everyday, a natural relish awakens within his tongue, and his disease is gradually destroyed at the root."

As it is further explained, "The Absolute Truth is Sri Krishna, and loving devotion to Sri Krishna exhibited in pure love is achieved through congregational chanting of the holy name, which is the essence of all bliss." [16]

When the happiness of chanting increases, it lifts the person up to a new level of joy, the likes of which he or she has not experienced before. "When a person is actually advanced and takes pleasure in chanting the holy name of the Lord, who is very dear to him, he is agitated and loudly chants the holy name. He also laughs, cries, becomes agitated and chants just like a madman, not caring for outsiders." [17]

Of course, it may take a little while for us to reach this stage of bliss, but it is not only possible, but is also described that this is what happens. In fact, many yogis and people who engage in spiritual activities like yoga, meditation, etc., try to find happiness in the peace of merging into the quiet within them, or in meditation on the Brahman. This can certainly have some positive effects, but it is described that higher than that is the bliss that emanates from the holy name of the Absolute Truth. "Compared to the ocean of transcendental bliss, which is tasted by chanting the Hare Krishna mantra, the pleasure derived from impersonal Brahman realization [*brahmananda*] is like the shallow water in a canal." [18]

When the devotee is attached to chanting the pure name, he or she will also have the knowledge of the *Vedas* revealed. Gradually, such a person will also attain Krishna *prema*, love of God. The *Vedas* unequivocally declare that by chanting the holy name, one experiences ecstatic bliss, as the holy name is the source of everything, including that supreme spiritual happiness. [19]

## SELF-REALIZATION THROUGH CHANTING

Another point is that by chanting the names of the Lord, one brings the mind under control and allows one to think and meditate on the Absolute Truth. This is much easier than the process of Raja and Astanga yoga in which we are meant to empty the mind of all thoughts and sensual stimulation, which eventually allows us to have a glimpse of our real identity. Only after understanding and perceiving our real identity as a spiritual being can we proceed to the next step, which is to perceive the Supersoul within us, which is the localized expansion of the Supreme Being, and then to realize what our connection or relationship is with the Supersoul. The chanting on the names of God brings our consciousness into the connection with God much more quickly, and is a much more attractive process. In fact, it is the names of God that is the vibration of God.

So, instead of trying to empty our mind, we fill it with transcendental and spiritual vibration, which uplifts our consciousness to this spiritual frequency. This not only purifies the mind, our consciousness, but opens the channels of perception so that we can also begin to perceive that same spiritual dimension. Meditation is meant to draw to us that which we meditate on, and such meditation of chanting the holy names brings that spiritual frequency to us very quickly. By chanting the Hare Krishna mantra, one immediately concentrates on the sound incarnation of the Lord and thinks of the Absolute Truth by this process. Thus, he or she can be very quickly elevated to the position of *samadhi* or trance in this way. The Hare Krishna mantra can be chanted by anyone, without the consideration of where to sit, or how to meditate. There are no such injunctions as you find in Raja or Astanga-yoga. You simply sit, with body straight, and chant and hear the Hare Krishna mantra. Or you can even stand or walk, and simply chant and listen to the mantra. You can't get much easier than that.

Even while singing and dancing to the melody of the Hare Krishna mantra in a congregational setting, which is called *sankirtana*, if we are open to receiving the vibration, we can begin to experience its potency very quickly, and our hearts can be filled with joy by the contact with such spiritual vibration and sound.

How the holy names bring one to the spiritual level of perception is described by Srila Bhaktisiddhanta Sarasvati Thakur in his *Anubhasya* commentary to the *Caitanya-caritamrita* (Adi.7.73): "The Name and the Named [meaning Krishna] is not different from one another. Therefore, just as Lord Krishna is the absolute reality, liberated, the embodiment of pure consciousness, a transcendental philosopher's stone, so to is His name. Only through the worship of the Holy Name (*nama-bhajana*) can both one's gross and subtle misidentifications be destroyed. The Vaikuntha name [meaning completely spiritual since the name comes from the spiritual world] alone can save the living being from absorption in thoughts of material sense gratification. Because it is powerful enough to do this, it is called the *mantra-sara*, the essence of all mantras. Every material thing has its name, form, attributes, characteristics, and functions, all of which are subject to arguments and experimental knowledge. The same is not true for the Vaikuntha name; the name, form, attributes, and associates of the Lord are all situated in nonduality." [20]

This means that the Lord, His characteristics, form, and name are all the same in spiritual substance. For this reason, chanting the holy names of the Lord, or discussing Krishna's characteristics, are the best means of understanding the Absolute Truth and becoming progressively spiritually realized. And one of the best ways to glorify and remember the Lord is to chant and sing His names. As it is explained, "O descendant of King Bharata, one who desires to be free from all miseries must hear about, glorify, and also remember the Personality of Godhead, who is the Supersoul, the controller and savior from all miseries." [21]

"O King, it is therefore essential that every human being hear about, glorify and remember the Supreme Lord, the Personality of Godhead, always and everywhere." [22]

"Devotional service, beginning with the chanting of the holy name of the Lord, is the ultimate religious principle for the living entity in human society." [23]

"Simply by chanting the holy name of Krishna, one is relieved from all the reactions of a sinful life. One can complete the nine processes of devotional service by chanting the holy name." [24]

The nine processes of bhakti-yoga or devotional service include hearing, chanting, remembering the Lord, serving, worshiping the Lord, praying, obeying, maintaining friendship with the Lord, and surrendering everything to the Lord. But simply chanting the holy names, which automatically includes hearing, is the way that completes every other of the nine processes. So the way to reach the heights of spiritual realization, along with everything else you may include, is through the chanting of the holy names. But this means that one must chant offenselessly, which we will discuss more later. As this continues, it awakens the dormant love of God in the heart. This is beyond merely realizing one's spiritual position as a soul within the body. This is the ultimate level of purity and spiritual realization, that by purely chanting the holy names we can be free from our karma, which paves the way to attain love of God.

"Simply chanting the Hare Krishna *maha-mantra* without offenses vanquishes all sinful activities. Thus pure devotional service, which is the cause of love of Godhead, Krishna *prema*, becomes manifest." [25]

"By chanting the holy name of the Lord, one dissolves his entanglement in material activities. After this, one becomes very attracted to Krishna, and thus dormant love for Krishna is awakened."[26]

The importance of this is further emphasized in the *Bhagavatam* (11.2.40), "By chanting the holy name of the Supreme Lord, one comes to the stage of love of Godhead. Then the devotee is fixed in his vow as an eternal servant of the Lord, and he gradually becomes very much attached to a particular name and form of the Supreme Personality of Godhead. As his heart melts with ecstatic love, he laughs loudly or cries and shouts. Sometimes he sings and dances like a madman, for he is indifferent to public opinion."

In this way, the bhakti-yogi realizes that he has reached the ultimate position of his or her psychological and spiritual development, the realization of which also gives the devotee great joy. He also realizes that the holy name is the most precious treasure in the Lord's storehouse. It is the chief means that awakens love of God, which is the prerequisite for attaining the spiritual domain. Furthermore, the Supreme Being has four characteristic features that can attract us, namely His name, form, qualities, and activities. But the name is original and superior because it is through the name that we are awarded the cognition of the other three features. Therefore, especially for a Vaishnava or Krishna devotee, chanting the holy name is the prime religious activity. It can accomplish everything else.

Since chanting the holy name of Krishna is so important, we should endeavor with great determination to take shelter of the holy name in all times and circumstances. The more we do this, the more the holy name, which is an incarnation of Krishna, will bestow His mercy on us and relieve us of all the unwanted things in our hearts and bring all auspiciousness. When we become purified and develop a love for Krishna's name, then feelings of *raga* also become possible, which is the feeling of attachment for a relationship with the Lord.

In one of the songs by Srila Bhaktivinoda Thakur in his song *"Krishna-nama dhare kata bala?"* in his book *Saranagati*, he says, "When the name is even slightly revealed, it shows me my own spiritual form and characteristics. It steals my mind and takes it to Krishna's side. When the Name is fully revealed, it takes me directly to Vraja, where it shows me my personal role in the eternal pastimes."

This means that as we purify or spiritualize our consciousness, our own devotional or Vraja mood is revealed, and how we fit into the eternal pastimes of Krishna in His supreme abode. This is and leads to the perfectional stage of spiritual realization. [27]

## THE SIGNIFICANCE AND MEANING OF
## THE HOLY NAMES OF THE LORD

Even in the early Vedic literature of the *Rig Veda* (1.156.3) we find the following prayers that describe many of the unique characteristics and potencies of the name of God, in this case in the name of Vishnu: "O Supreme Lord, Sri Vishnu! Your sacred *nama* [name] is absolutely cognizant and all-illuminating because the entire Vedic scripture have emanated from Him. Your name is the wellspring of supreme bliss, the embodiment of Brahman, is readily available, and is full of transcendental knowledge. We meditate upon the purport of Your name, discuss [Your] name amongst ourselves, and chant Your name continuously. In this way, we worship You.

"O Sri Vishnu, ever since our faith in You has become steadfast, our desire to gain Your direct audience has led us to offer incessant prayers at Your lotus feet, which are the purifying agents of the hearts of the devotees and replete with relishable transcendental pastimes. We always hear the glorification of Your unsurpassable qualities and praise them amongst ourselves. In this way, we have taken shelter of Your omnipotent and all-purifying name.

"O sages. Know for certain that the original primeval Supreme Personality of Godhead you seek is Sri Krishna. Worship Him in this realization, for He is the ultimate goal of the Vedas, the absolute essence. He is the embodiment of eternity, absolute knowledge, and divine bliss. The purpose of human life is to know Him, to describe Him and the wonderful pastimes of His incarnations. Let us eulogize and worship that Supreme Lord according to our natural spiritual emotions and taste. In this way, we shall crown our lives with paramount success and continuously chant *harinama* [the names of Hari, Lord Krishna who takes away all inauspiciousness], which is dynamic, variegated and omnipotent. To chant *harinama* is the most relishable activity, and the bestower of the greatest pleasure."

This description certainly gives great insight into the potencies of the holy names and how to unleash those potencies by the most blissful activity of discussing the nature of the Lord and to engage in the congregational chanting of the holy names, which is called *harinama sankirtana*.

To understand deeper meanings and significance of the name Krishna, or any of His holy names, we need to first accept the premise that the name of Krishna and Krishna Himself is composed of the same spiritual energy. There is no difference. All words have significance, but if I chant the name of water, I do not get the experience of water. My thirst remains unquenched. The point is that we can experience the presence of Krishna just by sincerely chanting

His name with faith and devotion. It will begin to reveal itself to us, and we can actually have the experience of Krishna's presence if we treat the name with the respect that it is due.

For example, the *Padma Purana*, as quoted in the *Caitanya-caritamrita* (Mad.17.133), explains it this way, "The sacred name of Krishna is transcendentally blissful. It bestows all spiritual benedictions, for it is Krishna Himself, the reservoir of all pleasure. Krishna's name is complete, and it is the form of all transcendental mellows. It is not a material name under any condition, and it is no less powerful than Krishna Himself. Since Krishna's name is not contaminated by the material qualities, there is no question of its being involved with *maya* [the temporary material energy]. The name of Krishna is always liberated and spiritual; it is never conditioned by the laws of material nature. This is because the name of Krishna and Krishna Himself are identical."

In the *Agni Purana* it is said, "Whoever chants the words 'Hare Krishna, Hare Krishna, Krishna Krishna, Hare Hare' even negligently will achieve the goal, without doubt."

Then in the *Brahmanda Purana* it is also said, "Whoever chants 'Hare Rama, Hare Rama, Rama Rama, Hare Hare,' is freed from all sins."

It was Sri Caitanya Mahaprabhu, the greatest preacher of the glories of the holy name, who combined these two statements, thereby issuing the words Hare Krishna and Hare Rama to drown the world in love of God, Krishna *prema*. Even though this mantra had been described previously in Vedic literature, Sri Caitanya Mahaprabhu taught His followers and the world to chant the sixteen-word mantra, Hare Krishna, Hare Krishna, Krishna Krishna, Hare Hare / Hare Rama, Hare Rama, Rama Rama, Hare Hare.

According to the *Agamas* and the *Gautamiya Tantra*, the root '*krs*' means 'to attract' and the suffix '*na*' means 'ultimate bliss.' Together these two roots form the word *Krishna*, which means the person who attracts, and the personification of the ultimate bliss. This is the Supreme Brahman or ultimate Supreme Being. So it would seem natural that if we are going to work for anything, why not simply work for the ultimate bliss?

The *Agamas* further explain that by uttering the syllable '*ra*', all sins are driven away. But in order to keep them from returning, the syllable '*ma*' is added, as if in closing the door. Also in the *Ramatapini Upanishad* the person who enjoys with Radha is called Rama. This refers to Krishna, who gives pleasure to the yogis, meaning the bhakti-yogis or devotees. [28]

There is still another point of significance to these names. The *Padma Purana* also explains that Rama means the all-conscious and all-blissful Divinity who permeates the whole world, and in whom the yogis find joy. The *Mahabharata* (Udyoga Parva, 70.5) also says that the syllable '*krs*' means existence, and '*na*' means joy or bliss. Thus the name Krishna also means the everlasting, immortal and eternal joy. Then the word *Hari* means one who takes away all sins or all inauspiciousness, and who burns all the sins of one who recites His name.

Therefore, while chanting this Hare Krishna mantra in *japa* or *sankirtana*, the *sadhaka* or practitioner should dwell on the meaning of these divine names, and should believe that the all-pervading Supreme Being has appeared before him in the form of the holy name. Thinking in this way and to consider the unfathomable opportunity a person has because of being introduced to the Lord in His name, gives increasing joy and peace of mind. In this way, the *sadhaka* can keep his mind fixed on the Divine Form of the Lord as his *Ishta-devata*, His chosen Divinity.

It is also through this name that Krishna calls out to all of His eternal servants, both devotees and the materially conditioned souls, like a cow who has lost her calf. He scatters His name amongst them through the mercy of the pure devotees in hope that they will get a glimpse of the supreme bliss that is available if they would only decrease their material attractions and look within to their true spiritual identity and to their Supreme Creator. He sees their suffering in the material world of repeated birth and death and wants them to be relieved, but it is their own free will as to whether they choose to remain attracted to the material energy or the spiritual. Nonetheless, He provides the necessary instruction such as *Bhagavad-gita* and asks everyone to take shelter of Him. But many are those who pay no attention, nor do they realize the ultimate bliss that is awaiting for them if only they would take up the chanting of the holy name and become receptive to all of the potencies that await them by doing so.

It is the eternal function of the individual soul, the *jivatma*, to be attractive to the all-attractive, infinite Supreme Soul, either directly or to His material energy. It is also the eternal function of the Supreme Being to provide various ways for the materially conditioned souls to become attracted to the Supreme Being and the multifaceted spiritual energy where they can get a taste of everlasting, infinite, supreme bliss and ecstasy. The easiest and most open doorway to this realm is through the invitation to take to the chanting of the holy name of the Supreme Lord. And this name is distributed throughout the material creation only by the mercy of the Lord's devotees who give this opportunity to as many people as possible. For those who do so and take it seriously, they can rise above the temporary passing pleasures derived from the limited material energy and can come in contact with the eternal, infinite and ultimate bliss that compares to an ocean of nectar. This is the significance of the holy name in the form of the Hare Krishna *maha-mantra*.

## HOW THE MAHA-MANTRA CAN DELIVER ALL LIVING BEINGS

We should emphasize this point, as explained, "In this age of Kali, the holy name of the Lord, the Hare Krishna *maha-mantra*, is the incarnation of Lord Krishna. Simply by chanting the holy name, one associates with the Lord directly. Anyone who does this is certainly delivered." [29]

Therefore, as a person associates with the Supreme Being through the sound of His holy names or hearing about His qualities, the Lord will begin to enter their hearts and changes their disposition and uplifts their spiritual awareness. This is confirmed in the *Srimad-Bhagavatam* (12.12.48), where it says, "When people properly glorify the Supreme Personality of Godhead or simply hear about His power, the Lord personally enters their hearts and cleanses away every trace of misfortune, just as the sun removes the darkness or as a powerful wind drives away the clouds."

So here we can understand that the holy names are so potent

for those who can sincerely chant them, but what about other living beings like the animals? What can be done for them?

Actually, this was answered in a discussion between Sri Caitanya Mahaprabhu and Haridasa Thakura. Sri Caitanya asked, "On this earth there are many living entities, some moving and some not moving. What will happen to the trees, plants, insects and other living entities? How will they be delivered from material bondage?"

Haridasa Thakura replied, "My dear Lord, the deliverance of all moving and nonmoving living entities takes place only by Your mercy. You have already granted this mercy and delivered them. You have loudly chanted the Hare Krishna mantra, and everyone, moving or not moving, has benefitted by hearing it. My Lord, the moving entities who have heard Your loud *sankirtana* have already been delivered from bondage to the material world, and after the nonmoving living entities like trees hear it, there is an echo. Actually, however, it is not an echo; it is the *kirtan* of the nonmoving living entities. All this, although inconceivable, is possible by Your mercy. When loud chanting of the Hare Krishna mantra is performed all over the world by those who follow in Your footsteps, all living entities, moving and nonmoving, dance in ecstatic devotional love." [30]

In this way, the Lord acts and provides facility so all living entities can advance spiritually, regardless of who or what they are, as also confirmed in the *Srimad-Bhagavatam* (10.29.16), "Krishna, the unborn Supreme Personality of Godhead, master of all of the masters of mystic power, delivers all living entities, moving and nonmoving. Nothing is astonishing in the activities of the Lord."

So, by such use of the Hare Krishna mantra, any living being that comes in contact with it gets spiritual benefit. But especially those who understand the significance of the mantra and use it faithfully and sincerely. This is why the spiritual aspirants, those who are advanced in spiritual pursuits, chant the holy names and discuss the pastimes and characteristics of the Supreme Being so devotedly. "Paramahamsas, devotees who have accepted the essence of life, are attached to Krishna in the core of their hearts, and He is the aim of their lives. It is their nature to talk only of Krishna at every moment, as if such topics were newer and newer. They are as attached to such topics as materialists are attached to topics of women and sex." [31]

# Chapter Nine

## THE MOST WORSHIPFUL OBJECT IS THE HOLY NAME

When Sri Caitanya Mahaprabhu was asking Ramanada Raya what is the most worshipable of all objects, Ramanada Raya replied, "The chief worshipable object is the holy name of Radha and Krishna, the Hare Krishna mantra." [32]

So, not only is this *maha-mantra* the vehicle by which we can infuse ourselves with the spiritual vibration of the spiritual world, but out of everything that we hold dear or that is worshipable, the holy name is to be held in the highest esteem. This is why some temples in India are centered around the holy name and have no specific deity. In this way, they chant, sing and discuss the nature of the holy name as their main function. Of course, many are those temples that do have Deities of Radha-Krishna and Krishna's various other forms, and where the chanting and singing of the holy names is one of the essential parts of the worship that goes on there, even having *sankirtana* 24 hours a day. But this shows the importance the holy name has, especially in the form of the Hare Krishna mantra. And as we have mentioned, there are no hard and fast rules to abide by regarding where and how to chant. It can be chanted anywhere, at any time, and in any condition.

Chanting the holy name is direct service to Krishna. And by chanting the names of Krishna in *sankirtana*, a congregational setting, or in solitary meditation in *japa*, a person will develop feelings for Krishna, up to and including Krishna *prema*, ecstatic and intense love. This is the ripened fruit of chanting the holy names. [33]

This is the ultimate fulfillment of all spiritual pursuits, beyond acquiring knowledge, Brahman realization, or liberation by merging into the Brahman. Attaining this love is what can uplift us to the stage in which we engage in the eternal pastimes of the Lord, either in the Vaikuntha planets or in Goloka Vrindavana. As the *Bhagavata Purana* (1.5.22) points out, "Learned circles have positively concluded that the infallible purpose of the advancement of knowledge, namely [through] austerities, study of the *Vedas*, sacrifice [or rituals], chanting of hymns and charity, culminates in the [hearing of] transcendental descriptions of the Lord, who is defined in choice poetry."

Such pastimes of the Lord can be found in such texts as the *Srimad-Bhagavatam*. Reading or listening to them is the very easy process that is incorporated in bhakti-yoga. This is also why the *Bhagavatam* (2.1.11) points out that for anyone who has developed some spontaneous attachment to the chanting of the holy names of the Lord, or the Hare Krishna mantra, is to be understood as having attained the highest perfectional stage of spiritual success. Also, in the *Adi Purana* Krishna says to Arjuna that anyone who is engaged in chanting My transcendental name must be considered to be always associating with Me. "And I may tell you frankly that for such a devotee I become easily purchased."

The *Padma Purana* also explains that the chanting of Hare Krishna is present only on the lips of a person who has been worshipping Vasudeva [Krishna] for many births. And that there is no difference between the holy name of the Lord and the Lord Himself. As such, the holy name of the Lord is as perfect as the Supreme Being Himself in fullness, purity and eternity. The holy name is no material sound vibration, nor has it any material contamination. [34]

The only thing to do then is to reach the stage of chanting offenselessly, wherein the potency of the name can be felt to the highest degree. Materialistic senses cannot properly chant the holy names of the Hare Krishna *maha-mantra*. But by adopting the chanting process, the name itself can purify the devotee so that he may very soon chant offenselessly. So until then, we can certainly have fun by chanting with other devotees and enjoy the saintly association while we help each other raise ourselves to higher and higher spiritual awareness until one day we can float in the ocean of nectar that emanates from Lord Krishna in the form of His names.

This is why Sri Caitanya has advised that everyone should chant this Hare Krishna mantra just to wipe away the materialistic dust from our hearts that has accumulated over many lifetimes. If this dust is cleansed away, then one can actually understand the importance of the holy name. However, if a person is not inclined to clean away the dust and wants to keep things the way they are in one's materialistic mindset, then it will not be possible to derive the transcendental result from chanting Hare Krishna. Therefore, we should be encouraged to associate with other devotees to maintain our interest and encouragement to develop our spiritual awareness, and our service attitude toward the Lord and His holy names, because this will help him be relieved of the troubles in material existence and experience a higher level of happiness.

This is why the holy names of Krishna are the most worshipable object within this world because hearing Them purifies the inner self. From there we can more easily begin to understand Krishna's form, qualities, characteristics, His associates and then His pastimes. From the chanting of the holy names, all other perfections of spiritual life will come to everyone. This is the conclusion of spiritual authorities. It is like the shortcut that cuts through all difficulties, both material and spiritual.

Then the most difficult thing to acquire or understand can be attained, which is the loving mood that the residents of the supreme spiritual abode of Goloka Vrindavana have for Lord Krishna. Invoking this mood is the key to being able to enter into the eternal pastimes that go on in Goloka. And this is all possible by sticking with the chanting of the Lord's names.

## THE MOST IMPORTANT PRINCIPLE IN BHAKTI-YOGA

The most important principle in the process of devotional service, bhakti-yoga, is the chanting and singing of the holy name. Of course, after we have given so much information on the potency and significance of the holy name, this should be obvious. It was Sarvabhauma Bhattacharya who asked Sri Caitanya Mahaprabhu, "Which item is most important in the execution of devotional service?" Sri Caitanya replied that the most important item was the chanting of the holy name of the Lord. [35]

So, even doing all of the other principles and activities of devotional service, the chanting of the holy names is the most significant. Everything else is like an extension of the chanting. That is the core engagement, spending a certain amount of time each day chanting the names of Krishna, and then we can engage in the other principles, such as remembering, serving, etc., which are actually highlighted by the chanting. They can become more perfected by being performed with the right attitude and mood after we have done our *japa* meditation. This is what we learn from this point.

So the next question would be how do we chant appropriately so we can invoke the deepest potential from our meditation on the holy names. This is what we answer next.

## HOW TO CHANT THE HOLY NAMES

In learning the best way to chant, the first thing to remember is that all it takes is faith to chant the holy names. It is said that one who has sufficient faith is eligible to chant it. But even without faith, anyone can try it and recognize the joy within the chanting. But with a little experience, a person will want to continue the process. And with this faith, a person will want to become more steady at it.

The *Vishnu-dharma* states that there are no hard or strict rules when it comes to chanting the holy names of the Lord. You can do it at any time or any place, as stated:

> *na desha-niyamas tatra*
> *na kala-niyamas tatha*
> *nocchishtadau nishehash cha*
> *shri-harer namni lubdhakaha*

"There is no restriction of place or time, nor any injunction forbidding the accepting of remnants of food, etc., when one has become greedy to chant the name of Sri Hari."

Also, the holy name is so powerful and complete that, "One does not have to undergo initiation or execute the activities required before initiation. One simply has to vibrate the holy name with his lips. Thus, even a man of the lowest class can be delivered." [36] Many Vedic mantras are not allowed to be given to a person without them being initiated by a guru into its chanting. It is this initiation which awakens one's transcendental knowledge by spiritual purification, or the means to invoke the power of the mantra. But for chanting the Hare Krishna mantra, initiation is not required. All that is required is

# Chapter Nine

faith. However, if a person does accept initiation and instruction for chanting, his spiritual consciousness will awaken much sooner.

Furthermore, anyone can certainly join a group for *sankirtana* chanting of the Hare Krishna mantra, or even pick up a set of beads to chant *japa* quietly for oneself. In any way you chant, it is beneficial and joyful. But there are a few things that will help you get the most out of your chanting, and to bring out the deepest effects of the holy names. So the second point is the mood in which you chant.

"To chant the holy name always, one should be humbler than the grass in the street and devoid of all desire for personal honor, but one should offer all respects to others." [37]

The attitude while chanting should be one of humility, that we are like infants crying for our mother, or praying to the Lord for guidance to know what to do in our life. We may have so much material facility, such as wealth, big house, fat bank account, beautiful wife or husband, but if we do not truly know who we are on a spiritual level, we are but fools. We have no reason whatsoever to be proud. It is only by the guidance from the Supreme that we may get the understanding of who we really are and where we are going, or where we should be going. And the only way we can get that is by getting the mercy of the holy name, which will then act on us to open our hearts to the higher wisdom it has to offer. And, in most cases, the only way we get the holy name is through the grace of the pure devotees. Then this will lead us or open us up to the directions that Lord Krishna gives in such texts as the *Bhagavad-gita* and others. And our mood of humility while chanting the holy names will help us attain that.

The best mood in which to chant is the mood of love, asking Krishna for the mercy to get closer to Him. Chanting God's holy names is also a type of admiration or worship, and if this is done with a loving feeling, then that will help open deeper levels of love for God. Of course, such love means without the desire for any personal motive or benefit. It should be done simply to please the Lord. In this way, the yogi should have no desire in his mind while chanting, other than love for the name itself, which is actually love for Krishna. The *japa* should be carried out with love, faith and reverence for the mantra. And the more love there is, the more inwardly focused will be the devotee. If the devotee thinks of anything while chanting, it should be of the form, qualities or pastimes of the Lord. Then the devotee's tongue, ears, and mind are all engaged in the chanting process, and his soul will float on the ocean of joy, peace and bliss. When one tastes such feelings, the meditation on the holy names can only go deeper and more inward.

For me, when I think of how kind the Lord has been to me in so many arrangements of my life that were made beyond my own capacity, but for getting closer to understand God, or freer from material impediments, or in awakening deeper levels of spiritual awareness, I cannot help but be overcome with emotion while chanting the holy names. It shows that the Lord has taken care of me better than I could take care of myself. It also shows the strong connection there has been throughout my life in my purpose to find God, and that my destiny was also there throughout whatever else I have done in this life. In this way, there is the realization that the Divine is all love, the very embodiment of love. Love is His very nature. He is all mercy, and merely waiting for us to turn toward Him so He can more easily display such compassion and care. Then, in this kind of mood, you can recognize the arrangement and power of God wherever you look. Anywhere in the world is the power of God and God's qualities of compassion, mercy, kindness, care, and concern, all of which we are meant to reflect in our own character the closer we get to God. And anything that does not reflect this is nothing but mankind's absence of God.

The next step is to try to chant without being distracted, especially for chanting *japa* for one's personal meditation. This means two things: first that your chanting is focused on the sound of the holy names, and second, that you start to chant a certain number of names or rounds on your beads every day. If you are distracted, you will be thinking of something else and will also likely just try to complete your chanting without much thought or devotion. It is important to concentrate on the quality of your chanting, and that the name should be pronounced distinctly. If you cannot understand the words you are calling for Krishna, it is likely that He may not understand them either, nor anyone else. Krishna should also be able to understand whose name you are chanting. This way you can begin to taste the nectar of the name. And that is important to increase your faith in the chanting.

If we can chant in the ways we have described so far, we can avoid what is called offensive chanting. So we must know what is offensive chanting, because this will nullify or greatly decrease whatever benefits we would otherwise derive from our chanting.

This is described in the *Hari-bhakti-vilasa* (11.527) as quoted from the *Padma Purana*, "Should someone utter the holy name of the Lord even once, or should he merely remember it or hear it in passing, it will certainly deliver him from material bondage, whether it is correctly or incorrectly pronounced, properly joined, or vibrated in parts. O brahmana, if one uses the holy name for the benefit of the material body, for material wealth and followers, or under the influence of greed or atheism–in other words, if one utters the name with offenses–such chanting will not produce the desired result with the same rapidity."

The fact is, offensive chanting is a likely stage of chanting we all go through when we first begin to chant. It is not uncommon. We all chant with the idea that it may improve my health, wealth, peace of mind, my interactions with others, and so on, which it will certainly assist in many ways. But that is not the prime purpose of it. However, if the beginner in chanting is not contaminated by atheistic concepts, he still has a good chance of going through this offensive stage and reach a higher level of chanting and feeling reciprocation with the holy name in due time. He is only ignorant of the potency of the name and the real purpose in chanting it. [38] And this can be easily corrected.

There are three stages to chanting: *namaparadha*, which is offensive chanting, then *namabhasa*, or the stage of less offenses or the reflection of the holy name when we are still not chanting properly but getting closer, and then *shuddha-nama*, when we reach the pure chanting of the holy name, which brings liberation.

A few of the offenses in chanting the holy names include chanting without focus or intention, or with a material conception of the holy name, or improper understanding (*sanketa*), chanting in jest or ridicule (*parihasa*), chanting derisively (*stobha*), or with disregard or neglect (*hela*). [39]

In fact, once we reach the *namabhasa* stage, it is not to be underestimated, for it still avails many positive benefits to the individual and increases his piety. It offers him great good fortune, more than religiosity, vows, yoga, rituals, and so on. By chanting, all one's sinful reactions become absolved, and he is freed from the effects of Kali-yuga. Even the miseries brought on by demons, ghosts, evil spirits, and malefic planetary influences can be averted by the power of the holy names. Even if one is destined for the hellish planets, such karma can be counteracted. It is even more powerful than visiting every pilgrimage place, studying all the *Vedas*, or performing all kinds of altruistic work. *Namabhasa* chanting even offers an eternal residence in the spiritual abode of Vaikuntha, especially during the age of Kali-yuga. [40] So even this stage offers great opportunity for spiritual advancement.

There are ten main offenses to the holy name that need to be avoided, and these are:

1. To blaspheme the devotees who have dedicated their lives to the propagation of the holy names of the Lord.
2. To consider the names of the demigods like lord Shiva or lord Brahma to be equal to, or independent of, the name of Lord Vishnu.
3. To disobey the orders of the spiritual master.
4. To blaspheme the Vedic literature or literature in pursuance of the Vedic version.
5. To consider the glories of chanting Hare Krishna as imagination.
6. To give mundane interpretation of the holy name of the Lord.
7. To commit sinful activities on the strength of chanting the holy names of the Lord.
8. To consider the chanting of Hare Krishna as one of the auspicious, ritualistic activities which are offered in the *Vedas* as fruitive activities (*karma-kanda*).
9. To instruct a faithless person about the glories of the holy name.
10. To not have complete faith in the chanting of the holy names and to maintain material attachments even after understanding so many instructions on this matter. It is also offensive to be inattentive while chanting.

By learning to avoid these ten offenses anyone will quickly achieve the desired success, which is Krishna *prema*.

One of the hardest of these offenses to give up is holding onto material attachments. This does not merely mean holding on to objects of desire, but to the idea of "me" and "mine," especially in regard to bodily designations of who and what we think we are. The main word in that last statement is "think," because keeping materialistic attachments is mostly a mental activity, like habitual thought patterns. We may think we are male or female, black or white, old or young, Russian or American, wealthy or poor, a celebrity or not, etc., but such designations in our mentality will only distract us from the path of devotion. These are only materialistic designations and are symptoms of spiritual immaturity, and deterrents to proper cultivation of devotional service and higher spiritual realizations. It is a sign that you still have not understood your spiritual identity as a soul within the body, which is a part and parcel of the Supreme Being, Krishna, and that you actually belong to the spiritual realm, not this limited and temporary world of constant cycles of birth and death. However, by taking instruction from the spiritual master and the Vedic texts, and continuing to chant the holy names, one will eventually rise above such concepts and can eventually enter the stage of purely chanting the holy names.

The only way one can attain the stage of offenseless chanting is to mix with other devotees and avoid bad association. By chanting with concentration in the association of devotees, the heart becomes pure and ignorance is destroyed, one becomes more enlightened, and the taste for chanting increases. By Krishna's mercy, the bhakti-yogi may take shelter of a pure devotee who has fully experienced the potencies of the holy names, and who can guide you along the path more effectively. Otherwise, a person may remain misguided and not advance as quickly.

When the name's nature becomes clear to the yogi, Krishna's spiritual form can also appear along with the name. Thus the perception of Krishna in the name drives away the modes of material nature, and pure goodness appears, which then bestows the realization of Krishna's spiritual qualities. According to the purity of the chanting, the Lord's pastimes can now also appear in the pure heart of the devotee who has awakened his natural spiritual vision. At that time, the material world takes on a whole different perspective, and one can see the spiritual energy that exists all around us. Thus, when the purified tongue glorifies the Lord with *japa* or simple recitation of the names, the mind can see Krishna's form, the heart perceives Krishna's qualities, and the soul in trance sees Krishna's pastimes. Such pastimes may be the activities in Vrindavana, as described in such texts as the *Bhagavatam*, or in the fact that the whole process of creation and annihilation of the material universes is itself a pastime of Krishna. [41]

Srila Bhaktivinoda Thakur explains the way in which we can reach pure chanting: "If the holy name is seriously chanted just once, even though impurely, or if it is simply heard without distraction, the sound penetrating within to the soul, then the living entity can be immediately liberated, regardless of his high or low caste. And beyond this, when the holy name is chanted in the clearing stage (*namabhasa*–the second stage when impurities are swept from the heart of the chanter), then the highest goal is attained after some delay. All the other auspicious and pious results, including liberation can be quite easily achieved, but the attainment of love of Godhead is suspended for a while. In the clearing stage of chanting, the *jiva* is absolved of all sins, and by following this path, he gradually reaches the highest stage of chanting: *shuddhanama* or the pure name. One obtains love of Krishna only after reaching this stage of pure chanting. When *namabhasa* is complete, all sins and *anarthas* (unwanted desires in the heart) are dissipated, and the devotee chants purely. Then *shuddhanama* (the name in pure goodness) offers the devotee the highest spiritual success: love of Krishna." [42]

When we reach the stage of pure chanting, it becomes a whole new experience of happiness and bliss. Pure chanting is described in the *Srimad-Bhagavatam* (3.15.25), "Persons whose bodily features change in ecstasy and who breathe heavily and perspire due to hearing the glories of the Lord [or His holy names] are promoted to the kingdom of God, even though they do not care for meditation and other austerities. The kingdom of God is above the material universes, and it is desired by Brahma and other demigods."

Furthermore, when we can purely chant the holy name, its power is fully revealed by our perception of its spiritual qualities. When a person takes complete shelter of the holy names, he or she becomes the recipient of the treasure of Krishna *prema*, or intense and ecstatic love for God. Therefore, when we reach this stage of offenseless chanting, the bhakti-yogi becomes eligible to receive Krishna's causeless mercy. What happens is that his chanting quickly awards him the divine fruit of *bhava*, the first stage of love of God. In this way, the bhakti-yogi is promoted from being a *sadhika* or simple practitioner to *bhava*, one who can experience spontaneous pure devotional service. From *bhava* comes *prema*, which is the mature fruit of pure devotion, the likes of which can allow the devotee to taste the same emotions as the residents of Krishna's supreme abode of Goloka Vrindavana. This is the result of offenseless chanting. [43]

This is greatly emphasized by Haridasa Thakur, the *acharya* of chanting the holy names. While discussing the glories of the holy name in an assembly of people in the village of Candapura, Haridasa clearly explained that regardless of all the other benefits that can be attained by chanting the holy names of the Lord, by actually chanting the holy name without offenses, one awakens his ecstatic love for the lotus feet of Krishna. This is the ultimate purpose and goal. [44]

When the devotees become offenseless or qualified in the remembrance of Krishna's name, or concentration on His form, meditation on His qualities, absorption in His pastimes, they can ultimately enter into the pastimes with the taste of Krishna *rasa*, or a relationship with Krishna in a trance-like state. This is *apana-dasa*, remembering the various pastimes of Krishna in the eight different times of the day. When the devotee becomes deeply absorbed in this practice, they attain their *svarupa-siddhi*, which is the attainment of their eternal spiritual form and identity. These devotees can then be known as natural *paramahamsas*, swan-like devotees who have attained their natural spiritual identity. By the mercy of Krishna, when such devotees leave their material body at the time of death, they become associates of Krishna in the Vraja or Vrindavana pastimes in their own spiritual body. This is called *vastu-siddhi*. This is the ultimate result of purely chanting the holy names of Krishna, called *prapana-dasa*. [45]

This is how the process of chanting the holy names works, from the stage of merely trying it, then practicing it, and all the way up to the complete realization of one's spiritual identity.

"Let there be all victory for the chanting of the holy name of Lord Krishna, which can cleanse the mirror of the heart and stop the miseries of the blazing fire of material existence. That chanting is the waxing moon that spreads the white lotus of good fortune for all living entities. It is the life and soul of all education. The chanting of the holy name of Krishna expands the blissful ocean of transcendental life. It gives a cooling effect to everyone and enables one to taste full nectar at every step." (*Siksastaka* 1, written by Sri Caitanya Mahaprabhu)

**CHAPTER NOTES**
1. *Caitanya-caritamrita,* Adi-lila, 7.74.
2. *Srimad-Bhagavatam,* 11.6.24.
3. *Caitanya-caritamrita,* Madhya-lila, 15.108.
4. Ibid., Antya-lila, 3.55.
5. *Srimad-Bhagavatam,* 6.2.15-16.
6. Ibid., 7.15.74.
7. *Sri Harinama Cintamani,* p.67.
8. *Srimad-Bhagavatam,* 6.2.18-19.
9. Ibid., 6.3.7.
10. Ibid., 6.2.8.
11. Ibid., 6.13.8.
12. *Bhakti-rasamrita-sindhu* 2.1.103.
13. *Caitanya-caritamrita,* Antya-lila, 3.63.
14. Ibid., Adi-lila, 7.72-3.
15. *Srimad-Bhagavatam,* 2.1.11.
16. *Caitanya-caritamrita,* Adi-lila, 1.96.
17. Ibid., 7.94.
18. Ibid., 7.97.
19. *Sri Harinama Cintamani,* p.59.
20. *Art of Sadhana,* p.147.
21. *Srimad-Bhagavatam,* 2.1.5.
22. Ibid., 2.2.36.
23. Ibid., 6.3.22.
24. *Caitanya-caritamrita,* Madhya-lila, 15.107.
25. Ibid., Adi-lila, 8.26 & *Cc.*Antya.lila, 4.70-1.

26. Ibid., Madhya-lila, 15.109.
27. *Art of Sadhana*, p.26.
28. *Sri Caitanya-Siksamrita*, p.227-8.
29. *Caitanya-caritamrita,* Adi-lila, 17.22.
30. Ibid., Antya-lila, 3.67-72.
31. *Srimad-Bhagavatam,* 10.13.2.
32. *Caitanya-caritamrita,* Madhya-lila, 8.256.
33. Ibid., Adi-lila, 1.7.83, 86.
34. *Nectar of Devotion*, pp.108-9.
35. *Caitanya-caritamrita,* Madhya-lila, 6.241.
36. Ibid., 15.108.
37. Ibid., Adi-lila, 17.26 & Antya.20.21 & *Sikshasthaka* text 3.
38. *Sri Harinama Cintamani*, p. 27.
39. Ibid., p.22.
40. Ibid., p.22.
41. *Sri Caitanya-Siksamrita*, p. 232-4.
42. *Sri Harinama Cintamani*, p. 16.
43. Ibid., p. 90-1.
44. *Caitanya-caritamrita,* Antya-lila, 3.178.
45. *Sri Caitanya-Siksamrita*, pp. 230-2.

# CHAPTER TEN

# *Getting the Right Instructions From a Proper Guru*

The principle of accepting a spiritual master is something we have touched on earlier, but it is so important that for those who are serious, it deserves its own chapter.

Taking to a spiritual path and learning spiritual knowledge means accepting information as given by someone else, whether it is from a personal teacher or from someone's book or video or some other media. Of course, this is the case in any field of study. So how do we find a qualified spiritual teacher? And do we need one?

When we talk about what a spiritual master is and whether we need one, there is often a tendency to think that there is no reason for us to have a personal spiritual guide advising us what we should or should not do. "After all," we may tell ourselves, "I've gotten this far on my own, why should I let anyone else cramp my style or tell me how to live? I'm getting along alright." Thus, due to pride and a large ego, we may dismiss the idea of trying to understand what a qualified spiritual master is and whether there is a need or benefit in having one.

The way to know who is an authorized spiritual master or teacher is to be informed about the character, qualities, and knowledge that one must have in order to be a qualified spiritual authority. Not just anyone can call themselves a spiritual teacher or guru.

### WHAT IS A SPIRITUAL MASTER

The first qualification one must have to be a bona fide spiritual master or qualified teacher is a complete understanding of the science of God. Regardless of one's social position or birth, if one is a pure devotee of the Lord, then he can teach others. This is verified in the *Caitanya-caritamrta* (*Madhya-lila*, 8.128) which explains that regardless of whether one is a *brahmana* (priest), *sannyasi* (renounced mendicant), or a *sudra* (laborer), if he knows the science of Krishna he can be a spiritual master.

The *Padma Purana*, however, mentions that even if one is a highly elevated brahmana, familiar with all the rituals of the scripture, if he is not purified, he cannot be a spiritual master.

The characteristics of one who is purified are stated by Sri Rupa Gosvami in his *Upadesamrta* (Text 1), in which he writes that a person is qualified to make disciples all over the world if he can control his mind, anger, tongue, belly, genitals, and the urge to speak. This means that such a spiritual master can control his senses, mind, anger, belly, and genitals because he is purified by transcendental knowledge and spiritual realizations. He is not just faking it by going through the motions and offering some lip service to maintain his honor and prestige. He actually knows he is not the body and, therefore, being completely self-realized, he is not bothered by bodily demands. If a spiritual leader cannot control his mind, his words, anger, belly, or genitals, then he obviously is not yet purified and not qualified to lead others. He still identifies with his body and, therefore, caters to bodily urges. For one to be a *svami* or master, he must be a master of his senses: a *gosvami*. If he cannot yet control his senses, then he is not yet ready to be a bona fide spiritual guide who can teach throughout the world. Instead, he must continue to accept instruction for his own purification from those who are more advanced. In other words, he cannot set others free as long as he is still tied up.

A few more of the characteristics of a qualified spiritual master are mentioned in the following verses:

"If one is seen to be unlimitedly merciful, perfectly complete, distinguished by all good qualities, fixed in activities for the benefit of all living entities, free from lust, possessing all types of perfections, all-knowing [in spiritual knowledge], and capable of slashing all doubts of the disciple while always remaining alert to be engaged in the service of the Lord, then such a person may be known as a guru."[1]

"When one has fully assimilated all the conclusions of the revealed scriptures and thereby establishes the codes of perfect behavior for others, himself also acting strictly according to those codes, such a knower of the Absolute Truth of perfect character is glorified by the title of *acharya*." [2]

The word *acharya* means one who teaches by example. So not only can he explain the spiritual truths to others, but he shows by his own example how to attain such a goal. Also, one should not pose as a spiritual master if he cannot deliver those who depend on him. The *Srimad-Bhagavatam* (5.5.18) explains that a person should not become a spiritual master, nor a father, husband, mother, or a demigod if he cannot deliver those who depend on him from the cycle of repeated birth and death in the material worlds.

The original spiritual master is actually God Himself. The Lord appears as both the *acharya*, the spiritual master, and as the Supersoul to deliver the living beings. As stated in *Srimad-Bhagavatam* (11.29.6), the Lord appears externally as the spiritual master and internally as the Supersoul in order to help guide the living being back to the Lord's spiritual abode.

Naturally, the Lord as Supersoul in the heart instructs and guides us from within, as confirmed in *Caitanya-caritamrta* (*Madhya-lila*, 8.265). So why not simply take guidance from the Supersoul? The problem is, as explained in *Srimad-Bhagavatam* (8.24.52), that although the Supersoul is always ready to instruct us, and is the dearmost friend and well-wisher of everyone, because we are filled with lusty desires for bodily pleasure, we cannot hear or understand the Lord. So to cure us of such misguided lusty desires which bind us to repeated birth and death in this material world, and causes us to forget the real goal of life, the Supreme manifests Himself externally in the form of the spiritual master and Vedic texts and instructs those of us who will listen. This is how the Lord is always ready to help us from within and from without. Thus, the pure devotee spiritual master, who can receive the message of the Supersoul within and deliver that pure sound vibration to his students in an untainted and unchanged form, is practically identical with God, as confirmed in *Caitanya-caritamrita* (*Adi-lila,* 1.61).

This is how God delivers the living entities from the material world through the bona fide spiritual master. Therefore, a real spiritual leader should not be considered an ordinary person. As explained in *Caitanya-caritamrta* (*Adi-lila*, 1.45, 47), the spiritual master and Krishna are nondifferent in that the Lord instructs the devotees through the pure representative. The *Padma Purana* also warns that any person who considers the authentic spiritual master to be an ordinary human is to be taken as a resident of hell.

## RECOGNIZING A QUALIFIED GURU

It is very important to be sure of the qualifications of the spiritual master. That is why it is suggested that you take the time to notice his qualifications and if he follows the proper codes of conduct as enunciated above. Lord Krishna in the *Bhagavatam* (11.17.22) also says, "My dear Uddhava, the spiritual master must be accepted not only as My representative but as My very self. He must never be considered on the same level with an ordinary human being. One should never be envious of the spiritual master, as one may be envious of an ordinary man. The spiritual master should always be seen as the representative of the Supreme Personality of Godhead, and by serving the spiritual master, one is able to serve all the demigods."

To accept a qualified spiritual master is the crucial point for advancement in spiritual life. Otherwise, simply being engaged in any kind of yoga cannot guarantee one's future to become free from material existence altogether. A person may certainly make some progress by such means, but to reach the real goal is not guaranteed. Therefore, one who is fortunate enough to come under the shelter of a genuine spiritual master is sure to traverse the path of spiritual success.[3]

So, what are the qualities to be observed in a saintly spiritual master? These are also further elaborated by Lord Krishna in the *Srimad-Bhagavatam* (11.11.29-32): "The Supreme Personality of Godhead said: O Uddhava, a saintly person is merciful and never injures others. Even if others are aggressive, he is tolerant and forgiving toward all living entities. His strength and meaning in life come from the truth itself, he is free from all envy and jealousy, and his mind is equal in material happiness and distress. Thus, he dedicates his time to work for the welfare of all others. His intelligence is never bewildered by material desires, and he has controlled his senses. His behavior is always pleasing, never harsh and always exemplary, and he is free from possessiveness. He never endeavors in ordinary, worldly activities, and he strictly controls his eating. He therefore always remains peaceful and steady. A saintly person is thoughtful and accepts Me as his only shelter. Such a person is very cautious in the execution of his duties and is never subject to superficial transformation, because he is steady and noble, even in a distressing situation. He has conquered over the six material qualities–namely hunger, thirst, lamentation, illusion, old age, and death. He is free from all desire for prestige and offers honor to others. He is expert in reviving the Krishna consciousness of others and, therefore, never cheats anyone. Rather, he is a well-wishing friend to all, being most merciful. Such a saintly person must be considered the most learned of men. He perfectly understands that the ordinary religious duties prescribed by Me in various Vedic scriptures possess favorable qualities that purify the performer, and he knows that neglect of such duties constitutes a discrepancy in one's life. Having taken complete shelter at My lotus feet, however, a saintly person ultimately renounces such ordinary religious duties and worships Me alone. He is thus considered to be the best among all living entities."

In this way, we can recognize a saintly devotee and spiritual master by these qualities. However, there are also internal qualities that are described. Such a guru should also be realized in knowing what his relationship is with the Supersoul, Krishna, or he cannot be a bona fide spiritual master. [4] This can only be discerned by the words and descriptions of the Lord's pastimes that the guru relates. Does he describe the pastimes, as related in *shastra*, as an observer who is merely reporting the events, or as a participant in the activities? This can give a sign to his understanding of his relationship with Krishna.

As explained in the *Bhagavatam* (4.29.51): "One who is engaged in devotional service has not the least fear in material existence. This is because the Supreme Personality of Godhead is the Supersoul and friend of everyone. One who knows this secret is actually educated, and one thus educated can become the spiritual master of the world. One who is actually a bona fide spiritual master, representative of Krishna, is not different from Krishna."

Therefore, when you have a genuine guru, consulting with him is no different than consulting with the Supreme Lord. This does not mean that the spiritual master will know all relative truths such as how many stars are there in the sky, or where exactly can we dig into the ground to get water, or how many hairs are there on the body of a cow, or where to invest our money, and things like that. What he is a master of is the process by which we can arrange our lives to follow the path of bhakti-yoga so we can attain the Supreme, and thus reach the real goal of human existence.

A real spiritual master teaches in accord with the previous saints and sages as well as the standard scriptural texts. For assuring ourselves of continued spiritual progress, these three guides of guru, *shastra* (scripture) and *sadhu* (saintly persons or advanced devotees) must be consulted. If we find that, for example, a spiritual teacher diverts in behavior or differs in the philosophical teachings that are set by the standard Vedic references or previous *acharyas*, then his authority should be questioned and he should be avoided, unless it is otherwise shown that his purpose is justified. As stated in the *Hari-bhakti-vilasa* (1.101): "One who [assuming the position of an *acharya*] delivers irregular speeches contradictory to the standard Vaishnava scriptures, as well as one [as a disciple] who hears such unauthorized speeches, are both destined for hell." Thus, comparing the three above mentioned sources of knowledge (guru, *sadhu* and *shastra*) as a system of checks and balances will enable us to be sure we remain on the right path.

Therefore, we must be cautious. If someone poses as a spiritual authority but is not qualified, he will only misdirect us on our path to spiritual progress. Regardless of how many rules he may supply for moral conduct and so on, the final and highest levels of spiritual advancement may not be available through such a person. This is clearly pointed out in the *Bhagavatam* (11.18.40-41): "One who has not controlled the six forms of illusion [lust, anger, greed, excitement, false pride, and intoxication], whose intelligence, the leader of the senses, is extremely attached to material things, who is bereft of knowledge and detachment, who adopts the sannyasa [renounced or priestly] order of life to make a living, who denies the worshipable demigods, his own self and the Supreme Lord within himself, thus ruining all religious principles, and who is still infected by material contamination, is deviated and lost both in this life and the next."

Therefore, in such a condition, a person cannot be a spiritual authority but actually needs spiritual guidance as much as anyone else. He should not mislead or cheat people by posing as something he is not, but should admit his own frailties and work for his own continued need for development.

So, we should carefully consider what is said in the *Katha Upanishad* (1.2.7), "Many persons cannot even hear about the soul, and even after hearing about him, many cannot have any realization of him; this is because an instructor who is a genuine seer of the truth is rarely found, and realization can only be obtained by becoming very expert. And since to receive instruction from such an expert spiritual master is rare, only a selected few can know the soul in truth."

Herewith, the significance of the true spiritual master has been explained. The gift of spiritual knowledge as given by the *acharya* is priceless. It is difficult to find authentic spiritual knowledge or a person who can actually explain it properly. And once found, it can be hard to understand, what to speak of knowing how to utilize it in our daily lives. But by the grace of the spiritual master, we not only are able to understand such knowledge, but we also learn how to practically apply it in our lives to solve all the problems of material existence, which is, namely, to attain freedom from it.

The authorized spiritual master does not make up anything new or change the message or alter Vedic knowledge. He simply repeats the same instructions given by the previous authorities. This is the authorized process as given through the disciplic succession. The spiritual master finds new ways to preach the same message so that it can be practically applied in the present times.

# Chapter Ten

## THE RARE GOOD FORTUNE OF MEETING A PURE DEVOTEE

Another important point is that it is only by the rare chance of meeting a bhakti-yogi, a devotee of the Lord, that a conditioned soul, who often has already spent many lifetimes wandering throughout the universe in various conditions and species of life, gets the seed of bhakti-yoga. Such a soul can then come closer to the Lord by learning the art of devotional service, which makes the external energy, *maya*, flee. [5]

This is why pure devotees, agents of reality, wander over the earth spreading the knowledge of bhakti-yoga so that others can benefit and also become enlightened. [6] In this way, they are servants of humanity, while having no interest in materialistic affairs. Sometimes they act as though undercover agents, reaching only the most inquisitive or qualified souls who may be in need of receiving such knowledge, while other pure devotees may be more easily recognized by their outgoing nature and followers.

It is only by such fortune of being favored by a pure devotee that one can attain to Krishna-bhakti and become eligible to be relieved from the entrapment of material existence. However, one must continue to receive the proper instructions on how to proceed if there will be success. This is why Krishna helps the conditioned soul as the *chaitya-guru*, or the spiritual master who resides in the heart as the Supersoul, instructing the inquiring person from within, as well as the guru from outside. [7]

As *Srimad-Bhagavatam* (4.30.34) describes, "Even a moment's association with a pure devotee cannot be compared to being transferred to heavenly planets or even merging into the Brahman effulgence in complete liberation. For living entities who are destined to give up the body and die, association with pure devotees is the highest benediction."

Even Lord Krishna explains in the *Bhagavatam* (11.12.1-2, 7, and similarly repeated in 5.12.12 & 6.1.16), "My dear Uddhava, by associating with My pure devotees one can destroy one's attachment for all objects of material sense gratification. Such purifying association brings Me under the control of My devotee. One may perform the astanga-yoga system, engage in philosophical analysis of the elements of material nature [sankhya-yoga], practice nonviolence and other ordinary principles of piety, chant the *Vedas*, perform penances, take to the renounced order of life, execute sacrificial performances and dig wells, plant trees and perform other public welfare activities, give in charity, carry out severe vows, worship the demigods, chant confidential mantras, visit holy places or accept major or minor disciplinary injunctions, but even by performing such activities one does not bring Me under his control... The persons I have mentioned did not undergo serious studies of the Vedic literature, nor did they worship great saintly persons, nor did they execute severe vows or austerities. Simply by association with Me and My devotees, they achieved Me."

"The path followed by pure devotees of the Lord, who are well behaved and fully endowed with the best qualifications, is certainly the most auspicious path in this material world. It is free from fear, and it is authorized in the *shastra*." [8]

"...Even half a moment's association with pure devotees within this world of birth and death is a priceless treasure for any man." [9]

"O Lord, who resembles the shining sun, You are always ready to fulfill the desire of Your devotee, and therefore You are known as a desire tree [*vancha-kalpataru*]. When acharyas [advanced devotee teachers] completely take shelter under Your lotus feet in order to cross the fierce ocean of nescience, they leave behind on earth the method by which they cross, and because You are very merciful to Your other devotees, You accept this method to help them." [10]

Here is another example of what and who is an *acharya*. It is one that not only is in contact with the Lord, but also gives guidance while he is present, and leaves behind the instructions after he leaves so that others can follow and reach the same goal.

## IS IT NECESSARY TO HAVE A SPIRITUAL MASTER?

Whether it is necessary or not to accept a spiritual master or recognize a spiritual authority from whom to take guidance is something that is often times unclear to people. But from the *Bhagavatam* (11.22.10) we learn that since a person cannot attain self-realization alone by his own effort, and since he has been covered by ignorance from the beginning of time, there must be another person who knows the spiritual truth and can impart this knowledge to him. In other words, though a person may be born with an intuitive awareness of God or have a natural tendency for searching out spiritual knowledge, one must approach an external source for enlightenment in order to fully awaken such spiritual consciousness. Furthermore, it has been understood by transcendental scholars that without the assistance of a genuine spiritual guide, one will not be able to fathom the depths of spiritual knowledge. Therefore, even in such ancient writings as the *Atharva-veda* (18.2.11, 14), it is recommended that we should take guidance from the learned masters:

"O man, pass with devotion, ever fleeting day and night, born of Dawn, pervading all the four directions, bright and dark in appearance! Go near the learned gurus, who remain in pleasure in the company of God. Few learned persons attain to prosperity, few realize the real essence of things. There are others who speedily imbibe the knowledge of God. O man, approach all these learned persons and derive knowledge from them."

However, if one is too rebellious to accept guidance and instruction from without, he will never become qualified to receive instruction from within, from the Supersoul, and will be forced to accept nothing more than his own speculations and foolishness. Therefore, Sri Krishna explains to Arjuna in *Bhagavad-gita* (4.34), "Just try to learn the truth by approaching a spiritual master. Inquire from him submissively and render service unto him. The self-realized soul can impart knowledge unto you because he has seen the truth."

In this way, the spiritual master, a pure devotee of the Lord, can give you the truth because he has seen it, and he knows how to attain it, and can guide you to do the same. But such knowledge is given in a reciprocal manner through the submissive inquiry and the service provided by the student. It is the execution of the instruction of the spiritual master that will bring the student perfection in his or her spiritual development.

The *Mundaka Upanishad* (1.2.12) also states: "To understand that transcendental science, one must approach an authentic spiritual master."

In this way, for understanding transcendental knowledge, there is no question that one must accept a spiritual master who can aid people in general with his mature spiritual realizations. This is further confirmed in *Srimad-Bhagavatam* (3.7.39) which emphasizes that a person cannot get the confidential knowledge of devotional service unless he is helped by the pure devotees. As also described in the *Bhagavatam* (11.3.21), a person must find and take shelter of a genuine spiritual master by initiation if he expects to find real happiness. A genuine spiritual master is one who knows the conclusions of spiritual knowledge and can teach them to others.

In the *Svetasvatara Upanishad* (6.23) it is further explained that all the conclusions of the Vedic literature are revealed to those great souls who engage in exclusive devotional service to the Supreme Lord, and also similarly serve the spiritual master. And the *Chandogya Upanishad* (6.18.2) states that a person who accepts initiation from the *acharya* and serves him with devotion knows the Supreme Absolute Truth.

The point to remember is that this life we are currently undergoing is nothing more than a moment on our great path towards spiritual realization. We have experienced the full range of problems that occur in material existence lifetime after lifetime. Now we find that we are not only still looking for happiness, but also searching for answers to our questions, solutions to our problems, an easier way to live, etc, etc. How many more lifetimes we continue with this process is up to us. But now that we are in the human form of life, we have particular advantages we can utilize. Some of these advantages are explained in *Srimad-Bhagavatam* (11.20.17), which says the human body, awarded by nature, is a rare achievement amongst the many species of life. The human form is like a strong boat, the spiritual master is the captain of the boat, and the instructions of the Supreme Being, as found in the Vedic literature, are compared to favorable winds that propel the boat on the proper course. A person who does not take advantage of such an opportunity to cross the ocean of material existence is comparable to one who kills his own soul.

This is the process for utilizing the human form of life properly in order to become free from fruitive activities which cause continued birth and death in the material world. Within this material creation, under the influence of the modes of nature and our accumulated karma, we are going up and down through various good or bad situations. But once we come in contact with a bona fide spiritual master, everything can change. Only the most fortunate, however, intelligently avail themselves of the association offered by the pure devotee spiritual master. This is further explained in the *Caitanya-caritamrta* (*Madhya-lila*, 19.151-164): Throughout the universe living beings are wandering amongst the lower and upper planetary systems because of their karma. Out of innumerable living entities, one is greatly fortunate if he meets a genuine spiritual master. Only by the mercy of such a master, and the mercy of the Supreme, does one get knowledge of bhakti (devotional service) to the Supreme. When he is given the seed of bhakti, he should plant it in his heart and care for it by watering it with hearing and chanting about Sri Krishna so the seed will sprout. If the creeper continues to grow with the practice of devotional service, it will grow beyond the boundaries of the universe and reach the spiritual world. There it grows more and enters the supreme spiritual planet Goloka Vrindavan and finally reaches the shelter of Krishna's lotus feet. There the creeper produces the fruit of love of God. When the fruit of love ripens, it falls and the gardener (the devotee) tastes the sweetness of this love with great happiness. This is the highest perfection of life and makes all other material perfections seem insignificant.

## THE IMPORTANCE OF APPROACHING A SPIRITUAL MASTER

When the student is ready, the teacher will appear. But in this case a qualified teacher appears by the grace of God and one's eagerness for answers. Then with sincerity a person will find a qualified teacher.

The *Skanda Purana* explains the meaning of the word *guru*:

"The syllable 'gu' refers to the darkness of ignorance; the syllable 'ru' means that which impedes it. Thus the guru is so named because he eradicates the darkness of ignorance in others." So, the meaning of guru is one who removes the darkness of ignorance and also one who is heavy with spiritual knowledge. So it is not just anyone who can accurately be named a guru, although the name gets used a lot for many purposes these days. Still, it is spiritual knowledge that is meant to be given, not just any kind of knowledge.

Secondly, there are two kinds of gurus, such as the *diksha* guru, or the one who gives you proper initiation into the sacred spiritual knowledge, and into the chanting of the holy names and the *diksha* mantra, which is usually the gayatri mantra. In this way, he imparts the essential spiritual conclusions to the disciple. The spiritual knowledge begins on the *sambandha-jnana* level, which is the knowledge of the identity of the soul and its relationship with the Supreme Lord.

Then there is also the *siksha* guru, one who can give instruction and elaborations on the sacred knowledge, but is not giving you initiation. There can be many *siksha* gurus that a person can accept, but there is only one diksha guru who gives you initiation. So the *diksha* guru is the main spiritual master in one's development. Both gurus should be respected properly. This is the key to spiritual success.

However, the difference in the importance of these kinds of gurus is especially indicated in a verse from the *Bhagavatam* (10.80.32) in which Sri Krishna says to His friend Sudama, "My dear friend, he who gives a person his physical birth is his first spiritual master, and he who initiates him as a twice-born brahmana and engages him in religious duties is indeed more directly his spiritual master. But the person who bestows transcendental knowledge upon the members of all the spiritual orders of society is one's ultimate spiritual master. Indeed, he is as good as My own self."

The *Upanishads* also explain the necessity to have a guru to give elucidation on spiritual topics: "To understand these things properly, one must humbly approach a spiritual master who is learned in the *Vedas* and firmly devoted to the Absolute Truth." [11]

"This realization, my dear boy, cannot be acquired by logic.

It must be spoken by an exceptionally qualified spiritual master to a knowledgeable disciple." [12]

It is further related that to be relieved of being lost in the never-ending cycle of repeated birth in death, wandering throughout this cosmic manifestation, an intelligent person should engage in bhakti-yoga, the devotional service to the Lord, under the guidance of a bona fide spiritual master. [13]

Even in the *Padma Purana* Lord Shiva tells his wife Parvati, "My dear Parvati, there are different methods of worship, and out of all such methods the worship of the Supreme Person is considered to be the highest. But even higher than the worship of the Lord is the worship of the Lord's devotees." [14]

This line of thinking is further elaborated in the *Bhagavatam* (3.7.19): "Let me become a sincere servant of the devotees because by serving them one can achieve unalloyed devotional service unto the lotus feet of the Lord. The service of devotees diminishes all miserable material conditions and develops within one a deep devotional love for the Supreme Person."

In fact, the importance of this cannot be underestimated, as concluded herein: "The value of a moment's association with a devotee of the Lord cannot even be compared to the attainment of heavenly planets or liberation from matter, what to speak of worldly benedictions in the form of material prosperity, which is for those who are meant for death [and continual rebirth]." [15]

So we can see that again and again in the Vedic literature it is recommended to take shelter of a genuine spiritual master, like Lord Krishna says, "...One should approach a bona fide spiritual master who is in full knowledge of Me as I am, who is peaceful, and who by spiritual elevation is not different from Me." [16]

## STAGES OF ASSOCIATION WITH PURE DEVOTEES

Now that we know the value of the association with such great devotees, how do we begin and develop such contacts?

Lord Krishna relates in the *Srimad-Bhagavatam* (11.18.38-39) that, "One who is [or is becoming] detached from sense gratification, knowing its result to be miserable, and who desires spiritual perfection, but who has not seriously analyzed the process for obtaining Me, should approach a bona fide and learned spiritual master. Until a devotee has clearly realized spiritual knowledge, he should continue with great faith and respect and without envy to render personal service to the guru, who is nondifferent from Me."

So the first stage is simply to listen to the pure devotee guru describe the information in the sacred texts like the *Bhagavad-gita* and *Srimad-Bhagavatam*. In the second stage, after the student becomes a little more advanced, he offers to follow the principles of devotional service under the guidance of the pure devotee. Then he may also accept such an advanced devotee as his spiritual master. In the third stage, under the guidance of his spiritual master, the new devotee executes regulative devotional service, and, thus, becomes freed from unwanted activities. After that, his faith becomes fixed and he develops a transcendental taste for such devotional activities in bhakti-yoga, then develops attachment, and then begins to experience ecstasies from such service and spiritual moods. In the last stage, he develops love for the Supreme. These are the stages in developing love for God in the association of the pure devotee. In this way, a person becomes completely transcendental to the ups and downs of material existence and paves his or her way to the spiritual realm. Only the most fortunate person can achieve such success in life. [17]

Associating with saintly devotees who move among us and shower us with affection, and asking them questions is easier and more practical and open to direct experience than engaging in most types of yoga processes. The very contact with such saints gives redemption for the soul, and gives imperceptible benefit and peace of mind, relief from material troubles, and accelerates the soul into the spiritual atmosphere. For those who lack the reception of the divine vibration coming from saintly people, they will not readily perceive the transcendental frequency being emitted by such advanced souls. But those who have will readily be effected by that divine effulgence coming from such saints.

## TRANSMITTING SPIRITUAL SOUND

The way this works is that the consciousness of the qualified spiritual master exists in the spiritual atmosphere, and he transmits from his lotus mouth the transcendental sound vibration of the spiritual planets in Vaikuntha. This is similar to a radio which transmits sounds from places many miles away. But to transmit the energy of the spiritual world, the master's consciousness must be completely purified. If one cannot control his senses, it shows that his consciousness is still on the material platform, at least to an extent. Therefore, he cannot deliver pure spiritual sound to his followers. Since the disciples or followers of a guru or spiritual leader generally cannot advance beyond the level of the teacher, such followers must be certain their teacher is qualified, or they should not accept him. "O Devi, there are many so-called gurus who amass wealth from their disciples, but the bona fide spiritual master who can destroy all the miseries of his disciples is rare." [18] Furthermore, "A person who by keeping disciples becomes desirous of receiving personal service and fame is certainly unfit to be considered on the platform of guru." [19]

The point is that when a pure devotee, whose consciousness lives in the spiritual platform, describes the pastimes of Krishna, especially Radha and Krishna together, he emanates that spiritual vibration which attracts the heart of those who are receptive to it, because the pure devotee and the pastimes of Radha and Krishna are imbued with divine love, for which everyone hankers. Then when a beginning devotee is convinced in his or her heart and mind that this type of love and happiness is what their soul has been longing for, then they will want more association with such a pure devotee and will also be inclined to offer various types of service to such a great soul. This solidifies the relationship and also the exchange of spiritual potencies between the neophyte or beginning devotee and the spiritual master. It is then through the blessings of the great saints that the neophyte devotee paves the way to develop love of God, or *bhava-bhakti*.

As this *bhava-bhakti*, love for the Lord, arises in the heart of the devotee, it is nourished only by the association of the advanced pure devotees. But this association must remain in the mood of love and respect, because if one happens to offend a pure devotee, then the priceless treasure of *bhava* gradually decreases and may even disappear. Then such an offender takes on inferior qualities and interests. If such an offense cannot be rectified, then such an offender will fade away from the path of bhakti-yoga altogether.

As it is described, "The mind is like an impetuous horse that even persons who have regulated their senses and breath cannot control. Those in this world who try to tame the uncontrolled mind, but who have abandoned the feet of their spiritual master, encounter hundreds of obstacles in their cultivation of various distressful practices. O unborn Lord, they are like merchants on a boat in the ocean who have failed to employ a helmsman." [20]

Therefore, our prayer to the Lord should be that He send to us a devotee who can describe the Lord's various pastimes and qualities so that our own faith and understanding become fixed. Then we can also become open to our own experiences in spiritual relations and reciprocation in our connection with God.

The *Vaishnavakhanda* (Vaishakhamasa-Mahatmya 16.18-19) explains, "O Lord, manifested in the form of the universe and possessed of infinite strength, when you show your strength to the individual soul, it is only then that it gets an opportunity to enjoy communion with high-souled ones, the virtue of which the ocean of mundane existence shrinks to the size of a cow's footprint [which can easily be stepped over]. And, Lord, it is only when one is blessed with such fellowship with pious souls that one comes to develop unwavering and implicit faith in You."

Gosvami Tulsidasa in the *Ramacharitamanasa* says, "The fellowship of genuine saints is attained only by those whom Sri Rama regards with favor."

Lord Rama also says in the *Ramacharitamanasa* (12.13-14), "Devotion is independent and a mine of all blessings; men, however, cannot attain it except through the fellowship of saints. Saints for their part are inaccessible without a stock of [pious] merit; the fellowship of the Lord's devotees in any case brings to an end the cycle of births and deaths."

In this way, as Lord Krishna summarizes, if one does not engage in devotional service with His devotees, which is given and made possible by His devotees, there is no effective means of escaping material existence. [21] "Unless one worships the lotus feet of great devotees, one will be conquered by the illusory energy, and his intelligence will be bewildered." [22]

Also in the *Adi Purana*, Lord Krishna addresses Arjuna, "My dear Partha, one who claims to be My devotee is not so. Only a person who claims to be the devotee of My devotee is actually My devotee." [23]

This shows the influence a devotee has with the Supreme. One should never think the pure devotee is an ordinary person. If someone offends the Supreme Being, the spiritual master can intercede with the Lord on behalf of the disciple. On the other hand, if a pure devotee spiritual master is angered by someone or his disciple, the Lord will not even turn to look at the offender. Therefore one should take great care to please the spiritual master. If one seeks the favor of a devotee instead of directly approaching the Supreme, he or she becomes easily successful more quickly. Without the favor of a pure devotee, one cannot easily approach Krishna directly, what to speak of engaging in the service to the Supreme.

The conclusion is that to attain the help of a pure devotee is to attain the grace of the Lord Himself. Therefore, having obtained the invaluable fortune of a human existence we should endeavor to shake off our attachment to this material body as well as to worldly enjoyments and diligently strive with all our resources to attain God-realization until our last breath. Otherwise, if we have had such an opportunity but neglect it, we shall suffer interminable regret in our future lives. And one of the best means of avoiding such a fate is through the association of pure devotees of the Lord.

The reason why this is so important is that living in the association of a yogi, one becomes like a yogi. And with further association, a person can actually become an advanced yogi. We become like that with which we associate. Likewise, when we associate with worldly men, we also become worldly-minded. But we have already been doing that for lifetimes. How many more lifetimes will we spend like this in the hopes of finding happiness and permanence? Such is not to be found within the illusory energy.

If we cannot attain the association with advanced devotees,

then we should strive for the association with others who are also trying to make spiritual progress, and who are following the instructions that come from such pure devotee spiritual masters. A person is greatly benefitted by cultivating the fellowship of those who are following a spiritual discipline with reverence and devotion as outlined by a pure devotee.

## TAKING INITIATION OF A QUALIFIED GURU

A spiritual master who can actually instruct others so they can attain the spiritual strata is considered the most respected and venerable of all persons. This is elaborated upon in the *Manu-samhita* (2.140), which says that a brahmana who teaches the pupil the Vedic spiritual knowledge and takes charge of him through the initiation process, called *upaniti*, is called the *acharya*. It is through the initiation ceremony that one gets closer to the guru. But the guru is like a parent training his children, and not someone who merely enjoys the facilities supplied by the disciples. Furthermore:

"Of him who gives natural birth and him who gives the knowledge of the *Veda*, the giver of the *Veda* is the more venerable father; for the birth for the sake of the *Veda* ensures eternal rewards both in this life and after death. Let him consider that he received a mere animal existence when his parents begat him through mutual affection, and when he was born from the womb of his mother. But that birth which a teacher acquainted with the whole *Veda*, in accordance with the law, procures for him through *Savitri* [initiation into chanting the *mantra*, specifically the *gayatri*], is real, exempt from age and death. The pupil must know that that man also who benefits him by instruction in the *Veda*, be it little or much, is called in these institutes his guru, in consequence of that benefit conferred by instruction in the *Veda*. That brahmana who is the giver of the birth for the sake of the *Veda* and the teacher of the prescribed duties becomes by law the father of an aged man, even though he himself be a child. [24] . . . For a man destitute of sacred knowledge is indeed a child, and he who teaches him the *Veda* is his father; for the sages have always said 'child' to an ignorant man, and 'father' to a teacher of the *Veda*. [25]... A man is not therefore considered venerable because his head is grey; him who, though young, has learned the *Veda*, the gods consider to be venerable." [26]

So, the next step is to take initiation from such a qualified spiritual master to accelerate one's spiritual progress. First of all, one verse that gives advice on both of these points is: "Therefore any person who seriously desires real happiness must seek a bona fide spiritual master and take shelter of him by initiation. The qualification of the bona fide guru is that he has realized the conclusions of the scriptures by deliberation and is able to convince others of these conclusions. Such great personalities, who have taken shelter of the Supreme Godhead, leaving aside all material considerations, should be understood to be genuine spiritual masters."[27]

"One should know the *acharya* to be My self and never disrespect him in any way. One should not envy him, thinking him an ordinary man, for he is the representative of all demigods." [28]

In this way, the guru is like the spiritual father of the disciple and should be treated in a similar manner. Disciples should be willing to render service to the guru in assisting him in his mission to spread spiritual knowledge, as well as in regular activities, such as cooking, getting water, and other simple tasks in the service to the guru. This humble service qualifies the disciple to receive further insights into the secrets of deep spiritual knowledge and experience. In this arrangement, the disciple accelerates his progress toward the spiritual realm.

The point is that no one goes back to the spiritual abode of the Lord, Krishna, without the blessings of another Vaishnava. And once a yogi has received such blessings from a pure devotee, his destination to the spiritual abode of the Lord, Goloka-Vrindavana, is guaranteed, either in this lifetime or the next. This is why a devotee, a bhakti-yogi, always desires the blessings of the previous Vaishnava *acharyas*. So he remains a humble servant in his attitude and actions, which prevents any offensive behavior, and which will please those senior devotees who offer spiritual favors in return.

"Unless they smear upon their bodies the dust of the lotus feet of a Vaishnava [who is] completely freed from material contamination, persons very much inclined toward materialistic life cannot be attached to the lotus feet of the Lord, who is glorified for His uncommon activities. Only by becoming Krishna conscious and taking shelter at the lotus feet of the Lord in this way can one be free from material contamination." [29]

Why do we say the "lotus feet" of the great devotees or the Lord? Because, like a lotus flower rises above the waters in which it is rooted, the Lord's feet also never actually touch the ground, nor are effected by the material energies in which He may appear. The great devotee spiritual masters also have lotus feet in the sense that he is always above the modes of material nature, but is above it in terms of his consciousness, which is always focused on the spiritual atmosphere or the Lord's pastimes.

This is also the importance of taking shelter of a spiritual master by initiation and becoming a disciple. This enables one to be more strongly connected to the previous *acharyas* in the line of disciplic succession, which descends all the way back to be connected with the Lord directly.

## THE SIGNIFICANCE OF THE PARAMPARA OR DISCIPLIC LINEAGE

The way the disciplic succession or *parampara* system works is that the bona fide guru is he who received the mercy of his guru. This goes on like this from generation to generation, extending back through time to Lord Krishna Himself. In other words, Krishna in the form of Lord Vishnu who originally taught this knowledge to Lord Brahma, who taught Narada, who taught Vyasadeva, and so on. Therefore, this knowledge is carefully handed down from person to person in the present form we have today. These persons in the disciplic succession are not ordinary, but are perfectly self-realized and are the transparent medium by which this knowledge descends. In this way, we can directly hear Lord Krishna speak, although it appears as if we are simply getting instruction from the present spiritual master. This is the mystery of the disciplic succession. By coming in contact with this *parampara* network, we can directly hear the unadulterated message of the Supreme. If one avoids the disciplic succession, then one's spiritual knowledge remains imperfect.

In the Vedic tradition, there are four recognized *parampara* systems called *sampradayas*. One *sampradaya* comes from Lord Brahma, one from Sri (the goddess of fortune), another one comes from the four Kumara brothers headed by Sanat-Kumara, and another *sampradaya* comes from Lord Shiva.

An example of an authorized and complete disciplic succession is the one we belong to, the Brahma-*sampradaya*. The list of personalities in it are as follows: (1) Lord Krishna, (2) Brahma, (3) Narada, (4) Vyasa, (5) Madhva, (6) Padmanabha, (7) Nrihari, (8) Madhava, (9) Aksobhya, (10) Jayatirtha, (11) Jnanasindhu, (12) Dayanidhi, (13) Vidyanidhi, (14) Rajendra, (15) Jayadharma, (16) Purusottama, (17) Brahmanyatirtha, (18) Vyasatirtha, (19) Laksmipati, (20) Madhavendra Puri, (21) Isvara Puri, (22) Lord Caitanya Mahaprabhu, (23) Rupa Gosvami (along with Svarupa and Sanatana), (24) Raghunatha and Jiva Gosvami, (25) Krishnadasa Kaviraja, (26) Narottama, (27) Visvanatha, (28) [Baladeva] Jagannatha, (29) Bhaktivinode, (30) Gaurakisora, (31) Bhaktisiddhanta, (32) and our own spiritual master, His Divine Grace A. C. Bhaktivedanta Swami.

The following verse relates the importance of Narada Muni, one of the early *acharyas* in this line: "Narayana, the Supreme Personality of Godhead, the well-wisher and friend of all living entities, formerly explained this transcendental knowledge to the great sage Narada. Such knowledge is extremely difficult to understand without the mercy of a saintly person like Narada, but everyone who has taken shelter of Narada's disciplic succession can understand this confidential knowledge." [30]

"O supreme form, we are always servants of Your servants, especially Narada Muni... It is by the grace and mercy of Narada Muni that we have been able to see You face to face." [31]

Lord Krishna also explained in the *Bhagavad-gita* (4.2-3) that one of His purposes in appearing on earth was to re-establish the sacred *parampara* or disciplic succession because even though He started it ages ago, it had become lost and He was here to continue it. He says, "This supreme science was thus received through the chain of disciplic succession, and the saintly kings understood it in that way. But in course of time the succession was broken, and therefore the science as it is appears to be lost. That very ancient science of the relationship with the Supreme is today told by Me to you because you are My devotee as well as My friend; therefore you can understand the transcendental mystery of this science."

So if one is considering a particular spiritual master or teacher, first find out what disciplic succession to which he belongs. If he is not a part of any authorized disciplic succession, then his teachings and whatever mantras he offers will lack potency and you will not get full benefit. Therefore, if one feels perplexed about how to find an authentic spiritual master, all one needs to do is first accept the Supreme as the original spiritual master and then seek out His pure representative. Simply understand what Krishna says in the revealed scripture, as presented in this chapter, and you will know what qualifications to look for in an authentic spiritual leader from whom you can take instruction and guidance. By coming in contact with a proper spiritual master, you will be able to understand transcendental knowledge which will answer all your questions and relieve you of your uncertainties. As stated in *Bhagavad-gita* (4.36, 39): even if a person is the worst of sinners, he can cross the ocean of material miseries by boarding the boat of spiritual knowledge. Such a man who is faithful and in control of his senses, quickly attains the supreme spiritual peace.

In this way, unless you are blessed by another devotee, you cannot acquire the information or insight to realize the position of the Supreme Being. This knowledge descends through the *parampara* or lineage of disciples that go back to Narada Muni, and to even Lord Brahma, and to Lord Vishnu or Krishna Himself. So if a person takes shelter of this lineage, he or she will be able to understand this confidential information. This is the power of taking shelter of the *parampara*, the line of spiritual masters who carefully hand down from one guru to another this rare spiritual knowledge for those who are sincere and qualified, and who want to be free from the ups and downs and the temporary happiness and distress of material existence. This is the wish of those who genuinely want to attain freedom from material life. When a person feels this way, they are eligible for taking initiation from the spiritual master.

# Chapter Ten

## THE SIGNIFICANCE OF INITIATION

*Diksha*, meaning one's spiritual initiation, is explained by Srila Jiva Gosvami in his *Bhakti-sandarbha* (868): "By *diksha* one gradually becomes disinterested in material enjoyment and gradually becomes interested in spiritual life."

How the potency of confidential levels of bhakti-yoga are transferred through the disciplic succession or lineage of spiritual masters to the new disciples is explained by Srila Bhaktivinoda Thakur in his book *Sri Harinam Cintamani* (page 33-34 of Chapter Four): "The potency or shakti of pure devotion is a blend of *hladini* (Krishna's pleasure-giving potency) and *samvit* (Krishna's knowledge-giving potency). The pure bhakti potency is instilled by a perfected pure devotee in the aspiring devotee; it is by this process that the bhakti potency is handed down. The bhakti potency reposes in the heart of a transcendentalist, and it uses him as a vehicle for further movement. When a *jiva* [entity] becomes free from envy and is inclined to devotional service, the bhakti potency is then transferred from a pure devotee's heart into that *jiva's* heart. This is a great mystery. The three great touchstones that offer [to most easily transfer] the mercy of a Vaishnava in attendance to bhakti are: the Vaishnava's eatable remnants, the water from his foot bath, and dust from his lotus feet.

"When one sits in the presence of a [pure devotee] Vaishnava for some time, one feels Krishna's potency exuding from his person. This potency enters the heart of a faithful person and impregnates it with bhakti. He experiences immediate ecstasy. Just by a moment's association with a Vaishnava, bhakti is invoked in the heart of a pious person. Immediately he will be inspired to chant Lord Krishna's name, and gradually the holy name will offer him all the spiritual qualities."

In this way, a pure devotee will effect the neophyte devotees with bhakti just by their association. The high frequency vibration will raise the consciousness of those who are nearby or who are willing to associate with him in some way. It is also explained that when the sacred mantra is given by the great devotee who chants it to the initiate, it is more powerful due to its descending from the advanced devotee. The Hare Krishna mantra is powerful by itself, but becomes more potent by the contact with and the dissemination by the pure devotee.

The mystery of the Supreme Being is unfolded before the eyes of the pure devotee because his eyes are anointed with love of God, which calls the Lord to reveal Himself. So this vision is not ordinary, to say the least. It is described that the transcendental name, form, characteristics, and pastimes are being televised into the heart of the pure devotee. No non-devotee can understand this. The spiritually developed person is able to have the television of the Kingdom of God, the spiritual realm, always reflected in his heart and consciousness. In this way, when he teaches, he is broadcasting the spiritual vibration from the transcendental abode to all who are willing to hear it. [32]

This is the significance of initiation, which is receiving pure knowledge of spiritual consciousness. This is highlighted by the formal ritual and, more importantly, the heartfelt feeling of accepting a pure devotee spiritual master, in which case the potency of the pure devotee can be accepted into the heart of the disciple, whose devotion and dedication brings him or her to the point wherein the disciple begins to experience the effects and personal realizations of spiritual life through the blessings of the guru. As described in the *Caitanya-caritamrita* (Antya-lila 4.192-3): "At the time of initiation, when a devotee fully surrenders to the service of the Lord, Krishna accepts him to be as good as He Himself." That is because the Lord transforms the devotee's body into spiritualized substance, and then the devotee worships the Lord in a spiritualized body. (We will talk more about this later in this book.)

At that time of initiation, the disciple can receive the full blessings to become spiritually purified and advanced to engage in bhakti-yoga without limitations, and then attain clear realizations of one's spiritual identity and relationship with the Supreme. Then his attitude should be one of confidence, as described in the *Bhagavatam* (7.9.18): "... I shall become completely uncontaminated from the association of the three modes of material nature and be able to chant the glories of Your Lordship, who are so dear to me. I shall chant Your glories, following exactly in the footsteps of Lord Brahma and his disciplic succession. In this way, I shall undoubtedly be able to cross the ocean of nescience."

"O my Lord, original spiritual master of the entire world, what is the difficulty for You, who manage the affairs of the universe, in delivering the fallen souls engaged in Your devotional service? You are the friend of all suffering humanity, and for great personalities it is necessary to show mercy to the foolish. Therefore I think that You will show Your causeless mercy to persons like us, who engage in Your service." [33]

This is the perfection one can attain by the grace of the spiritual master. Therefore, by receiving the blessings of the guru, one can become very powerful, both materially and spiritually. If, however, one does not take a spiritual master, he remains like a ship without a rudder with no possibility of reaching the proper destination. Thus, throughout the Vedic literature, it is always emphasized that one should accept a genuine spiritual master in order to keep advancing in one's spiritual development. "Unless one is initiated by a bona fide spiritual master, all his devotional activities are useless. A person who is not properly initiated can descend again into the animal species." [34]

Once initiated by a proper spiritual authority, one is connected through the *parampara* system to the Lord Himself, just as a light bulb is connected through the electrical line to the power house that charges it. If one adheres to the guidance of a bona fide spiritual master, nothing will prevent him from attaining complete spiritual perfection in this very life. One will not have to wait for his next birth, but can achieve everything in this present life in order to experience the Absolute Truth. Thus, by the grace of the Lord one gets a proper spiritual master, and by the grace of the spiritual master one gets the Lord.

What are the duties of the spiritual master and how does he or she treat the disciple? The guru's first duty is to see that his disciple is making advancement in spiritual life. And one type of duty is to help the disciple become released from past karma. In order to do this, sometimes the guru must take charge of the disciple's past sinful activities. This is part of the meaning of the initiation ceremony. If the guru becomes overly burdened by such karma, he will have to suffer some of the results, at least partially. Every disciple should be very careful not to commit further sinful activities after initiation. [35] This is also why the guru must have a strong connection with the parampara so that any such reactions go up through the line of gurus to Krishna who can then neutralize such reactions to protect the pure devotee. That is why it is very dangerous to be a guru and give initiation if one is not fully connected to the *parampara* or does not have a disciplic line with which he is connected.

"A saintly person, just like fire, sometimes appears in a concealed form [hidden from others] and at other times reveals himself. For the welfare of the conditioned souls who desire real happiness, a saint may accept the worshipable position of a spiritual master, and thus like fire he burns to ashes all the past and future sinful reactions of the worshipers by mercifully accepting their offerings." [36]

One point is that by initiation a disciple can be freed from sinful reactions. This is because when the spiritual master accepts a person as a disciple in the Vedic tradition, he takes the disciple's *karmic* reactions. *Karmic* reactions always affect us in various ways, but they also take the shape of continuous material desires which bind us to further material activities and their reactions. When the spiritual master takes our *karmic* reactions at the time of initiation, he paves the way for us to make spiritual progress without any hindrances. In this way, we are protected by the spiritual master. If, however, one takes a spiritual master and gets initiated and then goes off to engage again in the same materialistic activities as before, ignoring the guru's instructions, then this is extremely offensive on the part of the disciple and leaves him with no chance of making any advancement. It is like the example of the fan which spins around as long as it is connected to the electricity. Once it is unplugged, it slowly comes to a halt. Similarly, our karma continues as long as we remain connected to our sinful activities. But once we become disconnected from them, the karma becomes reduced and we slowly become free from such reactions by engaging in spiritual activities. Initiation is like unplugging ourselves from our past karma. But if we plug back into our sinful activities, then the fan of our karma begins to rotate again and pick up speed. So we want to remain unplugged from that.

The offenses and sinful activities of the disciple can also become an added burden for the spiritual master. Therefore, the disciple must take the process of initiation seriously.

However, the spiritual master must also be cautious in who he accepts as a student or disciple. A sannyasi or guru must examine the student to determine whether he or she is sincerely seeking spiritual knowledge. If he is not, he should not be accepted. So a guru does not take just anyone as a disciple. Nonetheless, in the line of Sri Caitanya Mahaprabhu, which is our line, those who understand the science of God can speak about this spiritual knowledge anywhere. From those who are listening, if someone is very sincere, he can be accepted as a disciple by a qualified guru. But in order to spread this science of bhakti-yoga, sometimes a guru will take the risk of accepting someone who is not thoroughly fit to become a disciple. But by the mercy of the spiritual master, the student may gradually become elevated. However, if a person continues to accept disciples for some prestige or false honor, the burden of karma, or his lack of a clear connection with the *parampara* may bring him down from his execution of bhakti-yoga, Krishna consciousness. This can be the danger in accepting too many disciples.

The essential characteristic of a disciple who has received initiation is a honest desire for faithful and loving service to the spiritual master, other devotees and Vaishnavas, and the Supreme Lord. The secondary characteristic is that he or she seeks to destroy and refrain from any further sinful activities, or those selfish acts which cause more karma, which becomes a burden for both the disciple and the guru. [37]

At the time of initiation, the disciple is usually taught how to chant the sacred mantra to awaken his spiritual vision. By the potency of the initiating process, one can immediately attain the level of a qualified brahmana. This is verified in the following verse: "By chemical manipulation, bell metal is turned into gold when touched by mercury; similarly, when a person is properly initiated, he can acquire the qualities of a brahmana." [38] The disciple is then considered to be twice-born. Initiation by the bona fide guru is the second birth, above and beyond one's ordinary birth from the womb of a mother.

Becoming twice-born is also mentioned in the Bible: "Jesus answered and said unto him, Verily, verily, I say unto thee, except a man be born again, he cannot see the kingdom of God." (*John* 3.3) Also, "Being born again, not of corruptible seed [from the womb], but of incorruptible, by the word of God [the spiritual mantra or scripture], which liveth and abideth forever." (*I Peter* 1:23) This simply refers to one's spiritual birth, as in the Vedic system of taking initiation from an authentic representative of God. In modern Christianity, this usually means accepting Jesus as one's personal saviour, along with being baptized, taking vows or going through catechism, and becoming a member of the Church. Of course, Christianity does not have an established *parampara* system as found in the Vedic culture, which has left the Bible open for many opinions and interpretations of what it means.

When someone is initiated by a genuine spiritual master and seriously engaged in bhakti-yoga, he is then considered to be a *madhyama-adhikari*, an intermediate level devotee of the Lord.

## HOW THE SPIRITUAL MASTER TEACHES

Because a saintly person is always interested in seeing everyone in society advance, he is always ready to teach transcendental knowledge. He also teaches by setting the proper example that everyone should follow. As stated in *Bhagavad-gita* (3.21): whatever is done by a great man, and whatever standard he sets by his actions, common men follow. Therefore, a guru must be ready to teach in many ways. Because the spiritual master is the authority on transcendental topics, he sets the correct standard in everything he does. However, if a guru cannot follow the appropriate standard or maintain the exemplary criterion in order to show others how spiritual life is meant to be performed, then we can understand that he is not a guru. He may be able to teach to a certain level, but is not suitable for giving initiation.

A true spiritual leader is always concerned about the

well-being of his followers and the people in general. He does not take the post of spiritual authority for his own benefit. This is one reason why he must maintain his purity. His duty is to train the disciple in a way that will enable the disciple to remain free from the influence of the illusory energy. The spiritual master recognizes the natural propensities of the student and instructs him how to use those propensities to make spiritual progress. Thus, the student becomes free from the modes of nature and can ultimately be released from the grip of material existence by acting according to his nature while under the guidance of his guru. This is how the bona fide spiritual master explains the scriptures so we can apply them in our lives in a practical way. For example, if one is an intellectual, one learns from the guru how to use that ability for spiritual progress. Or if one simply likes to work hard, the spiritual master can teach the disciple how to work so he does not unnecessarily waste his energy in useless endeavors and can make spiritual progress at the same time.

Some people have the idea that to receive enlightenment, the guru touches the disciple on the forehead and suddenly, in a flash of light, all the energy and knowledge of the guru is then transferred to the disciple. This is not exactly how it works, although coming in direct contact with a potent spiritual master can give the disciple special realizations and experiences. But in all cases, what is necessary is that the spiritual master be satisfied with the disciple. Only then is knowledge automatically manifest to the student of spiritual science. The point is that the spiritual teacher and student must both be genuine. The spiritual master must observe the potential disciple for some time to find out whether he is sincere and will be a qualified disciple. Then the spiritual master explains everything to the disciple on the authority of Vedic wisdom. This is the process as practiced for thousands of years. Furthermore, the disciple receives spiritual knowledge through the process of submissive inquiries and a good service attitude. This makes the relationship between spiritual master and disciple very strong, whereas knowledge given from the guru to disciple in exchange for money lacks potency and is not so effective.

When the spiritual master teaches, he must continue to give instructions even if the disciple is sometimes unable to follow them.

There is no benefit in compromising the authorized Vedic process in order to allow the disciple to justify continued engagement in faulty *karmic* activities. As questioned by Lord Rishabhadeva in *Srimad-Bhagavatam* (5.5.17), how can a person learned in spiritual knowledge engage someone in activities that will further entangle him in material existence? How can a gentleman allow a blind man to walk towards danger? No kind person will allow this. Therefore, the bona fide spiritual teacher must always explain the authorized and effective process for advancement regardless of whether everyone can perfectly follow it or not.

The spiritual master must also not become overly impatient with the disciple, otherwise the disciple may become too discouraged and give up or leave altogether. This, of course, is counterproductive. Everyone must be encouraged kindly and taught properly. This is further explained in the *Manu-samhita* (2.159-161): "Created beings must be instructed in what concerns their welfare without giving them pain, and sweet and gentle speech must be used by a teacher who desires to abide by the sacred law. He, forsooth, whose speech and thoughts are pure and ever perfectly guarded, gains the whole reward which is conferred by the Vedanta. Let him not, even though in pain, speak words cutting others to the quick; let him not injure others in thought or deed; let him not utter speeches which make others afraid of him, since that will prevent him from gaining heaven."

We should understand, however, that even if the spiritual master does seem forceful in the way he teaches, this should be considered his mercy on us to make us serious and determined. This side of the spiritual master's personality is usually shown only to the more advanced disciples who can follow all the orders of the guru. But it is only the spiritual master who reminds us that in spite of all we have or hope to accomplish, the clock keeps ticking away and with every tick our life decreases in its duration. Similarly, we may have worked hard to build a nice big house, and now we enjoy having our friends over and hearing their compliments about how beautiful our house is and so on. But the spiritual master can see that actually the house is on fire and will soon be destroyed. He may firmly tell us to get out quickly because if we do not we will be destroyed along with the house. If we argue with him and say, "Why should I leave this house? It's a nice house and I like it here," then we are simply securing our doom. Everything in this material world is continually approaching its end, and for this we must prepare ourselves, of which the spiritual master always reminds us. In this way, he is actually our best friend.

In *Srimad-Bhagavatam* (5.5.16), Lord Rishabhadeva says the materialistic person is ignorant of the real goal of life. He is simply interested in fulfilling his lusty desires. The foolish person does not realize that his selfish interest for sense gratification causes him to dive deep into the ocean of suffering. Therefore, we need to take guidance from a bona fide spiritual master who can remove our ignorance by instructing us about the real goal of life and how to achieve it.

## DUTY OF A DISCIPLE

Therefore, the humility of the student or disciple will show the guru or spiritual master one's sincerity. An example of this attitude is provided in *Srimad-Bhagavatam* (6.15.16) when King Citraketu, hopeful of his progress by the spiritual knowledge he has received, expresses himself to the great saintly devotees Narada Muni and Angira, "Because you are great personalities, you can give me real knowledge. I am as foolish as a village animal like a pig or dog because I am merged in the darkness of ignorance. Therefore, please ignite the torch of knowledge to save me."

When we have found a true saintly person, we should approach them with respect and be ready to hear their advice with open ears. The student receives knowledge from the spiritual master through aural reception, which also includes reading his books or using other media to receive spiritual information. In this way, the initiate learns how to proceed on the spiritual path while living in the material world.

Once having taken initiation from a spiritual master, you should never disrespect him or the articles used by him, such as his seat, bed, shoes, bathwater, etc. All such articles should be held in respect. Neither should one step on his shadow, or worship another person in front of him, nor give initiation to anyone while he is still alive, or try to impress others with one's spiritual knowledge in his presence. Whenever and wherever one sees his spiritual master, one should offer prostrated obeisances to him with his *guru pranam* (obeisance) mantra. Even the guru's name should be said with great reverence, and his orders should not be disobeyed. One should also honor any of his food remnants by eating them, and do not say anything that is displeasing or disrespectful to him. Simply by behaving thusly, one can easily develop a taste for devotional service like chanting the holy names, which in turn offers all perfection. [39]

The *Bhagavatam* (2.4.18) relates that it does not matter who you are or from what classification of society you come from, or how addicted you are to sinful activities, if you are sincere you can become purified by taking shelter of the pure devotees of the Lord, simply due to the Lord's supreme power. It is this power which emanates from the pure devotees in the form of proper teachings that allows anyone who follows such guidance to propel themselves to rise above all difficulties on the path of spiritual progress. By understanding our real identity, we can rise above all material limitations, which is the real condition of the soul which is beyond the body and all such identification.

There are several other qualities a disciple should acquire in order to properly serve the spiritual master. "To serve the spiritual master, the disciple should learn cleanliness, austerity, tolerance, silence, study of Vedic knowledge, simplicity, celibacy, nonviolence, and equanimity in the face of material dualities such as heat and cold, happiness and distress." [40]

The primary duty of a disciple is to follow the orders of the spiritual master. For one who does becomes very powerful. An example of this is King Citraketu, as described in the *Bhagavatam* (6.16.28-29). Citraketu attained the ruling position of the planet of the Vidyadharas because of his spiritual advancement after only one week of chanting the mantra that was given to him by his spiritual master. Within a short time he became more spiritually enlightened and attained the shelter of Lord Anantadeva.

We, of course, should not expect such rapid results in our own spiritual practice, but it is not impossible. The main point is that the disciple learns how to please the Lord and attain His shelter. This is verified in *Srimad-Bhagavatam* (11.3.22), which explains that the disciple should learn how to perform devotional service from the spiritual master. Since the Supreme Being reveals Himself to the pure devotee, if the disciple learns from the pure devotee how to favorably serve the Supreme, then the Lord will also reveal Himself to the disciple.

Nonetheless, steady service to one's guru and inquiring from him about spiritual knowledge will propel one to greater levels of advancement. Lord Krishna even explains, "I, the Soul of all beings, am not so satisfied by ritual worship, brahminical initiation, penances, or self-discipline as I am by faithful service to one's spiritual master." [41]

This is further described like so, "Accepting the bona fide spiritual master as one's life and soul and worshipable deity, the disciple should learn from him the process of pure devotional service. The Supreme Personality of Godhead, Hari, the soul of all souls, is inclined to give Himself to His pure devotees. Therefore, the disciple should learn from the spiritual master to serve the Lord without duplicity and in such a faithful and favorable way that the Supreme Lord, being satisfied, will offer Himself to the faithful disciple." [42]

This is how the disciple or neophyte devotee can attain the level of success in bhakti-yoga, which is when he or she also becomes a pure devotee, which has many benefits aside from one's own spiritual progress. It also benefits the whole family of the devotee, from many generations backward to many generations forward. As stated in the *Narada-Bhakti-Sutra* (71), when a person becomes a pure devotee, "The pure devotees' forefathers become joyful, the demigods dance, and the world feels protected by good masters."

## IF ONE REJECTS HIS SPIRITUAL MASTER

If, however, we accept a genuine spiritual master and then reject him, this is a great offense and all our spiritual advancement becomes null and void. The spiritual master should never be disrespected in any way. As the *Brahma-vaivarta Purana* states: "One pollutes his own intelligence and exhibits severe weakness of character when he rejects his own spiritual master. Indeed, such a person has already rejected the Supreme Lord Hari."

If a disciple begins to think independent of the spiritual master, he will become further and further misguided and will fail in his spiritual life.

Once we have been initiated by an authorized spiritual master who is qualified and who represents a bona fide disciplic succession, and if we are sincere and ready to take advice from him, then all our problems will be solved. Of course, the disciple should also observe the spiritual teacher for some time to make sure he is qualified before taking initiation from him. You cannot make much progress if you serve an unqualified guru. So, if we find the teacher is not so qualified, then it is best simply to wait and approach someone else later on who inspires us in our spiritual life and is a genuine spiritual guide.

## WHEN TO REJECT A GURU

On the other hand, if, in our neophyte stage, we are initiated by a spiritual master who we later find is not authorized or qualified, nor linked up to a bona fide disciplic succession, we should definitely reject him and take initiation from someone who is properly situated. This is confirmed in the *Narada-pancaratra* verse *avaisnavopadistena*, (also found in *Hari-bhakti-vilasa*, 4.366) which states: "One who is initiated into a mantra by a non-Vaishnava must go to hell. Therefore he should again be initiated properly, according to the prescribed method, by a Vaishnava guru." Or if the guru falls away from following a proper standard, then we are justified in leaving him.

As explained, one must abandon a professional, materialistic or ancestral imitationist guru and thus accept the shelter of a bona fide spiritual master who is a genuine guru. [43]

If someone poses as a great spiritual leader but is not qualified, he actually becomes a great disturbance to society. Not only are his instructions ineffective because they lack potency, but he cannot deliver the true, untainted message of God because he is not in tune with God. He will not be able to deliver himself, what to speak of those who depend on him for guidance. Therefore, the sign of a pure devotee is that he is one hundred percent always engaged in the service of the Supreme and has no other motive. The spiritual master never claims to be God, but is a servant of God. If he claims to be God, then you can know he is a number one fool. He simply wants to imitate God, which no one can do. No one should allow themselves to be exploited by such a fool.

It is enjoined that one must abandon a guru who is guru only in name, and who is polluted by sense enjoyment, a fool devoid of intelligence to discriminate between duty and non-duty, and who follows any path other than pure devotional service to the Lord. [44]

Unfortunately, many people unknowingly put faith in so-called spiritual authorities who are actually not of much help or are even misleading. In many cases people do not know what to look for in a spiritual leader. This is actually very dangerous, as pointed out in *Srimad-Bhagavatam* (7.5.31), those entrapped in the delusion of trying to enjoy material life and have accepted other blind men as their leader or guru cannot understand that the real goal of life is to engage in devotional service to the Lord and return to the spiritual realm. As one blind man follows another blind man into the ditch, one materialist follows another into the strong bonds of fruitive labor to suffer the miseries of materialistic life.

For example, a materially attached political leader may seem attractive to people because of the promises he makes or the jokes he relates in his speeches. Or a so-called guru may perform some magic tricks or speak some flowery philosophy to impress other foolish men. But such leaders actually keep people bound up in the clutches of material existence. They may offer the people some hope that things will get better, but generally there is no substantial variation in the usual course of events. Therefore, people gradually become frustrated and want to elect a new leader. But if one simply accepts the Supreme and the bona fide representative of God as their authority and guide, they will know what to do. They will not have to worry anymore about being cheated in their search for answers. As stated in *Srimad-Bhagavatam* (8.24.50-51), people who are ignorant of the goal of life accept other foolish men as their leader. A materialistic guru only teaches economic development and sense gratification, causing his followers to continue in materialistic life. But intelligent men seek guidance from the Supreme Personality who sees everything and who gives spiritual knowledge by which one can quickly regain his original spiritual position.

## CONCLUSION

Achieving the shelter of the Supreme is actually the ultimate goal of spiritual life and the reason for accepting a spiritual master. This success, however, depends on faith in both the Lord and the spiritual master. As it states in the Vedic verse, *yasya deve para bhaktir*: "Only unto those great souls who have implicit faith in both the Lord and the spiritual master are all the imports of Vedic knowledge automatically revealed." Therefore, the spiritual master must never be disrespected since he is, essentially, the door to such spiritual success. In fact, it is the genuine and authorized spiritual master who delivers us from the conditioned life of ignorance to the other side beyond birth and death, or to the life of freedom, by opening our eyes with spiritual knowledge. Therefore, if one is serious about making spiritual advancement, he or she should carefully consider whether to accept a spiritual master, and the qualities a master should possess. We hope we have provided the information that will point the way to discerning what to look for in a spiritual master.

**CHAPTER NOTES**
1. *Hari-bhakti-vilasa* 1.45,46, *Vishnu-smriti vacana.*
2. *Vayu Purana.*
3. *Nectar of Devotion*, p. 58.
4. *Srimad-Bhagavatam,* 3.28.2 pur.
5. *Caitanya-caritamrita,* Madhya-lila, 22.15.
6. *Srimad-Bhagavatam,* 3.4.25.
7. *Caitanya-caritamrita,* Madhya-lia, 22.44-50.

# Chapter Ten

8. *Srimad-Bhagavatam*, 6.1.17.
9. Ibid., 11.2.30.
10. Ibid., 10.2.31.
11. *Mundaka Upanishad*, 1.2.12.
12. *Katha Upanishad*, 2.9.
13. *Srimad-Bhagavatam*, 11.2.37.
14. *Nectar of Devotion*, p.103.
15. *Srimad-Bhagavatam*, 1.18.13.
16. Ibid., 11.10.5.
17. *Nectar of Devotion*, p.150.
18. *Purana-vakya*.
19. *Vishnu smriti*.
20. *Srimad-Bhagavatam*, 10.87.33.
21. Ibid., 3.7.39 & 11.11.48.
22. Ibid., 5.3.14.
23. *Nectar of Devotion*, p.103.
24. *Manu-samhita*, 2.146-150.
25. Ibid., 2.153.
26. Ibid., 2.156.
27. *Srimad-Bhagavatam*, 11.3.21.
28. Ibid., 11.17.27.
29. Ibid., 7.5.32.
30. Ibid., 7.6.27.
31. Ibid., 10.10.37.
32. Ibid., 2.9.35 pur.
33. Ibid., 7.9.42.
34. *Hari-bhakti-vilasa*, 2.6 from *Vishnu-yamala*.
35. *Srimad-Bhagavatam*, 9.9.5 pur.
36. Ibid., 11.7.46.
37. *Art of Sadhana*, p. 235.
38. *Bhakti-sandarbha*, 298, from the *Tattvasgara*.
39. *Sri Harinama Cintamani*, p. 53.
40. *Srimad-Bhagavatam*, 11.3.24.
41. Ibid., 10.80.34.
42. Ibid., 11.3.22.
43. *Bhakti-sandarbha sankhya* 210.
44. *Mahabharata*, Udyoga-parva, 179.25.

# CHAPTER ELEVEN

## *Starting to Get the Taste for Bhakti-yoga*

So as we accept the devotional principles and engage in the process of regulative bhakti-yoga and chanting of Hare Krishna, and our consciousness becomes increasingly spiritualized or purified from materialistic tendencies, we find that we start to get a taste for this spiritual process of engaging in devotional service to the Supreme. As Lord Kapiladeva explained to His mother, if one hears from devotees about the information and pastimes of the Supreme, the way of transcendental experience quickly opens to him, and gradually he attains a taste for knowledge that in due course develops into attraction and devotion. [1]

We see here that association is important. The vibration and insight and realization from senior seers and devotees will also effect us in a most positive way. This helps us become more attracted to the transcendental nature of Lord Krishna, by which we become increasingly indifferent to material attractions. However, if we do not become more attracted to the spiritual reality, then, naturally, we will remain attracted to different types of material enjoyment. This will keep us bound up in the world of repeated birth and death as dictated by our karma. This is what happens to any ordinary person.

Besides association, another means of acquiring the taste for bhakti is when a person becomes a little detached from material attractions, which is often brought on from recognizing all the problems that accompany material existence. The point is that material life comes as a whole package, meaning it includes both the joys and sorrows, the achievements and the losses, the pleasures and the problems. When a person begins to wonder if there is not something better, if this is all that there is, or if there is not something more than this, he or she becomes ready to enquire about a spiritual path and to understand the process of bhakti-yoga.

The *Bhagavad-gita* (2.44) explains that for a person who is too attached to enjoying his or her senses and material opulence and fascinations, and who is bewildered or overtaken by such things, the resolute determination to engage in devotional service does not take place. In other words, a person who is still enslaved by the dictates of the mind and senses cannot perceive the joy in the simple life of spirituality and bhakti-yoga. So they are condemned to continue to be pushed into temporary actions to try to please their mind and senses. But once a person begins to see the futility in that, they become open to something higher. Then if a person is lucky enough to enquire or even start the practice of serious bhakti-yoga, then the influence of *maya* or material darkness subsides. He or she is no longer so influenced by the illusion, the influence of the material energy. Krishna is compared to sunshine, bhakti-yoga is the path to reveal that sunshine, and wherever there is sunshine there can be no darkness. And the bliss of such sunshine becomes increasingly apparent.

"The transcendental qualities of Sri Krishna are completely blissful and relishable. Consequently the Lord's qualities attract even the minds of self-realized persons from the bliss of [impersonal Brahman] self-realization." [2]

Once a person accepts the regulative practice of bhakti-yoga, he or she can go on to acquire *rasa*, which means a taste for the spiritual practice that he or she does.

The taste for bhakti, or devotional service, *seva*, becomes stronger when the regulative bhakti gives way to *rasa*, meaning the divine bhakti which is the natural state of love for God. That is when the simplest task, whether it be washing the temple pots, cleaning the temple floor, or making flower garlands, becomes an ecstatic experience simply because of the mood with which the task is done. This is the mood of trying to make the Supreme, especially Radha and Krishna together, happy by our endeavors. This is what draws us closer to God, and draws the attention of God closer to us. Then it becomes an exchange. This can go on to develop into *bhava*, which is the preliminary awakening of dormant love of God, which naturally exists in everyone's heart because we are all spiritual parts and parcels of God.

If our attitude of servitude is what Lord Krishna appreciates and is what can give us the bliss of our service, then the opposite is also true, that doing something for our own selfish desires will be bereft of a service attitude and will not give us that higher taste. Such activities often become bland or boring if done often enough, whereas spiritual activities remain ever-fresh. This further means that before we do anything, we should ask ourselves and determine if Sri Krishna would like what we are going to do. Or would our spiritual master approve. If not, there is no reason to do it, and it may actually detract from the higher taste, the *rasa* with the Lord that we are seeking. This also means that such an activity may be an obstacle to our continued spiritual progress. So we should proceed with caution and care.

An example can be given in the act of *darshan*, which is often used to mean seeing the Deities in the temple, or getting *darshan* of our guru. But it is more than that. It is seeing the Deities and then, in return, being seen by the Deities. Then you feel that They also want to see you, and that They are happy that you have come to see Them. Then *darshan* becomes not merely an act you perform, but a spiritual exchange between you and Their Lordships in Their Deity form. This is over and above the regulative bhakti, and is when the grace of Radha and Krishna reveals the divine bhakti, which is the loving mood that draws in a closeness, a spiritual taste, a *rasa*, between you and the Deities.

This is when one's devotional service is done in a pure and selfless manner. This taste can become so strong that the devotee no longer wants anything from this mayic or illusory world, which becomes insignificant. He or she only wants to increase this ecstatic love for Radha and Krishna, and drown his or her heart and mind in this loving exchange, this relationship between himself or herself and Their Lordships. Nothing compares to it. And if a beginner devotee does not feel that way at first, he or she should know that this is what it can become. It all depends on developing the proper mood, which opens a person to the *rasa* or taste for the loving exchange, which becomes increasingly ecstatic as he or she progresses.

This is described in the *Narada-Bhakti-Sutra* (Sutra 66): "After breaking through the coverings of the three modes of nature [the *gunas*], one should act only in pure love of God, remaining perpetually in the mood of a servant serving his master, or a lover serving her beloved."

This is the spontaneous stage of the *rasa* or relationship of servitude or love toward the Lord. This is much deeper than merely going through the motions of service, knowing that the goal is *prema*, the divine and ecstatic love for the Lord. This love is the perfection of the spiritual world, and is what we should become accustomed to if we expect to reach the spiritual domain. This is the purpose of bhakti-yoga–to increasingly spiritualize our consciousness until we are on the same frequency level as the spiritual world.

This mood of servitude first appears in Lord Krishna's brother, Lord Balarama, who serves Lord Krishna in so many ways. [3] This mood also gives Lord Balarama ecstasy in His service to Lord Krishna. The point of this is clearly described like so: "The sweetness of Lord Krishna is not to be tasted by those who consider themselves to be equal to Krishna. It is to be tasted only through the sentiment of servitude." [4] In this way, those who think of the Lord with love and faith as servitors are more dear to the Lord, which creates a more intimate exchange of blissful relations between the Lord and the individual devotee.

In this way, a person who is on the path to become one with God, or to merge in with Him, or to attain *moksha* or liberation into the Brahman, simply cannot experience the sweetness of the Supreme like a bhakti-yogi, a devotee in the mood of simply wanting to serve the Supreme. But this is also the conclusion as expressed by other pure devotees, as well as what is described in the more elaborate levels of the Vedic texts, as confirmed in the *Caitanya-caritamrita* (Adi.6.104): "This conclusion of the revealed scriptures is also the realization of experienced devotees. Fools and rascals, however, cannot understand the opulences of devotional emotions."

Even in the pastimes of Lord Krishna's family, His own father, Nanda Maharaja, experiences ecstatic love towards Lord Krishna even though he does not know that Krishna is the Supreme Lord. This ecstasy makes Nanda Maharaja to feel himself a servant of his own son, Lord Krishna. Therefore, he too prays for attachment and devotion to his son, Lord Krishna. In this way, any progressing devotee who begins to feel *rasa*, or an ecstatic exchange with Lord Krishna, will pray that his or her mind becomes more attached to Krishna, and that such attraction simply increases. [5]

The *Bhakti-rasamrita-sindhu* (3.2.87) says: "That stage at which affection for the beloved converts unhappiness into happiness is called *raga* or attachment." That is the stage that we desire to attain, and which outweighs the need for all of the rules and regulations, by which all the rules are automatically included in such attachment to the Lord. [A detailed description of the different levels of attachment to Lord Krishna, as they develop from one to another, and their symptoms can be found in the *Caitanya-caritamrita*, Madhya-lila, 19.178-235.]

To summarize: our progress on this path all starts with the knowledge of the relationship between the *jiva* soul and Ishvara, the Supreme Being, which is called *Sambandha*. Then by using this knowledge, a bhakti-yogi engages in devotional service for the satisfaction of the Lord, which is called *Abhidheya*. This is what can develop or awaken one's original love of God which is naturally situated in the heart of the living being. From there it leads to *Prayojana*, which is the taste for expressing one's love, which can lead to deeper and deeper feelings of love for God. This is the topmost goal of the living being and of human existence.

Once a yogi becomes attached to his or her relationship with the Lord, there are eleven forms of attachment, as described in the *Narada-Bhakti Sutra* (82): "Although devotional service is one [meaning that any service is on the same spiritual level as another], it becomes manifested in eleven forms of attachment: attachment to the Lord's glorious qualities, to His beauty, to worshiping Him, to remembering Him, to serving Him, to caring for Him as a parent, to dealing with Him as a lover, to surrendering one's whole self to Him, to being absorbed in thought of Him, and to experiencing separation from Him [as in longing to meet and see Him]. This last is the supreme attachment."

All of these ways of becoming attached to the Lord will bring a taste for one's relationship with the Supreme, but feeling separation is like a lover always meditating on the beloved and being anxious to meet again. This is a meditation on God in which whatever a bhakti-yogi is doing is based on the idea of hankering to come into contact with the Lord, waiting to see Him.

This can lead to the supreme loving attitude which is *prema*, or the supremely divine love for Krishna which offers the deepest taste or *rasa* with the Lord. As explained in the *Sri Caitanya-Siksamrita* (page 238), the aspirant for *prema*, after following the regulative principles for devotional service, such as hearing about the Lord, chanting His holy names and pastimes, remembering them, etc., becomes pure in heart and attains *bhava*, or love. Then he or she can enter into the sweetness of loving relations. In Krishna's pastimes, all relations or exchanges are supremely sweet, regardless if it is in neutrality (*shanta*), servitude (*dasya*), friendship (*sakhya*), or parental affection (*vatsalya*). These all correspond to the devotee's personal qualities. But *madhurya-rasa*, the mood of a love for the beloved, is the most worshipable and relishable. This may not be for everyone, but in order to enter this mood there must be a loyalty to Radharani, otherwise there is no taste from this mood, nor can one enter into it.

All souls are the marginal energy of Krishna. The male and female identity of the gross material body are illusory conceptions, which originate in the material attachments or conceptions held within the subtle body, which consists of the ever-changing mind, intelligence and material ego. The internal and eternal pure soul is spiritual, with no relation to the material identity of male or female. [6] When a particular spiritual sentiment arises in relation to Krishna, it produces the appropriate body for the soul which is in accord to that relationship. In the *madhurya-rasa* or a love for the beloved, all souls in that relationship have a pure, spiritual female form and worship one male, Krishna.

The Supreme Being is the form of eternity, knowledge and bliss. It is explained that Krishna is the form of eternity and knowledge, but Radha is the form of bliss, the *hladini-shakti*. Radha and Krishna are, thus, one entity, but to distribute *rasa*, which is the bliss of eternal spiritual relations, They take two forms. Therefore, those bhakti-yogis who are greedy for the mood of the inhabitants of

Vraja, or Krishna's supreme abode of Goloka Vrindavana, they follow that Vraja mood. They follow in the footsteps and the mood of one of the inhabitants of Vraja who plays a part in Krishna's pastimes, to which the devotee is especially attracted. (This is called *raganuga-bhakti*, about which we will explain more later.) Thus, the aspirants for *prema* should follow this process for gaining entrance into and attain a position in the eternal pastimes of Radha and Krishna. [7]

In conclusion, this is the key to not only attaining a relishable taste for one's service to Krishna, but the means to go as deep as one's tendency and attraction will allow, even to that level as found in Krishna's supreme abode, Goloka Vrindavana. Therefore, if we have the right mood, we can feel spiritual ecstasy and enter the devotional disposition of the residents of Goloka Vrindavana, right here, right now, while still living in this material world.

**CHAPTER NOTES**
1. *Srimad-Bhagavatam* 3.25.25.
2. *Caitanya-caritamrita,* Madhya-lila, 17.139.
3. Ibid., Adi-lila, 6.88.
4. Ibid., 6.103.
5. *Bhagavatam* 10.47.66-67 & *Caitanya-caritamrita,* Adi-lila, 6.57-61.
6. *Svetasvatara Upanishad* 5.10.
7. *Sri Caitanya-Siksamrita*, p. 238.

# CHAPTER TWELVE

# *Feeling Reciprocation From Lord Krishna*

Getting a taste for our service in bhakti-yoga is a preliminary feeling before we start to get a real sense of reciprocation from the Supreme. Now we describe a closer connection and relation to God that we can get through the process of bhakti-yoga. This is when we feel a joyous reciprocation from the Lord Himself by the service we do. There are many examples of this, such as when we go before the Deity of Lord Krishna, or Radha and Krishna together, and for no apparent reason we just feel happy. There is a connection and a response between the devotee and the Deities. Or when we do some service for the Deities and can feel that They are approving of our service, or our attitude and mood of devotion, or both.

Another example is when my own spiritual master, Srila Prabhupada, asked the devotees who were with him how do they know Krishna is God? How can they be convinced? They responded with such answers that Krishna says so in the *Bhagavad-gita*, or the other *shastras* like the *Srimad-Bhagavatam* says so. To these replies, Srila Prabhupada said "No", that is not how you personally can tell that Krishna is God. Then he explained that it is by the reciprocation that you personally receive from Krishna that you can tell that Krishna is God. You experience it yourself. That is how you can know and be convinced.

The essence of this reciprocation can be said simply that the more a devotee sincerely loves Krishna, the more Krishna will reciprocate with that devotee, even to the level that a highly advanced devotee can talk with Krishna face to face, [1] or even hear Krishna give specific instructions for things to be done, or the way to do something.

In this way, receiving the reciprocation from the Lord, a bhakti-yogi can thoroughly understand the meaning and purpose of the process of loving devotional service.[2] It awakens the relationship between the living being and the Supreme. The devotee now experiences that by attracting the Lord with devotion, the Lord will reciprocate such devotion in many ways. The devotee only has to be advanced enough to be able to recognize such response that comes from the Lord. It is in this manner that Krishna paves the way for the devotee to come ever closer to Him.

However, the Lord may be trying to direct a person, but the person may have so many outside concerns he or she is attending to that he or she cannot get the message. The person may not be able to recognize the reciprocation that is coming from God. As explained in the *Bhagavatam* (8.24.52): "My Lord, You are the supreme well-wishing friend of everyone, the dearmost friend, the controller, the Supersoul, the supreme instructor and the giver of supreme knowledge, and the fulfillment of all desires. But although You are within the heart [as the Supersoul, Paramatma], the foolish, because of lusty desires in the heart, cannot understand You."

This describes the caring nature of Lord Krishna, even to those who may neglect Him.

As the *Caitanya-caritamrita* (Mad.8.90-91 & Adi. 4.177) explains: "Lord Krishna has made a firm promise for all time. If one renders service unto Him, Krishna correspondingly gives him an equal amount of success in devotional service to the Lord. According to Lord Krishna in *Bhagavad-gita* (4.11), 'All of them–as they surrender unto Me–I reward accordingly. Everyone follows My path in all respects, O son of Partha.'"

This means that we are all experiencing different levels of truth on our way back to the highest Truth. The material world is not false, but it is like a dream because it is temporary. A dream is real, it is a real experience. But it effects us only as long as we remain dreaming. But upon awakening from the dream we realize that it was just a temporary dream, and we look around to see our real situation. So as we experience this life in the material world, we are effected by it until we awaken with spiritual knowledge to understand our real situation as spirit souls that belong to a different level of reality, the spiritual reality. Then, instead of struggling to serve the Lord's material energy and various aspects of it, we can learn to turn our love and endeavors to serve Him directly and begin to connect with Him. Then as we develop love for Him, we can enter our real home where we belong in the spiritual domain. And the more we realize this, and the more we act in that way by engaging in bhakti-yoga, the more Krishna will pave the way for us to reach Him. Then the closer we attempt to get to Krishna, the closer He gets to us. For every step we take toward Krishna, He takes a hundred or a thousand steps toward us. This is the attractive nature of Lord Krishna, and the way He protects His devotee.

In this way, when the Supreme Lord Sri Krishna recognizes a devotee, He gives Him the intelligence and dictates how he may reach the spiritual realm.[3] This is also explained by Lord Krishna in the *Bhagavad-gita* (10.10): "To those who are constantly devoted and worship Me with love, I give the understanding by which they can come to Me."

This is further described in the *Bhagavatam* (7.9.27): "Unlike an ordinary living entity, my Lord, You do not discriminate between friends and enemies, the favorable and unfavorable, because for You there is no conception of higher and lower. Nonetheless, You offer Your benedictions according to the level of one's service [to You], exactly as a desire tree delivers fruits according to one's desires and makes no distinction between the lower and the higher."

This is very simply described by Lord Krishna Himself in the *Bhagavad-gita* (8.14) wherein He says, "For one who remembers Me without deviation, I am easy to obtain, O son of Partha, because of his constant engagement in devotional service."

Lord Krishna actually becomes indebted to the devotee by the service the devotee performs, and He blesses him for his devotion. From the *Bhagavatam* (3.8.26-27) we find this example: "The Lord showed His lotus feet by raising them. His lotus feet are the source of all awards achieved by devotional service that is free from material contamination. Such awards are for those who worship Him in pure devotion. The splendour of the transcendental rays from His moonlike toenails and fingernails appeared like the petals of a flower.

"He also acknowledged the service of the devotees and

vanquished their distress by His beautiful smile. The reflection of His face, decorated with earrings, was so pleasing because it dazzled with the rays from His lips and the beauty of His nose and eyebrows."

This is one of the ways that Lord Krishna begins to bless the sincere devotees. It is also explained that the Lord becomes so pliable to the devotee that He takes up residence in the heart of the devotee in the form that the devotee meditates on to accommodate his or her mood of devotion. "O my Lord, Your devotees can see You through the ears by the process of bona fide hearing, and thus their hearts become cleansed, and You take Your seat there. You are so merciful to Your devotees that You manifest Yourself in the particular eternal form of transcendence in which they always think of You." [4]

In fact, the Lord does not want to leave the hearts of such devotees. "O my Lord, persons who smell the fragrant aroma of your lotus feet, carried by the air of Vedic sound through the holes of the ears, accept Your devotional service. For them You are never separated from the lotus of their hearts." [5]

Plus, just as the Lord resides in the hearts of the devotees, the devotees similarly reside in the heart of the Lord. This is the reason for such reciprocal exchange between them. This is how the Lord can actually come under the control of the devotee by the love that is exhibited toward the Lord. Sukadeva Gosvami described this in his teachings in the *Bhagavatam* (10.9.19): "O Maharaja Pariksit, this entire universe, with its great, exalted demigods like Lord Shiva, Lord Brahma and Lord Indra, is under the control of the Supreme Personality of Godhead. Yet the Supreme Lord has one transcendental attribute: He comes under the control of His devotees..."

This explains the nature of and reasons for Krishna's varied pastimes within this material world. It is simply to please His associates and to attract all the living beings to His activities and characteristics. By such activities, Lord Krishna raises the consciousness of all humanity, but especially brings His devotees to the highest perfectional stage of spiritual development, explained as follows: "Nothing remains unachieved when the Supreme Personality of Godhead is pleased with someone. By transcendental achievement, one understands everything else to be insignificant. One who engages in transcendental loving service is elevated to the highest perfectional stage by the Lord Himself, who is seated in everyone's heart." [6]

## HOW THE LORD IS READY TO PROTECT HIS PURE DEVOTEES

The point of this is that if we can show our sincere devotion by our service to the Supreme, He will also be ready to assist us in various ways. There are many examples of this from which we can acquire inspiration.

The *Bhagavatam* (4.29.46) specifically explains that, "When a person is engaged in devotional service, he is favored by the Lord, who bestows His causeless mercy."

"The Lord is eternally very beautiful, and He is worshipable by all the inhabitants of every planet. He is ever youthful and always eager to bestow His blessings upon His devotees." [7]

In this way, we should always feel confident that the Lord is always aware of what spiritual progress a devotee is trying to achieve. The Lord gives the devotee blessings to pass through all kinds of challenges that are ordinarily encountered in life. Life can be difficult in order to motivate a sensible person to wonder why there is suffering and what to do about it. It is not that suffering has no purpose. So, what is the point of this, and how do we resolve it? It is not a matter of trying to simply make things better, like learning how to become a better swimmer while drowning in a stormy sea. The best thing is to get out of the ocean completely. Similarly, the best thing is to be released from the material existence once and for all, and to help others do the same. But for devotees, because they are constantly thinking of the Supreme Lord, they undergo life on a different level. This does not mean that there are no challenges. This is part of having a material body, such as with birth, disease, old age, and death. But the Lord can help by giving strength to the devotee to pass through these challenges with an equipoised mind, focused on the goal of life, which is to return to the spiritual strata. As Sri Kavi explained to King Nimi, "O King, one who accepts this process of bhakti-yoga to the Supreme Personality of Godhead will never blunder on his path in this world. Even while running with eyes closed, he will never trip or fall." [8]

Of course, we do not suggest running with your eyes closed, but the point is that even while unsure of how to proceed in life, like a blind man, if a person has taken up the path of bhakti-yoga, there is nothing but positive progress to be made. As Lord Krishna states in *Bhagavad-gita* (9.2), "The process of devotional service to the Supreme Personality of Godhead is eternal, and it is very joyfully and naturally performed." Why? Because it is the natural state of the soul. Therefore, regardless of what a person does, if he or she takes up this path, they are rightfully situated and will regain their true spiritual identity, beyond the limitations of the material body. And Lord Krishna reciprocates with such a devotee to help him or her find the way to continue their progress on this path back to Him.

Even if a bhakti-yogi strays or falls from the path of devotion, the Lord gives him or her protection so they may easily return and continue their course of progress. This is the causeless mercy that a devotee can receive. Why is it causeless? Because the Lord is not obligated to anyone, but He also understands the difficulties of this material existence and shows His love for those who love Him, or those who have tried to progress on the path of love and devotion toward Him. Therefore, as it is explained in several places to emphasize this point in the *Srimad-Bhagavatam* (10.2.33), "O Madhava, Supreme Personality of Godhead, Lord of the goddess of fortune, Lakshmi, if devotees completely in love with You sometimes fall from the path of devotion, they do not fall like nondevotees, for You will protect them. Thus they fearlessly traverse the heads of their opponents and continue to progress in devotional service."

This means that for one who has even once tasted the nectar of performing loving devotion to Krishna, even if he falls away from the path of bhakti-yoga, he still cannot completely forget that sweet taste. Somehow he remembers it, and after a short time, or even what may appear to be a long time, that person will again return to the path of devotional service to Krishna. Even if he stumbles on the path and does something wrong, there is protection given by the Lord so the person may continue his or her progress. As it is further described:

"One who has thus given up all other engagements and has

taken full shelter of the lotus feet of Hari, the Supreme Personality of Godhead, is very dear to the Lord. Indeed, if such a surrendered soul accidentally commits some sinful activity, the Supreme Lord, who is situated within everyone's heart, immediately takes away the reaction to such sin." [9]

This does not mean that devotees can do whatever they like and expect to be forgiven, but the word accidental is key in the above verse. It means that if for some reason one is distracted by some material attachment that they fall from the path, they are immediately rectified by their continued engagement in bhakti-yoga. In this way, the Lord can also change the karma of a devotee so that he or she does not undergo various difficulties that they were previously meant to experience. Say a person was meant to be in some serious car accident, but because of their practice of bhakti-yoga, their karma is reduced so that their injuries are not so serious. This is the potency of bhakti-yoga, but is also another example of the reciprocation the Lord gives to His devotees.

The ultimate protection is described in one of the concluding and important verses of importance in the *Bhagavad-gita* (18.66): "Abandon all varieties of religion and just surrender unto Me. I shall deliver you from all sinful reactions. Do not fear." In this way, Lord Krishna gives the ultimate protection by relieving us of our bad karma simply by surrendering to Him.

Through one's engagement in bhakti-yoga, a person begins to become aware and perceive God in all things. This awareness is a type of protection that the Lord gives to His devotees so that no matter what may take place and what dangers a devotee encounters, he or she is always in awareness of the Supreme Being. Thereby even at the moment of death the devotee remembers the Lord, and because of that remembrance the devotee returns to the place of the Lord to participate in His pastimes. This is explained like so: "Dhruva Maharaja rendered devotional service unto the Supreme, the reservoir of everything, with unrelenting force. While carrying out his devotional service to the Lord, he could see that everything is situated in Him only and that He is situated in all living entities. The Lord is called Achyuta because He never fails in His prime duty, to give protection to His devotees." [10]

This is the love Lord Krishna sends His devotees. This is also the spiritual protection that is allocated to the devotees, as Lord Krishna Himself further declares in the *Bhagavad-gita* (9.31), "O son of Kunti, declare it boldly that My devotee never perishes." In this way, Lord Krishna is always eager for His devotee to return to His abode. This is again reiterated as follows: "My dear Lord, O Supreme Personality of Godhead, Bhagavan, You are the Supreme Soul. If one meditates on Your transcendental body, You naturally protect him from all sources of fear, even the imminent danger of death." [11]

## SPECIAL ATTENTION FROM LORD KRISHNA

Sometimes Lord Krishna gives a devotee special attention, or motivation. Occasionally a sincere devotee who wants to reach Krishna and His spiritual abode is distracted by material assets or opulences. He may have a beautiful girlfriend who has specific demands from him. Or a bank load of money, which may be nice, but becomes a great distraction regarding what to do with it and how to protect it, or it creates a feeling of power over others, which is never good, especially for someone who is trying to make spiritual progress. So what is more important? The spiritual advancement for preparing for the next life and a higher destination, or to enjoy life now with all the gusto you can? So, Lord Krishna sometimes takes away such distractions in order to make it easier for the devotee to focus on what matters most, which is one's spiritual progress.

In Lord Krishna's response to Indra, He describes how, "A man blinded by intoxication with his power and opulence cannot see Me nearby with the rod of punishment in My hand. If I desire his real welfare, I drag him down from his materially fortunate position." [12]

I have seen this happen to devotees, or potential devotees, wherein whatever attachments they have that is holding them back in taking bhakti-yoga more seriously is taken away from them by special arrangements of Krishna. You may not understand what is happening while it is going on, but it simplifies the situation and removes unnecessary distractions or obstacles to one's spiritual progress. And that is always beneficial, at least in the long run. As Lord Krishna explains:

"The Personality of Godhead said: If I especially favor someone, I gradually deprive him of his wealth. Then the relatives and friends of such a poverty-stricken man abandon him. In this way he suffers one distress after another. When he becomes frustrated in his attempts to make money and instead befriends My devotees, I bestow My special mercy upon him.

"A person who has thus become sober fully realizes the Absolute as the highest truth, the most subtle and perfect manifestation of spirit, the transcendental existence without end. In this way, realizing that the Supreme Truth is the foundation of his own existence, he is freed from the cycle of material life." [13]

* * *

To conclude, anything done for the Lord, from direct devotional service, or rituals, penances, austerities, and so on, never go in vain and become a permanent asset in the form of spiritual merit that will always give a person beneficial results, even if it is over the course of many lives. [14]

However, you cannot understand the Supreme Being, Lord Krishna, by scholarship, study, austerities, etc., alone. It is only through serving the Lord in the proper mood that can attract the Lord to you. Then He will give you the blessings by which you can understand Him. This understanding itself is part of the reciprocation a yogi can receive as the direct blessings from the Lord. The Lord only reveals Himself when He is pleased by the devotee's service. [15]

**CHAPTER NOTES**
1. *Caitanya-caritamrita,* Madhya-lila, 4.95 pur.
2. Ibid., 6.244.pur.
3. Ibid., Adi-lila, 8.78 pur.
4. *Srimad-Bhagavatam,* 3.9.11.
5. Ibid., 3.9.5.
6. Ibid., 3.13.49.
7. Ibid., 3.28.17.

8. Ibid., 11.2.35.
9. Ibid., 11.5.42.
10. Ibid., 4.12.11.
11. Ibid., 7.10.29.
12. Ibid., 10.27.16.
13. Ibid., 10.88.8-10.
14. Ibid., 3.9.13.
15. *Bhagavad-gita.*7.25 & *Caitanya-caritamrita,* Madhya-lila, 6.82, 89.

# CHAPTER THIRTEEN

# *Beginning to Understand the Lord*

Now that we are beginning to advance in spiritual life, and even recognize various kinds of reciprocation that we receive from the Lord, we naturally begin to understand some of the Supreme's characteristics. With these realizations, we also begin to more clearly comprehend the reasons for devotional service and how it helps reawaken our connection with the Supreme Being, and how it is a natural condition for the soul.

As we begin to understand our own spiritual nature and true identity, we also begin to have deeper insights into the nature of the Supreme Being. It is through spiritual development that we begin to have a spiritual vision or perception, not only of our own true position, but also of the spiritual form of the Lord. This means we rise above the limited perception of things that is provided by the senses, which is bound to make mistakes in understanding the most basic of things. Then as we begin to have a perception of our own soul, we also begin to detect the nature of the Supersoul, the Paramatma in the heart. This further leads us to understand more about the nature of the Supreme Personality, Bhagavan. In order for Him to interact with us, either through His reciprocation or through a loving relationship as developed through bhakti-yoga, then it becomes increasingly apparent that He also must have a personality, which means He must be a person. Without that, then what is the meaning of this material creation wherein all living beings are struggling not only to survive, but to express themselves in so many ways? And the highest level of expression is that of love. If this was not the case, then why would there be a need for this material creation, or anything at all?

One point is that love is but a key element in the nature of the soul. We want to love somebody, otherwise we feel incomplete. Therefore, such a relationship is between two personalities. But the highest expression of love is to have a relationship with the Complete, the Supreme Being, the ultimate lover. The soul is already a part of the Supreme. So the connection and love only need to be reawakened. When it is, then our soul also feels complete. Then we are naturally satisfied and at peace. And in this way we can understand God as a person, the Supreme Person.

As explained in the *Caitanya-caritamrita* (Mad.20.164): "Only by devotional service can one understand the transcendental form of the Lord, which is perfect in all respects. Although His form is one, He can expand His form into unlimited numbers by His supreme will."

In this way, there are unlimited forms of God, beginning with His original form, that expand into the various *avataras*, and so on, all for engaging in various purposes and pastimes. All of these are described in the Vedic literature. But now in bhakti-yoga, we can directly understand how the Supreme Being interacts with His creation and the living beings, and especially with His devotees in a very personal way. He is not merely some spiritual force that exists without personal involvement. And now we can begin to perceive that on a personal level.

The point is that God is beyond the material nature. So unless we also transcend and rise above the limited consciousness of dull matter, as displayed in material existence, we also will not be able to understand the Supreme. Rising above the modes of material nature and entering the spiritual realm, or just getting a glimpse of it in the beginning of our spiritual development, is one of the goals of bhakti-yoga. This is what allows us to perceive the nature of spiritual existence.

As long as people try to approach Krishna with pride in material knowledge, without the prerequisite of humility and a serving attitude, Krishna will remain far from their reach. He is not obligated to reveal Himself in any way. But when people call out to Krishna with a humble heart, they can then begin to see Krishna, or at least recognize how His energies interact around us. Some people call this cosmic consciousness, but devotees in bhakti-yoga call it Krishna consciousness. And as they progress in bhakti-yoga, they can experience the Lord's unlimited bliss in the *rasa* or mellows of spiritual exchange. This is completely beyond the body, or any of its categories, like one's caste, birthright, wealth, beauty, power, influence, etc. So it is easy to understand why God seems far away or even non-existent to those people who are wrapped up in placing value on such materialistic forms of identity. None of these have anything to do with the real nature of the soul. Therefore, we have to rise above such labels and attachments to get a real glimpse of spiritual reality.

As most spiritual scholars know, there are three levels of understanding God: namely the Brahman, Paramatma and Bhagavan. The bhakti-yogi understands all three, but culminates in the realization of God as Bhagavan, the Supreme Personality.

Various forms of yoga focus on merging into the Brahman. The Brahman is the great white light, the *brahmajyoti* or the Brahman effulgence, which is actually the rays that emanate from the body of the Supreme. It is the form without qualities or personality, and is composed of innumerable *jiva* souls floating in its brilliance. This is the goal of yogis who try to merge into it. The bliss one attains by merging into the Brahman is mostly the bliss that comes from being completely free from all forms of material limitations and identity. It is not the bliss which comes from spiritual loving relations. So this form of God, the Brahman, is not the ultimate realization of God, nor the highest bliss.

As explained in the *Caitanya-caritamrita* (Adi.2.5, 12-15): "What the *Upanishads* describe as the impersonal Brahman is but the effulgence of His body, and the Lord known as the Supersoul is but His localized plenary portion. He is the Supreme Personality of Godhead, Krishna Himself, full with six opulences. He is the Absolute Truth, and no other truth is greater than or equal to Him.

"What the *Upanishads* call the transcendental, impersonal Brahman is the realm of the glowing effulgence of the same Supreme Person. As with the naked eye one cannot know the sun except as a glowing substance, [similarly] merely by philosophical speculation one cannot understand Lord Krishna's transcendental varieties. The opulences of the impersonal Brahman are spread throughout the millions and millions of universes. That Brahman is but the bodily effulgence of Govinda."

Also, from the *Brahma-samhita* (5.40) we have another glimpse in a description which says, "I worship Govinda, the primeval Lord, who is endowed with great power. The glowing effulgence of His transcendental form is the impersonal Brahman, which is absolute, complete and unlimited, and which displays the varieties of countless planets, with their different opulences, in millions and millions of universes."

However, the Brahman, which is very powerful, eternal, yet has no comprehensible qualities, is very difficult for the embodied living being to understand. We are always thinking of and acting in a world filled with various forms with qualities of numerous kinds. So it is not easy to try to grasp or realize that which has no qualities. Even Lord Krishna explains this in the *Bhagavad-gita* (12.5), where He says, "For those whose minds are attached to the unmanifested, impersonal feature of the Supreme, advancement is very troublesome. To make progress in that discipline is always difficult for those who are embodied."

That is why Lord Krishna advises that for making steady and easy progress in spiritual life, one should meditate on the ultimate goal to begin with, which is His own personal form through the process of bhakti-yoga: "The Blessed Lord said: He whose mind is fixed on My personal form, always engaged in worshiping Me with great and transcendental faith, is considered by Me to be most perfect." [1]

Paramatma is the second stage of God-realization, which is the Supersoul expansion in everyone's heart, but is also viewed as the universe. The Supersoul in the heart accompanies every living being in all stages of life and development. So God is always with everyone, but He is waiting for the *jiva* soul to finally turn toward Him and enquire about his or her real purpose in life. Once the enquiry is made, the Lord as the Supersoul begins to guide that person to make further advancement. Various forms of yoga, such as Raja-yoga, also try to provide the means for Paramatma realization, depending on one's philosophical school of thought.

On the third stage of realization, Bhagavan refers to that Supreme Personal aspect of God that is complete in beauty, strength, wealth, knowledge, renunciation, etc. He is endowed with unlimited energies, and is the source of all energies. He expands into various forms that work in various ways, from manifesting all of the spirit souls, the spiritual energies, and expanding into the material energy wherein the cosmic creation manifests. But His ultimate form of Sri Krishna is simply engaged in loving pastimes, and interacts with all of the spirit souls who develop love for Him. This is the essence of the Vaikuntha planets and Lord Krishna's personal abode known as Goloka Vrindavana.

Through the above descriptions, we should understand that the realization of Bhagavan is the culmination of the realizations of Brahman and Paramatma, which are incomplete realizations of the Lord. But the realization, and further interactions with the Lord, is only possible through the process of pure bhakti, which reveals the Lord's real form directly to the devotee.

Bhagavan is the ultimate objective of all the functions and tendencies of the soul, and bhakti ultimately encompasses all these functions, which is a natural loving tendency and all expressions that go with it, especially that which exists between the individual and the Supreme Being. Thus, bhakti yields the complete vision of the Lord as He is. [2]

In this way, by seriously practicing bhakti-yoga, one can attain the blessings of the Lord, which enables one to realize the Lord's form as it is. This is not through the process of speculation, but through the means of personal perception attained through steady progress on the path of bhakti. As explained in the *Bhagavatam* (10.14.29): "My Lord, if one is favored by even a slight trace of the mercy of Your lotus feet, he can understand the greatness of Your personality. But those who speculate to understand the Supreme Personality of Godhead are unable to know You, even though they continue to study the *Vedas* for many years."

Certainly, studying the Vedic literature is the basis for understanding the different aspects of the Absolute Truth. But one has to practice what they teach. You cannot simply reach the highest levels of realization without putting the teachings into one's life by proper *sadhana* or practice. It is only by uplifting one's consciousness by spiritualizing it through changing one's lifestyle does the means for attaining the perception of the ultimate reality exist. Then by receiving the blessings of the Supreme can a person be able to perceive the Absolute Truth, Lord Sri Krishna, as He is.

This is the self-awakening knowledge and perception that a devotee begins to attain when progressing on the path of bhakti-yoga. It becomes a normal course of events to become aware of the personality of the Lord and the Deities in the temple as a devotee's spiritual vision becomes increasingly clear. Furthermore, as one's spiritual sight grows, it becomes easier to be convinced of the nature of God and the potency of the process of bhakti-yoga, and ultimately enter into the spiritual domain. Lord Krishna specifically explains in the *Bhagavad-gita* (11.54-5) that it is through bhakti-yoga that a person, a yogi, can progress to reaching this awareness: "My dear Arjuna, only by undivided devotional service can I be understood as I am standing before you, and can thus be seen directly. Only in this way can you enter into the mysteries of My understanding. My dear Arjuna, one who is engaged in My pure devotional service, free from the contamination of previous activities [karma] and from mental speculation, who is friendly to every living entity, certainly comes to Me."

**CHAPTER NOTES**
1. *Bhagavad-gita* 12.2.
2. *Sri Caitanya-siksamrita*, p. 164-5.

# CHAPTER FOURTEEN

# *Attaining Love of God*

If we are making progress in our spiritual development, then we should now be feeling increased detachment from materialistic attractions. We should now start understanding how temporary the enjoyment of material or sensual pleasures can be, and that should give us the impetus to start increasing our taste for our spiritual practice. This also means that our attraction for Krishna should be increasing in proportion to our hearing and discussing His characteristics amongst other devotees.

So what is this attraction to Krishna? What is the love we are meant to attain, and may, indeed, be starting to experience?

The essence of the pleasure potency of the Lord [the *hladini-shakti*], and what gives Him pleasure is love. The essence of this love of God is emotion [*bhava*], which leads to emotional expression in one's devotional service. And the ultimate development of this emotion is called *maha-bhava*, or great or deep emotional feeling and expression to the Lord. [1]

So this love is dynamic, not static. It continues to give rise to expression and reciprocation between the individual soul and the Supreme Soul. This is what ultimately attracts the soul of everyone. We are all looking for this and it is what attracts the Lord to the individual who has and expresses such love for Him.

Normally, there are four main goals of life, which includes religiosity, economic development, sensual and mental gratification, and liberation from material existence. But developing love of God is the fifth and highest goal, which, once attained, makes the other four goals seem as insignificant as straw in the street. [2] This means that life without this fifth goal remains incomplete. Even a religious system that leaves out this fifth goal of attaining love of God through the devotional process is also incomplete. But only that person who is most fortunate attains this love of God. [3]

This love is the perfection of human existence, regardless of whatever else a person may accomplish. Why? Because for the living being it is the return to the constitutional nature and position of the soul, one's real identity beyond the temporary bodily position. As stated in the *Srimad-Bhagavatam* (1.2.8): "The occupational activities a man performs according to his own position are only so much useless labor if they do not provoke attraction for the message of the Personality of Godhead."

Lord Krishna further explains in *Bhagavad-gita* (4.10) that when a living being is freed from attachment, fear and anger, and then being absorbed in Him and taking refuge in Him, is how many, many persons in the past have become purified by knowledge of Him, and have all attained transcendental love for Him.

The eternal function of the individual *jiva* soul is to be attracted to the infinite consciousness of the Supreme Soul. And the eternal function of the Supreme Soul is to draw all the infinitesimal souls towards Him, and give them all a place in His spiritual abode where they can get a taste of the everlasting, infinite, supreme joy. This is what the living being is always looking for, and why the soul can never be completely happy with the temporary pleasures derived from limited and fleeting contact with the material energies. [4]

The individual and the Lord have a deep and eternal relationship. But for one who is materially bound in the bodily identification of life, this remains hidden. But by performing *sadhana*, or the regulative spiritual practice of bhakti-yoga, this relationship can be revealed. Therefore, if a person is firmly fixed in devotional service, whether he or she executes just one or many of the principles, the waves of love for God gradually awaken. [5]

Even the name of Krishna means the all-attractive state of being (*Krish*), and the supreme bliss (*na*). So if we are going to work for something, we should be interested in working for the greatest happiness, which is Lord Krishna. This is also why we are always looking for the ultimate level of happiness, which is within the form of Krishna. [6]

When a devotee becomes absorbed in deep love for the Lord, this may also manifest with bodily symptoms, a few of which are, "Perspiration, trembling, standing of one's bodily hairs, tears, faltering (of one's voice), fading, madness, melancholy, patience, pride, joy, and humility–these are various natural symptoms of ecstatic love of Godhead, which causes a devotee to dance and float in an ocean of transcendental bliss while chanting the Hare Krishna mantra." [7]

We should mention, however, that proper etiquette is that a devotee does not exhibit such symptoms wilfully. He or she keeps them hidden as much as possible. But when the ecstatic bliss is strongly felt, a devotee's heart melts and he may not be able to subdue such feelings or symptoms. Then he may even appear like a madman who is not easily understood by the general public who do not understand such feelings. But this is how spiritual ecstasy can occasionally manifest physically, as further explained, "It is a characteristic of love of Godhead that by nature it induces transcendental symptoms in one's body and makes one more and more greedy to achieve the shelter of the lotus feet of the Lord." [8]

This is elaborated in the *Bhagavatam* (11.3.32): "Having achieved love of God, the devotees sometimes cry out loud, absorbed in thought of the infallible Lord. Sometimes they laugh, they feel great pleasure, speak out loud to the Lord, dance or sing. Such devotees, having transcended material, conditioned life, sometimes imitate the unborn Supreme by acting out His pastimes. And sometimes, achieving His personal audience, they remain peaceful and silent."

In this way, a devotee may show various symptoms, either outwardly or inwardly, of the love he or she feels for Krishna. When such an advanced devotee feels this kind of ecstatic love for God, he or she may also feel a sense of separation from Krishna, which excels the desire to meet with Krishna. Such an emotion of love in separation can actually be stronger than the love a devotee feels when in the direct association of Krishna because either you strongly hanker to see Krishna, or you feel like at any moment Krishna will appear. This is in the highest stage of love for God, called *prema-bhakti*. But this is attained only after working on developing one's love through *sadhana* or the practice of the regulations in bhakti-yoga, while *prema* is the ultimate stage of relishing one's love for the Supreme.

When on the way to *prema*, one should learn to be very eager to become engaged in some particular type of service to the Lord, even to the point wherein a bhakti-yogi will cry tears to be engaged. This is the sign of great eagerness for meeting and serving the Lord. This is what will bring the devotee to the spiritual realm. [9]

*Prema* is the state of permanent spiritual emotion for Krishna. This is the final stage in devotional development. *Prema* is the goal of the soul, or the constant favorable attitude of love for Krishna. There is the aspiration for *prema*, and the attainment of *prema*. Having attained *prema*, there is no further development for the soul, or further spiritual realization of God. There is only a continuous taste and focus on Krishna, and nothing else.

In the aspiring stage, there are those who derive bliss from following the path of bhakti, namely the rules and regulations (the *viviktanandis*) and listening to discussions about the Lord, and then those who derive bliss from preaching (the *goshthyanandis*) and chanting the Lord's holy names. Some derive bliss from both activities. It is only through the process of surrender to Lord Krishna that *bhava* and later *prema* appear. This surrender is the process of simply accepting those things that are favorable to attaining *prema-bhakti*, and avoiding those things which are unfavorable. Such devotees think of Krishna as their only or ultimate protector. They sincerely feel themselves very fallen, and are convinced that they can do nothing except if Krishna desires. Thus, they are in constant thought and meditation on Lord Krishna.

Lord Krishna Himself says in the *Bhagavad-gita* (8.8): "He who meditates on the Supreme Personality of Godhead, his mind constantly engaged in remembering Me, undeviated from the path, he, O Partha [Arjuna], is sure to reach Me."

In this way, liberation from material existence is merely an automatic by-product of love of God. It is this pure devotional service that brings us to Lord Krishna's spiritual abode. This is related in the *Bhagavatam* (11.3.33), where it says that simply learning the science of devotional service and engaging in it in a practical way, is the means by which a devotee attains love of God. And by such complete devotion to the Supreme Personality, the devotee easily crosses over the illusory energy, *maya*, which is extremely difficult to cross.

Not only does this love of God through devotional service brings one to the spiritual realm, but it also brings one directly to Lord Krishna. It is very difficult to achieve Lord Krishna through any process except through love, bhakti-yoga. This is explained in the *Srimad-Bhagavatam* (11.12.9), where Lord Krishna says, "Even though one engages with great endeavor in the mystic yoga system, philosophical speculation [jnana-yoga], charity, vows, penances, ritualistic sacrifices, teaching of Vedic mantras to others, personal study of the *Vedas*, or the renounced order of life, still one cannot achieve Me [through these methods]."

Therefore, it is only through the means of pure devotion that a person can reach Krishna. But what is pure devotional service? This is explained in a simple way in the *Bhakti-rasamrita-sindhu* (1.1.11): "One should render transcendental loving service to Lord Krishna favorably and without desire for material profit or gain through fruitive activities or mental speculation. That is called pure devotional service."

So this is not impossible to attain. In fact, under proper guidance, it only needs to be reawakened since it is the natural, constitutional characteristic of the soul. It is like reuniting the spark with the fire, wherein the spark regains its power to burn, rather than fizzling out. It is like the drop of water that is saved from drying out in the desert and is carried by the river to reunite with the ocean. In the same way, the soul, reuniting with the Supreme through the process of bhakti-yoga, feels like it has returned to its real home, filled with truly loving pastimes with the Supreme Being that are the cause of eternal and unbounded bliss. Thus, the soul feels like it has returned home to where it has longed and searched to be for eons. In this way, the soul enters an ocean of happiness.

As said in the *Caitanya-caritamrita* (Madhya-lila, 2.49): "Unalloyed love for Krishna is like an ocean of happiness. If someone gets one drop of it, the whole world can drown in that drop. It is not befitting to express such love of Godhead, yet a madman must speak. However, even though he speaks, no one believes him."

"Even the most learned scholar cannot understand the activities and symptoms of an exalted personality in whose heart love of Godhead has awakened." [10]

Herein again we find that ecstatic symptoms of love of God are not to be exhibited in front of ordinary men, because they would not be able to understand it anyway, or worse, may even criticize and then make offences that will be detrimental for themselves. Furthermore, this experience can hardly be comprehended by anyone but another devotee. Nonetheless, devotees still try to see if anyone is interested to accept this process of bhakti-yoga, knowing the ecstatic experience that awaits those who pursue it without giving up. And such bliss for the soul is one of the goals of bhakti-yoga.

"The goal of love of Godhead is not to become materially rich or free from material bondage. The real goal is to be situated in devotional service to the Lord and enjoy transcendental bliss. In Vedic literature, Krishna is the central point of attraction, and His service is our activity. To attain the platform of love of Krishna is life's ultimate goal. Therefore Krishna, Krishna's service and love of Krishna are the three great riches of life. In all revealed scriptures, beginning with the *Vedas*, the central point of attraction is Krishna. When complete knowledge of Him is realized, the bondage of *maya*, the illusory energy, is automatically broken." [11]

So, it is this illusory energy which keeps us bound up in a limited perception of who we really are. It limits our potential and restricts our vision of what we can be, far and above merely improving our material or bodily situation, thinking this will give us happiness. We are spiritual beings, far beyond the material energy. And when we again awaken ourselves, awaken our consciousness to perceiving our spiritual identity, then we can not only be free from such limitations brought about by our material conditioning, but we can rise above such bondage and be free to enter the spiritual realm and taste that ocean of spiritual happiness that is in connection with the Supreme Being, the cause of all causes, source of all realities.

## HOW TO ATTAIN THE STAGE OF LOVE OF GOD

If we are still trying to attain or simply heighten our love for the Supreme Lord, the process is easily outlined in the following verses, and all we have to do is follow them:

"In the beginning there must be faith. Then one becomes interested in associating with pure devotees. Thereafter one is initiated by the spiritual master and executes regulative principles under his orders. Thus one is freed from all unwanted habits and becomes firmly fixed in devotional service. Thereafter, one develops taste and attachment. This is the way of *sadhana-bhakti*, the execution of devotional service according to the regulative principles. Gradually emotions intensify, and finally there is an awakening of love. This is the gradual development of love of Godhead for the devotee interested in Krishna consciousness." [12]

"The spiritually powerful message of Godhead can be properly discussed only in a society of devotees, and it is greatly pleasing to hear in that association. If one hears from devotees, the way of transcendental experience quickly opens to him, and gradually he attains firm faith that in due course develops into attraction and devotion." [13]

"If one actually has the seed of transcendental emotion in his heart, the symptoms will be visible in his activities. That is the verdict of all revealed scriptures." [14]

"When the seed of ecstatic emotion for Krishna fructifies, the following nine symptoms manifest in one's behavior: foregiveness, concern that time should not be wasted, detachment [from material attractions], absence of false prestige, hope [for continued spiritual progress], eagerness, a taste for chanting the holy name of the Lord, attachment to descriptions of the transcendental qualities of the Lord, and affection for those places where the Lord resides–that is, a temple or a holy place like Vrindavana. These are called *anubhava*, subordinate signs of ecstatic emotion. They are visible in a person in whose heart the seed of love of God has begun to fructify." [15]

The first stage in developing love for God is *shraddha*, or the stage of faith and attraction for the Supreme Lord. In order to develop this further, one associates with other devotees of the Lord. As we progress in this way, the taste for hearing about transcendental topics increases. Then we become even more attracted, which can lead to *bhava*, or the preliminary stage of love for God. This is when the bhakti-yogi develops affection for the Lord. The third stage is to practice the rules and regulations. This dissipates any misgivings about the process of bhakti-yoga and purifies our consciousness to propel our progress. As we become more surcharged with transcendental love, there develops a strong sense of separation from Krishna, which is the hankering for seeing, meeting or engaging in the service of Lord Krishna. This leads to various kinds of ecstasies.[16]

Herein, the emphasis is in the associating with Krishna by hearing about Him. Krishna explains this Himself, in speaking to the wives of the brahmanas and to the *gopis* who came to meet Him, in which He says, "It is by hearing about Me, seeing My Deity form, meditating upon Me and chanting My names and glories that love for Me develops, not physical proximity. Therefore please go back to your homes." [17]

This is a lesson for all of us, that it is the process of bhakti-yoga that matters most, not necessarily where we reside. However, residing where we can see the Deity in the temple and associate with devotees is always most beneficial.

Elevation to the stage of ecstasy can be done by the mercy of Lord Krishna, or through the blessings of the pure devotee, which is the usual way we can get there. But that means we must act according to the instructions that the pure devotee spiritual master may give us for our guidance. We cannot merely sit back and wait for the special mercy from Krishna, or think that being initiated is all we need. We need to continue to practice our *sadhana* for progressing forward in our devotional service. It is no different than bathing everyday if we want to be clean and not emanate a foul body odor. We have to bathe everyday. Similarly with our practice of bhakti-yoga, we have to engage in the method properly. [18]

The power of the pure devotee who is a *prema-bhakta*, one who is in the stage of divine love, is unlimited, and he is also very merciful. He can transfer his power or his mercy to any *sadhana-bhakta* [practicing devotee] that he chooses. That itself can be considered the mercy of Lord Krishna to the devotee. Then that devotee can move forward to acquire *rasa*, or a taste for his devotional service, and from there move on to *bhava*, the early stage of love of God.

As a person advances, his understanding of bhakti-yoga increases and his attachments to the material world decrease. By

## Chapter Fourteen

advancing in hearing and chanting, or reading and discussing about Krishna, his or her faith becomes more firmly fixed. His faith develops into a taste for doing bhakti-yoga or devotional service with attachment. When attachment becomes pure, meaning it is done without any material purposes or rewards, it begins to exhibit *bhava* and *rati*, preliminary stages of love and reciprocation. When this *rati* increases, it is called love of God. [19]

When *bhava* arises within the heart of a *sadhana-bhakta*, a practicing devotee, his or her life naturally becomes changed, and he or she purifies his or her lifestyle. Then the *bhava-bhakta*, the devotee who has attained the preliminary stage of love, naturally engages his whole life and all his assets in the service of the Lord. It may appear that they do not follow all of the rules of bhakti, but they have already attained the success of all the rules, which are now automatically included in their activities. So they should not be judged by neophyte devotees, or offenses can occur that will be detrimental to the younger devotee's progress. [20]

It is also described in the *Caitanya-caritamrita* (Mad.21.34) that when the stage of *bhava* is reached, a devotee has awakened the tendency or taste to chant and describe the transcendental qualities of the Lord. He has attachment for this process.

So, as we progress through *bhava* and the feelings of love become more intense or concentrated, we can reach *prema*. What is *prema*? *Krishna-prema* is pure, ecstatic divine love. Pure love is the eternal function of the soul. That is why when we are covered over by the material elements and bodily conceptions of life, we still look for love and the means to express that love, generally by finding another soul who will accept our love. Everything we do is ultimately to express our love, or is a cry out for love. Therefore, the only real religion is pure love and the process to awaken that pure spiritual love between the *jiva* soul and the Supreme Being. This is the final goal of any genuine religion. If that is not the intention of any religion, then it is incomplete and will not take you to the final goal, which is to awaken the real nature of the soul. Therefore, *prema* exists naturally in the innermost heart of the soul of every living being, and the object of that divine love is the Supreme Being, Krishna, who alone can fully reciprocate that love. None of the other *devas* or gods have ever shown the depth of love and loving relations that has been displayed in the pastimes and characteristics of Lord Krishna.[21]

As a bhakti-yogi develops into a pure devotee, his or her vision changes completely. A pure devotee knows that he or she is meant to serve the Supreme Personality, and that all things that exist can be utilized in such service. And because such pure devotees have been blessed from within the heart, due to their emotional exchange with the Lord, they can see that Supreme Lord wherever they look. In this way, life and the world are no longer anything like they were before the devotee had such a purified and spiritualized awareness.[22]

Then the spiritual dimension unfolds in front of them, and everything becomes the *lila* or pastimes of the Lord. Then they can actually begin to interact with those pastimes, even to the point wherein at the time of giving up their material body, they are immediately transferred to the place where Krishna's pastimes are going on. They also perfect their service to Krishna in the final preparation for going back to Krishna's personal spiritual abode. Then they no longer take a birth in this material world again.

**CHAPTER NOTES**
1. *Caitanya-ccaritamrita,* Adi-lila, 4.68.
2. Ibid., 7.84.
3. Ibid., 7.100.
4. *Art of Sadhana,* p.161.
5. *Caitanya-caritamrita,* Madhya-lila, 22.134.
6. *Art of Sadhana,* p.161.
7. *Caitanya-caritamrita,* Adi-lila, 7.89-90.
8. Ibid., 7.87.
9. *Nectar of Devotion,* p.84.
10. *Bhakti-rasamrita-sindhu* 1.4.17 & *Caitanya-caritamrita,*
    Madhya-lila, 23.39-40.
11. *Caitanya-caritamrita,* Madhya-lila, 20.142-144.
12. Ibid., 23.14-15.
13. *Srimad-Bhagavatam* 3.25.25.
14. *Caitanya-caritamrita,* Madhya-lila, 23.17.
15. *Bhakti-rasamrita-sindhu* 1.3.25-26.

16. *Srimad-Bhagavatam* 1.6.16 pur.
17. Ibid., 10.23.33 & 10.29.27.
18. *Nectar of Devotion*, pp.133-34.
19. *Teachings of Lord Caitanya*, p.137.
20. *Sri Caitanya-Siksamrta,* pp.146-147.
21. Ibid., pp.10-11.
22. *Teachings of Lord Caitanya*, p.245.

# CHAPTER FIFTEEN

# *Different Types of Love for God*

When we begin reaching love for God in our practice of bhakti-yoga, we should understand that there are different kinds of love, which leads us to understand how there are different kinds of activities that we can engage in to express these various emotional feelings in our service to the Supreme Being.

This is described in the *Caitanya-caritamrita* (Adi-lila. 4.19, 21, 24-25, 27-28, 32): "In whatever transcendental mellow My devotee worships Me, I reciprocate with him. That is My natural behavior... If one cherishes pure loving devotion to Me, thinks of Me as his son, his friend or his beloved, or regarding himself as great and considering Me his equal or inferior [as one friend to another], I become subordinate to him... Mother sometimes binds Me as her son. She nourishes and protects Me, thinking Me utterly helpless. My friends climb on My shoulders in pure friendship, saying, 'What kind of big man are You? You and I are equal'... Taking these pure devotees with Me, I shall descend [into the material world] and sport in various wonderful ways, unknown even in Vaikuntha. I shall broadcast such pastimes by which even I am amazed... I shall taste the essence of all these *rasas*, and in this way I shall favor all the devotees."

In this way, Lord Krishna engages in spiritual loving exchanges in all kinds of *rasas* or relationships, just to accommodate the expressions of the innumerable pure devotees that live in the spiritual world. And from time to time, He brings some of these devotees with Him to display these many pastimes to the residents of the material worlds just to attract them to Him, as further described, "Then, by hearing about the pure love of the residents of Vraja, devotees will worship Me on the path of spontaneous love, abandoning all rituals of religiosity and fruitive activity." [1]

This is the process of bhakti-yoga, to go deeper than mere rituals, and for that, Krishna sometimes displays His personal pastimes in this material creation with His numerous pure devotees. Then as we hear of these pastimes of Krishna, we go deeper and deeper into the feelings of devotion, which turn into feelings of love. This love, as it becomes more spontaneous, develops into *rasa*, or feelings in a particular form of expression. These are basically categorized in four different forms, which then develop in more personal distinctions, based on the mood of the devotee's pure love for Krishna. These are described as servitude [*dasya*], friendship [*sakhya*], parental affection [*vatsalya*], and conjugal love [*shringara*]. These are the four main transcendental mellows [*rasas*]. By the devotees who cherish these four mellows, Lord Krishna is subdued.[2]

There is a fifth mood of devotion called *shanta-rasa*, which means the mood of neutrality. This neutral stage is the feeling that God is great, but does not go much beyond this, nor displays loving exchanges like the other four *rasas*, which is what pleases Krishna the most. *Shanta-rasa* is the lowest among the relationships in the spiritual world. But it displays a pure sense of awe and veneration for the Lord, with an understanding of the relationship between the *jiva* soul and the Lord. So this is the elementary stage when loving relations may begin as when a devotee wants to be one of Krishna's cows, or His stick, or His flute, or His peacock feather, or one of the flowers that grow to be part of Krishna's flower garland, or any of the other things that serve various functions in the spiritual world. From there one goes to the *dasya-rasa*, the first stage of servitude, and engages in various pastimes with Krishna in that mood.[3]

Herein we can begin to see how there are different forms or moods of loving exchange between Lord Krishna and the pure devotees. And that even those things which seem to be inanimate are actually beings that are in the loving mood to Lord Krishna known as *shanta-rasa* or neutrality. In this way, the whole atmosphere of the spiritual world reverberates with spiritual love. Any of these *rasas* are glorious, but the point is that such love in any of these moods should be spontaneous. It is this spontaneous level of love when the purified soul displays its constitutional characteristic.

So, as we practice bhakti-yoga and begin to attain love of

God, we may develop an attraction to one of these *rasas* or moods of loving exchanges with Lord Krishna. The first stage is the neutral feeling, that we appreciate the greatness of the Supreme Being, and we increasingly become free from material contamination or attractions to the temporary as our attraction to that which is eternal grows. In the mood of *dashya* or servitude, the living entity appreciates his or her position as everlastingly subordinate to the Lord, and recognizes that he is eternally dependent on the causeless mercy of the Lord. In that mood, he or she begins to feel a natural affection for the blessings of the Lord and always wants to serve the Lord and is most happy doing so. In that mood one follows in the footsteps of devotees like Citraka, Patraka or Raktaka. In the third stage, in *sahkya-rasa*, transcendental love is developed, and one has the feeling as one friend to another on an equal level with the Lord as one of His associates. In this stage, there is relaxed exchanges as in joking and laughing, or playing in fraternal ways. If one is attracted to this mood, he can follow in the footsteps of devotees like Baladeva, Shridama or Sudama. At this stage, and with the Lord's arrangements, a devotee practically forgets his inferior position, but still has the greatest respect and love for the Supreme Person. But Lord Krishna especially loves this kind of relation with His many cowherd friends.

In the *vatsalya-rasa*, the fraternal affection grows into parental affection when the devotee feels the love of a parent of the Lord. At this stage, the devotee feels that he is superior than the Lord and shows his or her love by wanting to care of the Lord, especially in the Lord's form as baby Krishna. This form invokes a maternal or paternal emotion that makes the devotee feel that without his or her care, baby Krishna would be neglected. So the Lord allows Himself to be at the mercy of such devotees and puts Himself under their care. A devotee in this position attains the position in which they can hold and embrace the Lord and even kiss His head, like any parent with a child. In this mood, a devotee can follow in the footsteps of Krishna's parents, like Nanda Maharaja and Mother Yashoda.

The next stage is when the parental mood develops even further into *shringara* or *madhura-rasa*, which is the mood of love that exists between the lover and beloved. In this stage the devotees who take the form of the damsels of Vraja engage in affectionate glances between themselves and Lord Krishna, or in motions of the eyes, pleasant words, attractive smiles, etc. To perfect this mood, one can follow Srimati Radharani and Her girl friends, or Her serving maids (*manjaris*) like Rupa and Rati *manjaris*. [4]

It is in the *madhura-rasa*, the mood of a lover toward the beloved, wherein the devotee experiences the maximum extent of Krishna's sweetness. The devotee situated in the *madhura-rasa* attains the highest perfection of *prema*, the ultimate level of love for God. All sixty-four of the qualities of Krishna are present in the *madhura-rasa* of Vraja, and the devotees of Vraja manifest the same qualities of infinite sweetness. [5]

This is also confirmed in the *Caitanya-caritamrita* (Adi-lila 4.44-48): "But if we compare the sentiments in an impartial mood, we find that the conjugal sentiment is superior to all in sweetness. Increasing love is experienced in various tastes, one above another. But that love which has the highest taste in the gradual succession of desire manifests itself in the form of conjugal love. Therefore I call it *madhura-rasa*... Such love is found nowhere but in Vraja. This mood is unbounded in the damsels of Vraja, but among them it finds its perfection in Sri Radha."

To develop this kind of love for Krishna can only be possible for those who are already engaged in the regulative principles of bhakti-yoga, specifically in the worship of Radha and Krishna in the temple. Such devotees gradually develop a spontaneous love for the Deity. And by hearing of the Lord's exchange of loving affairs with the *gopis*, such devotees gradually become attracted to these pastimes. After this attraction becomes highly developed and becomes spontaneous in one's devotional service, he or she can begin to cultivate that loving mood. This mood has nothing to do with the body, or whether one is male or female. It is purely connected to the soul of the bhakti-yogi. A woman may develop an attitude for becoming a friend of Krishna, while a man may develop the mood of becoming a *gopi* in Vrindavana. [6]

Only those advanced devotees who are qualified for this *madhura-rasa* can taste this, or even begin to understand the depth of this topic. This is why the Lord has said in the *Caitanya-caritamrita*

(Madhya-lila 23.99): "The exchanges between Krishna and the different devotees situated in various transcendental mellows cannot be experienced by non-devotees. Only advanced devotees can understand and appreciate the different varieties of devotional service reciprocated with the Supreme Personality of Godhead."

However, it does not matter in which mood or *rasa* that a devotee is situated, he or she thinks that relationship with Krishna is the best. This is explained further in the *Caitanya-caritamrita* (Adi-lila 4.42-43): "Four kinds of devotees are the receptacles of the four kinds of mellows in love of God, namely servitude, friendship, parental affection, and conjugal love. Each kind of devotee feels that his sentiment is the most excellent, and thus in that mood he tastes great happiness with Lord Krishna."

This is how bhakti-yoga allows us to develop various loving moods and numerous types of activities in spiritual life, all of which gives unbounded bliss to the participant who attains such love for the Supreme Being.

**CHAPTER NOTES**
1. *Caitanya-caritamrita,* Adi-lila, 4.33.
2. Ibid., 3.11.
3. *Teachings of Lord Caitanya*, pp.40-41.
4. Ibid., p.35, & *Nectar of Instruction*, p.77.
5. *Sri Caitanya-Siksamrta*, p.58-9 & *Bhagavatam,* 9.4.66 & 10.29.14-15.
6. *Nectar of Devotion*, p.130.

# CHAPTER SIXTEEN

# *The Types of Devotees and Devotional Service and Rising to the Topmost Position*

As we have learned about different types of love for God in the previous chapter, and various moods that devotees can have in their activities of loving service, there are also different kinds of devotees on different levels of advancement. By understanding the different levels of devotees on the path of bhakti-yoga, we can also perceive what level we are on at this stage of our development. Then we know what we have accomplished so far, but what we still have to do.

## THE TYPES OF DEVOTEES PRACTICING BHAKTI-YOGA

Lord Krishna explains in *Bhagavad-gita* (7.16) that there are four types of pious men who approach Him and render devotion to Him, and that includes those who are distressed and looking for relief, those who desire wealth, those who are inquisitive about the mysteries of life, and those who are searching for knowledge of the Absolute Truth. However, Lord Krishna continues to point out in the following verses (*Bg*.7.17-18) that those who are wise and in full knowledge in union with Him are the best, for Krishna is very dear to him, and he is very dear to Krishna. All who approach Krishna are magnanimous souls, but he who is situated in knowledge of Krishna is considered to dwell in Krishna. Being engaged in Krishna's transcendental service, such a person attains Krishna.

Of course, Krishna also explains in *Bhagavad-gita* (7.15) that there are four kinds of men who will not approach or surrender to Him. These include those who are grossly foolish, the lowest of mankind, those whose knowledge has been stolen by illusion, and those who partake of the atheistic nature of demons. These are the people who cannot be helped and do not take up the path of bhakti-yoga even in the most elementary way, unless they are willing to change their habits.

When a person begins the path of bhakti-yoga, he is considered to still be affected by the modes of material nature, namely goodness, passion and darkness. As Lord Kapila explains about the means to work from the lower to the higher modes in one's practice of bhakti-yoga, "...there are multifarious paths of devotional service in terms of the different categories of the executor. Devotional service executed by a person who is envious, proud, violent and angry, and who is a separatist [which means seeing himself as separate from everyone else], is considered to be in the mode of darkness. The worship of Deities in the temple by a separatist, with a motive for material enjoyment, fame and opulence, is devotion in the mode of passion. When a devotee worships the Supreme Personality of Godhead and offers the results of his activities in order to free himself from the binding force of fruitive activities, his devotion is in the mode of goodness. The manifestation of unadulterated devotional service [in the mode of goodness] is exhibited when one's mind is at once attracted to hearing the transcendental name and qualities of the Supreme Personality of Godhead, who is residing in everyone's heart." [1]

So we can look at ourselves and analyze which category we fit into on the basis of these descriptions, and then understand how best to proceed forward in our practice to propel the rate of our advancement. The point is that simply worshiping, chanting mantras, reciting holy verses, observing the *arati* ceremony, or even dressing the Deities, etc., is not really devotion on the path of bhakti. But what actually makes it bhakti is the intention and mood with which we do these things. When we make a firm decision that we want to attain the perception of our connection with Radha and Krishna and awaken our love for Them, then our practice becomes real devotion. Then, no matter how faulty our attempts may be, it is the intention and love that is accepted by the Lord, and which continues to propel us to higher levels of devotion. This brings us to the next divisions of devotees to consider.

Beginning transcendentalists are further divided into three more basic kinds, the *sarva-kama*, the *akama*, and the *moksha-kama*, which means those, respectively, who still have material desires; those who have no material desires; and those who seek liberation. [2] Nonetheless, by taking up the path of bhakti-yoga can give them all a chance to rise above these categories and become even more spiritually purified.

There are an additional three basic kinds of devotees on the path of bhakti-yoga. As devotees progress, they may be called *kanishtha-adhikaris*, or third-class or materialistic devotees. These are the neophytes or beginners. Then there are the *madhyama-adhikaris*, or the second class devotees. And then are the *uttama-adhikaris* or *maha-bhagavatas*, which are those who are advanced or pure. These are first-class devotees.

The perception of reality differs between these kinds of devotees. This is explained in the Eleventh Canto (45-53) of the *Srimad-Bhagavatam*, which can be summarized as follows:

The advanced devotees see within everything the soul of all souls, Sri Krishna. In this way, he sees everything in relation to the Supreme Lord, and everything that exists is eternally situated within the Lord and His vast energies. Even while engaging his senses with their objects of attraction, like hearing, seeing, smelling, touching, and tasting, such a first-class devotee still sees the whole world as the energy of the Lord. Thus, he is not attracted nor repelled by anything. A devotee who can tolerate the birth and decay of the body, hunger and thirst, the constant struggle with material nature, the inevitable miseries of material existence, and who remains aloof from them simply by remembering the lotus feet of the Supreme Personality of Godhead is considered the foremost of devotees.

One who has actually taken shelter of the lotus feet of the Supreme Lord becomes freed from fruitive activities, both from performing them and from their karmic reactions. In fact, he or she is freed from lust, and the desire of the mind and body to enjoy material sense gratification. Plans for enjoying sex life, social prestige and money cannot develop in his mind because of his attraction to transcendental activities. He rises above bodily identification and becomes a part of divine consciousness. Thus, he is considered a pure devotee on the highest platform. Such a devotee is also freed from any sense of false prestige, even when born in an aristocratic family.

Furthermore, the first-class devotees are those who have realized the Supreme Person, which is the goal. [3] He is also expert in the study of the Vedic literature and in presenting their conclusions. He understands the ultimate goal of these texts and knows that Krishna is the ultimate object of love and devotion. He has strictly followed the rules and regulations under the training of a pure devotee spiritual master. In this way, he is fully trained to preach and become a spiritual master himself. Thus, he is considered first-class. He never deviates from the principles and conclusions of higher authority, and he attains firm faith in the scriptures by personal realization. He may have cultivated knowledge by his study, but he also has his own realized knowledge by personal experience.[4]

In this way, the consciousness of an advanced devotee is fully saturated in God consciousness, but in a practical way. In other words, he or she goes through the actions of life while still recognizing the Supreme Being as the basis of everything. As Lord Krishna says in *Bhagavad-gita* (18.54), "One who is transcendentally situated at once realizes the Supreme Brahman and becomes fully joyful. He never laments nor desires to have anything; he is equally disposed toward every living being. In that state one can attain pure devotional service to Me."

"For such a devotee never fears any condition of life. For them heavenly planets, liberation, or the hellish planets are all the same, for their interest is only in the service of the Lord." [5]

The second-class devotee offers his love to the Supreme Lord, and is a sincere friend to all the devotees of the Lord, shows mercy to the ignorant people who are innocent, but disregards those who are atheists or envious of the Supreme Being. [6]

The second-class are those who have partially realized the plenary portion of the Absolute, or the Supersoul presence in all living beings. [7] He may also not be very expert in arguing or presenting the conclusions of revealed scripture, but he has firm faith in the objective. Therefore, he is still undaunted within himself as to his decision that Krishna is the supreme object of worship. [8]

The third-class devotee may faithfully engage in the worship of the Deity in the temple, but may not always treat other devotees respectfully, and may not see the Lord situated in all other living beings outside the temple. He may also still be infatuated with material opulence. [9]

The third-class devotees are those who have barely realized any form of the absolute person, yet may still be aware of Him by spiritual knowledge, and may still be attached to material association of various kinds. His faith is not strong, and may not be aware of the conclusions of the Vedic literature. The neophyte's faith may be changed by someone else who has strong arguments opposing his position. [10]

The third-class devotees may have little spiritual knowledge but are still attracted to the preliminary levels of bhakti-yoga, such as hearing and chanting about the Lord and observing the worship of the Deity in the temple. They also may be more attracted to the material blessings one gets than by spiritual benefits. So the third-class devotee should strive to become a second-class devotee. Therefore, such a person should continue to focus on hearing the spiritual knowledge from *shastra*, like the *Srimad-Bhagavatam, Upanishads* and *Vedanta* from the pure devotee, *maha-bhagavata*. Without hearing such literature, or the instructions therein, one cannot make actual progress. This must be done along with the practice of the regulative principles. Without this, it only remains a show. [11]

A neophyte devotee may not have much taste for hearing from or respecting such authority as the Vedic literature or the spiritual master, but it is by this process that their heart will become purified and all doubts about the process will be evaporated. This leads the way for deeper and deeper realizations about the Absolute Truth. In this way, even a third-class devotee rises to become second-class, and then to first-class.

From these descriptions we may be able to discern where we are located in our progress, and what is best for us to do to continue our upliftment.

In this way, until we become fully purified, we may display different inadequacies in the performance of our progress. But that does not mean we cannot become a pure devotee. It may only take more time, or more sincerity and determination. Whatever service we do with the intent to please the Lord is most auspicious, and brings us ever closer to the Lord. This cannot help but purify or spiritualize our consciousness, which is the whole purpose of bhakti-yoga. So do not be distracted or dismayed or discouraged, and keep going forward until you reach the goal. It is not that difficult on this spiritual path.

As further explained, "Only a rare person who has adopted complete, unalloyed devotional service to Krishna can uproot the weeds of sinful activities with no possibility that they will revive. He can do this simply by discharging devotional service, just as the sun can immediately dissipate fog by its rays." [12] Elsewhere it is more succinctly stated by Lord Krishna, "My dear Uddhava, devotional service in relationship with Me is like a blazing fire that can burn to ashes all the fuel of sinful activities supplied to it." [13]

This is how easy it is. So, everything is automatically accomplished on the spiritual path of bhakti-yoga and simply by such engagement we will become purified of any faults.

As we associate with these three levels of devotees, how should we treat them? This is clearly explained in the *Upadeshamrita* (Text Five): "One should mentally honor the devotee who chants the holy name of Lord Krishna, one should offer obeisances to the devotee who has undergone spiritual initiation [*diksha*] and is engaged in worshiping the Deity, and one should associate with and faithfully serve that pure devotee who is advanced in undeviated devotional service and whose heart is completely devoid of the propensity to criticize others."

In this way, the devotee should recognize his own position and act accordingly with others, and not try to imitate more advanced devotees for gaining more respect or admiration. This is surely the beginning of falling down from any position on the path of bhakti-yoga. For example, a person should not assume the position of a great spiritual teacher or master if he is not an *uttama-adhikari*, or topmost devotee, who can deliver others. Someone on a lower platform, who is not a pure devotee, can certainly help spread the science of God and the path of bhakti-yoga according to his level of understanding. But for giving initiation or accepting disciples, the person should be on the topmost platform because the disciples often cannot advance more than the level of the teacher. [14]

Remember, bhakti-yoga is not a process that is based on blind faith. It is expected that with proper practice, you will enter a level in which you have your own realizations, reciprocations and connection with the Supreme Being. This leads to the position of simply wanting to serve the Lord out of love, without any mixed purposes. This is the goal and the status of the first-class devotee, which many others have achieved in the past. The bliss that one receives in such consciousness far outweighs what can be attained from any material pleasure.

As expressed in the *Bhagavatam* (3.27.27): "When a person engages in devotional service and self-realization for many, many years and births, he becomes completely reluctant to enjoy any one of the material planets, even up to the highest planet, which is known as Brahmaloka, [that is when] he becomes fully developed in consciousness."

This means that a bhakti-yogi becomes completely self-sufficient in his own spiritual happiness. He needs no external source of stimuli to feel pleasure or happiness. He can go anywhere and feel content, and hesitant to try to engage in any other source of joy. He is simply no longer attracted to anything else. So the question is, what are you waiting for? Is there something else more important? That is what you must decide.

So, as we develop on our path in bhakti, we can gradually but steadily become pure devotees. The *Caitanya-caritamrita* (Adi-lila 1.64) explains there are basically two kinds of pure devotees on the path of bhakti-yoga, "Such pure devotees are of two types: personal associates [*parshats*] and neophyte devotees [*sadhakas*]." This means there are those who are already purified and are considered as good as the Lord's associates, and then there are those who are still following the process of purification, *sadhana-bhakti*. But because they follow the path with pure intention, they are also considered pure devotees because it is only a matter of time when they also will be considered associates of the Lord.

Furthermore, the *Caitanya-caritamrita* (Madhya-lila, 22.100) points out two more kinds of devotees that are more advanced while still living in this material world: "There are two kinds of devotees–those who are fully satiated and free from all material desires, and those who are fully surrendered to the lotus feet of the Lord. Their qualities are one and the same, but those who are fully surrendered to Krishna's lotus feet are qualified with another transcendental quality–*atma-samarpana*, full surrender without reservation." This means that the latter are more dependent on the mercy of the Lord, and more giving to whatever He may wish, which means they have a closer relationship with the Lord. This is what we wish to attain.

These are the primary kinds of bhakti-yogis who are traversing the path, upon which is our primary focus in this book. But how are these devotees engaged while progressing on this path?

## KINDS OF DEVOTIONAL ACTIVITY

The beauty of bhakti-yoga is that there are many kinds of activities that are still part of the bhakti-yoga path. Just as there are different levels of devotees, there are various kinds of devotional activities. The process of bhakti is like a tree, with branches, leaves and fruits. Whatever aspect you are attracted to, it is still part of the same tree. And the many branches are the many different activities that a person can perform or engage in that are part of that tree. Whatever part you like, it is still as sweet as any other part. But which activity is most attractive to a particular devotee only depends on his or her taste. There can be decorating the Deity in the temple, or making and sewing outfits for the Deity to wear, or performing priestly duties like doing the *arati* ceremony, or attending the *arati* and worshiping and offering obeisances to the Deity, or dancing in the *kirtan*, or cleansing the floors of the temple, or cooking delicious food offerings for the Lord, or tending to the temple grounds, or making a garden to offer vegetables and flowers to the Deity, or giving classes to share knowledge of the process of bhakti-yoga or the Vedic philosophy.

There are also the preliminary activities like simply reading the books and hearing about the various qualities of the Supreme Being and discussing this with other devotees, and then remembering and meditating on the pastimes and qualities of the Lord, or offering worship and prayers, etc. These are called *sravana, kirtana, smarana, archanam,* and *vandanam*. [15] All of these activities are spiritual and in relationship with the Lord, and help the bhakta or devotee to make spiritual progress. But the point is that various devotees will be more attracted to certain activities than others. That is the beauty of bhakti-yoga because it offers so many varieties of engagement in which the devotee can become absorbed, all the while speeding toward the spiritual world.

However, working on the temple grounds in the heat of the day, or cooking in a hot kitchen, or preaching to challenging people may also appear to be austerities that may not be so easy, but such austerity provides spiritual merit and frees the devotee of material desires and false ego which purifies them of material existence. Why? Because it is the sentiment of love for the Lord that encompasses these activities, and this is what brings them to the stage of pure devotion and allows them to become a topmost devotee.

The basic activities for advancing in devotional service are varied, and any of these can bring a person to a higher level of spiritualizing themselves on the path of bhakti-yoga. These are described by Lord Krishna Himself in *Srimad-Bhagavatam* (11.19.20-24) as those activities that He considers to be the highest in devotional service. "Firm faith in the blissful narrations of My pastimes, constant chanting of My glories, unwavering attachment to ceremonial worship of Me, praising Me through beautiful hymns, great respect for My devotional service, offering obeisances with the entire body, performing first-class worship of My devotees, consciousness of Me in all living entities, offering of ordinary, bodily activities in My devotional service, use of words to describe My qualities, offering the mind to Me, rejection of all material desires, giving up [or utilizing] wealth for My devotional service, renouncing material sense gratification and happiness, and performing all desirable activities such as charity [like giving donations to the temple], sacrifice [using one's time in serving the Lord and His devotees], chanting, vows and austerities with the purpose of achieving Me–these constitute actual religious principles, by which those human beings who have actually surrendered themselves to Me automatically develop love for Me. What other purpose or goal could remain for My devotee?"

So these varied activities are all useful for spiritual progress when centered around Lord Sri Krishna.

While we are developing ourselves, all devotional service can be brought to two basic levels of devotional activity that we can recognize in the participants on the path of bhakti-yoga. As explained, "There are two kinds of devotional activity–spontaneous and regulative... By executing spontaneous devotional service in Vrindavana, one attains the original Supreme Personality of Godhead, Krishna... By executing regulative devotional service, one becomes an associate of Narayana [Lord Vishnu] attains the Vaikunthalokas, the spiritual planets in the spiritual sky." [16]

Both aspects of bhakti-yoga, namely regulative or spontaneous, will take the person to the spiritual world. And through regulative devotion a person can reach the spontaneous level of performing devotional service. We will discuss this further in a later chapter. But if a person stays sincerely engaged on the regulative level, he still attains the spiritual Vaikuntha planets that float in the Brahman effulgence, and where the residents engage in varieties of worship of Lord Narayana in the mood of awe and veneration. In this way, bhakti-yoga uplifts and can deliver all levels of devotees to the spiritual world.

However, "The Supreme Personality of Godhead, Krishna, the son of mother Yashoda, is accessible to those devotees engaged in spontaneous loving service, but He is not as easily accessible to mental speculators, to those striving for self-realization by severe austerities and penances, or to those who consider the body the same as the self." [17]

## VARIETIES OF ACTIVITIES AFTER LIBERATION

It is also described that there are another two classifications of devotees, one called the *nitya-siddhas*, or the eternally perfect associates of the Lord who practically never fall down to the material atmosphere unless they are assigned to do so with a particular purpose or mission, and then there are the *sadhana-siddhas*, or those who become perfect by their *sadhana* or practice of bhakti-yoga. [18]

So not only are there different categories of devotees on the path of bhakti, but even among the *nitya-siddhas* or eternal associates of the Lord there is a variety of activities that the devotees engage in for their service to Lord Krishna. In this way, by our practice of bhakti-yoga here and now, we can become eligible to enter into Krishna's supreme abode wherein we can engage in various loving activities. So even after liberation in Lord Krishna's abode of Goloka-Vrindavana, there are various categories of devotees who have different relationships with Krishna to which we may be attracted.

There are the eternal associates of the Lord in the mood of servitude. This is described as continual affection for and attraction to Lord Krishna. This is generally affection in the mood of reverence. The residents of Vaikuntha or worshipers of Lord Vishnu are usually in the mood of awe and reverence. The devotees in the mood in servitude are divided into four classes: appointed servants like Lord Brahma or Lord Shiva who manage various aspects of the material energy and the modes of passion and darkness; devotees in servitude who are protected by the Lord; devotees who are always associates in the spiritual world; and devotees who are simply following in the footsteps of the Lord. [19]

Then there are the devotees in the mood of friendship, which are of two basic kinds: one who is the confidential servant of the Lord and the other is the well-wisher of the Lord. In the material world these are often seen as the friend who is engaged in the various kinds of service to the Lord, and the other is the preacher who tries to give people knowledge of the spiritual world and Lord Krishna, and thus acts as a well-wisher to everyone. [20]

Within the transcendental realm of Vrindavana, Krishna has eternal friends of four kinds, the well-wishers, the ordinary friends, confidential friends, and intimate friends. Well-wishers are those who are a little older than Krishna and have some parental affection and try to protect Krishna from any harm. Ordinary friends are those who are a little younger than Krishna and who are very attached to Him and give Him all kinds of service, such as helping Him tend the cows in adventures around the forests of Vrindavana. They are called *sakhas*. There are so many stories of how Krishna plays in pastimes with his friends.

Confidential friends of Lord Krishna are those almost the age of Krishna and are called *priya-sakhas*. They act like they are on a equal level with Krishna, completely unaware of Him being God, or in need of any protection or servitude. There are also the *priya-narma* or intimate friends. One of the functions of the intimate friends is to be a connection between Krishna and His cowherd girl friends and the pastimes with Radharani. The basis of all of these friends is simply to give transcendental happiness to Krishna in various forms of comradery. [21] In this way, the whole mood of the abode of Vrindavana is simply transcendental enjoyment and bliss.

After that there are the devotees with the parental affection, such as those who play the parts of Krishna's parents, aunts and uncles, and friends of the parents, and His teachers. [22]

Higher than that are the cowherd girls who also play a part in spiritual conjugal pastimes with Krishna. But this is far different than ordinary, material love. These devotees are divided into further classes. First there is the topmost *gopi*, which is Radharani who is accompanied by Her immediate associates. There is also conjugal love in the feeling of separation, or in direct contact. This extends to so many different moods that lead to so many different classifications, that further lead to innumerable pastimes. This can be described elsewhere for now.

The point is that there are so many varieties of spiritual pastimes that go on eternally in the spiritual world that anyone will find a place where they belong and can feel extraordinary bliss and happiness. By studying Krishna's pastimes in the literature like *Srimad-Bhagavatam* we can identify a personality and pastimes in which we are especially attracted. That is a mood in which we can develop our own attachment and attraction to Lord Krishna.

This also indicates that only devotees on the path of bhakti-yoga can relish the ecstatic taste of devotion to the Supreme Being, Lord Krishna, or understand such pastimes centered around Him.

This also shows how rare it is to progress on the path of bhakti to attain such devotion.

## RISING TO PURE BHAKTI

So how do we attain this pure devotional mood? The point is that whatever is our situation, in whatever class of bhakti we may be, or whatever level of spiritual advancement we are in, we can continue to rise until we are also among those who are considered pure, or purely spiritualized as I like to say. At that time we are considered to be liberated from any further rounds of birth and death in this material existence.

As described in *The Nectar of Devotion* (Page 1), there are five kinds of liberation, which include to become one with the Lord, to live on the same spiritual planet as the Supreme Lord, the have the same spiritual features as the Lord, to enjoy the same opulences as the Lord, and to live as a companion of the Lord in one of the main *rasas* or relationships with the Lord. But a pure devotee not only rejects material sense gratification, but also does not want any of these five kinds of liberation. He or she is satisfied simply by engaging in loving service to the Lord. That is the characteristic of pure devotion. Why? Because of the reasons listed by Srila Rupa Gosvami.

He states there are six characteristics of pure devotional service, which include:

1. Pure devotional service brings immediate relief from all kinds of material distress.

2. Pure devotional service is the beginning of all auspiciousness.

3. Pure devotional service automatically puts one in transcendental pleasure.

4. Pure devotional service is rarely achieved.

5. Those in pure devotional service deride even the conception of the monistic or impersonal liberation of merging into the non-active state of being in the great Brahman effulgence. They feel the bliss there is only a fraction of what is attained by loving relations with the Supreme Being.

6. Pure devotional service is the only means to attract Sri Krishna.

This is the power of such bhakti, which is also described by Srila Kapiladeva in the *Srimad-Bhagavatam* (3.29.10), when instructing His mother in the science of bhakti-yoga, "My dear Mother, those who are my pure devotees, and who have no desire for material benefit or philosophical speculation, have their minds so much engaged in My service that they are never interested in asking Me for anything–except to be engaged in that service. They do not even beg to live in My abode with Me."

In other words, by reaching this level of devotion, which means this depth of a connection with Lord Sri Krishna, all other benefits seem inconsequential. Nonetheless, it is also explained that liberation follows the pure devotee just like a maidservant, ready to assist him or her in attaining the ultimate freedom from all forms of material bondage and existence.

Furthermore, such bhakti-yoga is so powerful that it is considered the most auspicious path even for a religious householder who can selflessly worship the Supreme Being with wealth honestly earned.[23] So, even for married people who are often so preoccupied that they have little time or interest in spiritual affairs, bhakti-yoga is, nonetheless, considered the path that can also bring them to the level spiritual liberation.

The fact is, this pure devotion, also called *shuddha-bhakti*, meaning bhakti in the mode of pure goodness, is nothing more than the pure activity of the soul in its completely spiritualized condition. It is its natural, constitutional position and engagement. Bhakti-yoga is nothing more than the process of uncovering this natural condition by peeling away all that prevents us from reaching it, or all the layers of *maya* that prevents us from realizing our normal condition that remains dormant as long we are influenced or attached to various material attractions, in spite of how inferior they are. In other words, we may know that our material habits and sensual attachments will not give us real happiness, but we are stuck with them because that is all we know. Therefore, we need to learn about spiritual happiness and how to attain it. In this way, bhakti-yoga is the process of transferring our attractions toward Krishna, and our loving relationships toward the supreme relationship with Krishna in which we can be truly happy.

So, by following the principles of bhakti-yoga, we can rise from the lowest level of bhakti or a *kanishta-adhikari* to the highest level of realization of that of an *uttama-adhikari*. This process is really not so difficult, even while traversing all of the problems of material existence. As related by Sukadeva Gosvami to Maharaja Pariksit, "My dear King, in the material world the conditioned souls are confronted by death at every step of life. Therefore, who among the conditioned souls would not render service to the lotus feet of Lord Mukunda [Krishna], who is worshipable even for the greatest of liberated souls?" [24]

So, how do we accomplish this? As Sri Havir said to King Nimi, "Within the material world, one's material body is always subject to birth and decay. Similarly, the life air [*prana*] is harassed by hunger and thirst, the mind is always anxious, the intelligence hankers for that which cannot be attained [in the form of various sensual pleasures], and all of the senses are ultimately exhausted by constant struggle in the material nature. [Yet] A person who is not bewildered by the inevitable miseries of material existence, and who remains aloof from them simply by remembering the lotus feet of the Supreme Personality of Godhead, is to be considered a *bhagavata-pradhana*, the foremost devotee of the Lord." [25]

This is further elaborated as follows: "Devotion, [which gives] direct experience of the Supreme Lord, and detachment from other things–these three occur simultaneously for one who has taken shelter of the Supreme Personality of Godhead, in the same way that pleasure, nourishment and relief from hunger come simultaneously and increasingly, with each bite, for a person engaged in eating." [26]

Therefore, "By chanting the holy name of the Supreme Lord, one comes to the stage of love of Godhead. Then the devotee is fixed in his vow as an eternal servant of the Lord, and he gradually becomes very much attached to a particular name and form of the Supreme Personality of Godhead. As his hearts melts with ecstatic love, he laughs very loudly or cries or shouts. Sometimes he sings and dances like a madman, for he is indifferent to public opinion." [27]

This is how an ordinary bhakti-yogi can develop into a

devotee of the topmost level who experiences the ultimate bliss in his spiritual position in direct connection with the Supreme Lord. No one is excluded from this experience. It is only a matter of using the tools that assist in this process, namely the instructions found in the Vedic literature and given by the pure devotee spiritual teachers, along with the association of other devotees.

Persons who have been thoroughly spiritualized by bhakti-yoga are always joyful, being situated in elevated consciousness, and are always attached to the studies of scripture like the *Srimad-Bhagavtam*. They are always cheerful in the association of devotees, have accepted Lord Krishna as the ultimate shelter, and are pleased to engage in all aspects of devotional service. They have in their hearts the transcendental ecstasy of attachment to Lord Krishna. When that ecstatic state of being is enriched with love of Krishna, one gradually attains to the mature state of spiritual life and transcendental experience. [28]

So, as a person continues the process, and as his experience and direct perception of his or her connection with God becomes all the more clear, one's faith also becomes more firm. As related in the *Caitanya-caritamrita* (Madhya-lila 22.69): "One whose faith is soft and pliable is called a neophyte, but by gradually following the process, he will rise to the platform of a first-class devotee." And what is the vision of the first-class devotee? As explained: "The lotus feet of the Supreme Personality of Godhead are sought even by the greatest of demigods, such as Brahma and Shiva, who have all accepted the Supreme Personality of Godhead as their life and soul. A pure devotee of the Lord can never forget those lotus feet in any circumstance. He will not give up his shelter at the lotus feet of the Lord for a single moment–indeed, not for half a moment–even in exchange for the benediction of ruling and enjoying the opulence of the entire universe. Such a devotee of the Lord is to be considered the best of the Vaishnavas." [29]

This is why the topmost devotees pray only for more service to the Lord. They do not even pray for the five types of liberation because they are satisfied simply by being engaged in Krishna's devotional service. [30] And this is what will deliver them to the spiritual world, our real home of love and bliss.

## CHAPTER NOTES
1. *Srimad-Bhagavatam* 3.29.8-11.
2. *Teachings of Lord Caitanya*, p.161.
3. *Srimad-Bhagavatam* 1.2.12, pur.
4. *Nectar of Devotion*, p.29.
5. *Srimad-Bhagavatam* 6.17.28.
6. Ibid., 11.2.46.
7. Ibid., 1.2.12, pur.
8. *Nectar of Devotion*, p.29.
9. *Srimad-Bhagavatam* 11.2.47.
10. *Nectar of Devotion*, p.29.
11. *Srimad-Bhagavatam* 1.2.12, pur.
12. *Srimad-Bhagavatam* 6.1.15.
13. Ibid., 11.14.19.
14. *Nectar of Instruction*, p.58.
15. *Srimad-Bhagavatam* 7.5.23-24.
16. *Caitanya caritamrita,* Madhya-lila, 24.84-87.
17. *Srimad-Bhagavatam* 10.9.21.
18. Ibid., 3.3.26.pur. & *Nectar of Devotion*, p.211.
19. *Nectar of Devotion*, p.299.
20. Ibid., p.97.
21. Ibid., p.329-335.
22. Ibid., Chapter 43.
23. *Srimad-Bhagavatam* 10.84.37.
24. Ibid., 11.2.3.
25. Ibid., 11.2.49.
26. Ibid., 11.2.42.
27. Ibid., 11.2.40.
28. *Teachings of Lord Caitanya*, p.147.
29. *Srimad-Bhagavatam* 11.2.53.
30. Ibid., 3.25.31 & *Nectar of Devotion*, p.42.

# CHAPTER SEVENTEEN

# *The Outlook and Behavior of a Devotee*

As we develop ourselves spiritually on the path of bhakti-yoga, it is typical to begin seeing changes in ourselves, our values, or the reduction of our material desires, and so on. This is how a bhakti-yogi or devotee grows, and the signs of how he or she is developing. But some devotees may seem to advance faster, which may only be a sign of how much they accomplished in a previous life. So we should not be overly critical of ourselves as we continue our practice.

However, in my experience, sometimes neophyte bhakti-yogis may get discouraged when they do not see themselves progress or change as fast as they would like. But I tell people not to look at themselves or make comparisons on their development on a day to day basis. But keep practicing and then compare how they are changing on a yearly basis. Day by day, not much may seem to be happening. But when you look at yourself as you were a year ago, you may notice a drastic decrease in sensual hankerings, material habits, fewer attachments, and deeper insights into one's spiritual view of things, or a more mature understanding of the spiritual and Vedic philosophy, or a more direct experience of your spiritual identity, and so on. This is a clear result of your continued practice of bhakti-yoga. And this progress will certainly continue as long as you do not give up.

How a devotee can view their progress is to compare one's position to descriptions in the Vedic literature. For example, a devotee learns what Krishna wants by learning from the pure devotee spiritual master. So, how much we are aspiring to learn from such a devotee will certainly be a determining factor in how we are advancing. [1]

An advancing devotee is also confident in performing his or her service, and knows that any sincere and humble devotion displayed by the devotee will be accepted by Lord Krishna who will reciprocate that devotion. Not only does Lord Krishna become attracted by such bhakti, but any devotee will start to feel and gradually fully experience the higher taste for such service since that is the real hankering of the soul. This becomes increasingly apparent as the devotee becomes more purified from materialistic attractions. This is like jaundice in which the disease makes sugar taste bitter, but once cured, the person will again taste sugar as sweet.

The same thing goes for devotional service to the Lord. A person who is overly attracted to materialistic pleasures will not feel much joy from bhakti-yoga. But as they become more spiritualized, the nature of the soul becomes more apparent to the point in which a person feels increasingly content and happy while engaged in the activities that are the very nature of the soul, which is to engage in eternal, loving relations with the Supreme loving person, which is the Supreme Being.

Another aspect that can be seen in a bhakti-yogi's progress is the humility that a devotee exhibits in his relations with others. A devotee never considers himself to be exalted or someone special. He always thinks others are more advanced than he is. He is always grateful for the mercy that has come to him or her in the form of knowledge about the process of bhakti-yoga, which is almost always from another devotee, or directly from a pure devotee of the Lord. He feels that his service to the Lord may be imperfect, but the intention is what is appreciated by the Lord. Even if a person is born in a rich or aristocratic family, that is only a material consideration, and anything material can change at any time. Therefore, it is the causeless mercy of the Supreme that any devotee is fortunate enough to continue on the path of bhakti-yoga. As stated in the *Shikshashtaka* prayers of Sri Caitanya (verse 3): "One can chant the holy name of the Lord in a humble state of mind, feeling himself lower than the straw in the street. One should be more tolerant than a tree, devoid of all sense of false prestige, and ready to offer all respect to others." [2]

With such an attitude, a person will be able to continue the path of bhakti-yoga. However, this does not mean that when danger arises that we do not protect other devotees or the Deity of the Lord. If such threats occur, and people try to attack us or our fellow devotees, or the temple and Deities of the Lord, it is also our devotional service to protect them. Devotees follow the path of *ahimsa*, or nonviolence. We never cause violence, nor do we look for it. But if violence should approach us, we should be courageous enough not to run away, especially when such threats are against other devotees, the spiritual master, the temple, or the Deities. Then we should act to protect them.

We should also be willing to protect the Vedic culture. It is the Vedic tradition, along with our freedom to participate in it, which will determine the future well-being of humanity, and the continuation of the deeper aspects of spiritual knowledge. When and if this comes under threat, then this should be protected and preserved for its perpetuation. This makes it possible for future generations to understand it and also participate in it, which paves the way for a better world. And the best way to protect the Vedic tradition is to understand it and explain it to others, or simply share it with all who are interested. Then they can also begin to realize the value of it and start to utilize whatever aspect of the philosophy that fits in their own lives.

In this way, the devotee is like the Lord by being a friend to all. And the best friend to all living beings, particularly other humans, is to tell them about their spiritual identity and who they really are. This in itself can help solve so many of the problems that many people face today, which stems originally from ignorance of who we are, the purpose of life, and where we are going by our present actions. Even the global pollution of many of the natural resources we need to survive comes from the original pollution of the false and materialistic aims of life, especially for profit, adoration and prestige. It is this spiritual knowledge that can help alleviate that.

Lord Krishna also explains it like this in *Bhagavad-gita* (12.13-14): "One who is not envious but who is a kind friend to all living entities, who does not think himself a proprietor, who is free from false ego and equal in both happiness and distress, who is always satisfied and engaged in devotional service with determination, and whose mind and intelligence are in agreement with Me–he is very dear to Me."

Furthermore, a devotee never works simply to accumulate material opulence. He or she knows that such material items and whatever glamor there may be in material existence are temporary. Not only are they here one day and gone tomorrow, as they say, but even as we age, things like our beauty, health, wealth, strength, etc., gradually disappears or leave us. But for a devotee, whatever material facilities he has are also considered spiritual because they are used in some way in the service to the Lord. Such items as a house, a car, or even refrigerator, and so on, are used to help the devotee in his or her engagement in bhakti-yoga, which again is the constitutional position of the soul. Just like a car is used to take the person to work, where he earns money for his own maintenance and also for giving donations to the temple, which makes the time he spends at work into spiritual activities. A house not only becomes a home, but when the person establishes a temple room in his house, it also becomes his personal temple. So these things that a devotee has are also used in a spiritual way. If they cannot be used in his or her service to the Supreme, then such a yogi is not interested in acquiring them. They serve no purpose. So he or she is simply not interested. This alone simplifies life to a great degree.

Plus, a devotee who does receive much material opulence accepts it as blessings from the Lord. Therefore, he is always grateful to the Lord for whatever he has, and also utilizes it for the higher purpose of serving the Lord, or utilizing his wealth to continue the activities in the temple, or in serving the devotees and Deities of the Lord, and to help preserve and protect the Vedic culture, which can be done in many ways.

It is the same way with friends. If a person is only a friend because of being a vehicle for sense gratification, or because of nothing more than sharing a similar interest in materialistic activities, such friendships are often so superficial that they will not last long. The mind is very fickle, and when the mind and interests change, the relationships based on such interests also change, or even end altogether. So a devotee, who can foresee such things, may be friendly with everyone, but he or she is very particular in making deeper friendly relations with those who are similarly spiritually interested. The soul is the essence of all that is eternal and truly meaningful. Therefore, the soul or the Supreme Being should be the central aspect of any friendship. All friendships should be based on truth, and truth is the divine knowledge of the soul. Without that, then what is the basis or value of any friendship? That does not mean that we cannot deal with anyone for business or work, or other reasons. But how much time we invest in relations with those who are simply materialists with no spiritual interest should be limited for obvious reasons. We will develop characteristics similar to those with whom we associate. Therefore, we may have friends on all levels, but we should try to develop deeper friendships with those who are similarly interested in spiritual topics or bhakti-yoga so we can share our activities with them. The more we organize our lives like this, then the more we will also continue to advance spiritually.

There are a number of other qualities that a person desiring to be a great soul should acquire, and these manifest in his or her character as he or she advances in bhakti-yoga. These are described by Lord Shiva to Parvati in the *Padma Purana*, as well as in a discussion between Bhumi and Yamaraja in the First Canto of *Srimad-Bhagavatam*. Such qualities include truthfulness, cleanliness, mercy, perseverance, renunciation or detachment, peacefulness, simplicity, control of the senses, equilibrium of the mind, austerity, equality, forbearance, placidity, learning, knowledge, chivalry, influence, strength, memory, independence, tactfulness, luster, patience, ability to talk nicely, gravity, steadiness, faithfulness, respectfulness, and lack of false egotism. [3]

Furthermore, a devotee who becomes purified becomes so powerful that he can purify the holy places visited by numerous pilgrims. As said in the *Bhagavatam* (9.9.6) when King Bhagirathi addressed the Ganga River, and said: "Those who are saintly because of devotional service and are therefore in the renounced order, free from material desires, and who are pure devotees, expert in following the regulative principles mentioned in the *Vedas*, are always glorious and pure in behavior and are able to deliver all fallen souls. When such pure devotees bathe in your water, the sinful reactions accumulated from other people will certainly be counteracted, for such devotees always keep in the core of their hearts the Supreme

Personality of Godhead, who can vanquish all sinful reactions."

We could include a number of other points regarding the changes, behavior and qualities of a bhakti-yogi, but the whole purpose is to continue to move toward attaining a taste for our devotional activities, and then developing further toward awakening love, *bhava*, within our heart for the Lord, Krishna. When *bhava* or love arises in the heart of a *vaidhi-bhakta*, or a practicing devotee, their lifestyle will naturally change. It will include all of the above-mentioned changes and qualities, as well as others. The change from one's practice of the principles of bhakti-yoga to attaining love for God is not abrupt, but continues to develop as long as a person follows the process.

When a person reaches love of God in the heart, then even more changes appear in the life and personality of the devotee. Nine of the most prominent changes include tolerance [to the ups and downs in life, or any causes of agitation], not wasting time, detachment [from material attractions], pridelessness, hope, eagerness, constant taste for chanting the name of the Lord, attachment to hearing topics about the Lord, and attraction for the places of Lord Krishna's pastimes.

Even if there are causes for disturbances, the *bhava-bhaktas*, the devotees who have achieved love for God, do not become disturbed. For example, even if someone becomes an enemy, or if a relative suffers or dies, if wealth is lost, if some family problem arises, if there is illness, the *bhava-bhaktas* may be involved with the immediate affair, but their hearts are not disturbed since they have fixed their mind on the Lord. It is as if they are watching the affairs that go on in this material world like watching a movie. And though they may feel empathy for the suffering of others, they still feel somewhat like a tourist going through the actions of life while still focusing on the ultimate reality, the Absolute Truth. So they still do not feel the usual anger, lust, greed, fear, lamentation, or illusion that others may endure while going through these various experiences. [4] However, what the devotee does feel is compassion at the misfortune of all who go through the ups and downs of life without the balancing affect that deep spiritual knowledge can provide.

In any case, these progressive changes are just some of the

results of our spiritual development and the changes that begin to manifest in the lives of the advancing bhakti-yogi. As we continue to make progress, we become increasingly absorbed in Krishna, until finally we display the symptoms and attain the vision of a topmost devotee, which is briefly described in the following verse from the *Srimad-Bhagavatam* (11.2.45): "The advanced devotee sees that all living entities are part and parcel of the Supreme Personality of Godhead. Everyone is in Krishna, and Krishna is also within everyone. Such a vision is possible only for a person who is very advanced in devotional service [bhakti-yoga]."

**CHAPTER NOTES**
1. *Caitanya-caritamrita,* Madhya-lila, 19.167 pur.
2. *Nectar of Devotion*, pp.16, 304.
3. Ibid., p.157.
4. *Sri Caitanya-Siksamrta*, p.146.

# CHAPTER EIGHTEEN

# *How the Lord Reveals Himself to His Devotee*

We have looked at how Krishna begins to reciprocate with new devotees in ways to help them along in their spiritual advancement, and how they can begin to get a deeper taste for Krishna, and so on. In this chapter we will look at how the Lord can more deeply reveal Himself to the devotee from within and how to make that happen.

First of all, the Lord reveals Himself through His pastimes that He displays at certain times in this world. *Srimad-Bhagavatam* (10.14.55) explains, "You should know Krishna to be the original Soul of all living entities. For the benefit of the whole universe, He has, out of His causeless mercy, appeared as an ordinary human being. He has done this by the strength of His internal potency."

It is through His appearance as Krishna, or any of His other *avatars*, that He exhibits His personality, qualities, attractiveness, and love for all of His devotees. This is how He also protects His devotees, gives them happiness and encouragement, and attracts the conditioned souls to realize there is a life that is much higher than mere material existence. This is clarified in the verse, "My dear master, although You have nothing to do with material existence, You come to this earth and imitate material life just to expand the varieties of ecstatic enjoyment for Your surrendered devotees." [1]

Furthermore, when the Lord appears in this way, He also leaves many instructions so everyone can uplift their lives and understanding of the true purpose of life. These directions can be found in such sacred texts as the *Bhagavad-gita, Bhagavata Purana*, and many others. So even if we cannot see Lord Krishna directly, we can still associate with Him through His instructions, along with the

*The Deity of Lord Krishna, allowing us to see Him.*

*The Deity of Srimati Radharani.*

reading of His pastimes and descriptions of His characteristics, qualities, personality, etc.

Secondly, Lord Krishna shows Himself to us in the form of the Deities. The Lord takes up habitation in the Deity after the *prana-pratishta* ceremony when we call the Lord to accept this *archa-vigraha* or Deity form, which is the form in which He accepts our care, service and worship in the temple. This form is His causeless mercy on the conditioned souls who may not be able to see the Lord through material senses. Therefore, He accepts inhabiting the Deity to receive our service, and so we can meditate on and think of the Lord in this way.

The Supreme is the controller of both material and spiritual energies, and can turn what is material into what is spiritual. Thus, He can also inhabit the form of the Deity and actually interact with the devotees in many ways. The Deity can and has shown Himself to talk to the devotees, walk, or even show Himself to dance to those with purified consciousness and spiritualized vision. In this way, the Lord is not a statue or a doll, or an idol, but is the *archa-murti*, directly the Supreme Being showing Himself through the worshipful Deity form. In fact, *shastra* states that one who sees the Deity as nothing but stone, paint, wood, or whatever, has a hellish mentality. In fact, I have written a book called *Krishna Deities and Their Miracles: How the Images of Lord Krishna Interact with Their Devotees*. This has numerous stories, both older and recent, of how the Deities displayed Their pastimes with Their devotees in numerous circumstances.

Thirdly, once we develop ourselves to go further in our spiritual perception, the Supreme will also reveal Himself from within ourselves. Lord Krishna can give us the knowledge and insight by which we can understand Him because He can control that, as He explains in *Bhagavad-gita* (15.15): "I am seated in everyone's heart, and from Me come remembrance, knowledge and forgetfulness..."

Then again He says, "To those who are constantly devoted to Me and worship Me with love, I give the understanding by which they can come to Me. Out of compassion for them, I, dwelling in their hearts, destroy with the shining lamp of knowledge the darkness born of ignorance..." [2]

In this way, the Supreme awakens the divine consciousness within the devotee so that he or she can comprehend the transcendental nature of the Lord.

Lord Krishna further explains this in *Srimad-Bhagavatam* (8.24.38), "You will be thoroughly advised and favored by Me, and because of your inquiries, everything about My glories, which are known as *param brahma*, will be manifest within your heart. Thus you will know everything about Me."

So as we progress in our bhakti-yoga, Lord Krishna takes notice of us and actually gives us guidance according to the love and surrender we have for Him. This is natural because it is this love, bhakti, which draws the attention of the Supreme Infinite to the infinitesimal. This is done because of the loving service performed by the devotee. As explained in the *Caitanya-caritamrita* (Adi-lila, 7.145), "The Supreme Lord, who is greater than the greatest, becomes submissive to even a very insignificant devotee because of his devotional service. It is the beautiful and exalted nature of devotional service that the infinite Lord becomes submissive to the infinitesimal living entity because of it. In reciprocal devotional activities with the Lord, the devotee actually enjoys the transcendental mellow quality of devotional service."

When this happens, the Supreme more deeply enlightens the devotee from within. One verse that points to this is, "The Supreme Personality of Godhead, who is situated in everyone's heart as the Supersoul, sells Himself to His devotees such as Narada Muni. In other words, the Lord gives pure love to such devotees and gives Himself to those who love Him purely. Great self-realized mystic yogis, such as the four Kumaras also derive great transcendental bliss from realizing the Supersoul within themselves." [3]

Consultation with the Supersoul is possible when the devotee is completely free from the distractions of ego and other material attachments. The Supersoul or Paramatma is always the *chaitya-guru*, or the guru within, and He also manifests before a person as the pure devotee spiritual master to give instruction. In this way, the devotee can also consult with the Supersoul in the heart. The ideal is to accept instructions from within, but if we are too proud to accept instructions from without, as through the spiritual master, we will never become qualified to recognize and accept instructions from within. But a sincere devotee is always assisted by the directions of the guru and the Supersoul. The Supersoul is the eternal friend of the living entity, in any species of life.

The above verses also begin to show that it is the Lord in the heart who brings transcendental realization to increasingly higher levels by directly enlightening the bhakti-yogi. And this is primarily based on the sincerity of the devotional service that the devotee offers to the Supreme. This is clearly described as follows: "O Lord, Your transcendental name and form are not ascertained by those who merely speculate on the path of imagination. Your name, form and attributes can be ascertained only through devotional service." [4]

Even in the *Padma Purana* the verse *atah shri-krishna-namadi* means, "One cannot understand the transcendental nature of the name, form, quality and pastimes of Sri Krishna through one's materially contaminated senses. Only when one becomes spiritually saturated by transcendental service to the Lord are the transcendental name, form, quality, and pastimes of the Lord revealed to him."

"My Lord, if one is favored by even a slight trace of the mercy of Your lotus feet, he can understand the greatness of Your personality. But those who speculate to understand the Supreme Personality of Godhead are unable to know You, even though they continue to study the *Vedas* for many years." [5]

This makes it clear that it is not the amount of study or erudite knowledge that a person has that qualifies him for understanding the Absolute Truth. No one can penetrate such understanding and perception without the will of the Lord Himself. And how do we attain that? As it is clearly stated in *Srimad-Bhagavatam* (10.9.21): "The Supreme Personality of Godhead, Krishna, the son of mother Yashoda, is accessible to devotees engaged in spontaneous loving service..." This shows the correct mood one should have to attract the Supreme Lord, and be successful on the path of bhakti-yoga, and begin to perceive the true greatness and glory of the Supreme Being. Without that, we can struggle for years or more and never get anywhere in our attempt to perceive the true nature of the Supreme Reality.

So you could say that God realization depends on intense

longing. It does not matter how many years we study the Vedic literature, how long we continue with our *sadhana*, and what else we may try to do. All of this may help, but the core feeling is that we cannot stand any further delay in realizing God. With that feeling, for every step we take toward God, He takes one thousand steps toward us. He cannot help it. He becomes motivated by our own longing to see Him. But this longing can be compared to the longing of a drowning man to reach the shore, knowing if he does not do that he will surely die. Or like the lover who cannot bear separation from the beloved. In the same way, when our only focus is to attain God, then He will surely begin to enlighten us on the nature of His transcendental qualities and pastimes, and on how to reach Him.

Then, by the combination of intense longing and the performance of our devotional service, we not only begin to perceive how the Lord is and has always been reciprocating with us, but we become illumined with transcendental knowledge from within. This is the power and intimate nature of bhakti-yoga. Even Lord Krishna admits this when He says, "My dear Uddhava, the unalloyed devotional service rendered to Me by My devotees brings Me under their control. I cannot be thus controlled by those engaged in mystic yoga, Sankhya philosophy, pious works, Vedic study, austerity, and renunciation. Only by practicing unalloyed devotional service with full faith in Me can one obtain Me, the Supreme Personality of Godhead. I am naturally dear to My devotees, who take Me as the only goal of their loving service. By engaging in such pure devotional service, even the dog-eaters can purify themselves from the contamination of their low birth." [6]

In an advanced stage, a pure devotee's interest and the Lord's are the same. Whatever the devotee does is for the interest of the Supreme. And whatever the Lord does is for the interest of His devotee. This is why such a devotee can receive instruction directly from the Lord. Of course, this is the intimate or close relationship between the Lord and His devotee. An expression of that is related by Lord Krishna when He says, "The devotees are My heart, and I am the heart of My devotees. My devotees do not know anyone but Me; similarly I do not know anyone but My devotees." [7]

In this way, the relationship between the devotees and the

Lord becomes closer and more intimate. The Lord invokes the illuminating knowledge within the heart of the devotees, and the devotees, upon understanding the Lord in deeper and deeper ways, become ever closer to the Lord. As King Citraketu explained in the *Srimad-Bhagavatam* (6.16.34), "O unconquerable Lord, although You cannot be conquered by anyone, You are certainly conquered by devotees who have control of the mind and senses. They can keep You under their control because You are causelessly merciful to devotees who desire no material profit from You. Indeed, You give Yourself to them, and because of this You also have full control over Your devotees."

The *Mundaka Upanishad* (3.2.3) also relates the means by which the Lord reveals Himself to a devotee, "The Supreme Lord is not obtained by expert explanations, by vast intelligence, or even by much hearing. He is obtained only by one whom He Himself chooses. To such a person, He manifests His own form."

Knowing this, we should engage in our *sadhana* or practice of bhakti-yoga while anticipating that at some time we will know and even see the Supreme Lord by His own will. How do we do this? To have the same desire to see the Lord as a drowning man desires to reach the shore. Even Sri Jiva Goswami writes in his *Bhakti Sandarbha* (277), "Sri Krishna will personally appear before the person who remembers Him and give Himself to him, which means that He is subdued by the devotee who remembers Him."

In conclusion, the general rule is that we can see the Lord when we are ripe for it. So the more we develop *prema*, or ecstatic love for God, the more we will attain the direct vision of the Lord. Until then, we can still use the facility of viewing and worshiping the Deity, and studying the *Bhagavad-gita* and *Srimad-Bhagavatam*, and taking instruction from the pure devotees. Just like when we go to the holy *dham* of Vrindavana or Mayapur, or bathe in the Ganga for purification, all of these actions will create a similar effect, which is to draw us ever closer to the direct association with the Supreme Lord Sri Krishna.

**CHAPTER NOTES**
1. *Srimad-Bhagavatam* 10.14.37.

2. *Bhagavad-gita* 10.10-11.
3. *Srimad-Bhagavatam* 5.24.21.
4. Ibid., 10.2.36.
5. Ibid., 10.14.29.
6. Ibid., 11.14.20-21.
7. Ibid., 9.4.68.

# CHAPTER NINETEEN

# *Attaining the Experience of God*

There is nothing so convincing for the practicing bhakti-yogi, or any spiritual person for that matter, than to have one's own experience of God. That is actually the purpose of the Vedic system, to allow one the means to purify or spiritualize one's consciousness to the point wherein that person begins to experience by direct perception the spiritual dimension, or the direct contact with God.

Naturally, we all may begin any path with faith, but faith alone is not enough. And any religion that does not go beyond faith remains incomplete. A genuine spiritual path is meant to help the follower such a perception, and give him or her the means or formula to attain the spiritual realm, which can be done right here, in this body, in this lifetime. This is what it is meant to do. And bhakti-yoga is meant to do that for the sincere practitioner who follows the path properly, and without giving up.

The first way we may begin to experience God is through the good graces of a pure devotee. "Since one cannot visually experience the presence of the Supersoul, He appears before us as a liberated devotee. Such a spiritual master is no one other than Krishna Himself."[1] It is through the instructions and guidance of such a sage who is already liberated by which we can attain the same spiritual vision he has. As we progress in this way, we also become closer to attaining our own spiritual experiences.

The point is, the more we advance in our devotional service, and in our hankering to see the Lord, the more we can see Him in His various reciprocations and blessings to us, up to and including seeing Him face to face. How does this happen? It may start with the recognition of the Lord being everywhere through His energies, or that all His energies are but an extension of the Supreme, but such consciousness increases continuously as we heighten our longing in our bhakti-yoga.

# Chapter Nineteen

One of the easiest ways to begin recognizing the presence of the Lord is by seeing His presence in all living beings and in the Deity in the temple. As the Lord explains, "All living entities, moving and nonmoving, are My expansions but are separate from Me. I am the Supersoul of all living beings, who exist because I manifest them. I am the form of the transcendental omkara [Om] and Hare Krishna Hare Rama, and I am the Supreme Absolute Truth. These two forms of Mine–namely the transcendental sound and the eternally blissful spiritual form of the Deity, are My eternal forms; they are not material." [2]

There are many verses that speak of how the Deity of the Lord is not a statue but is actually the *archa-vigraha*, an activated, worshipful form in which the Lord resides to accept our service. But a nice summary is given in the story of Sakshi-gopala, the walking Deity that was situated in Vrindavana and walked all the way to Jagannatha Puri, where He is now established in a small village a little ways to the north of town. He walked there only after being asked by a young brahmana who wanted the Deity to act as a witness to a promise that had been made to him by an older brahmana while in front of that Deity. The younger brahmana, when speaking to the Deity of Sasksi-gopala, told the Deity: "My dear Lord, You are not a statue; You are directly the son of Maharaja Nanda [Krishna]. Now, for the sake of the old brahmana, You can do something You have never done before." Sri Gopalaji then smiled and said: "My dear brahmana, just listen to Me. I shall walk behind you, and in this way I shall go with you." [3] And so the Deity reciprocated with the young brahmana and walked behind him all the way to Puri. This is how the Lord can manifest in the Deity in the temple, and react in various ways due to the devotion of the devotee. This is one of the easiest ways to begin recognizing the personal presence of the Lord. [You can check out my book *Krishna Deities and Their Miracles: How the Images of Lord Krishna Interact with Their Devotees* for many more such stories of how the Krishna Deities have interacted in various ways with Their devotees.]

So simply by walking into the temple we can see the spiritual form of the Lord as the Deity. It can be that simple. But then the Deity also becomes alive and reciprocates with us. He is not merely made of metal or stone. The presence of the Lord manifests there within the Deity after the installation process to make it easy for the devotees to focus on Him. Then we feel happy just to be in front of the Deity in such easy meditation. In fact, as it is described: "The beauty of Krishna has one natural strength; it thrills the hearts of all men and women, beginning with Lord Krishna Himself. All minds are attracted by hearing His sweet voice and flute, or by seeing His beauty. Even Lord Krishna Himself makes efforts to taste that sweetness. The thirst of one who always drinks the nectar of that sweetness is never satisfied. Rather, that thirst increases constantly."[4]

In this way, once we perceive the beauty of Lord Krishna, it captivates the mind over and above everything else. Our thoughts and meditation on the Lord increases, which guarantees our deliverance from the material creation and entrance into the spiritual realm.

The next methods of coming in contact with the Absolute are explained as follows: "There are three ways to attain the lotus feet of the Absolute Truth, Krishna. There is the process of philosophical speculation [jnana-yoga], the practice of mystic yoga [raja or astanga-yoga], and the execution of devotional service [bhakti-yoga]. Each of these has its different characteristics. The Absolute is the same, but according to the process by which one understands Him, He appears in three forms–as Brahman, Paramatma, and Bhagavan, the Supreme Personality of Godhead... If one follows the path of speculation, the Absolute Truth manifests Himself as the impersonal Brahman, and if one follows the path of mystic yoga, He manifest Himself as the Supersoul... By executing spontaneous devotional service [like] in Vrindavana, one attains the original Supreme Personality of Godhead, Krishna."[5]

So we can experience some aspect of the Absolute through jnana-yoga, which is the analysis of what is real and what is not, or through mystic yoga, which if used properly, can reveal the Paramatma or Supersoul within us all. But such mystic yoga requires a detailed process of meditation that not everyone can do, especially in this age of Kali-yuga which is full of distractions. This process goes through the steps of following the basic rules of the *yamas* and *niyamas* or what to do and not do, perfecting the *asanas* or physical positions, then *pranayama* or breathing exercises, then *pratyahara* or control of the mind and senses, then *dharana* or concentrating on the object of meditation, followed by *dhyana* or free flowing meditation on the object or goal, and then *samadhi*, which is oneness with the Supreme within. [You can check my book *Yoga and Meditation: Their Real Purpose and How to Get Started* for more information on this process.]

Nonetheless, whatever levels of meditation you can do will certainly have its benefits, which we do not discourage. But to reach the ultimate goal of self-realization through this path is not so easy. This is why bhakti-yoga is the easiest of paths to reach the Supreme. It accomplishes so many things all at once.

In any case, regardless of the path we take, to experience the Absolute Truth requires intense longing of the heart. It is no cheap thing. It cannot be done as an ordinary exercise to attain some ability. The intense longing that is mentioned should be the feeling a drowning man has when he does not know how to swim but desires to reach the river bank so he can be saved. Similarly, a person who desires to experience God should be longing to be free of this material creation by getting a glimpse of the Lord, which becomes the primary goal of his life.

As Lord Krishna says in *Bhagavad-gita* (12.6-7): "For one who worships Me, giving up all his activities unto Me and being devoted to Me without deviation, engaged in devotional service and always meditating on Me, who has fixed his mind upon Me, O son of Partha, for him I am the swift deliverer from the ocean of birth and death."

This is the longing we should have to attract Krishna to reveal Himself, which is the means to be lifted out of the ocean of repeated birth and death, and to then reach the spiritual world. Of course, let us remember that in bhakti-yoga, we can be doing an assortment of activities, and if they are connected with Krishna, then that itself is a form of meditation, simply by thinking about Krishna. And with every thought about Krishna, we get closer to Him.

Therefore, merely by eager and sincere service to the Lord, a bhakti-yogi can attain the vision of Him. Of course, this is no ordinary thing, as it is stated, "One who engages in Your devotional service twenty-four hours a day, desiring only Your mercy, will very soon attain shelter at Your lotus feet." [6] Bhakti-yoga is the path that allows us to utilize our activities in so many different ways as a service to the Lord, which is then a part of the yoga process.

So, the advanced devotee can immediately feel the presence of the Lord by focusing his or her mind and consciousness in a devotional way. "The Supreme Lord Sri Krishna, whose glories and activities are pleasing to hear, at once appears on the seat of my heart, as if called for, as soon as I begin to chant [or even think of] His holy activities." [7] And if one is not advanced, you should keep developing yourself in a steady way until you reach the goal.

Now we have to remember what Lord Krishna says in *Bhagavad-gita* (4.11): "All of them–as they surrender unto Me–I reward them accordingly. Everyone follows My path in all respects, O son of Pritha."

This means that all paths will ultimately reach Krishna if they are followed to their ultimate conclusion. Everyone is connected with the Supreme, Krishna, and to think otherwise is merely a mental construct based on false information or impressions, which must be corrected somehow or other, especially by following the proper path. But some paths are more direct than others. And to have an experience of God that leaves no doubts or confusion, requires that we give the instructions of Lord Krishna, or the pure devotee, the highest respect. Then we can be situated on the proper path.

However, what it takes is the surrender to the Lord, which means an intense service attitude. This was exhibited in the story of Narada Muni who was able to get a glimpse of the Lord by deep meditation, but only after he had received the blessings of the great sages. The Lord told him in the *Bhagavatam* (1.6.22): "O virtuous one, you have only once seen My person, and this is just to increase your desire for Me, because the more you hanker for Me, the more you will be freed from all material desires."

This is an example of how we must become purified to attain a glimpse of the spiritual strata, which means to enter the frequency level in which we can find or experience the Absolute Truth. When the material contamination of the modes of material nature are washed away by our spiritual practice, one's relation with God is revealed. [8] Furthermore, the closer we get to God, the feeling makes us want all the more to increase our transcendental view of the Supreme. This feeling is what helps propel us to again have an experience of the Supreme, not once but again and again, which can happen in many ways.

Another example includes how Srila Vyasadeva prepared himself to compile the Vedic knowledge into written form at his cottage at Shamyaprasa next to the Sarasvati River, "... he fixed his mind, perfectly engaging it by linking it in devotional service [bhakti-yoga] without any tinge of materialism, and thus he saw the Absolute Personality of Godhead along with His energy, which was under full control." [9] This was his inspiration to write the Vedic literature.

Even Lord Shiva, while talking to his wife Sati, said, "I am always engaged in offering obeisances to Lord Vasudeva in pure Krishna consciousness. Krishna consciousness is always pure consciousness, in which the Supreme Personality of Godhead, known as Vasudeva, is revealed without any covering." [10]

What do we learn from this? Herein it is made clear that when the yogi is free from materialism, and engages in service to the Supreme, he is uplifted to the state of Brahman, or the state of *suddha-sattva*, or the frequency of pure goodness of the spiritual dimension. It is this state of being wherein the Absolute Truth can be seen as He is without any interference or covering. When our material senses are purified, it paves the way to open our spiritual senses by which we can perceive the spiritual dimension, including Lord Krishna. This can also mean that our material senses become spiritualized to see beyond what is the normal view of our ordinary senses. But more importantly, it is by the devotee's sincerity in his or her service attitude which will bring forth the Supreme to reveal Himself to His devotees. Then He reveals Himself through His spiritual energy, and the devotee, by his or her spiritual vision, recognizes that energy and the Supreme who is the source of all such energy. Therefore, it is only through pure devotion to the Lord that we can attain the vision and awaken our relationship with the Lord.

When this happens, the knot of false identification with *maya* is pierced, and all misgivings about one's true identity and relationship with the Lord are cut to pieces, as explained in the *Bhagavatam* (11.20.30), "The knot in the heart is pierced [with spiritual knowledge], all misgivings are cut to pieces, and the chain of fruitive actions is terminated when I am seen as the Supreme Personality of Godhead."

So, for both the progressing and advanced devotee, the Lord can reveal Himself in many ways, and to whom He wants, and for whatever reason He wants. But as a bhakti-yogi increases his or her longing to love God, the Supreme also begins to reveal Himself in various ways. Even to the point of guiding that yogi, talking with that yogi, or showing Himself to that yogi for any number of reasons. Once that happens, attaining such an experience of God, the devotee is never the same, and his or her service reaches a new level of love and meaning and awareness. In this way, the path back to Krishna becomes ever more clear.

**CHAPTER NOTES**
1. *Caitanya-caritamrita,* Adi-lila,1.58.
2. *Srimad-Bhagavatam* 6.16.51.
3. *Caitanya-caritamrita,* Madhya-lila, 5.96-7.
4. Ibid., Adi-lila, 4.1479.
5. Ibid., Madhya-lila, 24.79-85.
6. Ibid., Antya-lila, 9.76.
7. *Srimad-Bhagavatam* 1.6.33.
8. Ibid., 9.19.25.
9. Ibid., 1.7.4.
10. Ibid., 4.3.23.

# CHAPTER TWENTY

# *Being Absorbed in God*

This is actually the goal of any saint, *sadhu*, holy man, or *bhakta*, to go through life and perform all of one's activities while being absorbed in thoughts and awareness of God–like a constant meditation. This is the means of bhakti-yoga by which we are always thinking of Lord Krishna in some way. This is the way we reach the spiritual strata.

"A grass worm confined in a hole by a bee always thinks of the bee in fear and enmity and later becomes a bee simply because of such remembrance. Similarly, if the conditioned souls somehow or other think of Krishna, who is *sat-chit-ananda-vigraha* [the eternal form of bliss and knowledge], they will become free from their sins. Whether thinking of Him as their worshipable Lord or as an enemy, because of constantly thinking of Him, they will regain their spiritual bodies. Many, many persons have attained liberation simply by thinking of Krishna with great attention and giving up sinful activities. This great attention may be due to lusty desires, inimical feelings, fear, affection, or devotional service..." [1]

The meaning of this verse is that it is the nature of the soul to love and be loved, and to offer service to the Supreme Soul. When the soul is engaged in its constitutional position and activities, naturally the effects of material life, such as karma, begin to evaporate and disappear. As a person progresses in this way, he or she begins to attain the perception of their real spiritual identity. And this is easily done simply by arranging one's life so that they can somehow think of Krishna all the time or as much as possible. This is the purpose of bhakti-yoga.

"O my Lord, master of all mystic yoga, this is the explanation of the yogic process spoken of by Lord Brahma [Hiranyagarbha], who is self-realized. At the time of death, all yogis give up their material body with full detachment simply by placing their minds at Your lotus feet. That is the perfection of yoga." [2]

If we are detached from this body, and are thinking of Krishna and His pastimes, qualities, characteristics, etc., when you leave your physical form, then we will naturally go to Lord Krishna's spiritual abode. But for materialists who have made no such endeavor, they will be thinking of material and bodily or sensual activities. Even if we leave this material body but then begin to hanker for the taste of some food, like chocolate or something, how can you enjoy the taste of such a thing without a material body? Therefore, such desires will bring us back into another material body in order to continue to pursue our material desires. But a person who brings his or her attention to Krishna throughout the day is already liberated, even while still existing in their material body. That is because their consciousness is being spiritualized, and enters into the same frequency as the spiritual dimension. One's devotion to God will automatically bring a person to thinking of God, which brings one to the object of their meditation.

For this reason, an advanced devotee sees the Lord everywhere, both as the Lord as Supersoul in the heart of every living being, and as the many types of energies of the material manifestation, all of which is the creation of the Lord. Thus, he sees God everywhere and is never forgetful of the Lord. Such a soul who sees the Lord everywhere is never lost.

As stated in the *Isha Upanishad* (Mantras 6 & 7): "He who sees everything in relation to the Supreme Lord, who sees all entities as His parts and parcels, and who sees the Supreme Lord within everything, never hates anything nor any being. One who always sees all living entities as spiritual sparks, in quality one with the Lord, becomes a true knower of things. What, then, can be illusion or anxiety for him?"

Herein we can understand that if we see all living beings as spiritual parts of the Lord, in the same spiritual quality, then we will be aware of the Supreme in everything. This is called spiritual or Krishna consciousness. This consciousness is the essence of bhakti-yoga, especially when such an awareness is tinged with love and devotion, as related in the *Narada-bhakti-sutra* (Sutra 55): "Having obtained pure love of God, one looks only at the Lord, hears only about Him, and thinks only about Him." It is this love that brings the Lord to one's full attention in such a way as described herein.

## REACHING TRANCE OR SAMADHI IN BHAKTI-YOGA

This is the position of being in a meditative trance or *samadhi* in bhakti-yoga. It is not something that has to be done by a special arrangement. The bhakti-yogi does not have to be in a special physical position, sitting posture or location, or engage in *pranayama* and so on, but only awakens his awareness of God everywhere.

This is expressed by Sri Havir to King Nimi in the *Srimad-Bhagavatam* (11.2.41): "A devotee should not see anything as being separate from the Supreme Personality of Godhead, Krishna. Ether, fire, air, water, earth, the sun and other luminaries, all living beings, the directions, trees and other plants, the rivers and oceans–whatever a devotee experiences he should consider to be an expansion of Krishna. Thus seeing everything that exists within creation as the body of the Supreme Lord, Hari, the devotee should offer his sincere respects to the entire expansion of the Lord's body." He continues to say (11.2.45), "The most advanced devotee sees within everything the soul of all souls, the Supreme Personality of Godhead, Sri Krishna. Consequently he sees everything in relation to the Supreme Lord and understands that everything that exists is eternally situated within the Lord."

Quite honestly, anyone who has this vision and maintains it is already residing in the spiritual world. It is only a matter of time before he automatically attains the supreme abode. As Lord Krishna describes in *Bhagavad-gita* (6.30): "For one who sees Me everywhere and sees everything in Me, I am never lost, nor is he ever lost to Me." In this way, this love not only draws us closer to God, but also draws God closer to us. Then the reciprocation and connection between ourselves and the Lord becomes all the more intense and blissful.

This is related by Sri Caitanya Mahaprabhu in His talk with Ramananda Raya, in which He said, "My dear Raya, you are an advanced devotee and are always filled with ecstatic love for Radha and Krishna. Therefore whatever you see–anywhere and everywhere–simply awakens your Krishna consciousness."

Furthermore, it is said by Sri Krishna Himself, "A highly elevated devotee can bind Me, the Supreme Personality of Godhead, in his heart by love. Wherever he looks, he sees Me and nothing else. Hari, the Supreme Personality of Godhead, who destroys everything inauspicious for His devotees, does not leave the hearts of His devotees even if they remember Him and chant about Him inattentively. This is because the rope of love always binds the Lord within the devotees' hearts. Such devotees should be accepted as most elevated." [3]

This is expressed a little differently by Sri Caitanya Mahaprabhu in His talk with Ramananda Raya as follows, "The *maha-bhagavata*, the advanced devotee, certainly sees everything mobile and immobile, but he does not exactly see their forms. Rather, everywhere he immediately sees manifest the form of the Supreme Lord." [4]

In this way, the progressed devotee does not merely see the world of forms, but sees the reality behind all these forms, which is the Supreme Creator. Therefore, we should cultivate the vision that everything we see is an expansion of the energies of the Lord, and that it is the Lord Himself who is sporting in the creation and annihilation of the material manifestation. We should be detached, knowing that nothing belongs to us, but we are only utilizing what we need in our own process of self-realization, and developing our service to the Supreme. If we can continue to progress in this process of bhakti-yoga like this, then we also will attain the vision of the advanced devotees. Then we will see further that we are also parts and parcels of the Supreme, engaged in offering loving service to the Lord. When this happens, there is no difference between what we do with our body and the intention and love we have in our soul. At that time we are no longer interested in engaging in activities merely to satisfy our mind and senses. We can see the futility of it, and are only interested in being fulfilled on the spiritual level. Being fixed in the service and awareness of God, such a person is in *samadhi*, and he becomes a *jivan-mukta*, a *jiva* soul who is already liberated while still in this material body.

# Chapter Twenty

## ATTAINING ONENESS WITH GOD ON THE PATH OF BHAKTI-YOGA

Such a person who has the constant awareness and vision that we have been discussing, is a devotee who attains oneness with God on the path of bhakti-yoga. He or she is absorbed in God and thinks of how to please the Lord or help carry out the wishes that God has for humanity. Then that yogi is considered spiritually awakened.

Just as a dream is real only as long as the dream continues, when we awake, we are free from the dream and come back into reality. Similarly, when we are free from material consciousness and rise to spiritual awareness, and work on that level, then there is no difference between what we do with our bodies and our soul. Everything is engaged in bhakti-yoga, the process of spiritual realization and performing our devotional service to the Supreme Lord. This is also when the subtle body of mind, intelligence and false ego, the false conception of who we are and the storehouse of our sensual desires, become evaporated by our spiritual development. Then there is no difference between our body and soul in our performance of our service to God. In fact, our bodies become spiritually surcharged because of the effects of our spiritual activities. This is another aspect of spiritual oneness on the path of bhakti. It is not that we give up our individuality and merge our identity or our souls into the great Brahman effulgence or into the body of the Supreme. No. Though maintaining our individuality, we no longer have separate interests from those of the Lord. It is that our interests are the same as Krishna's interests. Our activities are in line with the interests and wishes of Krishna's. And in this way, we are absorbed with God and act on the spiritual frequency as the Lord. That is the oneness or nonduality as found in bhakti-yoga.

This is summarized in the *Srimad-Bhagavatam* (4.22.27): "When a person becomes devoid of all material desires, liberated from all material qualities, he transcends distinctions between actions executed externally [with the body] and internally [as the soul]. At that time the difference between the soul and the Supersoul, which is existing before our self-realization, is annihilated. When a dream is over, there is no longer a distinction between the dream and the dreamer."

This is when a person could be said to be fully conscious, fully aware of his or her identity and connection with the Supreme. He is filled with love, joy and wonder or amazement, even to the point wherein the yogi is no longer concerned for his own existence, and is mainly focused on seeing God wherever he looks and in whatever he does. In such absorption of God, the devotee's voice may get choked, his eyes fill with tears, and his words may become slow. He becomes filled with unlimited bliss. Any non-devotee will not understand what is happening to him. But the devotee feels the constant presence of the Lord, and that is all that the devotee wants. Whatever it takes to keep this feeling, that is what he wants. He simply wants to do whatever service the Lord or the spiritual master wants him to do. For him, no obligation is left to be performed, no duty is left unaccomplished, and there is nothing more to be known. It is only the open road toward deeper levels of exchange with the Supreme and higher forms of bliss.

As Lord Krishna very simply explains in *Bhagavad-gita* (6.31), "The yogi that knows I and the Supersoul within all creatures are one, worships Me and remains always in Me in all circumstances."

This is why an expert devotee will mold his life so that he always remembers the Lord. While performing all kinds of duties for this life or the next, somehow he constantly remembers the Lord's names, qualities, pastimes, etc. Thus, he goes through life very differently than the common materialist who focuses mainly on his own goals, his own desires and wants, and how to achieve them. But a devotee is so absorbed in the bliss he gets from his connection with God that he is not interested in the grand prizes, possessions, riches, or fame that ordinary men desire. This is also pointed out in the *Srimad-Bhagavatam* (10.16.37), wherein the wives of Kaliya say in their prayers to Lord Krishna, "Those who have attained the dust of Your lotus feet never hanker for the kingship of heaven, limitless sovereignty, the position of Brahma, or rulership over the earth. They are not interested even in the performance of yoga or in liberation itself."

This is also why a devotee, especially one who has by now experienced a taste for his or her service to Krishna, or the reciprocation he has received from the Lord, sees nothing more important than Krishna. It is the Lord who he wants to serve, it is Krishna who he wants to experience, it is Krishna and His abode the devotee wants to attain. There is nothing more important and more joyful than this.

Even when a devotee enters a dangerous situation, or experiences some kind of loss, he accepts it as the mercy of the Lord because it is a good opportunity to think of the Lord very sincerely, in great earnest, and with undiverted attention. It is actually a test, a preparation in how to think of the Lord at the time of death. All fear is but the reflection of the ultimate fear, which is death. But if we can prepare for that and be able to think of the Lord at any time danger approaches, this practice will prepare us for thinking of the Lord even at the time when we leave this body. When we have conquered death in this manner, there is nothing left for us to be afraid of, knowing that Krishna will protect us. Thus, we may even welcome death.

Therefore, no material condition can stop the flow of devotional service to the Supreme Lord from the pure devotee. This is the example we should follow. In any circumstance, both good or bad, positive or negative, we can continue our loving thoughts of the Lord. After all, as it is said, any material obstacle or reversal in life is but a temporary illusion. So even if such an illusion should arise, why should it distract us from our natural spiritual position? We have to be able to discern between what is illusion and what is reality. The material condition is one of constant change, so that will continue around us for as long as we remain in this material world, or are affected by its nature of constant change. But the more we are firmly established in reality, which is the spiritual strata, then the freer we will be from identifying with the ever-transitioning material conditions.

A nice verse which relates this is in the *Bhagavatam* (3.29.12), which says, "Just as the water of the Ganges flows naturally down towards the ocean, such devotional ecstasy, uninterrupted by any material condition, flows toward the Supreme Lord."

Furthermore, in the mind of a person devoted to God, mental obstacles to our spiritual growth and evil cannot exist. Being sincerely absorbed in the Lord, as we have described herein, will gradually or rapidly obliterate the evil tendencies or bad habits that may be found there. Even Lord Krishna explains this point, "For him who constantly meditates upon My presence within all persons, the bad tendencies of rivalry, envy and abusiveness, along with false ego, are very quickly destroyed." [5]

Another verse points out that by absorbing ourselves in God, we can remain transcendental to the material changes that take place either within us or around us. "In this way, all the cowherd men, headed by Nanda Maharaja, enjoyed topics about the pastimes of Krishna and Balarama with great transcendental pleasure, and they could not even perceive material tribulations." [6]

Therefore, whatever problems that exist in our own mind, which is where they are perceived and stored anyway, cannot remain for long if we remain absorbed in Krishna.

## ABSORPTION IN GOD IS THE GOAL OF LIFE

During his or her lifetime, a pure devotee, or one who becomes purified, is always speaking of Krishna and engaging in His service. So as soon as he gives up his body, he immediately returns to the spiritual abode of Goloka Vrindavana where Krishna is personally present. He then meets Krishna directly. This is successful human life. [7]

This is how we become absorbed in God, in a constant meditation on the Supreme. Just as a man who puts on green glasses sees the whole world as green, even the whole universe will appear as a manifestation of the Supreme Being, Sri Krishna, of that person in whose heart is imbued with the presence of the Lord.

Such absorption in God is the highest achievement of human life, as even proclaimed by Lord Mahadeva, Shiva, when addressing the Lord in His form as Mohini, as found in the *Srimad-Bhagavatam* (8.12.6): "Pure devotees or great saintly persons who desire to achieve the highest goal in life and who are completely free from all material desires for sense gratification engage constantly in the transcendental service of Your lotus feet."

This goal of life, to see the Lord everywhere and in this way be absorbed in Him, was also specifically described by Prahlada Maharaja when he was trying to convince his materialistic and demoniac friends about what is the purpose of life when he said, "O sons of demons, in the same favorable way that one sees himself and takes care of himself, take to devotional service to satisfy Bhagavan Sri Krishna, the Supreme Personality of Godhead, who is present everywhere as the Supersoul of all living beings. Everyone... can revive his original, eternal spiritual life and exist forever simply by accepting the principles of bhakti-yoga. In this material world, to render service to the lotus feet of Govinda, the cause of all causes, and to see Him everywhere, is the only goal of life. This much alone is the ultimate goal of human life, as explained by all the revealed scriptures." [8]

**CHAPTER NOTES**
1. *Srimad-Bhagavatam* 7.1.28-30.
2. Ibid., 5.19.13.
3. *Caitanya-caritamrita,* Madhya-lila, 25.127-8 & *Bhagavatam* 11.2.55.
4. *Cc.* Madhya-lila, 8.274.
5. *Srimad-Bhagavatam* 11.29.15.
6. Ibid., 10.11.58.
7. *Caitanya-caritamrita,* Madhya-lila, 13.155, pur.
8. *Srimad-Bhagavatam* 7.7.53-55.

# CHAPTER TWENTY-ONE

# *Realizing the Highest Levels of Spiritual Knowledge*

When it comes to the realization or practical and personal perception of spiritual knowledge, there are various levels of realization that are possible. First is the understanding and then the perception of one's own spiritual identity as the spirit soul within the body, and that you are not the body. At this level, you can see that within the physical body, and deeper within the coverings of the subtle body, you are simply like a resident occupying this amazing but material vehicle. The body may change in so many ways, but you are the observer of the changes and not the changes themselves. You are above all that. You are the spark of consciousness that is eternal and transcends the birth, old age, disease and death that the body goes through. Nonetheless, the body is a great machine, a vehicle with the intelligence that can allow you to continue your spiritual development. Therefore, this opportunity should not be wasted. That is why yoga is necessary to peel away all the levels of illusion that affect our consciousness until the soul, our real identity, is revealed for us to directly perceive.

Of course, there are much more elementary levels of realizations as well, such as perceiving that you are not your mind. Or that you are not your thoughts, which come and go. Certain meditations are based on the idea of watching your thoughts come in, and then let them flow away while new ones again enter your awareness, while perceiving that they are not what determines who you are or what you must do. That you are more than your thoughts. People often think they are making great strides in their spiritual development by attaining such levels of realization. But if you continue, all such realizations gradually progress until you realize that you are not your mind or your body, and that you are actually the soul within.

After that is the realization of the Absolute Truth, which is of three levels. First is the realization of the Brahman effulgence, the great white light, the all-encompassing spiritual energy that pervades everything. This Brahman is made up of innumerable souls that float in that brilliant eternal existence of peace and bliss. Those yogis who follow the *advaita* or impersonalist philosophy and perfectly engage in the mystic yoga system can merge into that great Brahman.

Then there is the realization of the Paramatma, or the local expansion of the Supreme Being who appears as the Supersoul in everyone's heart, and who accompanies each and every soul on their journey through material existence. Those who practice the *dvaita* or personalist philosophy, meaning those who follow the premise that God is a person, and practice the raja or astanga yoga system with that objective, can engage in meditation in which they can realize the Paramatma within. With such a devout form of meditation on the realization of the Supersoul, they can achieve the Vaikuntha planets in the spiritual sky.

Then there is the realization of the Supreme as Bhagavan, the ultimate personality of the Supreme Being. This is also accomplished by following the *dvaita* or personalist philosophy and the yoga system that incorporates bhakti or devotion. In this process, we act in such a way that the illusion that affects us falls away so that we not only realize our own spiritual identity, but also the connection between ourselves and the Supreme Being, which is based on love and serving the Supreme in that loving mood. Then it is not merely an attempt made by our own spiritual strength to realize and experience the Divine, but it is our loving sentiment that also draws the Supreme Being closer to us, and who takes notice of our endeavors to reveal Himself to us, and also bring us back to His own abode. Otherwise, the doors to the spiritual world will hardly open all the way for us by our own initiative. We are hopelessly incapable of doing that, unless of course we have the assistance of the Supreme Being Himself, which is the whole point of following the process of bhakti-yoga.

Therefore, we may incorporate so many spiritual techniques

for raising our consciousness, or for gaining spiritual insight, but without adding or directly following the process of bhakti, it remains incomplete for attaining full realizations of our spiritual identity and our divine connection with the Supreme Reality, which ultimately is the Supreme Being, the most loving Lord Sri Krishna.

This is why Lord Krishna Himself explains in the *Srimad-Bhagavatam* (11.19.4-5), in His instructions to Uddhava, "That perfection which is produced by a small fraction of spiritual knowledge cannot be duplicated by performing austerities, visiting holy places, chanting silent prayers, giving in charity or engaging in other pious activities. Therefore, My dear Uddhava, through knowledge you should understand your actual self. Then, advancing by clear realization of Vedic knowledge, you should worship Me in the mood of loving devotion."

In other words, pious activities cannot do as much nor as quickly as using genuine spiritual knowledge to highlight our real identity. When this is mixed with the actual process for spiritualizing our consciousness, then it can awaken our perception of our natural, spiritual identity. But after that, as previously explained, by using the Vedic process in developing loving devotion to God, our connection with the Supreme Being will also become revealed.

So, who can actually reach the highest levels of understanding Vedanta? The bhakti-yogi who is attracted to understanding all aspects of the Supreme Being is easily able to understand all levels of realization that are described above. He or she wants to know his or her spiritual identity regarding the soul within the body, but also of the Supreme as Bhagavan, Paramatma and Brahman. However, we should remember that Brahman and Paramatma realizations are not complete by themselves. Therefore, a bhakti-yogi can delve deeply into any of these aspects of God, and realize all of them. It is not that such a yogi will limit himself, although he may certainly have a preference in the relations with the Supreme to which he is most attracted. This is not unlikely because Vedanta means the end of all knowledge, and the end means to arrive at realizing the ultimate source, the ultimate reality, which the Vedic literature establishes as Lord Sri Krishna, from whom comes many expansions or duplicates. So it is a matter of reviving a relationship with that ultimate person, or God. And the only yoga system that is centered around attaining such a relationship is bhakti-yoga.

Otherwise, what is the point of merely achieving *moksha*, liberation? That in itself is no ordinary thing, but after achieving it, then what? What's next? To float in an eternal ocean of effulgence, with little awareness of anything else? No activity, no emotions, no relations, no other beings to interact with? It is a supreme peace, bliss, and eternity, but no activity. And as the saying goes, variety is the spice of life. How can there be spiritual fulfillment with no variety? That is why bhakti-yogis are not often attracted to mere liberation, but are interested in establishing a loving relationship with the supreme reality, Lord Krishna.

The *Caitanya-caritamrita* (Adi-lila 7.146) clearly relates, "One's relationship with the Supreme Personality of Godhead, activities in terms of that relationship, and the ultimate goal of life [to develop love of God]–these three subjects are explained in every code of the Vedanta-sutra, for they form the culmination of the entire Vedanta philosophy."

Therefore, as the *Srimad-Bhagavatam* (1.2.12) continues this line of thinking, "The seriously inquisitive student or sage, well equipped with knowledge and detachment, realizes the Absolute Truth by rendering devotional service in terms of what he has heard from the Vedanta-shruti."

The *Bhagavatam* (11.3.40) takes this thought even further, "When one seriously engages in the devotional service of the Personality of Godhead, fixing the Lord's lotus feet within one's heart as the only goal of life, one can destroy the innumerable impure desires lodged within the heart as a result of one's previous fruitive work within the three modes of material nature. When the heart is thus purified, one can directly perceive both the Supreme Lord and one's self as transcendental entities. Thus one becomes perfect in spiritual understanding through direct experience, just as one can directly experience the sunshine through normal, healthy vision."

In this way, it becomes clear that it is through pure devotional service attained through bhakti-yoga which can give the highest levels of enlightenment and experience of the ultimate reality. This is also confirmed in a verse in the *Srimad-Bhagavatam* (11.26.30), wherein Lord Krishna explains, "What more remains to be accomplished for the perfect devotee after achieving devotional service unto Me, the Supreme Absolute Truth, whose qualities are innumerable and who am the embodiment of all ecstatic experience?"

The point is that once a seeker or yogi reaches this level of understanding and realization, there is nothing left to know, but only to proceed into deeper levels of such realization by direct perception and experience. Lord Krishna explains this in the *Bhagavad-gita* (9.2): "This knowledge is the king of education, the most secret of all secrets. It is the purest knowledge, and because it gives direct perception of the self by realization, it is the perfection of religion. It is everlasting, and it is joyfully performed."

Furthermore, Lord Krishna says in *Bhagavad-gita* (6.47), "And of all yogis, he who always abides in Me with great faith, worshiping Me in transcendental loving service, is most intimately united with Me in yoga and is the highest of all."

Or as the *Bhagavatam* (11.29.32) further explains, "When an inquisitive person comes to understand this knowledge, he has nothing further to know. After all, one who has drunk the most palatable nectar cannot remain thirsty."

Herein is a partial revelation that such a realization and experience leads us to taste the greatest happiness, when the soul, the individual, finally reconnects to its constitutional position and nature, like finding the home a person has been looking for all his life. But not just this life, but for many millions of lifetimes of wandering around this universe, through various planets and through innumerable species. And now, at long last, he reaches the ultimate platform of realization, peace, comfort, bliss, and connection with Divine Love. The hankering for this has motivated all of us to seek out our real nature for many lifetimes, and now upon attaining this knowledge we have found our real home.

The point is that once reaching this level of realization, and abiding in the consciousness which delivers such perception, then the frequency level in which our consciousness operates begins to blend with the same frequency of the spiritual dimension, and also attracts the Supreme Being to assist us in our entrance into the spiritual domain. As Lord Krishna explains in *Bhagavad-gita* (18.55), "One can understand the Supreme Personality as He is only by devotional service. And when one is in full consciousness of the Supreme Lord by such devotion, he can enter into the kingdom of God."

Lord Krishna goes on to say, "And whoever, at the time of death, quits his body, remembering Me alone, at once attains My nature. Of this there is no doubt. (*Bg*.8.5)... But those who worship Me with devotion, meditating on My transcendental form–to them I carry what they lack and preserve what they have. (*Bg*.9.22)... For one who worships Me, giving up all his activities unto Me and being devoted to Me without deviation, engaged in devotional service and always meditating upon Me, who has fixed his mind upon Me, O son of Pritha, for him I am the swift deliverer from the ocean of birth and death." (*Bg*.12.6-7)

So here we have Lord Krishna's promise that as we fix our mind upon Him, not only does our consciousness become more focused on the Supreme Reality, the Supreme Person, and the supreme destination, but because of our intentions and sincerity, which is really the essence of bhakti-yoga, He will also deliver us to the spiritual abode, in spite of whatever traits we lack. This is the rarest of opportunities and blessings that can be received by the engagement in bhakti-yoga.

So, what is the best process for reaching the highest stages of spiritual realization? This is related in numerous verses, but summarized as follows from the *Srimad-Bhagavatam* (11.14.26): "When a diseased eye is treated with medicinal ointment it gradually recovers its power to see. Similarly, as a conscious living entity cleanses himself of material contamination by hearing and chanting the pious narrations of My [Lord Krishna's] glories, he regains his ability to see Me, the Absolute Truth, in My subtle spiritual form."

Then in the *Srimad-Bhagavatam* (11.20.37) Lord Krishna concludes in this way: "Persons who seriously follow these methods of achieving Me, which I have personally taught, attain freedom from illusion, and upon reaching My personal abode they perfectly understand the Absolute Truth."

This means that as we understand the Supreme Reality through the process of bhakti-yoga, we can see the Supreme Being as we are cleared of impurities and become more spiritualized, to the point that when we reach the abode of the Lord, we are already able to understand the nature of God and our relationship with Him, and can fit into the spiritual world without difficulty. At that time, there is nothing left to be revealed, having attained the most complete level of spiritual realization.

# CHAPTER TWENTY-TWO

# *Attaining Your Bliss*
# *The Highest Happiness is in*
# *Spiritual Activities*

Spiritual realizations can bring to a person immense joy and bliss, but there is still a pleasure and happiness that is beyond religiosity, pious activities, or even direct spiritual understandings. It is the loving connection with the Supreme that is based on offering our devotional sentiments to the Lord in His form of Krishna, the God of love, and especially to both the Lord and His feminine potency Radharani. That is why many devotees are devoted to both, Radha and Krishna, the culmination of all loving expression and pastimes, and the emanation of all delightful affection and unbounded spiritual bliss.

However, we should ask why is this the case. Why is spiritual activity the basis of the highest happiness? This is fully explained in the Vedic literature, of which we will provide an overview here in this chapter.

The first thing to understand is that the nature of the soul itself is one of bliss. The more we become aware of our real spiritual identity as the soul within the material body, the happier will we be. The soul is a different substance than the material body, and its natural disposition is to be blissful. This is why we are always looking for happiness and fun while living in this material world. The point is that misery exists only within the illusion, the wrong aim of life, the wrong perception of who we are, while there is only growing bliss and happiness in the reality, which means the spiritual perception of who and what we are.

When the soul is covered by the gross and subtle bodies by

material association, the needs of the soul become interpreted as being the needs of the mind and senses. This turns into temporary or flickering happiness, which then often leads to distress, or the desire for more, or the lamentation for what we have lost. Distress and anxiety become the normal condition in material existence. But when the miseries are reduced, we feel we are happy. And that is mostly what material happiness is, the tingling sensation given to the senses which is interpreted as pleasure by the mind, or a temporary forgetfulness of the suffering we are forced to endure. But when the soul is truly revealed for what it is, and we become fully aware of our real identity, then the transitory nature of distress and happiness ceases as we enter deeper into constant bliss on the spiritual level.

The complete composition of the soul is explained in the *Sri Caitanya-Shiksamrita* (p.179) as follows: "From the *sandhini-shakti* arises the spiritual body, from the *samvit-shakti* arises [the eternal] knowledge and will, and from the *hladini-shakti* comes bliss. When these three energies combine in the soul, the soul manifests completely. The soul's body is a particle of spirit of the *sandhini-shakti*, the soul's will is a particle of *samvit-shakti*, and the soul's bliss is a very small portion of the *hladini-shakti*. This is the true identity of the soul, or his *dharma*."

In this way, bliss, love and attraction to the most lovable object, which is the Lord, is the inherent nature of the soul, our real identity. This is why the motivation and search for love, for happiness, and for attaining God, or the pursuit for understanding the mysteries of life, is part of the never-ending quest for any individual in this material world. Therefore, we are all the same in our deepest purpose in this life. But this is the primary purpose of life, to understand our spiritual identity.

As Lord Krishna says in *Bhagavad-gita* (3.17), "One who is, however, taking pleasure in the self, who is illumined in the self, who rejoices in and is satisfied with the self only, fully satiated–for him there is no duty." In other words, because he has fulfilled the purpose of life, there is nothing else to accomplish.

Now when we combine those energies of the soul with the Supreme Soul, this brings the greatest ecstasy. This is why it is recommended for the Krishna *bhakta* or devotee to reside in a holy place like Mathura or Mayapur, worship the Deity of the Lord, study and hear the *Srimad-Bhagavatam*, serve and associate with the devotees, and chant the holy names of the Lord, especially as found in the Hare Krishna *maha-mantra*, because by combining the soul with these processes is so potent, that even a little attachment to them can arouse devotional ecstasy even in a beginner. [1] Why? Because it connects the soul with the Supreme Being through these devotional activities. All kinds of happiness as found in other sources automatically follow the pure devotee.

In fact, for a devotee who delves deeply into the practice of devotional service and begins to feel a taste for it, can also reach the feeling of ecstasy in such activity. This is also related in the *Narada-Bhakti-Sutra* (6), "One who understands perfectly the process of devotional service in love of Godhead becomes intoxicated in its discharge. Sometimes he becomes stunned in ecstasy and thus enjoys his whole self, being engaged in the service of the Supreme Self."

However, this taste is increased when we perform such devotion with the right attitude of loving service. This means to follow the service attitude of those who have already attained a relationship with Sri Krishna in Vrindavana, like those who are the Lord's associates in Vrindavana, as described in the *Bhagavatam* and other revealed scriptures. This means to first follow the basic principles of our *sadhana* or practice of bhakti-yoga, and then to further follow in the mood of the residents of Vraja, or Vrindavana. Then we can also enter into the joy of such loving service to the Supreme Beloved. This is where the highest bliss can be relished.

This is further described in the *Caitanya-caritamrita* (Adi-lila 6. 44-47): "The conception of servitude to Sri Krishna generates such an ocean of joy in the soul that even the joy of oneness with the Absolute, if multiplied ten million times, could not compare to a drop of it. He [meaning Sri Advaita Acharya] says, 'Nityananda and I are servants of Lord Caitanya.' Nowhere else is there such joy as that tasted in this emotion of servitude. The most beloved goddess of fortune resides on the chest of Sri Krishna, yet she too, earnestly praying, begs for the joy of service at His feet. All the associates of Lord Krishna, such as Brahma, Shiva, Narada, Shuka, and Sanatana, are very much pleased in the sentiment of servitude."

Let us remember that being a servant of the Supreme Lord is so auspicious and blissful that even Lord Krishna Himself descended as Lord Caitanya to accept the emotions of His own devotee. He set the example of how to enter into the devotional mood and service attitude by which a bhakti-yogi can attain the ecstasy of devotional service to the Supreme, who is the center of all such forms of happiness.

In this way, there is no higher bliss than this. It is because this loving mentality invokes the pleasure of the Lord, which, the Lord being the root of each individual soul, heightens the pleasure of the soul, like a spiritual competition. This means that the more pleased the Lord becomes, the more joy is experienced by the devotee, who then hankers to dive even more deeply into the loving mood which is then displayed by his or her service.

The *Narada-Bhakti-Sutra* (60) explains that bhakti is the embodiment of peace and supreme ecstasy. Why? Because it is the constitutional nature of the soul. It is what the soul desires to attain. Thus, why would a person not want to dive into this as deeply as possible when one can become completely satisfied through such a process? Even Shri Yamunacharya says in his *Stotra-ratna* (43), "By serving You [the Supreme Lord] constantly, one is freed from all material desires and is completely pacified. When shall I engage as Your permanent eternal servant and always feel joyful to have such a fitting master?"

So this is basically the question in this verse, that if this is how to attain the highest bliss, then what are we waiting for? This is the purpose of the path of bhakti-yoga, and is also the natural result of attaining love of God.

Even simply praying to the Lord or discussing and remembering His characteristics in a serving attitude can bring the yogi into unlimited bliss that knows no bounds. As it is said, "Unalloyed devotees, who have no desire other than to serve the Lord, worship Him in full surrender and always hear and chant [or talk] about His activities, which are most wonderful and auspicious. Thus, they always merge in an ocean of transcendental bliss...Thus, I pray to that Supreme Personality of Godhead, who is eternally existing, who is invisible, who is the Lord of all great personalities, such as Brahma, and who is available only by transcendental bhakti-yoga." [2]

In fact, this is one of the purposes of the Supreme Lord, to come into this world and exhibit pastimes that attract not only the devotees, but also the common persons to draw them closer to Him and to the desire to go to their real home in the spiritual world. Plus, this is not merely for the time in which Lord Krishna or any of His expansions appeared, but also for the future of Kali-yuga, which is why such pastimes were recorded and described in sacred texts like the *Srimad-Bhagavatam*, as further explained, "To show causeless mercy to the devotees who would take birth in the future in this age of Kali, the Supreme Personality of Godhead, Krishna, acted in such a way that simply by remembering Him one will be freed from all the lamentation and unhappiness of material existence. Simply by receiving the glories of the Lord through purified transcendental ears, the devotees of the Lord are immediately freed from strong material desires and engagement in fruitive activities." [3]

As it is further explained in this line of thinking in the *Caitanya-caritamrita* (Antya-lila, 5.47), "Tasting the transcendental, effulgent, sweetly ecstatic love of Krishna, such a person can enjoy life twenty-four hours a day in the transcendental bliss of the sweetness of Krishna's pastimes."

Sri Krishna explains the significance of this kind of spiritual happiness and the means to attain it to His devotee Uddhava: "O learned Uddhava, those who fix their consciousness on Me, giving up all material desires, share with Me a happiness that cannot possibly be experienced by those engaged in sense gratification. One who does not desire anything within this material world, who has achieved peace by controlling his senses, whose consciousness is equal in all conditions, and whose mind is completely satisfied in Me finds only happiness wherever he goes." [4]

It is this happiness and inner spiritual bliss that becomes the goal of all those who begin to have even a glimpse of that ecstasy, which is attained by full absorption in the loving mood of serving the Supreme. This means that when a person actually feels this inner ecstasy, he or she loses interest in many of the issues or attractions or temptations that used to be very important to them, whether it be sports, politics, economics, current events, etc. Such a person gives up all kinds of materialistic distractions and begins to focus more and more steadily on that bliss and whatever it takes to maintain it, which automatically outweighs all other forms of entertainment and mental preoccupations that a person had previously found of interest.

In this way, devotees bathe themselves in devotional service in order to be relieved from the various tribulations of material existence. By doing this, the devotees enjoy supreme bliss, and liberation personified comes to serve them by delivering them from further rounds of material existence. But the devotees do not even care for this, even when it is offered by the Supreme Lord Himself, because liberation is not very significant to the devotee. Having attained the Lord's transcendental loving service, they feel they have attained everything they could possibly want, and have transcended all material desires. [5]

This is further described, "A person fixed in the devotional service of the Supreme Lord, Hari, the Lord of the highest auspiciousness, swims in the ocean of nectar. For him what is the use of the water in small ditches?" [6] Similarly, material happiness is like a temporary dream, or the happiness found in small ditches, while real happiness is found in the soul in the engagement of its natural condition of service to the Supreme, which is considered like an ocean of nectar. [7]

Not only are material pleasures rendered insignificant by the taste of the devotional ecstasy, but so is the pleasure of mystic perfections. As stated in the *Bhagavatam* (9.4.25), "Those who are saturated with the transcendental happiness of rendering service to the Supreme Personality of Godhead are uninterested even in the achievements of great mystics, for such achievements do not enhance the transcendental bliss felt by a devotee who always thinks of Krishna within the core of His heart."

This is why devotees do not accept any other process but the path of bhakti-yoga, devotional service. Even though the path of bhakti is explained to varying degrees throughout the Vedic literature, because devotees can relish such bliss, they are not interested in the processes of mental speculation, jnana-yoga, mystic yoga, unnecessary austerity, or even pious rituals. [8]

## SYMPTOMS OF ECSTATIC EMOTIONS

So how does transcendental love develop into ecstasy? To get a better understanding of how this works, this is described by Srila A. C. Bhaktivedanta Swami Prabhupada in his book *Teachings of Lord Caitanya* (p.33): "There are three stages of devotional service: The first is the beginning stage of cultivation, the second is the realization of service, and the third, the supreme stage, is the attainment of love of Godhead. There are nine different methods of cultivating devotional service–such as hearing, chanting, remembering, etc.–and all these processes are employed in the first stage. If one is engaged in chanting and hearing with devotion and faith, his material misgivings gradually become vanquished. As his faith in devotional service gradually increases, he becomes assured of a higher perfectional position. In this way one can become firmly fixed in devotion, increase his taste for it, become attached and feel ecstasy. This ecstasy occurs in the preliminary stage of love of Godhead. Attainment of ecstasy is produced by execution of devotional service. When one continues the process of hearing and chanting, attachment grows and assumes the name of love of Godhead.

"When one attains the third stage of transcendental love of God, there occur further developments known as transcendental affection, emotion, ecstasy, and extreme and intense attachment. These are technically known by the terms *raga*, *anuraga*, *bhava* and *mahabhava*. The progress from one stage to another can be compared to the thickening of sugar candy juice. In the first stage sugar candy juice is like a thin liquid. When, by evaporation, it becomes thicker and thicker, it turns into molasses. Finally it turns into granules and becomes sugar, rock candy and so on. Just as liquid sugar juice progresses from one stage to another, similarly transcendental love for the Supreme Lord develops by stages."

As a devotee begins to dive deeply into the feelings of love of God, which is the goal of the path of bhakti, it can be like a strong intoxicant. "The fruit of love of Godhead distributed by Caitanya Mahaprabhu is such a great intoxicant that anyone who eats it, filling his belly, immediately becomes maddened by it, and automatically he chants, dances, laughs and enjoys." [9] In this way, it is like staying high forever, but in a natural and spiritual high that it actually the ecstatic constitutional position of the soul.

Additional ecstatic symptoms are also described, "When one's transcendental loving service to the Lord is actually awakened, it generates transformations in the body such as perspiration, trembling, throbbing of the heart, faltering of the voice, and tears in the eyes." [10]

Someone absorbed in such ecstasy may indeed seem like a crazy person. Therefore, because others may not understand such symptoms, although advanced devotees may feel great ecstasy in their loving mood and attachment to the Lord, these symptoms are often curbed and prevented from being exhibited, which is part of the etiquette among other devotees, and not show such symptoms except only in the company of other advanced devotees. Otherwise such symptoms are kept internally.

One quality of such bliss is that all differences between devotees on this level of bhakti become inconsequential or meaningless. The bliss from our bhakti or devotion to the Supreme becomes the main focus, the great equalizer, and we help each other maintain that attitude. The more devotees gather in the same mentality and bliss, the more powerful it becomes.

As it is stated, "Love for Krishna has this one unique effect: it imbues superiors, equals and inferiors with the spirit of service to Lord Krishna." [11] This means that all differences become nullified when we become absorbed in the spiritual ecstasy of loving service to the Lord. This also means that when we are engaged in our meditation, or our *japa*, or other devotional activities and are still not feeling the right connection with it and the higher energy that comes from the association of Lord Krishna, we have to adjust our attitude or mindset, and our cooperation with other bhaktas.

To make the right connection, we have to be in the mood of servitude, which means that whatever actions I am performing, I am doing them to serve the higher cause, the higher purpose, for the pleasure of the Supreme Being. Then we can begin to feel that we are all connected in the right way, like a light bulb connected in the right way through the power lines to the power house, which provides the energy the light bulb needs to give its brilliance. When we are connected in the right way, through the attitude of servitude to the Supreme Soul, then the little *jiva* soul also becomes energized and enlightened and enlivened with the brilliance of spiritual knowledge and perception, and the bliss that naturally comes from the proper approach to the spiritual path. This paves the way for recognizing the spiritual unity between us all, and the means to attain the highest bliss in connection with the Supreme Lord.

## WHY THE EARLY VEDIC TEXTS OFTEN DO NOT DESCRIBE THIS BLISS

Each part of the Vedic *shastra* or literature has a specific purpose, and forms what could be described as a gradual ladder of development from one level of understanding to another. In this way it is a library that covers all aspects of the Absolute Truth. However, as we start from the early texts of the *Vedas*, and up through to the *Upanishads* and then on to the *Puranas*, the descriptions provide information that increasingly reveals the more personal aspects of the Supreme. And as the revelations become more personal, the relationship between the individual souls and the Supreme Soul also becomes more personal. Therefore, the bliss from personal loving relations with the Supreme may be alluded to in the earlier texts, but they become more prominent and descriptive as we develop into the later texts like the *Puranas*.

In the *Rig Veda*, the realm of Lord Vishnu is mentioned, which means such early texts only include the vision of the Vaikuntha planets in the spiritual sky, which are the residences of the different forms of Lord Vishnu. The Vaikuntha planets, where the residents worship in awe and reverence, do not have the more intimate pastimes of Vrndavana.

One prayer from the *Rig Veda* which refers to the abode of Lord Vishnu is this one:

*(om) tad vishno paramam padam*
*sada pashyanti surayaha*
*diviva chakshur-atatam*

> *tad vipraso vipanyavo*
> *jagrivam sah samindhate*
> *vishnor yat paramam padam*

"Just as those with ordinary vision see the sun's rays in the sky, so the wise and learned devotees always see the supreme abode of Lord Vishnu. Because those highly praiseworthy and spiritually awake brahmanas can see that abode, they can also reveal it to others." [*Rig Veda Samhita*]

Another of the most important prayers in the *Rig Veda* (10.90.1-16) which points the way to the realm of Lord Vishnu is the Purusha Sukta, which is a most commonly used Vedic Sanskrit hymn. It is recited in many Vedic rituals and ceremonies. It is often used during the worship of the Deity of Vishnu or Narayana in the temple, installation and fire ceremonies, or during the daily recitation of Sanskrit literature, or for one's meditation.

The *Purusha Sukta* also appears in the *Taittiriya Aranyaka* (3.12,13), the *Vajasaneyi Samhita* (31.1-6), the *Sama Veda Samhita* (6.4), and the *Atharva Veda Samhita* (19.6). An explanation of parts of it can also be found in the *Shatapatha Brahmana*, the *Taittiriya Brahmana*, and the *Shvetashvatara Upanishad*, and in the *Mahabharata* (Mokshadharma Parva 351 and 352). The *Mudgalopanishad* gives a nice summary of the entire Purusha Sukta. However, the contents of the Sukta have been elaborated in the most understandable way in the *Bhagavata Purana* (2.5.35 to 2.6.1-29).

The Purusha Sukta is a rather difficult text to explain in a modern way. This is primarily because of the archaic language that cannot always lend itself to interpretations based on the classical Sanskrit, and many of the words can be taken in several different ways, both literal and symbolic.

In any case, the emphasis of these early Vedic texts is twofold: to outline the rituals and use the hymns whereby we address the different gods who can supply the blessings for our material needs, and the means to attain *moksha*, or liberation, which is often mentioned as attaining freedom from further rounds of birth and death. But this liberation usually means entering into the Brahman effulgence or into the Vaikuntha planets which float in the Brahman.

Such texts may know of the abode of Lord Krishna, but they do not describe the blissful *lilas* or pastimes that go on there.

When we reach the *Upanishads*, they generally refer to the Absolute in an impersonal way, but they also begin to establish that the Supreme Reality has form, or, in other words, is a person, and that there is a divine abode, although the details of it are not always clearly provided. So as we go through the Vedic texts, we get clearer and clearer views of the nature of the Supreme Being.

The *Isa Upanishad* in particular indicates that the Supreme Absolute is both impersonal and personal. Other *Upanishads* describe the Absolute as, "He who created the worlds," or, "Who is luminous like the sun," "beyond darkness," "the eternal among eternals," etc. In fact, the basic method used in most *Upanishads*, as explained in the *Hayasirsa Pancharatra*, is to first present the Absolute Reality in an impersonal way and then present the personal aspects.

Yet, as we study the *Upanishads*, there are numerous references that go on to describe very clearly the spiritual nature and characteristics of the Supreme. The *GopalaTapani Upanishad* from the *Atharva Veda* has numerous verses which explain the nature of the Absolute Truth, such as the following verse (1.22): "Sri Krishna is that Supreme Divinity, the Paramount Eternal Reality among all other sentient beings, and the fountain-source of consciousness to all conscious beings. He is the only reality without a second, but as the Supersoul He dwells in the cave of the hearts of all beings and rewards them in accordance with their respective actions in life. Those men of intuitive wisdom who serve Him with loving devotion surely attain the summum bonum, supreme goal of life. Whereas those who do not do so never gain this highest beautitude of their lives."

Another verse from the *GopalaTapani Upanishad* (2.23) that further explains the nature of the Supreme is this one: "Sri Krishna has got no birth and no old age, He is always in His adolescence without any change. He is ever most effulgently shining so gloriously more than the sun. He is fond of remaining with the divine cows of Goloka Vrindavana. He is eternally fond of being with the *gopas*, cowherd boys, as He feels pleasure tending the cows. He is the very object of the *Vedas*, He as the Supersoul ever dwells in the heart of every living being, and He is the only Sustainer of all. He is the beloved sweet-heart of you all."

Not only do the *Upanishads* provide explanations of the impersonal Brahman and personal Bhagavan realizations, but as we can see they also speak of the Paramatma (Supersoul or Lord in the heart) realization. Especially in the *Katha, Mundaka,* and the *Svetasvatara Upanishads*, one can find statements explaining that within the heart of every individual in every species of life reside both the individual soul and the Supersoul, the localized expansion of the Lord. It is described that they are like two birds sitting in the same tree of the body. The individual soul, which is called the *atma* or *jiva,* is engrossed in using the body to taste the fruits of various activities that result in pleasure and pain. The Supersoul is simply witnessing the activities of the *jiva*. If, however, the *jiva* begins to tire of these constant ups and downs of material life and then looks toward his friend next to him, the Supersoul, and seeks His help, the *jiva* soul can be relieved of all anxieties and regain his spiritual freedom. This freedom is the spiritual oneness shared by the *jivatma* and Paramatma when the *jiva* enters into the spiritual atmosphere by submitting to the will of the Paramatma. This is achieved by the practice of yoga and by being guided by a proper spiritual master. It is not said that the individual soul loses his individuality, but both the *jiva* and Paramatma remain individuals.

In any case, the *Upanishads* present a much clearer approach to understanding the ultimate reality than the four primary *Vedas.*

However, going further, there is also the *Krishna Upanishad* that directly reveals that the most divine form of bliss dwells in the supremacy of love of Lord Krishna. It elaborates that when Lord Krishna descended to Earth in Braja Mandala, Vrindavana, the other eternal and divine personalities and powers also came with Him in order to serve Him and taste the sweetness of that divine love.

The *GopalaTapani Upanishad* goes much further in explaining things in this direction. It has only two chapters with a total of 172 verses. In the first chapter it explains that Lord Krishna is the absolute bliss. He is the Supreme God and the embodiment of eternal life, knowledge and bliss. This is elaborated throughout the chapter. Chapter Two explains how Lord Krishna is the supreme and most beautiful form of God. No other god or portion of this material creation can compare to His beauty. Therefore, it is recommended that we need to remember and adore Him, by which we can experience His divine love, which is like an ocean of nectar.

It is important to point out that the Sanskrit term for the experience of Krishna's divine love is *rasa*. It is the *Bhagavata Purana* [*Srimad-Bhagavatam*] that begins to explain the *rasa-lila* or bliss pastimes of Lord Krishna with His numerous associates. The word *rasa* is never used in connection with Lord Vishnu, Lord Shiva, Goddess Durga, or any of the other Vedic personalities in any of the *Upanishads*. That is because, though we may engage in respectful worship to these Divinities, the pleasure pastimes wherein there is such a deep exchange of divine bliss and love is not to be found in anyone but Lord Krishna. Even the expansions of Lord Krishna, such as Lord Vishnu or Lord Rama, may be forms of unlimited bliss, but the deep exchanges of loving bliss with Them do not have the potential that is found within Lord Krishna. Therefore, the conclusion is that Lord Krishna is the Supreme Personality in which is found all other forms of Divinity, and from whom comes the Absolute Truth and Absolute loving bliss.

The *Radhika Upanishad* explains this a little further. Therein it is described that only within Lord Krishna is there the *hladini* power, which is the pleasure or bliss potency. The other forms of the Lord are but parts or expansions of the Lord, and although They may be the same in power, They are lacking in the level of bliss potency that is found within Lord Krishna. This means that the supreme sweetness in loving exchanges is manifested from Lord Krishna. In this way, you have the sweet, sweeter and sweetest levels of loving bliss established in the different levels of the spiritual reality, until it culminates from the Brahman and to Vaikuntha on up to Goloka Vrindavana, the spiritual abode of Lord Krishna. Or from the *brahmajyoti* to the Vishnu forms up to the supremacy of Sri Krishna. This is what is established by fully understanding the purport of the *Upanishads*.

Herein we find the assortment of information that can be found in the main *Upanishads*. For the most part, except for the more specialized and detailed *Upanishads* that were referred to at the end, they only briefly indicate the personal traits of the Supreme Personality and the Divinity of Krishna and His abode. Mostly they provide knowledge only up to the Brahman or Vaikuntha, not beyond. They express the non-material, spiritual nature of God, but do not know or present much information on the personality and pastimes of the Supreme Being. The end or conclusive result of knowledge in the *Upanishads* is to attain liberation from material existence. But what such liberation consists of is often left out. So, information on the pastimes and nature of the abode of God and the spiritual domain, namely Goloka Vrindavana, is generally absent.

This is the case with most all of the *Shruti* texts, which consist of the four *Vedas*, the *Brahmanas, Aranyakas*, and *Upanishads*. Once you get beyond the rituals and methods for acquiring material needs by worship of the Vedic gods, the *Shruti* texts primarily contain knowledge of the futility of material existence, the temporary nature of the material creation, the bondage of the *jiva* souls in this existence of birth and death, and the spiritual nature of the individual and the Supreme Being. In parts, they may also describe that the goal of life is liberation from this material manifestation and the need to return to spiritual existence through the understanding of karma, spiritual knowledge, renunciation, and devotion to God (bhakti). However, they are unaware of much beyond this, or at least the finer details. They do not deliver information about the bliss of spiritual activities and the pastimes of Goloka Vrindavana, the most intimate and confidential abode of the Lord who is a spiritual being, a personality. Because of this basic deficiency, additional information is supplied elsewhere, which must be sought and understood. As we can see, this is a progressive ladder of education, in which case one should not stop with the *Upanishads*.

From here we go to the *Puranas*, which explain much more about Goloka and Radha-Krishna, such as in the *Skanda, Padma, Brahma, Brahmananda, Narada, Brahma-Vaivarta Puranas,* and the *Devi Bhagavatam,* as well as the *Narada Pancharatra* and the *Brahma Samhita*. Then there is also the *Vishnu Purana* which has many of the same pastimes as described in the *Bhagavata Purana*. The difference is that many of these *Puranas*, like the *Vishnu Purana,* describe the pastimes of Radha-Krishna and Their associates in Vrindavana like a reporter views news events and simply relates what happened. But the *Bhagavata Purana* describes it from the perspective of a participant in the pastimes. It is therein you can also enter into these pastimes if you have the proper mentality and, in this way, experience the bliss that they contain. This is the potency of the *Bhagavata Purana*, which is considered to be Srila Vyasadeva's own final commentary on all of the Vedic literature he had composed, as well as being the literary incarnation of the Supreme.

After Srila Vyasadeva composed the Vedic literature, he gave different portions of them to his disciples, each one handing the knowledge down to others. But when he wrote the *Bhagavata Purana*, he could see no one else who could contain the bliss within it. The only person who was worthy was Shukadev Goswami, who spoke the *Bhagavatam* to Maharaja Pariksit at the location of what is now called Shukratal. This was after Pariksit asked an assembly of sages what was best for him to do since he had only seven more days to live. Then Shukadeva entered the assembly of sages and was given the seat to explain and recite the *Bhagavata Purana* to Maharaja Pariksit. It was the *Bhagavatam* which could deliver a person to the spiritual abode in only seven days. But Shukadeva recited it in such a state of ecstasy that he could not even say the name of Radharani or he would go into a long deep trance. But he could not afford to do that because time was of the essence since Pariksit had only seven days left to live. If Shukadeva went into trance, it could be days before he came out of it. Therefore the full name of Radharani is not mentioned in the *Bhagavatam* but is only implied, where we can now insert the name ourselves to get a better view of the pastimes of Radha-Krishna.

This is why we can now illustrate the potency of bhakti-yoga in its full glory and relish the sweetness and ecstasy of the pastimes of Vraj, Goloka Vrindavana, and Radha-Krishna and Their associates by using the texts that we do. This is also how we learn to become one of the associates of Sri Sri Radha and Krishna, and be able to enter into Their pastimes. It is the *Bhagavatam* and special commentaries on it by the Vrindavana Goswamis, such as Rupa Goswami, Sanatana Goswami, Jiva Goswami, Krishnadas Kaviraja, Sri Caitanya Mahaprabhu, and others, that reveal the sweetness and intimate Divine Bliss of Radha-Krishna, and the supremacy of loving relations with Krishna above all other forms of God.

For a more detailed analysis and review of the Vedic literature and how they fit together and what information they provide, leading from the four *Vedas* up to the *Srimad-Bhagavatam*, you can see my book *Complete Review of the Vedic Literature*.

**CHAPTER NOTES**
1. *Nectar of Devotion*, p.110.
2. *Srimad-Bhagavatam* 8.3.20-21.
3. Ibid., 9.24.61-2.
4. Ibid., 11.14.12-13.
5. Ibid., 5.6.17.
6. Ibid., 6.22.22.
7. Ibid., 10.70.28.
8. *Caitanya-caritamrita,* Adi-lila, 13.65.
9. Ibid., 9.49.
10. Ibid., 8.27.
11. Ibid., 6.34-42.

# CHAPTER TWENTY-THREE

## *Attaining Realization of One's Spiritual Identity*

The level of realization of which we are dealing with here is more than realizing that you are not your material body, but that you are the soul within and far beyond the physical and subtle elements. Many are those yogis who have attained direct perception that they are the boundless and unlimited soul. This in itself is a level of liberation from material existence. But what we are discussing in this chapter is realizing your relationship with the Divine, Lord Krishna. How do we reach that level of realization?

First of all, through bhakti-yoga we begin to spiritualize ourselves, which includes surcharging both our body and our consciousness. This is done by first following the regulative principles of bhakti-yoga, taking instructions from the pure devotees, and engaging our mind and senses in the service of the devotees and Lord Sri Krishna. This means we begin to change the vibrational frequency in which we operate, including physically, mentally, intellectually, and spiritually. This also changes the frequency in which we can see things around us. The point to understand is that the more spiritual we become, the more we can see that which is spiritual. When that begins to happen, our whole state of being begins to change. Our body becomes spiritualized, and our consciousness begins to perceive the spiritual realm, allowing us to see or at least recognize the spiritual dimension all around us. When this happens, we enter a more advanced level of our practice of bhakti-yoga. This is when the external or superficial vision of the world subsides or even disappears, and an inward-looking vision arises.

This is partially explained by Prahlada Maharaja when he was addressing his friends when he said, "O my friends, O sons of demons, everyone, including you (the Yakshas and Rakshasas), the unintelligent shudras and cowherd men, the birds, the lower animals and the sinful entities, can revive your original, eternal spiritual life, and exist forever simply by accepting the principles of bhakti-yoga."[1]

In other words, no one is bereft of the opportunity to make spiritual advancement and reach the level of understanding their true spiritual identity, in which case they can live eternally in the spiritual world. However, the point is that it is by devotional service, bhakti-yoga, which uncovers the real nature, position and identity of the person or soul within the body.

As Lord Krishna Himself explains in *Srimad-Bhagavatam* (11.14.25), "Just as gold, when smelted in fire, gives up its impurities and returns to its pure brilliant state, similarly, the spirit soul, absorbed in the fire of bhakti-yoga, is purified of all contamination caused by previous fruitive activities and returns to its original position of serving Me in the spiritual world."

So far we have been discussing the means to uncover the identity of the soul, but that is not the only thing we want to do. As our mood of love and devotion to Lord Krishna continues to increase, He also begins to reveal more of Himself to us so that we not only understand His spiritual nature, but can also comprehend and perceive His glories and characteristics. Then we also begin to understand our connection with the Supreme Being, which is based on love.

That love is especially exhibited through our desire to increasingly associate with the Lord through His divine names, such as the Hare Krishna mantra. As we chant more purely, meaning without the offenses to the holy name, the name, which is Krishna's own vibrational form, will further awaken one's love for Krishna, and continue to propel one into that spiritual dimension. As Srila Bhaktivinoda Thakur has written in his song *Sharanagati*, "When the name is even slightly revealed, it shows me my own spiritual form and characteristics. It steals my mind and takes it to Krishna's side. When the name is fully revealed, it takes me directly to Vraja, where it shows me my personal role in the eternal pastimes."

This is the power of Krishna's names when we can chant purely. It takes us, by revelation, to see and act in the spiritual dimension in our own capacity in the eternal pastimes of Lord Krishna. By becoming spiritually purified through the chanting of the holy names of Krishna, one's natural spiritual mood or *rasa* becomes revealed, which is the natural attraction for the soul. Thereafter, the devotee can meditate on doing service in that mood. If we have been cultivating a particular mood in our loving service to Krishna, the service and role we play in those pastimes of the spiritual world can also begin to be revealed by the power of the holy names.

Upon leaving the material body, as the perfected devotee begins to enter Lord Krishna's abode of Goloka Vrindavana, the five relationships established in devotional service shine supreme, which are neutrality, servitude, friendship, parental affection, and conjugal love. After having come to the level of engaging in one of these moods, the devotee will develop or enter a transcendental spiritual body that suits that mood, and then enter the pastimes for which he or she has prepared, and upon which he has meditated.

To qualify yourself for this eligibility, you must practice the correct devotional mood and cultivate the relationship with Krishna that attracts you the most, and constantly drink in the nectarine sweetness of *krishna-nama*, the name of Krishna by associating with it through chanting, either congregationally in a group, or in personal meditation as in *japa*. The devotee should also meditate on the eightfold daily pastimes (*ashta-kaliya-lila*) of Lord Krishna. Then the devotee becomes increasingly familiar with Krishna's eternal pastimes, and through such meditation, along with the association of the holy names, the devotee can easily attain the *vastu-siddhi*, or his or her transcendental spiritual form. It is with that form that the devotee can enter into the eternal pastimes in which the devotee is meant to be engaged. By practicing this method of bhakti-yoga, one can remain transcendental to material existence until the end of his life, at which time he fully enters into the spiritual realm. [2]

However, as Srila Bhaktivinoda Thakur further explains, it is only upon attaining complete liberation from the body does this cultivation or meditation become completely pure. By cultivating the loving nature of the soul (*svadharma*), does the soul's spiritual identity (*chit-svarupa*) and its essential loving nature of pure ecstatic love, *prema*, gradually attain a completely pure state. [3]

How this ultimate stage of realizing one's spiritual form is attained through this devotional meditation is further explained by Srila Bhaktivinoda Thakur in his *Sri Harinama Cintamani* (pages 112-3). I will paraphrase it as follows:

In the *raganuga* or spontaneous stage of bhakti, our meditation is in the form of remembering the various pastimes of the Lord, which is called the *smarana* or remembering stage. At that time we should also recall the sentiments of the *gopis*, or the devotional mood of the eternal devotee to whom we are most attracted. This we can do by hearing the pastimes of Krishna as given in the *Srimad-Bhagavatam* and other scripture, and also hearing of the different devotees who interact with the Lord in the way to which we are most attracted. We should do that while remembering the eight phases of Krishna's daily pastimes, which is called the *ashta-kaliya lila*. Of course, at first we may not always remember these sentiments, but if we work at it and practice, we can more frequently remember the mood we are drawn towards in our service to and meditation on Krishna. By regular practice of such remembrance, we become steady. This is the *dharana* stage, meaning our mind becomes so focused on Krishna that we become automatically withdrawn from external or materialistic affairs.

When this develops into a fixed meditation, then it is the *dhyana* stage of bhakti-yoga. When *dhyana* becomes continual, it is the *anusmriti* stage. Beyond that we reach the *samadhi* stage of bhakti-yoga. This is when the bhakti-yogi has no interest in anything other than to be absorbed in remembering the pastimes of Lord Krishna. From *samadhi*, we enter into the *apana* stage of bhakti-yoga, which is the stage when we can perfectly invoke the devotional mood of our meditation.

Let me say here that the difference between other yogas and bhakti-yoga is the additional stages of meditation and spiritual development. Raja or Astanga-yoga has eight steps that the yogi takes in developing himself spiritually. These are as follows:

1. The *yamas*–the moral commandments or practice, which are the things to avoid.

2. *Niyamas*–the disciplines or things to do.

3. *Asanas*–postures for meditation as in hatha-yoga.

4. *Pranayama*–breath control and exercises.

5. *Pratyahara*–control of the senses and curbing the activity of the mind.

6. *Dharana*–concentrating on the object of meditation and becoming oblivious to everything else.

7. *Dhyana*–undisturbed flowing meditation and drawing the object of meditation toward you or you toward it.

8. *Samadhi*–becoming one with Infinity or the Supreme, the object of meditation.

However, in this form of yoga, you cannot proceed to the next stage before perfecting the step before it. But in bhakti-yoga, we can utilize all of these steps in meditation, but we do not always put much emphasis on the first four of the above steps. We can utilize all of them, but we start putting more emphasis on step five, controlling the senses and curbing the mind, which is done automatically when we focus our mind on the Supreme in His form of Krishna or any of His *avatars*, and in the service we perform for His pleasure. Practically, any manner which helps our focus on Krishna is considered a type of meditation. However, once we attain *raganuga-bhakti*–spontaneous love for Krishna achieved by practice of our *sadhana*–we go through the following steps in our meditation as described in the previous paragraphs, which include:

*Sravana*–hearing the pastimes and characteristics of the Lord.

*Smarana*–remembering the pastimes of the Lord.

*Dharana*–when the mind becomes so focused on remembering Krishna's pastimes that other activities and awareness of anything else become dim.

*Dhyana*–fixed meditation on Lord Krishna, His pastimes, qualities, characteristics, etc.

*Anusmriti*–continual or nonstop *dhyana*, or meditation on Lord Krishna.

*Samadhi*–when the bhakti-yogi has no interest other than remaining fixed in thought of Krishna. It is also at this stage when the soul can begin to understand his original constitutional position, and his eternal relationship with Krishna.

*Apana*–when the bhakti-yogi not only meditates on Krishna all the time, but also perceives and invokes his or her loving and devotional mood in his or her service to Krishna.

*Sampatti*–when the devotee can separate himself from all of his temporary designations and is steadily fixed in that original spiritual identity for which he yearns.

This is the difference in the meditation in bhakti-yoga. We are not interested in becoming one with the Infinite, but when we reach the stage of *apana*, we are always focused on our natural loving sentiment while engaged in the activities we perform for pleasing the Supreme. This is what takes us into the eternal pastimes on the spiritual planets. This is further explained by Srila Bhaktivinoda Thakur as follows:

Beyond *samadhi* is when we are no longer merely absorbed in our object of meditation, but now we become absorbed in the loving devotional sentiment toward our object of meditation, Krishna. At that stage we lose our awareness of being connected with the material body, and our spiritual identity becomes predominant. Intermittently, our eternal spiritual body manifests, and in that body we experience sublime ecstasy in rendering devotional service to Sri Sri Radha and Krishna in Vraj, Goloka Vrindavana. Gradually, the devotee experiences longer periods of being absorbed in Vraj in this way, even interacting with other spiritual beings or devotees in his *vraja-svarupa*, or spiritual body in his service in Goloka Vrindavana. He also sees the holy *dham* of Goloka Vrindavana and the transcendental pastimes going on there.

In this elevated stage, constant service and association with the holy name of Lord Krishna will inevitably bring about a face-to-face meeting with the blessed Lord Symasundara, Krishna. By the Lord's merciful will, all trace of the devotee's subtle body of mind, intelligence and false ego will be extinguished with the demise of the physical body of five elements.

This is when the devotee's pure spiritual form and identity fully manifests, minus all material coverings. Then, in the mood of pure *bhava* or spontaneous, pure and ecstatic devotion, he takes up his eternal service to Sri Sri Radha-Krishna in the transcendental holy land. He thus becomes a *sadhana-siddha*, meaning one who spiritually perfected himself by his devotional practice after having once been a materially conditioned soul. The devotee now becomes reinstated in his *siddha-svarupa* or perfected spiritual body through service (*bhajana*) and continued spiritual practice (*sadhana*). He now serves the Lord in the company of other eternal associates (*nitya-siddhas*) of the Lord who were never materially conditioned or fallen from their spiritual positions.

This is how one can become spiritually perfect on the path of bhakti-yoga and begin to enter the spiritual world before even having exited from the material body. But upon leaving the material body, one's position, identity and service becomes completely pure and steady within the eternal and blissful pastimes of Lord Krishna in Goloka Vrindavana.

**CHAPTER NOTES**
1. *Srimad-Bhagavatam* 7.7.54.
2. *Sri Caitanya-Siksamrta* p.321.
3. Ibid., p.181.

# CHAPTER TWENTY-FOUR

# *Entering Raganuga Bhakti Spontaneous Devotional Attraction*

The first thing to understand is that *raganuga* means that we follow a particular *raga* or devotional mood in a relationship with Krishna. This mood should be naturally attractive to us, which is why it becomes a spontaneous desire to relate with Krishna in this way. This further means that we follow in the footsteps of a devotee who is eternally established in that mood that we are most attracted to.

This spontaneous attraction can be compared to a man dying of thirst while thinking of getting water. He has to have it. The sooner the better. So, *raganuga* bhakti has been described as spontaneous attraction for something while completely absorbed in thoughts of it with an intense desire of love. This is the development of a relationship with the Supreme in a way that also attracts Lord Krishna. This is attained in the purified stage of our development of bhakti. Those who have attained *raganuga* bhakti are considered already perfectly developed in all the preliminary regulative principles and activities of basic *sadhana,* and with diligence have now achieved the steady, continuous and spontaneous loving service to the Supreme Being. The residents of Vrindavana who have attained *raganuga* bhakti have passed all the tests of regulative principles in their previous lives and have now been elevated to the position of direct association with Krishna as one of His dear friends. In other words, the bhakti-yogi must reach a level of perfection in following the regulative principles before he can come close to attaining *raganuga* bhakti.

The ultimate goal of *raganuga* bhakti is to enter into the eternal pastimes of Radha and Krishna in the spiritual abode of Goloka Vrindavana. It is the means to be with Krishna right now through our meditations of serving Him in the mood or *raga* of one of His eternal associates that also serves in the mood in which we are most attracted. This is accomplished primarily through hearing about Lord Krishna, chanting, and discussing His pastimes, and then meditating on the mood of our favorite devotee as we engage in our own service to Krishna, or the meditation on such service.

So how do we find our favorite *raga*? By regularly hearing about Krishna's pastimes is the way in which we hear of all the different types of devotees who interact with Krishna. Then we can develop an attraction for a specific *Vraja-bhakta*, or devotee in Vrindavana, and the relationship he or she has with Radha and Krishna. The more we immerse ourselves in hearing and meditating on these pastimes, the more likely we will be to find the particular *raga* or mood of devotion that moves our heart, and the particular devotee to follow to acquire that *raga* or devotional mood. Then we can enter *raganuga* bhakti, which is the way to enter into Krishna's eternal pastimes in Goloka Vrindavana.

Perfecting ourselves through the regulative principles of bhakti-yoga can take us up to the spiritual world to become a resident in one of the innumerable spiritual Vaikuntha planets where Krishna in His form of Lakshmi and Narayana are worshipped. This can even take us to the spiritual area of Dwaraka where Krishna is worshipped with His queens, or to Mathura where Krishna is worshipped in all of His youthful pastimes. In all of these places, Krishna is recognized as the Supreme Being. But in Goloka Vrindavana, all of the residents simply love Krishna and do not even recognize Him as God. This is where Krishna simply plays and has fun. And the only way you can enter this area of the spiritual dimension is through *raganuga* bhakti.

Therefore, this *raganuga* is the ideal we want to achieve if we want to reach Goloka Vrindavana, and we can do it simply by following the bhakti-yoga process. But if we are still engaged in making sure we are following the regulative principles, then it is still not pure devotion. However, when we attain this spontaneous love, then it is pure bhakti. Only when our affection for Krishna comes to the platform of spontaneous love is it counted in the category of pure devotional service.¹

For the regulative devotee (the *sadhana-bhakta*), his every mood and thought during meditation and remembrance of Lord Krishna should be based on scriptural references to make sure of its authenticity. Gradually, his *shraddha* or faith leads to *nishtha*, or firm and steady faith, and then to *ruchi* or taste or attraction for his devotional activities, and then to *asakti*, which is attachment. Then, as he continues to purify himself, he moves to *bhava*, or love of God, in which he can move toward a spontaneous attraction to Krishna. After this, he can be elevated to the stage of *apana-dasa*, when the bhakti-yogi not only meditates on Krishna all the time, but also invokes the devotional mood he is attracted to in his or her service to Krishna.²

The original inhabitants of Goloka Vrindavana, Lord Krishna's supreme abode, are easily and automatically attached to Krishna spontaneously in loving devotional service. Nothing can compare to such spontaneous devotion. When we follow in the footsteps of one of these devotees, our devotional service will also develop into *raganuga* bhakti. The primary characteristic of such spontaneous love is deep attachment to the Supreme Lord. Absorption in thought of Him is a marginal but steady characteristic. If the bhakti-yogi follows in the footsteps of the inhabitants of Vrindavana out of such transcendental desire to serve in such a way, that is the perfection of all preliminary rules and regulations, for which he no longer cares. The attachment and love outweighs them. That is the nature of *raganuga* bhakti.³

When an advanced or realized devotee hears about the affairs of the devotees of Vrindavana, either in the mood of neutrality, servitude, friendship, as a parent, or as a lover, he becomes inclined in one of these ways, and his intelligence becomes attracted. Indeed, he begins to covet that particular type of devotion. He wants to attain such feelings. When such desire is awakened, one's intelligence no longer depends on the instructions of *shastra* or on logic or argument.⁴ The devotee simply wants to dive ever more deeply into that particular loving relationship with Lord Krishna. Then he or she meditates on serving the Lord in this way.

"There are two simultaneous processes by which one executes this *raganuga* bhakti: external and internal. When self-realized, the advanced devotee externally remains like a neophyte and executes all the *shastric* injunctions, especially hearing and chanting. However, within his mind, in his *siddha-deha* (spiritual body) he serves Krishna in Vrindavana in his particular way [in the devotional mood that attracts him. In this way] He serves Krishna twenty-four hours a day." [5]

Serving day and night, or twenty-four hours a day, also means constant meditation or *samadhi* on one's service to Radha and Krishna once the bhakti-yogi has attained *bhava*. Therein he has the spiritual energy to continue his meditation always. Then he can enjoy service to Radha and Krishna throughout the day and night. Even his sleep is done for keeping his body healthy for his service to Sri Radha and Krishna. Thus, it also becomes a part of the bhakti-yoga process, and not a separate activity.

## HOW TO ATTAIN RAGANUGA BHAKTI

The key to entering into *raganuga* bhakti is the purification that a bhakti-yogi acquires by properly chanting the holy names of the Lord, especially in the Hare Krishna *maha-mantra*. As it is said by Sri Caitanya Mahaprabhu in the *Caitanya-caritamrita* (Antya-lila 20.21), "One who thinks himself lower than the grass, who is more tolerant than a tree, and who does not expect personal honor but is always prepared to give all respect to others, can very easily chant the holy names of the Lord constantly."

Not only can one easily chant the holy names when the bhakti-yogi feels this way, but this attitude is the way one should feel in order to attain the highest realizations brought by such chanting. If a person does so, he or she can develop deep longings, also described as greed for the eternal attachment to Lord Krishna that the residents of Vrindavana have for Krishna. This greed is the price that one must pay to attain a consciousness imbued with spontaneous loving devotional sentiments. This is called *raganuga* bhakti, and it is the merciful manifestation of Krishna's pleasure potency, *hladini-*

*shakti*, manifesting in the devotee's heart. [6] It is this pleasure potency which gives the act and mood of devotion so much bliss.

In the course of worshiping Krishna in the mood of the residents of Vraj, Vrindavana, the bhakti-yogi intensely desires to attain the mood of one of those devotees and prays to the residents, "I pay my repeated obeisances to all those devotees who meditate with great eagerness on the Lord as their husband, son, companion, brother, father, or friend." [7]

With this kind of respect toward the devotees in Vrindavana, the *raganuga-bhakta* or devotee begins to develop and can attain a spiritual body appropriate to his selected service. Thereafter, upon attaining perfection in the bhakti-yoga process, he or she attains the personal association of Krishna in the type of spiritual body that allows him or her to most appropriately engage in that loving mood.

However, it is also explained in *Padyavali* (text 14 & *Cc.* Madhya, 8.70), "Since Krishna consciousness soaked with devotion cannot be achieved even after the practice of hundreds of thousands of pious acts, one must pay the only price by which it can be bought: intense greed to have it. Should one come across this greed, one should grab it eagerly."

Therefore, this *raganuga* bhakti is based on faith that has intense desire to attain the association of Krishna. This kind of desire is very rare, so if we see even a glimpse of it, we should be ready and willing to grab it, and develop ourselves to keep it. So when the bhakti-yogi hears the sweet pastimes of the Lord from a pure devotee or from the *Srimad-Bhagavatam*, he becomes affected by the delightful moods that are expressed by these eternally perfected associates of the Lord, along with the beauty of the Lord's form, His attributes, character, personality, etc. Then the devotee's desire to experience this sweetness and to go deeper into it becomes automatic. This is the result of this kind of transcendental greed or spontaneous attraction. Then he seeks out more information in order to facilitate his longing to attain the object of his desire, which is Lord Krishna.

Therefore, this is described as the selfless loving service to Radha-Krishna with a desire to please Them and to love Them in the mood of the Vrajavasis, those eternally perfect devotees in Goloka Vrindavana, and to be one of Their loving associates in that supreme abode. This is *raganuga* bhakti, or what could be called the consciousness of divine love. This develops into a constant and natural longing for Krishna. When the devotee has further developed into the mood of *bhava* (divine affection) or *prema* (intense divine love), even a moment without the vision of Krishna is unbearable. As further explained, such spontaneous loving service is the highest perfection of bhakti-yoga, and, thus, the highest perfection of human life. [8]

However, there are only two causes for the appearance of such longing or greed for the emotions of the eternal associates of the Lord, and that is the direct mercy of the Lord, or the blessings of the pure devotee. Such mercy from the devotee can be from the blessings given in a previous life, or the good wishes in this present life. In either case, the devotee must take shelter of a similar *raganugiya* devotee guru. Some also call this *pushti-marga*, or the path of grace, meaning to receive the grace of the pure devotee.

Besides acquiring the blessings to attain the desire for *raganuga* bhakti, or to invoke the emotions of the *nitya-siddhas* or eternally perfect devotees within ourselves, the means to attain this consciousness consists of the standard processes of hearing, chanting, and all the other limbs of *vaidhi-bhakti*, meaning regulative devotional service. Srila Rupa Goswami describes the steps to attain *raganuga* bhakti in three verses of his *Bhakti-rasamrita-sindhu* (1.2.294-6):

"Remembering one's own beloved Nandanandana Krishna and His dearmost associates of one's own choice and taste, being attached to speaking about them, and, if possible, living with one's body in Sridhama Vrindavana, and if not, always living in Vraja at least mentally.

"In the transcendental realm of Vraja [Vrindavana] one should serve the Supreme Lord, Sri Krishna, with a feeling similar to that of His associates, and one should place himself under the direct guidance of a particular associate of Krishna and should follow in his footsteps. This method is applicable in [both] the stage of *sadhana* [spiritual regulative practices] and in the stage of *sadhya* [God realization], when one is a *siddha-purusha*, meaning a spiritually perfect [God realized] soul."

*A closeup of the Deity of Kunjabihari, meaning Krishna who sports in the groves of Vrindavana.*

# Chapter Twenty-Four

*A closeup of the Deity of Srimati Radharani.*

"All the items that were discussed for *vaidhi bhakti* [or the practice of devotional service by following the regulative principles] are also practiced and depended upon in *raganuga* bhakti. The wise devotees practice the items that are proper for their own [devotional] mood, but they do not act contrary to their own mood."

In this way, the advanced devotees continue to develop the particular loving mood that suits them, even if it appears they are simply doing the basics of bhakti-yoga. However, this shows that simply by sincerely continuing the process of bhakti-yoga, we can reach the stage of spontaneous attraction to the Supreme Lord in the devotional mood of Goloka Vrindavana. What is so special about that? We answer that next.

## RAGANUGA BHAKTI BRINGS THE DEVOTEE TO KRISHNA

The *Srimad-Bhagavatam* (10.9.21) conclusively explains, "The Supreme Personality of Godhead, Krishna, the son of mother Yashoda, is accessible to those devotees engaged in spontaneous loving service, but He is not as easily accessible to mental speculators [those still trying to analyze what is the Absolute Truth], or to those striving for self-realization by severe austerities and penances, or to those who consider the body to be the same as the self."

This means that by attaining the same loving feelings of the associates of the Lord is what brings the bhakti-yogi into the direct association of Lord Krishna. Srila Bhaktisiddhanta Sarasvati Thakur also explains it this way, regarding one's mood of devotion: "*Raganuga* bhakti, or spontaneous devotional service, can be executed in the *shanta-rasa* [mood of neutrality] when one aspires to be like Krishna's cows, or the stick or flute in the hand of Krishna, or the flowers around Krishna's neck. In the *dashya-rasa* [mood of servitude] one follows in the footsteps of servants like Citraka, Patraka or Raktaka. In the friendly [mood] of *sakhya-rasa* one can become a friend like Baladeva, Shridama or Sudama. In the *vatsalya-rasa*, characterized by parental affection, one can become like

[Krishna's parents] Nanda Maharaja or Yashoda, and in the *madhurya-rasa*, characterized by conjugal love, one can become like Srimati Radharani or Her lady friends such as Lalita and Her serving maids (*manjaris*) like Rupa and Rati. This is the essence of all instruction in the matter of devotional service."[9]

From these relations with Krishna, there are many kinds of ecstatic symptoms that the devotees experience. They are categorized in many ways as described in the *Caitanya-caritamrita* (Madhya-lila 23) and *Bhakti-rasamrita-sindhu*, which we will not explain here. But the point is that as a devotee enters into increasingly closer ties with Krishna, the center and cause of all ecstasies, the bliss also rises to higher levels of intensity. To give a hint of how this expands, here is a short description given in the *Caitanya-caritamrita* (Madhya-lila, 23.42-49):

"Love of Godhead increases and is manifest as affection, counter-love, love, attachment, sub-attachment, ecstasy, and sublime ecstasy. This development is compared to sugarcane seeds, then sugarcane plants, sugarcane juice, molasses, crude sugar, refined sugar, sugar candy, and then rock candy. Just as the taste of sugar increases as it is gradually purified, one should understand that when love of Godhead increases from *rati* [strong attraction in ecstatic love of God], which is compared to the beginning seed, its taste increases. According to the candidate possessing these transcendental qualities [like strong affectionate attachment and so on], there are five transcendental mellows [or relationships]–neutrality, servitorship, friendship, parental love, and conjugal love. These five transcendental mellows exist permanently. The devotees may be attracted to one of these mellows, and thus he becomes happy. Krishna also becomes inclined toward such a devotee and comes under his control [by such love]. When the permanent ecstasies [found in neutrality, servitorship, and so on] are mixed with other ingredients, devotional service in love of Godhead is transformed and becomes composed of transcendental mellows [or relations]. The permanent ecstasy becomes a more and more tasteful transcendental mellow through the mixture of special ecstasy, subordinate ecstasy, natural ecstasy, and transitory ecstasy. [An example of this is] Yogurt mixed with sugar candy, black pepper and camphor is very palatable and tasty. Similarly, when permanent ecstasy mixes with other ecstatic symptoms, it becomes unprecedentedly tasty."

For some, this may be a little difficult to understand, but it gives a view of the progressive levels of spiritual ecstasies derived from various loving activities as a devotee engages in closer and closer levels of relations with Krishna. From here, the descriptions go much deeper than this. This means that we can hardly fathom the deeper spiritual ecstasies of bhakti-yoga, loving devotional service.

## DEVOTION IN THE FEELING OF SEPARATION

One of the ways to develop the deep divine love is in the mood of separation, always hankering to see the Lord, and hoping that such a vision of the Lord will happen soon. Many of the most advanced devotees have cultivated such a mood, as exhibited by the mood of Madhavendra Puri who used to recite this verse at the end of his life: "O My Lord! O most merciful master! O master of Mathura. When shall I see You again? Because of my not seeing You, My agitated heart has become unsteady. O most beloved one, what shall I do now?" [10]

This verse would be expressed by Sri Caitanya Mahaprabhu who would then fall to the ground unconscious, overwhelmed with ecstatic emotion. This kind of worship in separation is considered one of the highest moods of the love one can have for the beloved Lord. The devotee feels himself to be neglected and lost, and being given the chance to see the Lord is the only cure. It is only by the mercy of the Lord that there is any way to feel better. So the mood of separation is the sentiment of always asking for the Lord's compassion, which itself brings about a feeling of closeness with the Lord, that He may appear at any time to offer assistance because of the love He feels coming from the devotee. Srimati Radharani would feel this way. All the devotees in the line of the Gaudiya-Madhva-*sampradaya* accept this principle of devotional service. This is why Lord Gaurahari, Sri Caitanya, would feel this loving mood and pray:

"My dear Krishna, only You and I know the strength of Your beautiful features and, because of them, My unsteadiness. Now, this is My position; I do not know what to do or where to go. Where can I find You? I am asking You to give direction." [11]

In this way, we are expressing the sentiment of our dependence on Lord Krishna in a mood of loving separation. This was also in the mood of the *gopis*, the cowherd maidservants of Lord Krishna, of which Srimati Radharani is the topmost. As it is said in the *Srimad-Bhagavatam* (10.32.2), after Krishna had disappeared from the *rasa* dance, the *gopis* became so overwhelmed due to His separation and their intense love for Him that He could not remain absent, and, "Suddenly, due to the feelings of separation, Lord Krishna appeared among them dressed in yellow garments and wearing a flower garland. His lotus face was smiling, and He was directly attracting the mind of Cupid."

So, this example shows how the love of the devotee can draw Krishna to appear before him or her. But there are various levels of love that pull Lord Krishna more strongly than others.

To explain further, as we develop ourselves from the regulative principles of bhakti-yoga, we develop faith (*shradha*), then steadiness (*nishtha*), taste for our service (*ruchi*), and then attachment (*asakti*) also begins to open. When these fully develop, it brings us to divine love, or *bhava*. Then we enter into *bhava-bhakti*, the next stage in a fully developed consciousness. When *bhava-bhakti* becomes complete or perfected, it become *prema-bhakti*, which is the ecstatic level of divine love. When devotees are in *prema-bhakti*, they conclude their life free from all material connection and liberated from any further slavery to the material energy, and reside eternally in the pure spiritual realm. [12]

Any aspect of worship of Lord Krishna in which *prema* is not present, or not attainable, will not result in or bring ourselves to the direct vision of the Supreme Person. [13] This shows the importance of attaining *prema*, which is pure love for Krishna with deep ecstatic emotional feelings, devoid of all material desires or attractions. This *prema* or intense, ecstatic love is found in all of the five main relationships, but increases from servitude, friendship, parental affection, to conjugal love.

It is true that whatever relationship a devotee has with the Lord is the best for that devotee, who is completely satisfied in that relationship. But when we study all the different methods of service from a neutral position onward, we can understand that there are higher and lower degrees of love. [14]

"Increasing love is experienced in various tastes, one after another. But that love which has the highest taste in the gradual succession of desires manifests itself in the form of conjugal love."[15]

In this way, there is a gradual order of improvement in the transcendental relationships from the initial ones to the later ones. In each subsequent relationship or mellow, the qualities of the previous ones are collectively manifest in those that follow. In other words, as the qualities increase, so the taste in the relationship also increases. Therefore the qualities found in the relationship of neutrality are also in servitude, which are also found friendship, all of which are found in parental affection, and all of those qualities are found in the deeper relation of conjugal love for the Lord, which has higher ecstasies not found in the relationships before it. Complete attainment of the lotus feet of Lord Krishna is made possible by love of God, specifically *madhurya-rasa* or conjugal love. Lord Krishna is indeed captivated by the devotee who has this standard of love. [16]

This is why Lord Krishna told the *gopis* in *Srimad-Bhagavatam* (10.82.45), "The means for attaining My favor is loving service unto Me, and fortunately you are all thus engaged. Those living beings who render service unto Me are eligible to be transferred to the spiritual world and attain eternal life with knowledge and bliss."

In this way, Lord Krishna has made a firm promise for all time. If one renders service unto Him, Krishna correspondingly gives him or her an equal amount of success in devotional service to the Lord. [17]

As Lord Krishna also says in *Bhagavad-gita* (4.11), "All of them, as they surrender unto Me, I reward them accordingly." However, in *Srimad-Bhagavatam* (10.32.22) it is said that Lord Krishna cannot proportionately reciprocate the devotional service in the mood of *madhurya-rasa*; therefore He remains always a debtor to such devotees.

"Although Krishna's unparalleled beauty is the topmost sweetness of love of Godhead, His sweetness increases unlimitedly when He is in the company of the *gopis*. Consequently Krishna's exchange of love with the *gopis* is the topmost perfection of love of Godhead." [18]

So how can we also attain such a fortunate position? This is the quintessential question. And for this we have the answer, as found in the *Caitanya-caritamrita*:

"One who is attracted by that ecstatic love of the *gopis* does not care about the regulative principles of Vedic life or popular opinion. Rather, he completely surrenders unto Krishna and renders service unto Him. If one worships the Lord on the path of spontaneous love and goes to Vrindavana, he receives the shelter of Vrajendra-nandana, the son of Nanda Maharaja. In his liberated stage the devotee is attracted by one of the five humors [or main types of relationships] in the transcendental loving service of the Lord. As he continues to serve the Lord in that transcendental mood, he attains a spiritual body to serve Krishna in [the supreme abode of] Goloka Vrindavana." [19]

"Therefore, one should accept the mood of the *gopis* in their service. In such a transcendental mood, one should always think of the pastimes of Sri Sri Radha and Krishna. After thinking of Radha and Krishna and Their pastimes for a long time, and after getting completely free from material contamination, one is transferred to the spiritual world. There the devotee attains an opportunity to serve Radha and Krishna as one of the *gopis*." [20]

"Without the help of the *gopis*, one cannot enter into these pastimes. Only he who worships the Lord in the ecstasy of the *gopis*, following in their footsteps, can engage in the service of Sri Sri Radha-Krishna [together] in the bushes of Vrindavana. Only then can one understand the conjugal love between Radha and Krishna. There is no other procedure for understanding. The pastimes of Sri Radha and Krishna are self-effulgent. They are happiness personified, unlimited and all powerful. Even so, the spiritual humors of such pastimes are never complete without the *gopis*, the Lord's personal [cowherd girl] friends. The Supreme Personality of Godhead is never complete without His spiritual potencies; therefore unless one takes shelter of the *gopis*, one cannot enter into the company of Radha and

Krishna. Who can be interested in Their spiritual pastimes without taking their shelter?

"There is an inexplicable fact about the natural inclinations of the *gopis*. The *gopis* never want to enjoy themselves with Krishna personally. The happiness of the *gopis* increases ten million times when they serve to engage Sri Sri Radha and Krishna [together] in Their transcendental pastimes." [21]

In this way, the greatest joy for these associates is to bring Radha and Krishna together. There is no materialistic lust in them. They have no desire to be alone with Krishna. They prefer to see Sri Sri Radha and Krishna displaying Their love between each other and simply assisting in that way.

Then what are the duties that the *gopis* are meant to perform in their service to Sri Sri Radha and Krishna? This also depends on what group of *gopis* in which you may belong. Within the group of *gopis* there are the *sakhis*, which are confidential associates, and the *manjaris*, who are most confidential associates, both of whom serve to make the atmosphere more conducive for the pastimes of Sri Sri Radha and Krishna.

Srila Rupa Goswami explains in his *Ujjvala-nilamani* that one who expands the conjugal love of Krishna and His enjoyment among the *gopis* is called a *sakhi*. Such a person is a confidential *gopi* in the conjugal affairs. Such assistants are like jewels in the form of Krishna's confidence. In the conjugal pastimes of Krishna, Krishna is the hero (*nayaka*) and Radhika is the heroine (*nayika*). The first business of the *gopis* is to chant the glories of both the hero and the heroine. Their second business is to create gradually a situation in which the hero may be attracted to the heroine and vice verse. Their third business is to induce both of Them to approach one another, to bring Them together. Their fourth business is to surrender unto Krishna, and their fifth is to create a jovial atmosphere. The sixth order of activity is to give Them assurance to enjoy Their pastimes, the seventh is to dress and decorate both hero and heroine, the eighth is to show expertise in expressing the desires that Radha and Krishna have, the ninth is to conceal the faults of the heroine, the tenth is to keep their respective relatives from missing their association, the eleventh is to educate, the twelfth is to enable both hero and heroine to meet at the proper time, the thirteenth is to fan both hero and heroine, the fourteenth is to sometimes reproach the hero and heroine in joking ways, the fifteenth is to set conversations in motion between Sri Radha and Krishna, and the sixteenth is to protect the heroine by various means. [22]

This is described to help give a good direction to our own meditation while we engage in our *sadhana*, our spiritual practice and personal devotional service to Radha and Krishna. As we become more purified, this mood will become increasingly clear and ever-present in our own meditations, as we have been describing.

However, materialists and cheaters, or those who take things cheaply (*sahajiyas*), may still misunderstand these transcendental pastimes, or think that they are already equal to being a *gopi* or *sakhi*, but this is only mental concoction. Even thinking oneself an associate of the Lord without accepting the procedure of following in the footsteps of the Lord's associates is as offensive as thinking oneself to be God. This is what will destroy your spiritual development and any possible relationship you may have with Lord Sri Krishna.

Therefore, if we want to reach the epitome of all devotional service and sentiments of love, we must sincerely and humbly engage in the service of the Lord's associates as described here in this chapter. Then genuine success will be revealed.

However, let us remember that many devotees will have an attraction to simply serve as one of Krishna friends or relatives, or as a servant. Or they may even have a parental affection for Sri Krishna. They may not be so interested in entering the association of the *gopis* and serving Sri Radha and Krishna in the forests of Vrindavana. And such loving relations also give Lord Krishna much transcendental pleasure, as the *Bhagavatam* describes, while the devotee also thinks he is perfectly situated in such blissful and ecstatic association with Krishna. So there is a perfect place for every devotee and every level of loving sentiment in the pastimes among the residents of Goloka Vrindavana.

This is our real home for which all of us have been endlessly searching. Now let us use this human form of life to accomplish our real mission and attain that supreme abode.

*In the spiritual world, there is nothing but transcendental bliss and enjoyment in loving activities, all evolving around the Supreme source of all bliss.*

\* \* \*

Naturally, there is much more to this topic of *raganuga* bhakti than we could express here. It is an intimate and confidential topic that few can fully understand until such bhakti-yogis have actually entered into *raganuga* bhakti. This is also why we provide at the end of this book a reading list of additional books you can read for further study and advancement, if you are interested and when you may be ready.

**CHAPTER NOTES**
1. *Nectar of Devotion*, p.121-2.
2. *Sri Harinama-Cintamani*, p.112.
3. *Caitanya-caritamrita,* Madhya-lila, 22.149-153.
4. *Sri Caitanya-Siksamrta* p.53-4 & *Bhakti-rasamrita-sindhu*
   1.2.270.
5. *Sri Caitanya-Siksamrta,* p.54 & *Caitanya-caritamrita,*
   Madhya-lila, 22.156-7.
6. *Art of Sadhana*, p.4.
7. *Bhakti-rasamrita-sindhu* 1.2.308 & *Caitanya-caritamrita,*
   Madhya-lila, 2.163.
8. *Caitanya-caritamrita,* Madhya-lila, 8.71.
9. *Nectar of Instruction*, p.77.
10. *Caitanya-caritamrita,* Madhya-lila, 4.197.
11. Ibid., 2.62.
12. *Sri Caitanya-Siksamrta,* p.176-7.
13. *Art of Sadhana*, p.18.
14. *Caitanya-caritamrita,* Madhya-lila, 8.83.
15. *Bhakti-rasamrita-sindhu* 2.5.38.
16. *Caitanya-caritamrita,* Madhya-lila, 8.85-88.
17. Ibid., 8.90.
18. Ibid., 8.94.
19. Ibid., 8.220-2.
20. Ibid., 8.228-9.
21. Ibid., 8.204-208.
22. Ibid., 8.205.pur.

# CHAPTER TWENTY-FIVE

# *Attaining Liberation and Entering the Spiritual World*

The goal of all yoga is to attain *moksha* or liberation from material existence, often called freedom from the repetitive cycle of birth and death, or *samsara* in Sanskrit. This is the ultimate reason why we practice yoga. But there are different views on what is liberation depending on the various schools of Vedic thought or yoga processes.

First there is the liberation into the Brahman, the great effulgence. Many yogas or divisions within the Vedic philosophy view this sort of liberation as the highest form of freedom from bodily existence. This is the aim when you feel that there is no personal God, or that God has no form, and that the Absolute Truth is ultimately a highly brilliant force that we merge into when we are able to attain *moksha*, liberation. Merging into the Brahman effulgence is like entering an eternal ocean of bliss as a spiritual spark floating in the smooth waves of energy composed of other innumerable spiritual sparks. That is considered the ultimate oneness by many. But to accomplish this, you must learn to control the mind and meditate on the formless light for long periods of time. This is the goal of the mystic yoga process. Then you must use the proper technique necessary to merge into the Brahman at the very end of your life.

Yet, it is also described that in Kali-yuga this is a very difficult path to take. It is not easy to meditate on the Brahman or that which has no form. Lord Krishna explains this in *Bhagavad-gita* (12.5), "For those whose minds are attached to the unmanifested, impersonal feature of the Supreme, advancement is very troublesome.

To make progress in that discipline is always difficult for those who are embodied."

However, Krishna goes on to relate that, "For one who worships Me, giving up all his activities unto Me and being devoted to Me without deviation, engaged in devotional service and always meditating upon Me, who has fixed his mind upon Me, O son of Pritha, for him I am the swift deliverer from the ocean of birth and death." [1]

So herein we see where Lord Krishna advises us to meditate on His personal form, which is not only easier to do, but also brings one to the level of liberation very quickly. Lord Krishna again confirms this in *Bhagavad-gita* (12.2) by saying, "He whose mind is fixed on My personal form, always engaged in worshiping Me with great and transcendental faith, is considered by Me to be most perfect."

However, what kind of liberation do we achieve if we are successful in our worship of Lord Krishna? This is clearly explained in the *Caitanya-caritamrita* (Adi-lila, 3.17-8), where it says, "By performing such regulated devotional service in awe and veneration, one may go to Vaikuntha and attain the four kinds of liberation. These liberations are *sarshti* [achieving opulences equal to those of the Lord], *sarupya* [having a four-armed form the same as the Lord's], *samipya* [living as a personal associate of the Lord] and *salokya* [living on a Vaikuntha planet]. Devotees never accept *sayujya*, however, since that is oneness with Brahman."

Herein are listed the four types of liberation that a devotee attains when they enter into the Vaikuntha planets that float in the spiritual sky of the Brahman. These planets are the residences of the innumerable forms of Lord Vishnu and Lakshmi, the goddess of fortune. This is why devotees are not interested in the *sayujya* form of liberation of merging into the Brahman where there are no spiritual activities. It is only like floating as a dazzling spiritual particle in an eternal light of bliss with no activities, no relations, no forms of expression, and so on. But devotees or bhakti-yogis want activities based on the spiritual loving relations connected with serving the Supreme.

The *Caitanya-caritamrita* (Adi-lila, 5.37-38) goes on to

describe, "Thus in the spiritual sky there are varieties of pastimes within the spiritual energy. Outside the Vaikuntha planets appears the impersonal reflection of light [the *brahmajyoti*]. That impersonal Brahman effulgence consists only of the effulgent rays of the Lord. Those fit for the *sayujya* liberation merge into that effulgence."

"Where it has been stated that the Lord's enemies and devotees attain the same destination, this refers to the ultimate oneness of Brahman and Lord Krishna. This may be understood by the example of the sun and the sunshine, in which Brahman is like the sunshine and Krishna Himself is like the sun." [2]

So it is this spiritual sunshine that the impersonalist yogis try to attain, which is composed of innumerable souls that float in the brightness of that unlimited effulgence. In a corner of the Brahman is a cloud that consists of the Karana Ocean where the cosmic creation is manifested. This is where all of the materially conditioned souls exist. When the Supreme desires to exercise His desire to engage in battle, He does not perform such pastimes in the spiritual realm, but engages in them while visiting the material world. But when He kills any demons who battle with Him, they also become purified by His touch and are then eligible for liberation, in which case they can also enter the Brahman. They cannot enter into the Vaikuntha realm because they have not learned the art of devotional service or bhakti, which is the only way a living being can become qualified to enter the Vaikuntha planets.

As explained in the *Srimad-Bhagavatam* (10.82.45), "Lord Krishna told the *gopis*: 'The means of attaining My favor is loving service unto Me, and fortunately you are all thus engaged. Those loving beings who render service unto Me are eligible to be transferred to the spiritual world and attain eternal life with knowledge and bliss.'"

This is actually what everyone is searching for, life without end in full knowledge and bliss. It is almost instinctual in the sense that this is the nature of the soul, so it is natural that the individual is only trying to uncover or realize his or her spiritual constitutional position. This is really the purpose of any spiritual path. But some are more complete in knowledge than others.

In the Vaikuntha planets the modes of material nature do not exist, so there is also no effects of time, such as past, present and future. It is said that time is conspicuous by its absence. There is only present time, where things go on indefinitely but without the lamentation of the past or the worry about the future. It is only bliss. And since there is no mode of darkness or ignorance, there is no destruction. And since there is no passion, there is no creation of anything. It is all perpetual and eternally existent.

Everything there is also self-illuminating, so there is no need for a sun or moon, or fire or electricity. The bodies of the residents are fully spiritual, in the same quality as the Supreme, and once attaining that realm, they never come back to the material worlds. Their spiritual bodies are delicate and attractively built, with four arms, and their eyes are like the petals of a lotus flower. The residents have no awareness of the material planets or the activities that go on there. They are only focused on the bliss of the loving spiritual activities in relation to the Lord that is shared by all of the residents of the Vaikuntha planets.

Farther than the Vaikuntha planets is the supreme abode of Lord Krishna called Goloka Vrindavana, or Krishnaloka. This is where the Lord manifests His two-armed form and where the residents do not display the mood of awe and reverence, but all engage in spontaneous devotion in the mood of servitude, friendship, parenthood, and conjugal love. This is the most intimate atmosphere, and the most confidential of pastimes and ecstatic bliss.

## HOW WE REACH THE SPIRITUAL WORLD

The process for reaching the spiritual world consists of following the same regulative principles we have already been discussing, which is called *sadhana-bhakti* or *vaidhi-bhakti*, regulative devotional service. This is so we can become increasingly spiritualized to the point of developing attraction for Lord Krishna, then love or *bhava*, and then *prema*, the loving consciousness that helps us to always think of Lord Krishna, especially at the time we leave this body. The importance of this is explained in many places in the Vedic literature, such as these examples:

"And whoever, at the time of death, quits his body, remembering Me alone, at once attains My nature. Of this, there is no doubt. Whatever state of being one remembers when he quits his body, that state he will attain without fail. Therefore, Arjuna, you should always think of Me in the form of Krishna and at the same time carry out your prescribed duties... With your activities dedicated to Me and your mind and intelligence fixed on Me, you will attain Me without doubt." [3]

"For one who remembers Me without deviation, I am easy to obtain, O son of Pritha, because of his constant engagement in devotional service." [4]

"Anyone, even a person in an impure state, who absorbs his mind in Him for just a moment at the time of death burns up all traces of sinful reactions and immediately attains the supreme transcendental destination in a pure, spiritual form as effulgent as the sun." [5]

However, we should not expect special favors to pave the way back to the spiritual world. But being patient and persevering is the way we make progress. This sentiment is clearly stated in the *Bhagavatam* (10.14.8), "My dear Lord, any person who is constantly awaiting your causeless mercy to be bestowed upon him, and who goes on suffering the resultant actions of his past misdeeds, offering You respectful obeisances from the core of his heart, is surely eligible to become liberated, for it becomes his rightful claim."

This is the guideline for any sincere devotee, that we should not expect immediate relief from our past misdeeds, though it can happen. But we should be tolerant and go on in our practice of bhakti-yoga, which will help free us from our material activities and the karmic reactions that we have accumulated from them. Even if there may be impediments or reversals in our life, we should simply tolerate them and keep moving forward in our spiritual development which can completely free us from any further entanglement in material existence.

Therefore, if we are going to accomplish anything truly extraordinary, we pray that we can leave this material world once and for all and have entrance into the spiritual domain, which all Vedic literature proclaims as the real goal of life. Here is an example of such a prayer as given in the *Srimad-Bhagavatam* (5.3.12): "Dear Lord, we may not be able to remember Your name, form and qualities due to stumbling, hunger, falling down, yawning, or being in a miserable diseased condition at the time of death when there is a high fever. We therefore pray unto You, O Lord, for You are very affectionate to Your devotees. Please help us remember You and utter Your holy names, attributes and activities, which can dispel all the reactions of our sinful lives."

In this way, the practice of remembering the pastimes and characteristics and the holy names of the Lord in the process of bhakti-yoga makes it more likely that we will be able to do so when we die. That is what can deliver or propel us into the spiritual world. This is especially emphasized in the descriptions by Sukadeva Goswami in the *Srimad-Bhagavatam* (10.90.50), "By regularly hearing, chanting and meditating on the beautiful topics of Lord Mukunda [Krishna] with ever-increasing sincerity, a mortal being will attain the divine kingdom of the Lord, where the inviolable power of death holds no sway. For this purpose, many persons, including great kings, abandoned their mundane homes and took to the forest [or wherever is best to cultivate bhakti-yoga]."

However, we should not think that this is only for a few special people that can do this. Many people have previously attained the abode of the Lord simply by thinking of Him in one way or another. This is explained in the instructions of Narada Muni to Maharaja Yudhisthira where he says, "Many, many persons have attained liberation simply by thinking of Krishna with great attention and giving up sinful activities. This great attention may be due to lusty desires, inimical feelings, fear, affection, or devotional service. I shall now explain how one receives Krishna's mercy simply by concentrating one's mind upon Him. My dear King Yudhisthira, the *gopis* by their lusty desires, Kamsa by fear, Shishupala and other kings by envy, the Yadus by their familial relationship with Krishna, you Pandavas by your great affection for Krishna, and we, the general devotees, by our devotional service, have obtained the mercy of Krishna. Somehow or other, one must consider the form of Krishna very seriously. Then, by one of the five different processes mentioned above, one can return home, back to Godhead...

Therefore, one must think of Krishna, whether in a friendly way or inimically." [6]

Of course, the best way to think of Krishna is in a positive and loving way. But the point is to somehow think or meditate on Krishna. This is the means to reach His supreme abode. Obviously, devotees engaged in hearing Krishna's glories with pure and mature faith are more quickly purified than those who harbor personal desires even while worshiping, hearing explanations of the Vedic learning, studying the scriptures, giving in charity, performing penances, or engaging in other ritual processes of purification. [7]

Therefore, for a person who is suffering in the fire of countless miseries in this material existence and who desires to cross the insurmountable ocean of material life, there is no more suitable a boat than that of cultivating and relishing the transcendental taste and joys of hearing Krishna's pastimes. [8]

There is also the example of the practicing devotee being a gardener. When devotees obtain the seed of devotional service by the mercy of the guru and Krishna, they should see to it that the seed develops into a creeper of bhakti, called the *bhakti-lata-bija*. This grows as they advance in their devotional service. The devotees plant the seed of bhakti in the core of their own hearts, which is called the field. Before planting a seed in the field, it is necessary to first plough the field to make it suitable for sowing and raising the plant. The fortunate soul receives from the true guru instructions to give up the quest for *bhukti* (material enjoyment), *mukti* (desire for liberation), and *yoga-siddhi* (mystical yogic perfections). In this way, the devotees cleanse the field. This is also helped by devotee association. Without pride, they give respect to all living beings, and become qualified to receive and recite the holy names of the Lord. As if subduing a wild horse, the devotees must trick the mind into submission. We want to be devotees, but often the mind, being the center of the senses and always wanting sensual activity, is no devotee. It wants to do something else. Therefore, we must stifle the mind so it does not distract us.

The devotional creeper gradually grows by the watering process of hearing about Krishna, chanting His holy names, discussing His characteristics, remembering Him, and other devotional activities. Through this process the creeper grows beyond the material realm, passes the Viraja River, pierces the effulgence of the Brahman, and arrives in the spiritual world on the Vaikuntha planets or Goloka Vrindavana, until it reaches the lotus feet of Lord Krishna Himself. However, if the creeper is still bound in the material world, attached to taste, smell, touch, sound, the senses, the mind, the elements, or the modes of goodness, passion and ignorance, there will be obstacles to its growth. But when it attains the spiritual world by the strength of its own nature, it cannot be broken or cut, and ascends even higher.

At the feet of Lord Krishna, there is no fear that it may decay, and the creeper spreads out and bears its fruit of *prema-bhakti*, ecstatic loving devotional service to the Lord. When this happens, the devotee, though still engaged within this material world, can travel the length of the creeper at will and be in trance in thought and meditation on the feet of Lord Krishna. In this way, he may still be seen in this world, but his consciousness is dwelling in the spiritual realm. In such a state of consciousness, that bhakti-yogi is already liberated.

## HOW A DEVOTEE ATTAINS A SPIRITUAL BODY

We have to understand that as we engage in the process of bhakti-yoga and our consciousness becomes increasing spiritualized, and our attraction to the Lord also increases, the more we are qualified for liberation from further rounds of birth and death, and the more we are ready to gain entrance into the spiritual strata. The great devotee Bilvamangala Thakur once said that if one develops unalloyed devotion to the Lord, liberation will follow the devotee as his maidservant. [9] In other words, when the bhakti-yogi is sincere, liberation is automatic, just as a maid follows to assist.

Lord Kapila, while instructing His mother in the process of Krishna bhakti, related to her this point, "My dear mother, the path of self-realization which I have already instructed to you is very easy. You can execute this system without difficulty, and by following it you shall very soon be liberated, even within your present body." [10]

Now we begin to understand that we do not have to wait until death to be qualified or to attain liberation. We can be liberated right here and right now. By endeavoring to perfect our path of bhakti-yoga, and serving the pure devotee and accepting instruction from him, we can become purified enough to be eligible for liberation from this material life. It then follows us just like a maidservant. This is what it means. By continuing to focus our attention on serving the Supreme as much as we can while dealing with our material affairs, we still rise in our spiritual life, and the more our consciousness and our bodies become saturated with spiritual vibration.

A bhakti-yogi's body becomes spiritual by his or her service to the Lord. This is also clearly related in the *Bhagavatam* (11.3.31), "Pure devotees develop a spiritual body and symptoms of ecstatic love simply by remembering and reminding others of the Supreme Personality of Godhead, Hari, who takes away everything inauspicious from the devotee. This position is attained by rendering devotional service according to the regulative principles and then rising to the platform of spontaneous love."

In other words, the spiritual body is already developing while we engage in spiritual activities. It is simply part of the process, which is another point in how bhakti-yoga accomplishes everything that is necessary for our spiritual progress. Alternative endeavors are not needed. We only need to stay the course.

The body of a devotee also becomes more and more spiritualized to the point wherein it is no longer material. This is the case with anything that we use for spiritual purposes, such as in the service of pleasing the Lord. That item becomes spiritualized because it is engaged in the natural function of any portion of the Lord's energy, which is in His service. Even Srila Bhaktisiddhanta Sarasvati Thakur gives his opinion that the body of a devotee who tried his or her best to work hard for the satisfaction of Lord Krishna by fully engaging in the Lord's service must be accepted as transcendental.[11]

This is confirmed by Sri Caitanya Mahaprabhu Himself who says, "The body of a devotee is never material. It is considered to be transcendental, full of spiritual bliss. At the time of initiation, when a devotee fully surrenders unto the service of the Lord, Krishna accepts him to be as good as Himself."[12]

"The living entity who is subjected to birth and death, when he gives up all material activities, dedicating his life to Me for executing My order, and thus acts according to My direction, at that time he reaches the platform of immortality, and becomes fit to enjoy the spiritual bliss of exchanges of loving mellows [or relations] with Me." [13]

In this way, the devotee's body becomes spiritual. Of course, a humble devotee will never think in this way of himself, but it can be viewed that he or she is attaining the position wherein the body itself is spiritualized by the constant meditation on or service to the Supreme Being. In other words, the vibrational level of both the consciousness and the physical body changes to the point wherein it is saturated with spiritual vibration. And like when you squeeze an orange fruit, orange juice comes out, similarly all that comes out of such a devotee is the awareness of Krishna. Then he or she also encourages others to think or meditate on the Supreme in various ways. Therefore when the yogi is freed from material connections in this way, his body becomes spiritual, and Krishna accepts his service. When a devotee no longer has any desire for material sense enjoyment, his spiritual identity and consciousness awakens. This also makes the body spiritual, and he or she rises in bhakti and becomes fit to render service to the Supreme.

One point to understand is that all material and spiritual energy emanates from the Supreme Being. He is the Supreme Controller. This means that He can convert matter into spirit, and spirit into matter. Therefore, a material thing can be turned into spiritual energy by the will of the Lord. The necessary condition for such a change is to employ so-called matter in the service of spirit, especially the Supreme Spirit. This is also the way to elevate ourselves to the spiritual plane. When we do this with everything around us, we can also become increasingly aware that in reality, there is nothing but the Supreme Being. As the saying goes, "What is not God?" Everything is the Supreme or the energy of the Supreme. We simply have to develop that awareness.

When Narada was discussing his experience with Srila Vyasadeva, he explained, "And so, O Brahmana Vyasadeva, in due course of time I, who was fully absorbed in thinking of Krishna and who therefore had no attachments, being completely freed from all material taints, met with death, as lightening and illumination occur simultaneously. Having then been awarded a transcendental body befitting an associate of the Personality of Godhead, I quit the body made of five material elements, and thus all acquired fruitive results of work [karma] stopped." [14]

Lord Krishna also explains it this way, "Just as gold, when smelted in fire, gives up its impurities and returns to its pure brilliant state, similarly, the spirit soul, absorbed in the fire of bhakti-yoga, is purified of all contamination [or karma] caused by previous fruitive activities and returns to its original position of serving Me in the spiritual world." [15]

Therefore, as we progress spiritually, all of our karma comes to an end. We are purified of all our karma, and we also do not acquire any more. Our karma does two things: it keeps us motivated to experience our material tastes and desires, and it also keeps us bound to further rounds of birth and death to continue our endeavors to satisfy our sensual and mental wants. It is the spiritual life of bhakti-yoga that continues to burn all of those desire seeds, like frying seeds in a pan, making them unable to sprout and grow any further. This is also part of the process by which a devotee changes his or her material body into a spiritual body.

However, bhakti-yoga goes a little farther. Just as it dissolves our karma, it also dissolves the subtle body, which is what our karma clings to. Without the subtle body, which is composed of mind, intelligence and false ego, the container of our karma and material desires or interests also disappears. As it is explained in the *Bhagavatam* (3.25.33), "Bhakti, devotional service, dissolves the subtle body of the living entity without separate effort, just as fire in the stomach digests all that we eat."

This is another example of how a bhakti-yogi does not have to try by separate endeavor for liberation. The very process of bhakti, which is service to the Supreme Personality, is the means for liberation. It is the means by which the soul attains its natural position.

Another question we should ask is what are the activities on the Vaikuntha planets and on Goloka Vrindavana. The answer is that all of the residents are offering various forms of worship and loving service to the Supreme Being. This gives pleasure to the Lord who in return shows His numerous forms to interact with His devotees in various ways for the pleasure of His devotees. In other words, the process of devotional service is what is going on in the spiritual world. This is how bhakti-yoga prepares us for entering the spiritual domain by training us in the ways devotees act in the spiritual world. It delivers the spiritual realm to the devotees in the material world.

This is why it is said that material existence, at least in regard to one's consciousness or interest, comes to an end when one attains love for Krishna. "As a result of bhakti, one's dormant love for Krishna awakens. When one is so situated that he can taste the association of Lord Krishna, material existence, the repetition of birth and death, comes to an end." [16] This is why it is also said that those who have attained love of Krishna have attained the topmost form of liberation. [17]

In this way, it becomes clear that becoming a devotee and entering the spiritual world is the perfection of life. No higher accomplishment can be attained. Everything else is temporary and full of ups and downs. This is the soul's natural position for which we search over the course of numerous lifetimes. And once we have attained the spiritual domain, there is no need to ever return, as Lord Krishna says in *Bhagavad-gita* (8.15): "After attaining Me, the great souls, who are yogis in devotion, never return to this temporary world, which is full of miseries, because they have attained the highest perfection."

## ATTAINING A SPIRITUAL BODY IN THE MOOD OF YOUR DEVOTION

This brings us to our next level of understanding, that a devotee can get a spiritual body according to one's love for Krishna. This begins to be explained as follows: "If one worships the Lord on the path of spontaneous love [or *raganuga* bhakti] and goes to Vrindavana, he receives shelter of Vrajendra-nandana, the son of Nanda Maharaja [Krishna]. In his liberated stage the devotee is attracted by one of the five humors [or *rasas*] in the transcendental loving service of the Lord. As he continues to serve the Lord in that transcendental mood, he attains a spiritual body to serve Krishna in Goloka Vrindavana [in that mood]. Those saintly persons who presented the *Upanishads* are vivid examples of this. By worshiping the Lord on the path of spontaneous love, they attained the lotus feet of Vrajendra-nandana, the son of Maharaja Nanda [Krishna]." [18]

So, one can go to Vaikuntha by perfectly performing regulative bhakti, but it is only by spontaneous love in one of the moods of love, or *rasas*, namely in neutrality, as a servant, friend, parent, or love interest, does one go to Goloka Vrindavana. There the devotee gets a spiritual body to engage in direct service to Krishna according to that mood.

The importance of the spontaneous devotional attitude is further described by Srila Prabhupada in the *Teachings of Lord Caitanya* (p. 332): "There are various kinds of personal devotees of Lord Krishna in the transcendental abode. For example, there are servants of Krishna like Raktaka and Patraka and friends of Krishna just like Sridama and Sudama. There are also parents of Krishna, like Nanda and Yashoda, who are engaged in the service of Krishna according to their respective transcendental emotions. One who desires to enter into the supreme abode of Krishna can take shelter of one of such transcendental servitors. Then, through the execution of loving service, one can attain transcendental affection for Krishna. In other words, the devotee in this material world who executes loving service in pursuance of the activities of those eternal associates with Krishna also attains the same post when he is perfected."

Therefore, a bhakti-yogi should engage in his or her service in the mood of the associate of Krishna to whom he is most attracted. In such a transcendental mood, one should always think of the corresponding pastimes of Sri Sri Radha and Krishna. After thinking of Radha and Krishna and Their pastimes for a long time and after getting completely free from material contamination, one is transferred to the spiritual world. There the devotee attains an opportunity to serve Radha and Krishna in the mood they have developed, such as in the mood of the *gopis*. [19]

So, as it is related by Srila Rupa Goswami, "The devotee

should always think of Krishna within himself, and one should choose a very dear devotee who is a servitor of Krishna in Vrindavana. One should then constantly engage in topics about that servitor [or devotee] and his loving relationship to Krishna, and one should live in Vrindavana. However, if one is physically unable to go to Vrindavana, he should mentally live there." [20]

In this way, even if we cannot live in the holy place of Vrindavana, we can mentally meditate on being there and live as if we are there. For example, living in an ashrama or in a temple where we can engage in service, or even making our home into a temple or having a temple room in our home, or arrange our house to remind us of Vrindavana, is a means by which we can easily feel a closeness to the holy land. Then we engage in service to our Deities, read the stories of Krishna's pastimes, focus on the activities of the devotees we like the most, and meditate on that mood in our own service to Krishna.

This is further explained like so: "The advanced devotee who is inclined to spontaneous loving service should follow the activities of a particular associate of Krishna in Vrindavana. He should execute service externally [with his physical body] as a regulative devotee as well as internally [in his mind and devotional mood] from his self-realized position. Thus he should perform devotional service both externally and internally." [21]

There are two processes by which one may execute this *raganuga* bhakti, or spontaneous devotion–external and internal. When self-realized, the advanced devotee externally remains like a neophyte and executes all the *shastric* injunctions [rules and regulations], especially hearing and chanting. However, within his mind, in his original purified self-realized position, he serves Krishna in Vrindavana in his particular way. Thus, he serves Krishna twenty-four hours a day.

So what does it mean by spontaneous? It means the same attraction to Krishna as a boy is spontaneously attracted to a girl, or as a girl may be spontaneously attracted to a boy. This is reference to the natural attraction the soul has for the Supreme Soul, especially when it becomes free from all forms of material distractions or attachments. And what does it mean to serve Krishna twenty-four hours a day? It means that whatever we are doing, somehow Krishna is connected to that, and we are trying to please Krishna by what we do. Even if we work a job, our mentality is that we do it to earn money to engage it in Krishna's service. Or even sleeping is part of our service to Krishna. Obviously, we cannot stay awake all the time, but we sleep so that we take care of our body and mind so we can engage it nicely in Krishna's service. Without enough sleep we may become too drowsy and get into a car accident, or something like that. How will that please anyone? So we have to take everything in moderation and do it with the right attitude, and use it so that we can be efficient in our acts of devotion.

## ENTERING KRISHNA'S PASTIMES IN ANOTHER UNIVERSE

When a person is ready to go back to the spiritual pastimes of Krishna in the spiritual world, they may first take birth in the Vraja that is manifested in the material realm at the time when Krishna is performing His pastimes. There, they take birth in a family of devotees who have the mood that has attracted that devotee. Any last imperfections are cleared away, and they are trained in perfecting their service, and then after leaving that body they enter the supreme Goloka Vrindavana to have direct experience of the spiritual pastimes of Krishna. This is explained like so in *Caitanya-caritamrita* (Madhya-lila, 20. 397), "The eternal pastimes of Krishna are continually taking place in the original Goloka Vrindavana planet. These same pastimes are gradually manifest within the material world, in each and every *brahmanda* [or universe]."

Srila Bhaktisiddhanta Sarasvati Thakur explains that Krishna's pastimes, in order to attract the conditioned souls and bring pleasure to His devotees, are manifest in one universe after another. The Vedic literature describes how there are millions of universes, and the Lord appears in each and every one of them. After Krishna leaves one universe, He starts His pastimes in another. In this way, all of Krishna's pastimes are being exhibited eternally in the spiritual sky, and in the material worlds. Just as the sun continuously appears to rise and set, it is always shining somewhere. This is the same with Krishna's pastimes. [22]

Krishna's earthly pastimes include both the eternally perfect, or *nitya-siddha* devotees, as well as those who are *sadhaka* devotees, meaning those who have become perfect by their spiritual practice. "After leaving the material body, the perfect devotee takes birth in the womb of a *gopi* on a planet [or universe] where Krishna's pastimes are going on. This may be in this universe or another universe. This statement is found in the *Ujjvala-nilamani*, which is commented upon by Vishvanatha Chakravarti Thakur. When a devotee becomes perfect, he is transferred to the universe where Krishna's pastimes are taking place. Krishna's eternal associates go wherever Krishna manifests His pastimes. As stated before, first the father and mother of Krishna appear, then the other associates. Quitting his material body, the perfect devotee also goes to associate with Krishna and His other associates." [23]

In this way, an advanced devotee, upon leaving the present body, goes to the universe where Krishna is appearing, and through the birth in a family of Krishna's associates, enters into Krishna's direct service in His pastimes. Therein, the devotee learns all about the services that he or she will perform, which other devotees they will associate with, and all the other intricacies of their transcendental situation. It is thereafter when the devotee leaves that body from such earthly pastimes, he or she goes to the original Goloka Vrindavana planet in the spiritual sky. This is further elaborated in the purport of *Srimad-Bhagavatam* (9.11.22) by A. C. Bhaktivedanta Swami Prabhupada: "After giving up his body, the devotee who becomes perfect enters that particular universe where Lord Ramachandra or Lord Krishna is engaged in His pastimes. Then, after being trained to serve the Lord in various capacities in that *prakata-lila* [the Lord's pastimes in the material universe], the devotee is finally promoted to *sanatana-dhama*, the supreme abode in the spiritual world. One who enters the transcendental pastimes of the Lord is called *nitya-lila-pravishta* [a participant in the eternal pastimes]."

This is one of the reasons why we find the principle in bhakti-yoga to live in a holy place like Vrindavana or Mathura if possible. However, a place like Vrindavana is considered to be both *sadhaka-*

*bhumi* and *siddha-bhumi*. In other words, Vrindavana is for both devotees who are practicing to become spiritually perfect, and those who are already spiritually perfect. They all act according to their level of spiritual realization. Plus the holy *dham* reveals itself according to the level of spiritual advancement and perception of the devotee.

However, the point is that when living in Vrindavana, when our *sadhaka* body perishes, meaning the body we are using to practice bhakti-yoga, even if we are not quite perfect yet, the Lord will allow us to take birth in a family of devotees there so that we can continue our practice in the holy *dham* and make rapid development.

## ENTERING THE SPIRITUAL REALM

First we need to understand a little more about the spiritual realm. Now we are in the material creation, in one of the universes that float in the spiritual water called the Karana Ocean, or casual ocean. What separates the material energy from the spiritual world, according to the *Padmottara-khanda* (225.57), is the Viraja River, the unusual water which surrounds the cosmic creation. This Viraja River is the goal of those who seek nirvana, or the merging into nothingness because it is neither in the spiritual or material worlds. Beyond the Viraja River is the spiritual sky, the Brahman effulgence, in which unlimited spiritual planets known as Vaikunthalokas are located. *Vaikuntha* means no anxiety, lamentation or fear. On each Vaikuntha planet lives an expansion of the Supreme Personality of God in His Vishnu or Narayana form, accompanied by Lakshmi, the goddess of fortune. All of the devotees in Vaikuntha engage in service to the Lord in the mood of awe and reverence, and are full in the six opulences of strength, knowledge, beauty, fame, wealth, and renunciation.

The Vaikuntha planets are also of a size that is incomprehensible. These are clearly described in a few verses of the *Caitanya-caritamrita* (Madhya-lila, 21.4-8, 43-52) like so: "The breadth of each Vaikuntha planet is described as eight miles multiplied by one hundred, by one thousand, by ten thousand, by one hundred thousand, by ten million. In other words, each Vaikuntha planet is expanded beyond our ability to measure. Each Vaikuntha planet is very large and is made of spiritual bliss. The inhabitants are associates of the Supreme Lord, and they have full opulence like the Lord Himself. Thus they are all situated. Since all of the Vaikuntha planets are located in a certain corner of the spiritual sky, who can measure the spiritual sky? The shape of the spiritual sky is compared to a lotus flower. The topmost region of that flower is called the whorl, and within that whorl is Krishna's abode. The petals of the spiritual lotus flower consist of many Vaikuntha planets. Each Vaikuntha planet is full of spiritual bliss, complete opulence and space, and each is inhabited by various forms [of the Lord]. If Lord Brahma and Lord Shiva cannot estimate the length and breadth of the spiritual sky and the Vaikuntha planets, how can ordinary living entities begin to imagine them?"

"The internal abode [of Lord Krishna] is called Goloka Vrindavana. It is there that Lord Krishna's personal friends, associates, father and mother live. Vrindavana is the storehouse of Krishna's mercy, and the sweet opulences of conjugal love. That is where the spiritual energy, working as a maidservant, exhibits the *rasa* dance, the quintessence of all pastimes.

"Vrindavana-dham is very soft due to the mercy of the Supreme Lord, and it is especially opulent due to conjugal love. The transcendental glories of the son of Maharaja Nanda are exhibited here. Under the circumstances, not the least anxiety is awakened within us.

"Below the Vrindavana planet is the spiritual sky, which is known as Vishnuloka. In Vishnuloka there are innumerable Vaikuntha planets controlled by Narayana and other innumerable expansions of Krishna. The spiritual sky, which is full in all six opulences [namely strength, knowledge, beauty, fame, wealth, and renunciation], is the interim residence of Lord Krishna. It is there that an unlimited number of forms of Krishna enjoy Their pastimes. Innumerable Vaikuntha planets, which are just like different rooms of a treasure-house, are all there, filled with all opulences. Those unlimited planets house the Lord's internal associates, who are also enriched with the six opulences.

"Below the planet named Goloka Vrindavana are also the planets known as Devi-dham, Mahesha-dham and Hari-dham. These are opulent in different ways. They are managed by the Supreme Personality of Godhead, Govinda, the original Lord. I offer my obeisances to Him." [24]

So, in the above verse, we get the idea that the spiritual world is divided into various levels for various purposes and for accommodating many different levels of liberated souls. As we have mentioned, beyond the Viraja River is the Brahman, which is for those who merge into the impersonal aspect of the Supreme. This is part of the spiritual nature, which is indestructible, eternal, inexhaustible, and unlimited. It is the supreme abode consisting of three fourths of the Lord's energies. It is known as *paravyoma*, the spiritual sky. Within the Brahman effulgence is the Vaikuntha planets, the abodes of Lakshmi-Narayana, where They are worshiped with awe and reverence, and everyone lives in great opulence. Beyond those planets is Madhurya-dham, the place of ultimate sweetness based on transcendental love. That realm is like a vast lotus flower with various petals for particular divine and spiritual pastimes that go on. The outer petals consist of one area called Ayodhya-dham for those devotees who are dedicated to Sita and Lord Ramachandra and Their associates. Deeper in is another area called Dwaraka-dham, where Lord Krishna lives with His devotees in more opulence than found in Vaikuntha. In the inner petals we can find Mathura-dham for the devotees of Krishna's youthful pastimes, and the center whorl of that lotus is Goloka-dham, the supreme abode of Lord Krishna wherein He engages in His most sweet pastimes and loving exchanges with His devotees. Even though all of these manifest as holy places in the material world, their spiritual locations are the most magnificent.

The abode of the external energy on the other side of the Viraja River is called Devi-dham, which is considered one-fourth of the Lord's opulences, and its inhabitants are the conditioned souls. Therein is the material energy, personified by goddess Durga. Even though we are in the material manifestation, we want to enter the spiritual world and reach the Vaikuntha planets or even Krishna's abode of Goloka Vrindavana. The spiritual world is the abode of the pastimes of the eternal spiritual energy. This includes the qualities of forgiveness, compassion, peace, equanimity, justice, and especially all-encompassing love, which is the core relationship between all residents of Vaikuntha and the Lord Himself. This is the glory of the divine abode. No one leaves this abode or goes back to the material world. If for some reason a devotee does, he goes with the Lord to display divine pastimes, or he has a mission to do in the material worlds on behalf of the Lord. If the latter is the case, it is not like a fall down into the material world at all, but he takes with him special powers, and his birth, actions, intellect, personality, and body are in themselves spiritual. Though his body may be produced by the material energy, the use of that body is purely spiritual and engaged in the service of his Lord. Therefore, he has the same qualities as found in the divine abode, as mentioned above.

Residents of the divine, spiritual abode of the Lord have bodies that are purely spiritual, which means they endure no decay, disease, birth, death, or any modifications as found in the material worlds. They are divine in essence, full of consciousness, knowledge, transcendence, and endowed with all virtues. All the mysteries and secrets connected with God and His abode which we cannot understand while we are in the cosmic creation and covered in a body of the material elements, can be wholly comprehended when we go to the Supreme Abode. As soon as one enters there, he fully perceives the secret of God's eternal nature and His abode in reality. He also now fully understands the secret of his own eternal identity. Even when entering the pastimes of the Lord, we see that they are quite different than what we had tried to understand them to be. In this way, the devotee experiences what was previously beyond experience and understanding. Of course, such are the limitations of being encased in a dense, material body. But by following the path of bhakti-yoga we can start refining our consciousness to where we can begin getting glimpses into understanding this knowledge, and even begin to perceive our own eternal nature and the spiritual dimension all around us.

## ADDITIONAL DESCRIPTIONS OF VAIKUNTHA

In the *Srimad-Bhagavatam*, Third Canto, Fifteenth Chapter, there is the following additional information on the kingdom of God: "In the spiritual sky there are spiritual planets known as Vaikunthas, which are the residences of the Supreme Personality of Godhead and His pure devotees, and are worshiped by the residents of all the material planets. In the Vaikuntha planets all the residents are similar in form to the Supreme Personality of Godhead. They all engage in devotional service to the Lord without desires for sense gratification.

"In the Vaikuntha planets is the Supreme Personality of Godhead, who is the original person and who can be understood through the Vedic literature. He is full of the uncontaminated mode of goodness, with no place for passion or ignorance. He contributes religious progress for the devotees.

"In those Vaikuntha planets there are many forests which are very auspicious. In those forests the trees are desire trees [trees that fulfill all desires], and in all seasons they are filled with flowers and fruits because everything in the Vaikuntha planets is spiritual and personal.

"In the Vaikuntha planets the inhabitants fly in their airplanes, accompanied by their wives and consorts, and eternally sing of the character and activities of the Lord, which are always devoid of all inauspicious qualities. While singing the glories of the Lord, they deride even the presence of the blossoming *madhavi* flowers, which are fragrant and laden with honey. When the king of bees hums in a high pitch, singing the glories of the Lord, there is a temporary lull in the noise of the pigeon, the cuckoo, the crane, the *chakravaka*, the swan, the parrot, the partridge, and the peacock. Such transcendental birds stop their own singing simply to hear the glories of the Lord. Although the flowering plants like the mandara, kunda, kurabaka, utpala, champaka, arna, punnaga, nagakesara, bakula, lily, and parijata are full of transcendental fragrance, they are still conscious of the austerities performed by tulasi, for tulasi is given special preference by the Lord, who garlands Himself with tulasi leaves.

"The inhabitants of Vaikuntha travel in their airplanes made of lapis lazuli, emerald, and gold. Although crowded by their consorts, who have large hips and beautifully smiling faces, they cannot be stimulated to passion by their mirth and beautiful charms. The ladies in the Vaikuntha planets are as beautiful as the goddess of fortune herself. Such transcendentally beautiful ladies, their hands playing with lotuses and their leg bangles tinkling, are sometimes seen sweeping the marble walls, which are bedecked at intervals with golden borders, in order to receive the grace of the Supreme Personality of Godhead.

"The goddesses of fortune worship the Lord in their own gardens by offering tulasi leaves on the coral-paved banks of transcendental reservoirs of water. While offering worship to the Lord, they can see on the water the reflection of their beautiful faces with raised noses, and it appears that they have become more beautiful because of the Lord's kissing their faces.

"It is very much regrettable that unfortunate people do not discuss the description of the Vaikuntha planets but engage in topics which are unworthy to hear and which bewilder one's intelligence. Those who give up the topics of Vaikuntha and take to talk of the material world are thrown into the darkest region of ignorance.

"Lord Brahma said: My dear demigods, the human form of life is of such importance that we also desire to have such life, for in the human form one can attain perfect religious truth and knowledge. If one in the human form of life does not understand the Supreme Personality of Godhead and His abode, it is understood that he is very much affected by the influence of external nature.

"Persons whose bodily features change in ecstasy and who breathe heavily and perspire due to hearing the glories of the Lord are promoted to the kingdom of God, even though they do not care for meditation and other austerities. The kingdom of God is above the material universe, and it is desired by Brahma and other demigods."

This description provides a little insight into the nature of the spiritual world. Just as there are husbands and wives and planets and airplanes in this universe, you will find a similar arrangement in the spiritual world. But there is a big difference between the two. It is stated that the material world is simply a perverted reflection of the spiritual world. Whatever beautiful things we see here are just reflections of the real beauty in the spiritual sky. There, everything is based on attraction to the Supreme, while here everything is based on attraction to these dull, material bodies, especially in the form of sex life. The temporary sex pleasure enjoyed by the residents of this material creation cannot compare to the eternal bliss that is available to those in the spiritual world.

## DESCRIPTIONS OF THE LORD'S SUPREME ABODE

The point is that the spiritual nature of the Lord's abode is beyond the ability of the understanding of the mind and intelligence, which are but material products. Therefore, the more we spiritualize our consciousness, the more we can perceive that which is spiritual. And the more we can understand or even begin to perceive the spiritual dimension, including the pastimes of the Lord that take place in the holy places. This is the potency of bhakti-yoga, which calls the Lord by our love to reveal Himself to us. Especially in the sacred abode of Goloka Vrindavana, where Krishna reveals His love for His devotees like no where else. It is there where the most intimate part of Krishna's love and care for His devotees are displayed, the likes of which are rarely described in any Vedic literature. It is confidential and meant to be experienced only by those who develop the deepest love for Krishna. But this is the nature of the Lord and His eternal abode–where love is the all-pervasive sentiment and frequency in which all residents exist and act. Krishna reveals His intimate self and feels blissful in attending to the desires of His loving devotees in His boundless love, and they feel ecstasy in serving Him in a similar fashion. Thus, the spiritual competition of increasing love between the Lord and His devotees knows no end.

This is the loving freedom that goes on in Goloka Vrindavana, where such love is slightly inhibited in the Vaikuntha planets where it is displayed in awe and veneration, or respect and admiration. In the Vaikuntha planets the loving mood of friendship, or parental expression or conjugal love are not displayed. But the great intimacy in love and friendship in the relationships in Goloka Vrindavana outweigh the mood of awe and respect. Therefore, Krishna can display aspects of His unlimited love that are not shown elsewhere. This is also part of the difference between Krishna in His four-armed form as Lord Vishnu or Narayana, and in His original two-armed form of Govinda, Krishna. Just as Arjuna was a close friend of Lord Krishna and treated Him in a casual and unceremoniously way at many times, when Arjuna saw Krishna's universal form that expanded throughout the universe, he became afraid. But no such fear of the Lord exists in the loving pastimes with Lord Krishna. This is the mood of Goloka Vrindavana.

The fact is that the love that pervades Goloka Vrindavana is so attractive that even residents of the wealthy and opulent Vaikuntha planets may also develop affection for Krishna. When that happens, they can become promoted to the Goloka Vrindavana planet. In the beginning, a devotee may want the spiritual opulences of the Vaikuntha planets, but at a more mature stage, if the dormant love for Krishna is awakened, Vrindavana becomes prominent in their hearts. Such a devotee is never attracted by the wealth and opulence of Vaikuntha. [25]

The majesty of the Lord presides in Goloka, but does not predominate. Rather sweetness and eternal bliss predominates. The wealth is that love is everywhere. Flowers emanate the fragrance of love, bees vibrate love, the birds sing with love, all the groves and forests are filled with love, and this is all an expression of love for Krishna. In this way, Krishna feels happiness, and that is reflected back to all the residents who also feel the highest bliss.

In this world, with the result of successful *sadhana* or spiritual practice, one can attain *svarupa-siddhi* (the realization of the true nature of the spiritual world). And whoever attains this, upon giving up the body quickly attains his *vastu-siddhi* by the grace of Krishna. (*Vastu-siddhi* is the final spiritual body suitable for the spiritual world.) In the material world, only a shadow of that supreme stage of existence can be experienced, but that is enough to motivate one to keep going. The preliminary stage of this is called *mukti*, which is liberation and the attainment of the permanent state of the living being after giving up the material body. But the final stage is *prema*, ecstatic love for Krishna that allows the yogi to enter into Krishna's pastimes and activities. (This is what requires the *vastu-siddhi*.) [26]

To explain this in another way, understanding the real nature of the complete spiritual realm is called *svarupa-siddhi*, the perfected spiritual body which includes realization of *sambandha-jnana*, which is knowledge of the relationship between the individual and the Supreme Being. If *sambanda-jnana* is realized, then *abhideya* (the process of cultivating ecstatic love for Krishna, or *prema*) and *prayojana* (which is the goal, meaning *prema* itself) can be attained. Krishna's spiritual abode, name, qualities, and pastimes are all particular aspects of the realizations in *prema*, ecstatic love for Krishna. [27] This is the abode of Goloka Vrindavana, a realm saturated and manifested from *prema*, or ecstatic love. As we have been saying, developing and being absorbed in this ecstatic love through the process of bhakti-yoga is the means for entering the spiritual world, which is a complete manifestation of this *prema*. Again, this is why it is important to develop this level of love so that we can enter into the world of love, *prema*, which is Goloka Vrindavana.

This is the beauty of the supreme abode of Lord Krishna. By meditating on doing our service to Krishna in the mood of the residents of Vrindavana, which is called *raganuga* bhakti, is the way we get our *siddha-deha*, our spiritual body that accommodates that mood.

## MORE DESCRIPTIONS OF GOLOKA VRINDAVANA

The Vedic texts further describe that in the center of all the spiritual Vaikuntha planets is the planet known as Krishnaloka or Goloka Vrindavana, which is the personal abode of the original Supreme Personality of God, Sri Krishna. Krishna enjoys His transcendental bliss in multiple forms on that planet, and all the opulences of the Vaikuntha planets are found there. This planet is shaped like a lotus flower and many kinds of pastimes are taking place on each leaf of that lotus, as described in *Brahma-samhita*, verses two and four: "The superexcellent station of Krishna, which is known as Gokula, has thousands of petals and a corolla like that of a lotus sprouted from a part of His infinitary aspect, the whorl of the leaves being the actual abode of Krishna. The whorl of that eternal realm, Gokula, is the hexagonal abode of Krishna. Its petals are the abodes of *gopis* [friends] who are part and parcel of Krishna to whom they are most lovingly devoted and are similar in essence. The petals shine beautifully like so many walls. The extended leaves of that lotus are the garden-like *dhama*, or spiritual abode, of Sri Radhika, the most beloved of Krishna."

The only business that Sri Krishna has in the spiritual realm is transcendental enjoyment. The only business of Krishna's eternal servants or devotees is to offer enjoyment to Him. The more enjoyment the devotees offer to Krishna, the happier He becomes. The happier Krishna becomes, the more His devotees become enlivened and taste eternal, transcendental ecstasy, which is the reflection of Krishna's happiness. In this way, there is an ever-increasing competition of spiritual ecstasy between Krishna and His parts and parcels. This is the only business in the spiritual world, as confirmed in *Brahma-samhita*, verse 6: "The Lord of Gokula is the Transcendental Supreme Godhead, the own Self of eternal ecstacies. He is superior to all superiors and is busily engaged in the enjoyments of the transcendental realm and has no association with His mundane [material] potency."

All of the inhabitants of Goloka Vrindavana have the most intense, pure love for Krishna. This is what controls Krishna in this spiritual abode. Krishna is controlled by the love of His devotees. He cannot resist the attraction of His devotee's love, so He reciprocates in a way in which all of the devotees feel completely fulfilled. This is where God goes when He does not want to be God. None of the devotees there know that He is God. They are simply attracted to Him and treat Him according to each devotee's loving mood. There, the spiritual force of *yogamaya* (personified by Paurnamasi devi) arranges all the details of the pastimes so that Krishna can experience every level of *raga* or devotional love that the devotees have for Him. This is all that goes on in this realm. It is this love that is constantly expanding, flowing in every way and expressed by every aspect of existence there. No one can comprehend the depth of loving ecstasy that is experienced there, certainly not anyone who is still bound in a material body and mind. It is so far beyond our conception that we cannot fathom it. Nonetheless, by this process of bhakti-yoga, and the power of our intense desire and depth of our love, we can also begin to enter into these all-loving and eternally blissful pastimes.

There are many stories in the Vedic literature which narrate how Krishna engages in loving activities with His friends and relatives and how He performs amazing feats which thrill and astonish everyone. Descriptions of the many activities and pastimes which go on in the spiritual world are found in such texts as *Srimad-Bhagavatam*, *Caitanya-caritamrta*, and Sanatana Goswami's *Brihat Bhagavatamritam*, which explain the many levels and unlimited nature of the spiritual realm. Indeed, the body of the Lord is described as full of eternal bliss, truth, knowledge, the most dazzling splendor, and source of all that exists.

Though it is not possible to experience spiritual pastimes or to see the form of the Supreme with ordinary senses, by spiritualizing our senses by the practice of yoga we can reach the platform of perceiving the Supreme at every moment. At that time we start becoming Krishna conscious and can begin to enter into the pastimes of Krishna, although situated within this material body. If we become fully spiritualized in this manner, there is no doubt that when we give up this material body, we will return to the spiritual world. Until then, we can continue studying the Vedic texts to remember and be conversant about the beauty and loveliness of the spiritual world, as described as follows:

"Vrindavana-dham is a place of ever-increasing joy. Flowers and fruits of all seasons grow there, and that transcendental land is full of the sweet sound of various birds. All directions resound with the humming of bumblebees, and it is served with cool breezes and the waters of the Yamuna River. Vrindavana is decorated with wish-fulfilling trees wound with creepers and beautiful flowers. Its divine beauty is ornamented with the pollen of red, blue and white lotuses. The ground is made of jewels whose dazzling glory is equal to a myriad of suns rising in the sky at one time. On that ground is a garden of desire trees, which always shower divine love. In that garden is a jeweled temple whose pinnacle is made of rubies. It is decorated with various jewels, so it remains brilliantly effulgent through all seasons of the year. The temple is beautified with bright-colored canopies, glittering with various gems, and endowed with ruby-decorated coverings and jeweled gateways and arches. Its splendor is equal to millions of suns, and it is eternally free from the six waves of material miseries. In that temple there is a great golden throne inlaid with many jewels. In this way one should meditate on the divine realm of the Supreme Lord, Sri Vrindavana-dham." [28]

"I worship that transcendental seat, known as Svetadvipa where as loving consorts the Lakshmis, in their unalloyed spiritual essence, practice the amorous service of the Supreme Lord Krishna as their only lover; where every tree is a transcendental purpose-tree; where the soil is the purpose-gem, water is nectar, every word is a song, every gait is a dance, the flute is the favorite attendant, effulgence is full of transcendental bliss and the supreme spiritual entities are all enjoyable and tasty, where numberless milch-cows always emit transcendental oceans of milk; where there is eternal existence of transcendental time, who is ever present and without past or future and hence is not subject to the quality of passing away even for the duration of half a moment. That realm is known as Goloka only to a very few self-realized souls in this world." [29]

By studying and hearing about the beauty of the spiritual world, we will understand that everything we are looking for in life has its origin in that eternal realm. There, it is described, one finds freedom from all pains and suffering, and the atmosphere is unlimitedly full of ever-expanding beauty, joy, happiness, knowledge, and eternal, loving relationships. It is a world full of recreation only, without the struggle for maintaining our existence. There is never any hunger, and we can feast and never get full. Neither is there any lamentation over the past or fear of the future. It is said that time is conspicuous by its absence. Thus, the needs of the soul for complete freedom and unbounded happiness and loving association are found in the spiritual atmosphere. That is our real home.

*A miniature painting showing Radha and Krishna in the forests of Vraja being assisted by Their associates, the gopis.*

# Chapter Twenty-Five

*A miniature painting showing Radha and Krishna dancing near the forests and lakes of Vrindavana.*

## ENTERING KRISHNA'S CONFIDENTIAL PASTIMES

As we have stated previously, not everyone will have a desire to enter into these most confidential pastimes of Lord Krishna. There are many devotees who may simply want to reach the Vaikuntha planets, or attain Ayodhya-dham, or Dwaraka-dham, or even be with Krishna in Mathura-dham. And there may be those devotees who may want to be devoted as Krishna's servant, or His friend, or develop an affection similar to His parents or elders. And that is perfectly all right. There are innumerable such devotees, and they all please and have relations with Krishna in various ways. But for those who want to enter the pastimes of Krishna's most confidential devotees, there is a method to follow.

So, let us have a short review of what we must do to enter Goloka Vrindavana and then go further into those most confidential pastimes. First of all, to enter the eternal realm of Goloka Vrindavana, one must follow the path of bhakti-yoga to rise to the level of *bhava* while still in the material body.

The stages of developing bhakti or devotional service from the level of practice to the topmost and final achievement of human life are nine steps. These go from:

1) *shraddha* (starting with and developing faith);
2) *sadhu-sanga* (association with other devotees);
3) *bhajana-kriya* (devotional action or *sadhana-bhakti*, such as hearing about Krishna, chanting His holy names, and the other basic steps);
4) *anartha-nivritti* (the process of purification, specifically eradicating activities and behaviors unfavorable to bhakti);
5) *nishtha* (unshakable faith and steadiness, when one becomes firmly steady in one's spiritual practice and thoughts of Krishna, and when the main endeavor in life is for spiritual advancement, and when material aspirations have become less important or even abandoned);
6) *ruchi* (attaining spontaneous taste and attraction for Krishna and for one's *sadhana* or spiritual practice);
7) *asakti* (deep attachment to Krishna, and chanting, hearing, and remembering Krishna's names and pastimes);

8) *bhava* (ecstatic emotion, divine love in a particular mood, the seed of *prema*, and realization of one's eternal spiritual identity and service, and direct vision of Krishna); and then
9) *prema* (exclusive and deeply ecstatic devotional love for Krishna).[30]

After attaining *bhava* is when the devotee will also realize his or her desired spiritual identity. It is when it becomes clear what *raga* or devotional mood to which one is most attracted, and then meditates on serving Krishna in that mood. This is when the devotee develops his or her *siddha-deha*.

The *siddha-deha* is explained by both Jiva Gosvami and Vishvanatha Chakravarti as a mentally conceived, spiritually perfect body, while one is still engaged in *raganuga-sadhana* (or *raganuga* spiritual practices), and is still in the final stages of undergoing *anartha-nivritti* (the process of getting rid of the last bits of our material or faulty tendencies). It is definitely a spiritual body and is suitable to render service internally (*manasi-seva*) to Radha and Krishna, but it is conceived in meditation. The *siddha-deha* is created by the force of the devotee's spiritual desires in the way he or she wishes to serve Krishna. The *siddha-deha* is the transcendental medium between doing your spiritual practice in your physical body and your *siddha-svarupa*, which manifests as you progress through the final stages of your *raganuga* bhakti meditations.

The next step is attaining your *siddha-svarupa*, which is the perfected spiritual form given or awarded by Krishna. Your *siddha-svarupa* is only attained after reaching the deeper stage of *bhava*, or the beginning phase of Krishna *prema*, and is the first fully transcendental manifestation of your spiritual identity. It is in this form that the devotee can get his first personal *darshan* or view of Lord Krishna and begin to perceive the spiritual abode of Goloka Vrindavana. This is about as developed as a person can get while still in the material body, and before he or she gets the *vastu-siddhi*.

Then, by developing and experiencing one's eternal relationship with Krishna, the bhakti-yogi can attain *prema*. This is attained by constantly meditating on one's eternal identity in the *siddha-svarupa*, or one's perfected spiritual form in relationship with Krishna, during the last phases of *raganuga* bhakti. *Prema* is developed by one's internal meditation on Krishna. This *prema* is required in order to enter into Krishna's eternal pastimes in Goloka Vrindavana. Otherwise, we may have to return to another material body to continue our progress in bhakti-yoga. If that happens, whatever our next situation may be, it will be an arrangement wherein we can continue our spiritual development from wherever we left off.

The full extent of *prema* and the conditions it presents cannot be fully experienced while in the material body. So at this time, when the devotee leaves the body behind, the devotee takes birth in a devotee family somewhere in a universe where Krishna's pastimes are being performed. This is the attainment of one's *vastu-siddhi*, or one's transcendental body and identity.

The *vastu-siddhi* is attained when one is completely disconnected with the present material body, and when one's identification with the new spiritual form takes over completely. Now the devotee resides in the pure spiritual form and engages in service to Radha and Krishna directly under the auspices of other Vraja devotees. Therein, the devotee becomes completely identified with the new spiritual identity, and accustomed to and thoroughly trained in the service upon which he or she has meditated for so long.

It is in the *vastu-siddhi* spiritual body that the devotee attains all of the required elements for their new identity, such as parents, siblings, village of birth, husband, and so on. It is in this birth that the devotee perfects the highest levels of their *prema* and becomes completely qualified to enter the eternal pastimes in Goloka Vrindavana. Entering these earthly pastimes of Krishna, or the *bhauma-lila*, is practically the same as going back to Krishna's supreme, eternal abode in the spiritual realm. But after our *prema* for Krishna is fully perfected here, we are easily transferred to the spiritual world and the eternal pastimes in that final, eternal spiritual body.

After that life in the *bhauma-lila*, one is swiftly transferred to Goloka Vrindavana, the supreme abode. This is the final stage of the journey when your fully developed spiritual identity and form, along with your relationship with Radha and Krishna and your *sakhi* group leader, and with your most desired services, are completely fulfilled far beyond whatever you could have imagined. This is when you accept the *Sampatti-dasa*, meaning the final stage of accepting one's spiritual form in Krishna's eternal pastimes in Goloka Vrindavana.

Therefore, to enter into the most confidential pastimes of Radha and Krishna, the bhakti-yogi needs to meditate on doing service in the mood of the *gopis*, Lord Krishna's cowherd maidservants. As it is explained in the *Caitanya-caritamrita*, (Madhya-lila, 8.201-205): "The pastimes of Radha and Krishna are very confidential. They cannot be understood through the mellows [or relations] of servitude, fraternity or parental affection. Actually, only the *gopis* have the right to appreciate these transcendental pastimes, and only from them can these pastimes be expanded. Without the *gopis*, these pastimes between Radha and Krishna cannot be nourished. Only by their cooperation are such pastimes broadcast. It is their business to taste the mellows [meaning the sweet taste that emanates from these activities].

"Without the help of the *gopis*, one cannot enter into these pastimes. [Therefore] Only he who worships the Lord in the ecstasy of the *gopis*, following in their footsteps, can engage in the service of Sri Sri Radha-Krishna in the bushes of Vrindavana. Only then can one understand the conjugal love between Radha and Krishna. There is no other procedure for understanding."

Thus, by following in the *gopis* footsteps, and following in their loving mood, one can realize and enter into the ultimate goal of service to Radha and Krishna in the bowers of Vrindavana. The natural love of the *gopis* for Krishna is not mundane sensuality. Rather, they like to serve Radha and Krishna together, and work to bring Radha and Krishna together from whatever other pastimes They may be performing. Even if Radharani is cooking or picking flowers, or if Krishna is playing with the cowherd boys, the *gopis* still like to bring Radha and Krishna together and in that way assist in Their pastimes. That is when the *gopis* feel the most happiness. And this is the quintessential stage of bhakti-yoga.

Furthermore, those who expand or increase the pleasure pastimes between Radha and Krishna are known as *sakhis*, the most confidential of the young servants of the Divine Couple. A notable feature of the *sakhis* and Radharani's girlfriends is that they have no desire to enjoy Krishna's company alone. Their innocent and highest pleasure is derived entirely from seeing the Divine Couple interact together, and helping Them to experience the joy of being together. This is the ever-increasing loving activities that go on in the deepest levels of Sri Sri Radha and Krishna's pastimes with Their confidential associates in the bushes of Goloka-Vrindavana.

## CONCLUSION

Even though Lord Krishna has countless devotees and associates with whom He can interact in pastimes of love and enjoyment, the Lord is still always seeking the means to attract the fallen or conditioned souls to His abode. In fact, without His devotees, Krishna has little need to enjoy His spiritual abode. As He says, "O best of the brahmanas, without saintly persons for whom I am the only destination, I do not desire to enjoy My transcendental bliss and My supreme opulences." [31] So, though Lord Krishna does not need anything to complete Himself for He is the complete whole, He still likes to interact in all kinds of ways with His loving devotees.

Therefore, we should be very thankful to the Supreme Lord Krishna for all He does to try and attract us to Him, as there is no means of ever repaying Him for His benedictions to us, and for the pure devotees who are always trying to enlighten us regarding our true identity and real home in the spiritual world. We are like helpless children trying to make our way out of a darkened room. It is only through the guidance supplied by the Supreme Lord and His pure devotees that we can start to make sense of it all, cure our materialistic addictions, and figure out who we are, where we are, how we got here, and where we belong, and then make our way to the eternal, spiritual home filled with light and love for which we are always hankering.

**CHAPTER NOTES**
1. *Bhagavad-gita* 12.6-7.
2. *Bhakti-rasamrita-sindhu* 1.2.278.
3. *Bhagavad-gita* 8.5-7.

# Chapter Twenty-Five

4. Ibid., 8.14.
5. *Srimad-Bhagavatam* 10.46.32.
6. Ibid., 7.1.30-32.
7. Ibid., 11.6.9.
8. Ibid., 12.4.40.
9. *Nectar of Devotion*, p.120.
10. *Srimad-Bhagavatam* 3.33.10.
11. *Caitanya-caritamrita*, Antya-lila, 4.173 pur.
12. Ibid., 4.192-3.
13. *Srimad-Bhagavatam* 11.29.34.
14. Ibid., 1.6.27-28.
15. Ibid., 11.14.25.
16. *Caitanya-caritamrita*, Madhya-lila, 20.141.
17. Ibid., 8.249.
18. Ibid., 8.221-223.
19. Ibid., 8.228-9.
20. *Bhakti-rasamrita-sindhu* 1.2.294 & *Caitanya-caritamrita*, Madhya-lila, 22.160.
21. Ibid., 1.2.295 & Ibid., 22.158.
22. *Caitanya-caritamrita*, Madhya-lila, 20.397, pur.
23. Ibid., 20.397, pur.
24. *Brahma-samhita* 5.43.
25. *Nectar of Devotion*, p.44.
26. *Srimad-Bhagavatam* 2.10.6 & *Sri Caitanya-Sikshamrta*, p.226.
27. *Sri Caitanya-Sikshamrta*, p.226.
28. *Gautamiya Tantra* 4.
29. *Brahma-samhita*, 56.
30. *Bhakti-rasamrita-sindhu* 1.4.15-17.
31. *Srimad-Bhagavatam* 9.4.64.

# CHAPTER TWENTY-SIX

# *How Devotional Yoga Benefits Others*

We may think that we are doing bhakti-yoga just for our own benefit and advancement, but when we practice it, it affects so many others at the same time in so many ways. So we will look at how that happens.

Of course, one way it works is that as we spiritually raise our own consciousness, it also spreads to others in our own sphere of influence, however great or small that may be. The people around us may simply notice that we are more peaceful, more equipoised, easier to get along with, and show the qualities of tolerance, grace, forgiveness, kindness, compassion, etc. People may appreciate that. But there can also be a subtle form of communication between ourselves and those we interact with wherein the frequency in which we operate, especially in our consciousness, may also affect the consciousness of those around us. It has an uplifting nature that others also absorb, whether it be our children, spouse, neighbors, co-workers, and so on.

This is also why if there is a certain percentage of people in the world who uplift themselves in this way, it will begin to affect the whole planet. If one percent raises their consciousness, then the world can begin to change just because of this one percent. But then if five percent, and later ten percent begin to uplift themselves, the general masses of people in the world will also raise their vibrational or frequency level to uplift the planet even more.

In this way, bhakti-yoga, or the performance of devotional service to the Lord, does not merely affect ourselves, but it is like watering the root of the tree wherein all the leaves of the tree also get benefit. We may act in ways to help a certain group of people, but does that mean we are neglecting everyone else? If we serve the

Lord, and if He is pleased, then that spreads to everyone else because He is in the heart of everyone as the Supersoul, and no one is neglected.

That does not mean that we stop any other altruistic activities, such as food distribution, giving classes on anger management, or providing care for others, and so on. No. But the food we can distribute can also be *prasadam*, meaning the food that has been first offered to the Lord or the Deities in the temple, which spiritually surcharges anyone who eats it. Or we may also give classes to allow others to realize that we are more than these bodies or the situation we find ourselves in, and, therefore, can overcome all challenges by utilizing this perception of our real spiritual identity. Anyway, such examples can go on and on.

This is also why it is said that devotional service to the Lord takes care of all obligations. Even obligations to our forefathers, parents, community, the great sages for the wisdom they have provided, etc., are fulfilled because by taking up the natural activity of the soul to engage in service to the Lord, that yogi has achieved the ultimate goal of life, and anyone who has helped him along the way is also benefitted for doing so. This means that whatever others have done to help him in life, are all rewarded in some way because he has reached the highest position and achievement that all understanding, education and assistance can provide.

This is further explained in the *Srimad-Bhagavatam* (11.5.37) in which Karabhajana Muni addresses Maharaj Nimi as follows: "My dear King, if somebody gives up his occupational duty as prescribed for the different *varnas* and *ashramas* [or stages of life], but takes complete shelter in surrendering himself to the lotus feet of the Lord, such a person is no more a debtor, nor has he any obligation to perform the different kinds of activities we render to the great sages, ancestors, living entities, and family and society members. Neither has he any need to bother executing the five kinds of *yajnas* [rituals] for becoming free from sinful contamination [or past karma]. Simply by discharging devotional service to the Lord he is freed from all kinds of obligations."

This is similar to what Krishna says in *Bhagavad-gita* (18.66): "Abandon all varieties of religion [or *dharma*] and just surrender unto

Me. I shall deliver you from all sinful reaction. Do not fear."

In Vedic and Hindu society, it is accepted that we have so many duties to deal with, such as taking care of our parents, grandparents, children, etc. Of course, this should not be neglected. But becoming a devotee who engages in the devotional service of the Lord helps them in ways that they may not understand. But when they leave their body at the time of death, they will then experience the benefits of their son or daughter having engaged in the direct service to God. It is like giving your relatives frequent flyer miles so that they will more easily attain a higher spiritual destination than they would have without your assistance from devotional service. Then they will be glad, instead of merely being temporarily proud that their son or daughter was a doctor, or engineer, or something like that. Not that accomplishing such positions should be criticized in any way, but adding devotional yoga to one's life is what makes the difference. As instructed in Vedic *shastra*, it is the higher goal of life.

The point to consider is explained in a verse spoken by Prahlada Maharaja wherein he says, "One may be born in a brahmana family and have all twelve brahminical qualities, but if he is not devoted to the lotus feet of Lord Krishna, who has a navel shaped like a lotus, he is not as good as a *chandala* [person born in a low class family] who has dedicated his mind, words, activities, wealth, and life to the service of the Lord. Simply to take birth in a brahmana family or to have brahminical qualities is not sufficient. One must become a pure devotee of the Lord. If a *sva-pacha* or *chandala* is a devotee, he delivers not only himself but his whole family, whereas a brahmana who is not a devotee but simply has brahminical qualifications cannot even purify himself, not to speak of his family."[1]

There are two things we learn from this verse; first that the social status of a devotee makes no difference. Even a person who comes from the lowest of social statuses has every right to learn the art of devotional service to the Lord, in which case he becomes exalted. "The Supreme Personality of Godhead, Krishna, is always favorable to the humble and meek, but aristocrats, learned scholars and the wealthy are always proud of their positions."[2] This indicates that wealth and high status is often what keeps such people from wanting to learn the art of devotional yoga. Thus, they use up their good karma for this life, which has allowed them to reach a materially high position, and in the next life they will start over with nothing.

The second and most important point we learn from the above description is that even a lowborn person who is a devotee can purify his whole family. In other words, the position of pleasing the Supreme Being is so powerful, that such a devotee can bring his whole family to the spiritual destination. In the *Skanda Purana* (Mahesvara Kaumarikhanda, 45.140), for example, it explains, "He whose heart gets merged in that infinite knowledge, the ocean of bliss, the Supreme Being, his family line gets sanctified, his mother's object of existence is fulfilled, and the earth itself attains purity through him."

In this way, a pure devotee serves the interest of his family more efficiently than those who may only be interested in fulfilling ordinary family duties. The Lord gives special interest and protection to the family members and descendants of a devotee, even if such members are non-devotees. Even the great demon Hiranyakashipu was awarded liberation simply for being the father of the great devotee Prahlada Maharaja. In this way, the Lord, who can do as He likes, is so kind that he gives special protection to the family members of His devotee. [3]

So a devotee purifies his family, but how much of his family is explained by Lord Narasimhadeva when speaking to Prahlada Maharaja in regard to his father who was the worst of demons, "The Supreme Personality of Godhead said: My dear Prahlada, O most pure, O great saintly person, your father has been purified, along with twenty-one forefathers in your family. Because you were born in this family, the entire dynasty has been purified. Wherever and whenever there are peaceful, equipoised devotees who are well behaved and decorated with all good qualities, that place and the dynasties there, even if condemned, are purified." [4]

So herein our whole dynasty, farther back and including more people than we can even know, can all be qualified for a spiritual destination if we simply become sincere and purified devotees. It is also stated that it is not only twenty-one generations back, but also another twenty-one generations forward. This is for a pure devotee, wherein some places have said that even an average devotee will still purify seven generations back and forward of his family.

Not only do we please or purify our family by such devotional service to the Supreme Being, of which we are all spiritual parts and parcels, but we also please the many demigods by such sincere action. The demigods or higher beings control various energies of nature. And the Vedic texts describe various rituals to invoke their blessings so we can attain the facilities to live comfortably. But a devotee engaged in serving the Supreme God automatically pleases the other *devatas* and demigods. This is also explained in the *Bhagavatam* (4.31.14), "As pouring water on the root of a tree energizes the trunk, branches, twigs, and everything else, and as supplying food to the stomach enlivens the senses and limbs of the body, simply worshiping the Supreme Personality of Godhead through devotional service automatically satisfies the demigods, who are parts of that Supreme Personality."

It can be further explained in this way, as found in the *Bhagavatam* (5.18.12): "All the demigods and their exalted qualities, such as religion, knowledge and renunciation, become manifest in the body of one who has developed unalloyed devotion for the Supreme Personality of Godhead, Vasudeva [Krishna]."

The point is that if such a bhakti-yogi can attract and please the Supreme Person, he can also please the whole universe because Krishna is the ultimate cause of the whole universe. This is why if more devotees can engage in such bhakti in this way, the more it will create a force of spiritual well-being that is felt by the whole world. No one is likely to see this force, or understand its cause, but it will nonetheless have its impact.

If we expand this effect of devotional service further, we can say that we love everyone by loving Krishna, and by loving Krishna we love everyone. Everyone is a part of Krishna. So, again we can say that it is like the process of watering the root of the tree, by which when worshiping Krishna, it nourishes everyone. As stated in the *Padma Purana*, "A person who is engaged in devotional service in full awareness of Krishna, is to be understood to be doing the best service to the whole world, and to be pleasing everyone in the world.

In addition to human society, he is pleasing even the trees and animals because they also become attracted by such actions." [5]

Therefore, we may be doing so many activities that can benefit the planet and its residents in so many ways, but one of the greatest forms of welfare work is the performance of pleasing the Lord. Lord Krishna Himself explains this as follows: "A devotee whose speech is sometimes choked up [in ecstasy], whose heart melts, who cries continually and sometimes laughs, who feels ashamed [considering himself most fallen] and cries out loudly and then dances–a devotee thus fixed in loving service to Me purifies the entire universe." [6]

In this way, the more people who take up this process of bhakti-yoga, the more this world and the people in it will become truly happy. The devotees become uplifted, and all others, not only humans but all species, will also become uplifted in various ways and can attain happiness. However, a godless society which is detached or disconnected from the purpose of a real civilization, which is the attainment of devotional service to the Supreme Being, only becomes more and more hellish, with an increase of misdirection, problems, hatred, envy, heartlessness, lack of cooperation, and so on. This makes no one happy, and only increases the suffering and misery found in the world, regardless of how much plan-making, politics, or social arrangements are made to assist society. That will never help much, as we can plainly see.

What we need is a deeper level of spirituality, which is being offered through this knowledge of bhakti-yoga, devotional service to Lord Krishna. All of society can reach a higher level of happiness, contentment and fulfillment when there is an increase of people practicing this simple but enlightening form of spiritual development.

**CHAPTER NOTES**
1. *Srimad-Bhagavatam* 7.9.10.
2. *Caitanya-caritamrita,* Antya-lila, 4.68.
3. *Srimad-Bhagavatam* 1.19.35. pur.
4. Ibid., 7.10.18-19.
5. *Nectar of Devotion*, p.7.
6. *Srimad-Bhagavatam* 11.14.24.

# CHAPTER TWENTY-SEVEN

# *Telling Others About Bhakti-Yoga*

When it comes to the idea of telling others about the process of bhakti-yoga, we find that the *Caitanya-caritamrita* (Adi-lila 7.26) says that this process of bhakti-yoga, or love of God, Krishna consciousness, will spread around the world, no matter whether a person be a gentleman, a rogue, or even be lame, blind or an invalid. No exact schedule for this is given, so it may take some time for this to happen. But we can already see that in many major cities around the world, there are already temples that advocate and explain this process and show how to do it. As this spreads, the world will see an upliftment of consciousness.

The point is that the pure devotee always wants to expand the number of devotees in the world. This is not only to increase the Lord's happiness, but also to help show people the real goal of life. To spread such knowledge of self-realization is the greatest welfare work for humanity and all living beings. This relieves people from the difficult path of material existence, and also shows how people can enter a higher level of peace, contentment and happiness. This is the way to show kindness and compassion to all living entities by enlightening them in the ways of Vedic culture and devotional service.

However, Lord Krishna does present some cautionary advice as follows: "This confidential knowledge may not be explained to those who are not austere, or devoted, or engaged in devotional service, nor to one who is envious of Me."[1]

Nonetheless, if a devotee does explain this transcendental knowledge to those who are interested, Krishna gives that person special blessings, and he or she becomes the dearmost servant of the

Supreme Lord, as Krishna Himself says in *Bhagavad-gita* (18.68-9): "For one who explains this supreme secret to the devotees, devotional service is guaranteed, and at the end he will come back to Me. There is no servant in this world more dear to Me than he, nor will there ever be one more dear."

Even if one is not very educated in the ways of material knowledge, if he works to allow others to understand this spiritual science, such a person is actually the best well-wisher of all others. As related in the *Srimad-Bhagavatam* (8.7.39), "People in general, being bewildered by the illusory energy of the Supreme Personality of Godhead, are always engaged in animosity toward one another. But devotees, even at the risk of their own temporary lives, try to save them."

The characteristic of the bhakti-yogi, a Vaishnava, is that he or she is unhappy to see the problems and distress of others. Materialistic life is considered like a blazing forest fire. One day you may be happy, and another day you are depressed. One day you may have everything you ever wanted, and another day you may have lost all that matters to you. One day you are dealing with others who want to make the world a better place, and another day you see people who could not care less about the reactions to their activities and how it affects others. It is never steady or stable. That is simply the nature of the material world. But it is also an impetus for people to ask themselves why they are suffering, or why are there so many problems. If they take that question far enough, this will lead them to the understanding that they are actually spiritual beings and will never be fully at home or completely comfortable in this material existence. Then what to do about it? This is where the Vedic instructions and the Lord's directions as found in *Bhagavad-gita* come in very handy. And these are provided to give humanity solace, and to show them what to do with their lives to improve things and get out of darkness. For this reason, devotees will accept miserable conditions if it means they can help raise others from their suffering condition.

*Srimad-Bhagavatam* (8.7.44) relates, "It is said that great personalities almost always accept voluntary suffering because of the misery of people in general. This is considered the highest method of worshiping the Supreme Personality of Godhead, who is present in everyone's heart."

This is similarly related in the *Bhagavad-gita* (18.68-9) where Krishna says, "One who preaches the *Bhagavad-gita* to My devotees is most dear to Me. No one can excel him in satisfying Me by worship." This is basically because a devotee wants to help in Krishna's mission to guide the conditioned souls toward spiritual life. Lord Krishna greatly appreciates this sentiment. Popularizing the philosophy of the *Bhagavad-gita* is certainly helping in the work of God, which can also bring much joy and peace to those who work in this way. Even just helping in such a devotee's mission also has the same value and appreciation by the Lord. If, however, a person does not feel peace, joy, enthusiasm, or illumination in helping spread the message of the *Gita*, then he should look into his heart and analyze the motivation therein. If one is sincere, then even if it is challenging, or if one undergoes hardship to do so, then he or she will feel reciprocation from the Lord for what is done, and also accumulate spiritual merit in their progress of bhakti-yoga.

Lord Krishna explains further, "The devotees of the Lord, peacefully fixed in absolute knowledge, are the ultimate shelter for those who are repeatedly rising and falling within the fearful ocean of material life. Such devotees are just like a strong boat that come to rescue persons who are at the point of drowning. Just as food is the life of all creatures, just as I am the ultimate shelter for the distressed, and just as religion is the wealth of those who are passing away from this world, so My devotees are the only refuge of persons fearful of falling into a miserable condition of life. My devotees bestow divine eyes [to see the spiritual dimension all around us], whereas the sun allows only external sight, and that only when it is risen in the sky. My devotees are one's real worshipable deities and real family; they are one's own self, and ultimately they are nondifferent from Me." [2]

In fact, Krishna says that to whomever tries to spread this transcendental knowledge, He will give Himself to that person. In this way, it is like Krishna is saying He becomes indebted to such a person. Plus, the more a devotee explains this information to others, the more purified he or she becomes, as Krishna explains, "One who liberally disseminates this knowledge among My devotees is the bestower of the Absolute Truth, and to him I give My very own self. He who loudly recites this supreme knowledge, which is the most lucid and purifying, becomes purified day by day, for he reveals Me to others with the lamp of transcendental knowledge. Anyone who regularly listens to this knowledge with faith and attention, all the while engaging in My pure devotional service, will never become bound by the reactions of material work." [3]

However, it is explained that unless one practices bhakti-yoga or devotional service to the Lord, he cannot have the empowerment to teach it to others. This conclusion is indeed confirmed throughout the *Gita* and *Bhagavatam*. [4] Of course, the question is why would anyone want to spread this message if they do not understand it, or are not enlivened by it? The person would not have the interest or the potency to do so. Even if a person earns a living by professionally reciting the *Bhagavatam*, which some people do in India, the potency that would enliven others with the proper understanding will not take effect. The message of the *Gita* or *Bhagavatam* and other conclusive Vedic texts can only be delivered from one heart to another. The power to deliver it in that way is not there unless the messenger is purified. And if someone is empowered to do so, then he can also empower others to take up the mission of understanding and then spreading the message of the *Gita*.

As Lord Krishna further relates: "And I declare that he who studies this sacred conversation [of the *Bhagavad-gita*] worships Me by his intelligence. And one who listens with faith and without envy becomes free from sinful reaction and attains the planets where the pious dwell." [5] So here Lord Krishna assures us that even if people are not devotees, by patiently and faithfully listening or reading these instructions of His, then they are still bound to enter into the heavenly planets of the pious after this life. This is a very positive result from such a simple act. Thus, we can only begin to imagine how much more powerful are the results from directly acting in devotional service to the Lord.

Nonetheless, it does not matter what one's position is, even if a person is a married householder with obligations, a person can still learn and repeat this message of the *Gita* to help others learn about Krishna and be relieved from the forest fire of material existence. As Sri Caitanya Mahaprabhu explained in the *Caitanya-caritamrita* (Madhya-lila, 7.126-8) when the brahmana Kurma asked to be shown special favor and allow him to go with Sri Caitanya and leave materialistic life, His reply was, "Don't speak like that again. Better to remain at home and chant the holy name of Krishna always. Instruct everyone to follow the orders of Lord Sri Krishna as they are given in *Bhagavad-gita* and *Srimad-Bhagavatam*. In this way, become a spiritual master and try to liberate everyone in this land."

Later Sri Caitanya Mahaprabhu clarified this even more when He said, "Whether one is a brahmana, a sannyasi or a shudra–regardless of what he is–he can become a spiritual master if he knows the science of Krishna." [6] In this case, to be a spiritual master may not mean you must give initiation to others, but you can certainly help instruct those who are interested about the message of Krishna and be an instructing or *siksha* spiritual master.

In conclusion, the essence of this instruction is that a person trying to reach the perfection of bhakti-yoga should understand it to the point wherein he or she can explain it to others. It does not matter who you are or what your position may be. To whatever degree one knows this science of bhakti, one can share it with others. Therefore, simply accept and practice the principles that are taught by the guru and preach them in the mentality of service to him. One should never take on the attitude that this is all coming from one's own power, grace or ability. A true messenger always gives all the credit to his own pure devotee spiritual master, and accepts that whatever mercy he has, is due to the mercy being delivered through his own guru as it descends down through the *paramapara*, or line of previous spiritual masters. If one's attitude is faulty, his message will be weakened. But if his dedication and devotion are firm, and acts accordingly, Krishna will give him or her the facility to do his or her part in helping deliver to the world this spiritual knowledge.

As pointed out in the prayers to Lord Krishna by the *gopis* in the *Srimad-Bhagavatam* (10.31.9), "The nectar of Your words and the descriptions of Your activities are the life and soul of those suffering in this material world. These narrations, transmitted by learned sages, eradicate one's sinful reactions and bestow good fortune upon whoever hears them. These narrations are broadcast all over the world and are filled with spiritual power. Certainly those who spread the message of Godhead are most munificent."

**CHAPTER NOTES**
1. *Bhagavad-gite* 18.67.
2. Srimad-*Bhagavatam* 11.26.32-4.
3. Ibid., 11.29.26-28.
4. *Caitanya-caritamrita,* Adi-lila, 3.21.
5. *Bhagavad-gita* 18.70-1.
6. *Caitanya-caritamrita,* Madhya-lila. 8.128.

# CHAPTER TWENTY-EIGHT

# *How God Came to Give Love*

All of Lord Krishna's various *avatars* or incarnations descend into this world to display pastimes and engage in purposes to help humanity and all living beings, and to attract us to His characteristics and personality. This helps motivate us to understand the spiritual world and the reasons for wanting to attain it. As the *Bhagavatam* explains (10.29.15): "O King, the Supreme Lord is inexhaustible and immeasurable, and He is untouched by the material modes because He is their controller. His personal appearance in this world is meant for bestowing the highest benefit on humanity."

You can read more about this and the various avatars in my book, *Avatars, Gods and Goddesses of Vedic Culture*, which gives the finer details on this topic.

In the meantime, there is a more recent *avatar* of Lord Krishna who helped bring more attention to two main things; one of which was to establish the authority of the process of bhakti-yoga and attaining love of God as a primary goal of human existence, and the second was emphasizing the path of *sankirtana* or congregational chanting of the Lord's holy names, specifically in the form of the Hare Krishna *maha-mantra*. That *avatar* is known as Sri Caitanya Mahaparabhu.

This is explained in the *Caitanya-caritamrita* (Adi-lila 3.14, 19-40), wherein Sri Caitanya says: "For a long time I have not bestowed unalloyed loving service to Me upon the inhabitants of the world. Without such loving attachment, the existence of the material world is useless." This is the whole purpose of the cosmic creation, that the inhabitants can, at some point, reach a stage of becoming exhausted of material life and turn toward understanding their spiritual nature, and then go further to attain love for the Supreme

Creator in a way that goes deeper than mere pious sentiment. And to spread this love is the purpose of the appearance of Sri Caitanya.

As He further explains, "I shall personally inaugurate the religion of the age–*nama-sankirtana*, the congregational chanting of the holy name. I shall make the world dance in ecstasy, realizing the four mellows [or relationships] of devotional service. I shall accept the role of a devotee, and I shall teach devotional service by practicing it myself. Unless one practices devotional service himself, he cannot teach it to others. This conclusion is indeed confirmed throughout the *Gita* and *Bhagavatam*. 'Whenever and wherever there is a decline in religious practice, O descendant of Bharata, and predominant rise of irreligion–at that time I descend Myself. To deliver the pious and to annihilate the miscreants, as well as to reestablish the principles of religion, I Myself appear, millennium after millennium.'

"If I did not show the proper principles of religion, all these worlds would fall into ruin. I would be a cause of unwanted population and would spoil all these living beings." (*Bhag.3.24.21*) Herein Lord Caitanya admits that a duty of the Lord is to at least supply to humanity the means for spiritual upliftment. It is up to them to accept it or not, but at least He has fulfilled the means to offer the methods by which humanity can progress forward to their ultimate spiritual purpose.

"My plenary portions can establish the principles of religion for each age. No one but Me, however, can bestow the kind of loving service performed by the residents of Vraja [Vrindavana]. There may be many all-auspicious incarnations of the Personality of Godhead, but who other than Lord Sri Krishna can bestow Love of God upon the surrendered souls? Therefore, in the company of My devotees, I shall appear on earth and perform various colorful pastimes.

"Thinking thus, the Personality of Godhead, Sri Krishna Himself, descended at Nadia [in Mayapur] early in the age of Kali. Thus, the lion-like Lord Caitanya has appeared in Navadvipa. He has the shoulders of a lion, the powers of a lion, and the loud voice of a lion. May that lion be seated in the core of the heart of every living being. Thus with His resounding roar may He drive away one's elephantine vices.

"Knowing Him [Lord Caitanya] to be the reincarnation for the Kali-yuga, Gargamuni, during the naming ceremony, predicted His appearance... The religious practice for the age of Kali is to broadcast the glories of the holy name. Only for this purpose has the Lord, in a yellow [or golden] color, descended as Lord Caitanya."

## THE STORY OF SRI CAITANYA MAHAPRABHU

Sri Caitanya Mahaprabhu [pronounced Chaitanya] (February 27,1486 to 1534 A.D.) was born in Navadvipa, Bengal, on a full moon night during a lunar eclipse. It is typical for people to bathe in the Ganges during an eclipse and chant the Lord's holy names for spiritual purification. So, everyone in the area was chanting the holy names when He was born. His parents, Jagannatha Misra and Sachidevi, gave Him the name of Vishvambhara, meaning the support of the universe, because astrologers had predicted His super human qualities and that He would deliver the people of the world. He was also nicknamed Nimai because He had been born under a nima tree.

During His childhood He exhibited extraordinary qualities, even having philosophical discussions with His mother. While growing, His brilliant intelligence began to become apparent. While still a child, He mastered Sanskrit and logic to the point of defeating local pundits, and established the truth of His spiritual and Vedic philosophy. He became so well known that many logicians of various religious and philosophical persuasions began to fear His presence and refused to debate with Him. Thus, Sri Caitanya established the authority of the Vaishnava tradition through the process of debate and logic.

Then, when Sri Caitanya went to Gaya on the pretext to perform ceremonies for the anniversary of His father's death, He received Vaishnava initiation from Ishvara Puri. Thereafter, He lost all interest in debate and simply absorbed Himself in chanting and singing the names of Lord Krishna in devotional ecstasy. Upon returning to Navadvipa, He gathered a following with whom He would engage in congregational singing of the Lord's holy names.

Thus, He started the first *sankirtana* (congregational devotional singing) movement, and established the importance of chanting the names of God in this age as the most elevated of spiritual processes, and the prime means for liberation from material attachments.

At first, His chanting with people was for the few participants who were a part of His group, but then Sri Caitanya ordered that the ecstasy of love of God be distributed to all people of the area. He gave no recognition for the privileges of caste, or for position, or type of philosophy a person had, or yogic asceticism. He only emphasized the devotional chanting of the Lord's holy names, using the Hare Krishna mantra (Hare Krishna, Hare Krishna, Krishna Krishna, Hare Hare / Hare Rama, Hare Rama, Rama Rama, Hare Hare) which can bring out the natural loving sentiments for God. In this way, He threw open the storehouse of love of God to the inhabitants of this earth.

It was at the age of 24 when He shaved His head and took the order of sannyasa, the renounced stage of life, when He accepted the name of Krishna Caitanya from Keshava Bharati during the initiation. He then spent four years traveling through South India, and also visited Vrindavana and Varanasi. During this time he also gave special instructions to Rupa and Sanatana Gosvamis, who then also spread the glories of the Divine Love for Radha and Krishna. They settled in Vrindavana where they spent their years in writing many books, elaborating the instructions of Lord Caitanya and the glories of bhakti for Radha and Krishna. They also revealed the places where Radha and Krishna performed many varied pastimes in that land of Vrindavana, which have remained special spots where devotees can become absorbed in the bliss of love of Radha and Krishna.

Lord Caitanya spent His remaining years in Jagannatha Puri. During this time He was absorbed in ecstatic devotion to Krishna in the loving mood of Radharani, in which He would lose all external consciousness. He freely distributed the divine nectar of this love for Krishna to everyone and anyone, day and night. Even His presence or mere touch could transform everyone that came near Him into the same devotional mood. He remained like this until He finally left our vision at the age of 48.

Lord Caitanya is considered and was established by Vedic scripture as the most recent incarnation of God. The Lord always descends to establish the codes of religion. This is confirmed in *Bhagavad-gita* (4.6-8) where Lord Krishna explains that although He is unborn and the Lord of all living beings, He still descends in His spiritual form in order to re-establish the proper religious principles and annihilate the miscreants whenever there is a decline of religion and a rise in irreligious activity.

Though there are many *avatars* or incarnations of God, all incarnations are known and predicted in the Vedic literature. Each incarnation performs many wonderful pastimes. But in Kali-yuga, the Lord descends in the form of His own devotee as Sri Caitanya in order to show the perfect example of how devotional service should be performed, and to stress the chanting of the Hare Krishna mantra for this age by inaugurating the process of the *sankirtana* movement for congregational chanting.

Predictions of the appearance of Lord Caitanya can be found in many Vedic texts. One of the oldest prophecies concerning Sri Caitanya's appearance in this world is found in the *Atharva-veda* verse, starting as: *ito 'ham krita-sannyaso 'vatarisyami*. In this verse the Supreme Lord states: "I will descend as a sannyasi, a tall, fair, and saintly brahmana devotee, after four to five thousand years of Kali-yuga have passed. I will appear on earth near the Ganges shore and with all the signs of an exalted person, and free from material desires. I will always chant the holy names of the Lord, and, thus, taste the sweetness of My own devotional service. Only other advanced devotees will understand Me."

Also, in a verse from the *Sama-veda*, starting as: *tathaham krita-sannyaso bhu-girbanah avatarisye*, the Supreme Being says that He will descend to earth as a brahmana-sannyasi at a place on the shore of the Ganges. Again and again He will chant the names of the Lord in the company of His associates to rescue the people who are devoured by sins in the age of Kali.

The *Mundaka Upanishad* (3.3) also relates the prophecy of Sri Caitanya in a different way. It states, "When one realizes the golden form of Lord Gauranga, who is the ultimate actor and the source of the Supreme Brahman, he attains the highest knowledge. He transcends both pious and impious activities, becomes free from worldly bondage, and enters the divine abode of the Lord."

Another prophecy of the appearance of Sri Caitanya is found in two verses in the *Bhavishya Purana*. It states:

*ajayadhvamaja yadhvam na sansayah*
*kalau sankirtana rambhe bhavisyami saci sutah*

"The Supreme Lord said: 'In Kali-yuga, I will appear as the son of Saci, and inaugurate the *sankirtana* movement. There is no doubt about this.'"

*anandasru-kala-roma-harsa-purnam tapo-dhana*
*sarve mam eva draksyanti kalau sannyasa-rupinam*

"O sage whose wealth is austerity, in the Kali-yuga everyone will see My form as a sannyasi, a form filled with tears of bliss and bodily hairs standing erect in ecstasy."

Another is from the *Svetasvatara Upanishad* (3.12):

*mahan praburvai purushah sattvasyaisha pravartakah*
*sunirmalamimam praptim ishano jyotiravyayaha*

"He is the most Benevolent Supreme Divinity [Mahaprabhu or the great master], as [through *sankirtana*] He graciously instigates [or bestows] intuitive wisdom in the *jiva* soul unto its fully developed cognition or purest attainment. This attainment of purest state or immortality is possible only by His grace as He is the Supreme Propeller and Imperishable Transcendental Enlightening Force."

Another is from the *Vayu Purana*: "In the age of Kali I shall descend as the son of Sachidevi to inaugurate the *sankirtana* movement." This is also confirmed in the *Srimad-Bhagavatam* (11.5.32) where it states: "In the age of Kali, intelligent persons perform congregational chanting to worship the incarnation of Godhead who constantly sings the names of Krishna. Although His complexion is not blackish [like that of Lord Krishna], He is Krishna Himself. He is accompanied by His associates, servants, weapons and confidential companions."

The great classic *Mahabharata* (Vishnu-sahasra-nama-stotra, 127.92.75) confirms that Sri Caitanya Mahaprabhu is not different from Lord Sri Krishna: "The Supreme Lord has a golden complexion [when He appears as Lord Caitanya]. Indeed, His entire body, which is very nicely constituted, is like molten gold. Sandalwood pulp is smeared all over His body. He will take the fourth order of life [sannyasa] and will be very self-controlled. He will be distinguished from Mayavadi sannyasis in that He will be fixed in devotional service and will propagate the *sankirtana* movement."

The *Caitanya-caritamrita* (Adi-lila, 3.19-20) also explains how the Supreme Lord Himself describes how He will appear as His own devotee to perform and teach devotional service by inaugurating the *sankirtana* movement, which is the religion for this age.

How He is the "great master" or will "bestow spiritual intelligence" is described in another *Upanishad*. This is one of the lesser *Upanishads* known as the *Chaitanyopanishad*, or *Sri Caitanya Upanishad*. This comes from the ancient *Atharva Veda*. In this description there is not only the prediction of His appearance but a description of His life and purpose, and the reasons why His process of spiritual enlightenment is so powerful and effective in this age of Kali. The *Chaitanyopanishad* is a short text with only nineteen verses. All of them are very significant.

The *Sri Caitanya Upanishad* (texts 5-11) explains that one day when Pippalada asked his father, Lord Brahma, how the sinful living entities will be delivered in Kali-yuga and who should be the object of their worship and what mantra should they chant to be delivered, Brahma told him to listen carefully and he would describe what will take place in the age of Kali. Brahma said that the Supreme Lord Govinda, Krishna, will appear again in Kali-yuga as His own devotee in a two-armed form with a golden complexion in the area of Navadvipa along the Ganges. He will spread the system of devotional service and the chanting of the names of Krishna, especially in the form of the Hare Krishna *maha-mantra*; Hare Krishna, Hare Krishna, Krishna Krishna, Hare Hare/Hare Rama, Hare Rama, Rama Rama, Hare Hare.

Another interesting story about the prediction of the appearance of Lord Caitanya in Kali-yuga is related in a lengthy conversation between Murari Gupta and Damodara Pandita, two contemporaries of Sri Caitanya. It is found in the *Sri Caitanya Mangala*, a biography of Sri Caitanya by Srila Locana Dasa Thakura. Among the many things they discuss are the symptoms and difficulties found in the age of Kali, how Lord Krishna appears on earth in this age, His confidential reasons for doing so, and how He revealed to Narada Muni His form as Lord Gauranga that He would accept while appearing on earth in this age. In this form He would distribute love of God to everyone He met by chanting the holy names. This conversation is very enlightening.

Within this conversation they further relate an incident recorded as the Vishnu-Katyayani Samvada of the *Padma Purana*. This is a conversation between Lord Vishnu and Katyayani (Parvati), Lord Shiva's wife. The story is that one time the great sage Narada Muni acquired the *maha-prasada*, personal food remnants of Lord Narayana, Vishnu, and gave a morsel to his friend Lord Shiva. Shiva tasted it and he began to dance in ecstasy, to the point of disturbing the earth. When he was approached by Parvati about why he was dancing so, he explained what happened. However, she was unhappy and angry that he did not share any with her. Being devoted to Lord Vishnu and concerned for the spiritual well-being of all conditioned souls, she then vowed that if she should get the blessings of Lord Vishnu, she would see to it that the Lord's *maha-prasada* was distributed to everyone. Just then Lord Vishnu Himself appeared and conversed with her. He assured her that He would appear in the world as Sri Caitanya Mahaprabhu in the age of Kali and would keep her promise and spread His mercy in the form of *maha-prasada*, food that has been offered to Him, and the chanting of His holy names to everyone, distributing His mercy everywhere.

Another book is the *Sri Hari-bhakti-vilasa* by Sanatana Gosvami. Sanatana lived about 500 years ago in Vrindavana, India and was a great scholar of the Vedic scripture. A portion of the book contains an anthology of an amazing assortment of verses from the Vedic texts which predict the appearance of Lord Caitanya. Besides some of the quotes we have already cited, he includes verses from such texts as the *Chandogya Upanishad, Krishna Upanishad, Narada Purana, Kurma Purana, Garuda Purana, Devi Purana, Nrisimha*

*Purana, Padma Purana, Brahma Purana, Agni Purana, Saura Purana, Matsya Purana, Vayu Purana, Markandeya Purana, Varaha Purana, Vamana Purana, Vishnu Purana, Skanda Purana, Upapuranas, Narayana-Samhita, Krishna-yamala, Brahma-yamala, Vishnu-yamala, Yoga-vasistha,* and the *Tantras,* such as *Urdhvamnaya-tantra, Kapila Tantra, Visvasara Tantra, Kularnava Tantra,* and others.

These and other predictions confirm the fact that Sri Caitanya Mahaprabhu would appear to specifically propagate the chanting of the holy names. Furthermore, in the Fourth Chapter of the Antya-lila of the *Caitanya Bhagavata,* which is a biography of Sri Caitanya Mahaprabhu written by Sri Vrindavan dasa Thakura who is said to be an incarnation of Srila Vyasadeva, Lord Caitanya explains: "I have appeared on earth to propagate the congregational chanting of the holy names of God. In this way I will deliver the sinful material world. Those demons who never before accepted My authority and lordship will weep in joy by chanting My names. I will vigorously distribute devotional service, bhakti, which is sought after even by demigods, sages, and perfected beings, so that even the most abominable sinners will receive it. But those who, intoxicated with education, wealth, family background, and knowledge, criticize and offend My devotees, will be deprived of everything and will never know My true identity." Then Sri Caitanya specifically states (Antya-lila 4.126): "I declare that My name will be preached in every town and village on this earth."

This verifies the fact that the chanting of the *maha-mantra* is the rare and special opportunity given by God for all to be relieved from the problems of the age of Kali and of material life in general. As confirmed in the *Caitanya-caritamrita* (Adi-lila, 3.77-78), it is Sri Krishna Caitanya who inaugurates the congregational chanting of the holy names, which is the most sublime of all spiritual sacrifices. Intelligent people will worship Him through this means, while other foolish people will continue in the cycle of repeated birth and death in this material world.

In another place of the *Caitanya-caritamrita* (Antya-lila, 20.8-9), Sri Caitanya specifically tells Svarupa Damodara and Ramananda Raya that chanting the holy names is the most practical way to attain salvation from material existence in this age, and anyone who is intelligent and takes up this process of worshiping Krishna will attain the direct shelter of Krishna.

He also strongly opposed the impersonalist philosophy of Shankaracharya and established the principle of *acintya-bhedabheda-tattva*. This specifies that the Supreme and the individual soul are inconceivably and simultaneously one and different. This means that the Supreme and the *jiva* souls are the same in quality, being eternally spiritual, but always separate individually. The *jivas* are small and subject to being influenced by the material energy, while the Supreme is infinite and always above and beyond the material manifestation.

Sri Caitanya taught that the direct meaning of the Vedic *shastras* is that the living entities are to engage in devotional service, bhakti, to the Supreme, Bhagavan Sri Krishna. Through this practice there can develop a level of communication between God and the individual by which God will lovingly reveal Himself to those who become qualified. In this understanding the theistic philosophy of Vaishnavism reached its climax.

As previously explained, there is a system of self-realization especially recommended for each age. In the age of Kali, people are not attracted to spiritual pursuits and are often rebellious against anything that seems to restrict or stifle their freedom to do anything they want. Since in this age we are so easily distracted by so many things and our mind is always in a whirl, we need an easy path. Therefore, the Vedic *shastra* explains that God has given us an easy way to return to Him in this age. It is almost as if He has said, "Since you are My worst son, I give you the easiest process." The *Caitanya-caritamrita* (Adi-lila, 3.40) confirms this and says that the Supreme Being descends as Sri Caitanya, with a golden complexion, to simply spread the glories of chanting the holy names, which is the only religious principle in this age of Kali. In this way, God Himself has given the method of chanting His holy names as the most effective means to reach His spiritual abode.

Sri Caitanya Mahaprabhu did not become much involved in writing. In fact, He only wrote eight verses, but His followers compiled extensive Sanskrit literature that documented His life and fully explained His teachings. For more complete descriptions and elaborations on His life, activities, and philosophy, as written by His close associates, these books that you can order are presently available through various outlets.

### Sri Chaitanya Bhagavat
### (Adi Lila, Chapter Three)
### By Srila Vrindavan Das Thakur

We will include a few additional descriptions from the *Sri Caitanya Bhagavat* that deals with Sri Caitanya's appearance and the prediction of His importance.

Even before He took his birth, the Lord propagated the chanting of His holy name. Streams of people went for their bath in the Ganga at the time of the eclipse and all the way they chanted the Lord's name. Some, who from their birth never once uttered the Lord's name, now chanted that name on their way to the Ganga. The sound of chanting emanated from every direction and the Supreme Lord, the best of the brahmanas, smiled to Himself as He made His appearance.

Sri Jagannatha Misra and Srimati Sacidevi glanced at their child's beautiful face and were overcome with unbounded joy. Ladies stood around the child not knowing what to do; fussily they ululated in jubilation. Relatives and friends hurried to see the new born child; Sri Jagannatha Misra's house was a scene of great exultation.

Srimati Sacidevi's father, Sri Nilambara Cakravarti, found esoteric and wonderful signs in every house of the child's astrological chart. Sri Cakravarti was astounded by the baby's beauty and saw all divine symbols on His person.

A much accepted prophesy in Bengal was that someday a king would be born in Bengal as a brahmana's son, so Sri Cakravarti thought that only the future would prove whether this was the child. In the presence of all, Sri Nilambara Cakravarti, an expert astrologer, began explaining the ramifications of different astrological signs in the Lord's chart. The further he delved into the child's exalted chart, the more difficulty he found in describing the Lord's position. The child will conquer Brhaspati (the sign for learning and education) and be a scholar; He will be a natural repository of all divine qualities.

Present in that gathering was a great saint in the guise of a brahmana who made predictions on the Lord's future. The brahmana said, "This child is the Supreme Lord Narayana Himself. He will establish the essence of all religion. He will initiate a wonderful preaching movement and deliver the whole world. He will give everyone that which is forever desirable even by Lord Brahma, Lord Shiva or Srila Sukadeva Gosvami. Upon seeing Him people will feel compassion for all living entities and become callous toward material pains and joys. This will be the great benediction for the whole world. Not to mention ordinary men, even hard-core atheists will worship the child's lotus feet. He will be glorified throughout the entire creation and people from all orders of life will come to worship Him. He is the personification of pure Bhagavata religion (eternal religion), the benefactor of brahmanas, cows and devotees, and the affectionate, devoted son of His parents.

"This child has come to accomplish great works, just as the Supreme Lord Narayana incarnated to re-establish religious principles. Who can explain the imports of this child's exalted astrological and esoteric symptoms? How fortunate you are, Sri Jagannatha Misra, a leader amongst men. I offer my obeisances to you, the illustrious father of this child. I feel greatly fortunate that I could calculate his astrological chart. His name accordingly will be Sri Visvambhara. He will be known to all as Navadvipa-chandra (the moon of Navadvipa). He is spiritual bliss personified."

The brahmana did not speak further about Lord Caitanya's pastime of accepting the renounced order of sannyasa since that would disturb the loving emotion of His parents.

Sri Jagannatha Misra was enthralled with ecstasy over the descriptions of his son. He immediately wanted to offer gifts to the brahmana. He was a poor man with few possessions, yet feeling great jubilation Sri Misra fell at the brahmana's feet and cried. The brahmana also caught Sri Misra's feet, and everyone present shouted "Hari, Hari" in great joy.

The relatives and friends were all praise for the child, and they blessed Him as they heard the super-natural predictions about

His future. Soon the musicians arrived playing their respective instruments -- clay drums, flutes and shanhai (a reed instrument) -- and filled the air with wonderful music. Ladies from the higher planets mingled freely yet unnoticed with the ladies from earth in this wonderful gathering. The mother of the demigods (Aditi) smiled and placed her right hand holding auspicious grass and paddy on the child's head to bless him saying, "Long life."

"Please remain eternally in this material world and manifest Your pastimes." This explained the expression "Long life."

Srimati Sacidevi and the others noticed the extraordinary beauty of these ladies but they hesitated to inquire about their identity. The demigods respectfully took the dust from Sacidevi's feet, and she lost her speech in extreme exultation.

Neither the *Vedas* nor Lord Ananta Sesa could describe the waves of jubilation that drowned Sri Jagannatha Misra's house. Entire Nadia seemed to be present at Sacidevi's house to experience that undescribable joy. Wherever the people were -- in their houses, or on the banks of the Ganga, or on the streets -- they all loudly chanted the Lord's name. Everyone jubilantly celebrated the Lord's birth, unknowingly thinking the festivity was actually for the lunar eclipse.

Lord Caitanya appeared on the full moon night of the month of Phalguna; this day is the most worshipable by Lord Brahma and other great personalities. This day of the Lord's appearance is the holiest of holy occasions; this day is devotion personified.

Lord Caitanya appeared on the full moon night of Phalguna and Lord Nityananda appeared on the 13th night of the waxing moon. Both these days are all auspicious and transcendental occasions. If one properly follows these two holy occasions, he develops love of Godhead and cuts asunder the knots of material illusion. The appearance days of pure Vaisnava devotees like the appearance day of the Supreme Lord, are also all-auspicious and transcendental.

Whosoever hears the narrations of Lord Caitanya's birth is freed from all miseries in life and in death. Anyone who hears Lord Caitanya's pastimes immediately gets love of God and becomes his eternal servitor; he comes with the Lord each time He advents in this material world.

The Adi Khanda text is wonderful to hear because it contains descriptions of Lord Caitanya's appearance. The Vedic literature describes these pastimes of the Lord as eternal, although He sometimes appears and sometimes disappears.

Lord Caitanya's pastimes have no beginning and no end; I write them down by the mercy of the Lord. I offer my humble obeisances at the Lord's feet and at the feet of all His devotees. I pray that I may be excused from all offenses. I, Vrndavana dasa, offer this song to the lotus feet of my life and soul, Lord Sri Krsna Caitanya and Lord Sri Nityananda Prabhu.

# READING LIST

This is for those who want to do more in-depth study of the deeper aspects of bhakti-yoga, especially *raganuga* bhakti, which includes details that are not fully described in this book.

Must Read Books:
Everyone should read *Srimad-Bhagavatam*, translated by A. C. Bhaktivedanta Swami, Bhaktivedanta Book trust, New York/Los Angeles, 1972.

*Caitanya-caritamrta*, translated by A. C. Bhaktivedanta Swami, Bhaktivedanta Book Trust, Los Angeles, 1974. This has all the basics from *Srimad-Bhagavatam* but goes more deeply into the pastimes and teachings of Lord Caitanya and into the proper steps of *raganuga* bhakti.

*The Manifestation and Realization of Your Eternal Identity*, by Uttamashloka dasa (Ron Marinelli), 2012. This is a great summary of the works by our acharyas on the means to engage in *raganuga* bhakti. You can get this book at: http://raganugabhakti.freeforums.net/thread/3/link-book-2-articles, and specifically at:
https://www.hightail.com/sharedFolder?phi_action=app/orchestrateSharedFolder&id=bDW7Q2Tezyg0Ji31LV1O_-ss_jH1QDrW8gqAH9zTJXI

*Sri Brihad-Bhagavatamrita*, by Srila Sanatana Gosvami, translated by Gopiparanadhana dasa, Bhaktivedanta Book Trust, Los Angeles, 2002.

*Bhakti Rasamarita Sindhu*, by Srila Rupa Gosvami, trans. by Bhanu Swami, Sri Vaikuntha Enterprises, Chennai, 2003.

*The Nectar of Devotion, The Complete Science of Bhakti-yoga*, A. C. Bhaktivedanta Swami Prabhupada, The Bhaktivedanta Book Trust, Los Angeles, 1970. (This is a summary study of the *Bhakti Rasamrita Sindhu* by Srila Sanatana Gosvami.)

*Jaiva Dharma, The Essential Function of the Soul*, Srila Bhaktivinoda Thakura, translated by Sarvabhavana dasa, Brihat Mrdanga Press, Vrindavana, India, 2004.

*Sri Caitanya-siksamrta, The Nectarean Teachings of Sri*

Reading List

*Caitanya*, Srila Bhaktivinoda Thakura, translated by H. H. Bhanu Swami, Brihat Mrdanga Press, Vrindavana, India, 2004.

*Sri Harinam Cintamani*, Srila Bhaktivinoda Thakura, trans. by Sarvabhavana dasa, Bhaktivedanta Books, Mumbai, 1990.

*Sri Bhajana-rahasya*, Srila Bhaktivinoda Thakura, Published by Pundarika Vidyanidhi dasa, Vrindavana.

Other books that also help.

*Ujjval Nilmani*, by Srila Rupa Gosvami, translated and published by Puri Maharaja, Goudiya Vaishnava Association, Mayapur, Nadia, India, Feb. 24, 2000.

*Sri Prema Bhakti-candrika, The Moonrays of Loving Devotion*, Narottama Dasa Thakur, commentary by Visvanatha Cakravarti Thakur, trans. Bhumipati dasa, Touchstone Media, Vrindavana, 1999.

*Sri Radha-Krsna-Ganoddesa-Dipika, A Lamp to See the Associates of Sri Sri Radha-Krisna*, Srila Rupa Goswami, Trans. by Kusakratha dasa, 2009.

*Gaura Govindarena-smarana-paddhati*, by Dhyanacandra Goswami, translated by Haridhama dasa.

*Govinda Lilamrita*, by Krsnadasa Kaviraja, Advaita dasa, Rasbihari Lal & Sons, Vrindavana, India.

*Madhurya Kadambini*, Srila Visvanatha Cakravarti Thakur, trans. by Dina Bandhu dasa, Vrinda Trust, Nandagram, 1993.

# GLOSSARY

*Acharya*--the spiritual master who sets the proper standard by his own example.

*Acintya-bhedabheda-tattva*--simultaneously one and different. The doctrine Lord Sri Caitanya taught referring to the Absolute as being both personal and impersonal.

*Advaita*--nondual, meaning that the Absolute Truth is one, and that there is no individuality between the Supreme Being and the individual souls which merge into oneness, the Brahman, when released from material existence. The philosophy taught by Sankaracharya.

*Agni*--fire, or Agni the demigod of fire.

*Agnihotra*--the Vedic sacrifice in which offerings were made to the fire, such as ghee, milk, sesame seeds, grains, etc. The demigod Agni would deliver the offerings to the demigods that are referred to in the ritual.

*Ahankara*--false ego, identification with matter.

*Ahimsa*--nonviolence.

*Akarma*--actions which cause no *karmic* reactions.

*Akasha*--the ether, or etheric plane; a subtle material element in which sound travels.

*Ananda*--spiritual bliss.

*Ananta*--unlimited.

*Anuraga*--That raga which makes the object of love experienced in ever-fresh ways and itself becomes ever-fresh; gives an experience of the hero with his form, qualities and sweetness, as if previously inexperienced; transforms by special thirst; experienced as if not experienced before. It is based on extreme strength of thirst and produces the perception of an object's absence when it is present.

*Apana-dasa*--The stage of accepting one's spiritual form (also called prapti)

*Apara-prakrti*--the material energy of the Lord.

*Aranyaka*--sacred writings that are supposed to frame the essence of the *Upanishads*.

*Arati*--the ceremony of worship when incense and ghee lamps are offered to the Deities.
*Arca-vigraha*--the worshipable Deity form of the Lord made of stone, wood, etc.
Ardhanarishvara--Shiva as half Shiva and half Parvati.
Aryan--a noble person, one who is on the Vedic path of spiritual advancement.
*Asana*--postures for meditation, or exercises for developing the body into a fit instrument for spiritual advancement.
*Asat*--that which is temporary.
*Ashrama*--one of the four orders of spiritual life, such as *brahmacari* (celibate student), *grihastha* (married householder), *vanaprastha* (retired stage), and *sannyasa* (renunciate); or the abode of a spiritual teacher or *sadhu*.
Ashvamedha–a Vedic ritual involving offerings to God made by brahmana priests.
*Astanga-yoga*--the eightfold path of mystic yoga.
*Asura*--one who is ungodly or a demon.
*Atma*--the self or soul. Sometimes means the body, mind, and senses.
*Atman*--usually referred to as the Supreme Self.
*Avadhuta*–a person who is so transcendental that he is beyond the normal rules and regulations of spiritual life.
*Avatara*--an incarnation of the Lord who descends from the spiritual world.
*Avidya*--ignorance or nescience.
*Aum*--*om* or *pranava*
Ayodhya--the birthplace of Lord Rama in East India.
*Ayurveda*--the original holistic form of medicine as described in the Vedic literature.
*Babaji*--wandering mendicant holy man.
Bhagavan--one who possesses all opulences, God.
*Bhajan*--song of worship, or personal devotional service.
*Bhajan kutir*--a small dwelling used for one's worship and meditation.
*Bhakta*--a devotee of the Lord who is engaged in *bhakti-yoga*.
*Bhakti*--love and devotion for God.
*Bhakti-yoga*--the path of offering pure devotional service to the

Supreme.

*Bhava*--Literally means that by which something is made known, or a transformation of the mind. A term generally used to convey specific moods, emotions, feelings and ecstatic experiences. One of the stages of attaining divine love for God. A ray of *prema*, or preliminary stage before *prema*.

Brahma--the demigod of creation who was born from Lord Vishnu, the first created living being and the engineer of the secondary stage of creation of the universe when all the living entities were manifested.

*Brahmacari*--a celibate student, usually five to twenty-five years of age, who is trained by the spiritual master. One of the four divisions or *ashramas* of spiritual life.

*Brahmajyoti*--the great white light or effulgence which emanates from the body of the Lord.

Brahmaloka--the highest planet or plane of existence in the universe; the planet where Lord Brahma lives.

Brahman--the spiritual energy; the all-pervading impersonal aspect of the Lord; or the Supreme Lord Himself.

*Brahmana* or brahmin--one of the four orders of society; the intellectual class of men who have been trained in the knowledge of the *Vedas* and initiated by a spiritual master.

*Brahmana*--the supplemental books of the four primary *Vedas*. They usually contained instructions for performing Vedic *agnihotras*, chanting the *mantras*, the purpose of the rituals, etc. The *Aitareya* and *Kaushitaki Brahmanas* belong to the *Rig-veda*, the *Satapatha Brahmana* belongs to the *White Yajur-veda*, and the *Taittiriya Brahmana* belongs to the *Black Yajur-veda*. The *Praudha* and *Shadvinsa Brahmanas* are two of the eight *Brahmanas* belonging to the *Atharva-veda*.

*Brahminical*--to be clean and upstanding, both outwardly and inwardly, like a *brahmana* should be.

*Brijbasi*--a resident of Vraja, Vrindavan.

*Caitanya-caritamrta*--the scripture by Krishnadasa Kaviraja which explains the teachings and pastimes of Lord Chaitanya Mahaprabhu.

*Candala*--a person in the lowest class, or dog-eater.

# Glossary

Causal Ocean or Karana Ocean--is the corner of the spiritual sky where Maha-Vishnu lies down to create the material manifestation.

Chaitanya Mahaprabhu--the most recent incarnation of the Lord who appeared in the 15th century in Bengal and who originally started the *sankirtana* movement, based on congregational chanting of the holy names.

*Chakra*--a wheel, disk, or psychic energy center situated along the spinal column in the subtle body of the physical shell.

Chandra--the moon.

*Chit*--eternal knowledge.

*Darshan*--the devotional act of seeing and being seen by the Deity in the temple.

Dashavatara--the ten incarnations of Lord Vishnu: Matsya, Kurma, Varaha, Narasimha, Vamana, Parashurama, Rama, Krishna, Buddha, and Kalki.

Deity--the *arca-vigraha*, or worshipful form of the Divinity in the temple.

*Deva*--a demigod, or higher being.

*Devaloka*--the higher planets or planes of existence of the *devas*.

Devaki--the devotee who acted as Lord Krishna's mother.

*Devas*--demigods or heavenly beings from higher levels of material existence, or a godly person.

*Dham*--a holy place.

*Dharma*--the essential nature or duty of the living being.

*Dharmashala*--a shelter or guesthouse for pilgrims at temples or holy towns.

*Diksha*--spiritual initiation.

Dualism--as related in this book, it refers to the Supreme as both an impersonal force (Brahman) as well as the Supreme Person.

Durga--the form of Parvati, Shiva's wife, as a warrior goddess known by many names according to her deeds, such as Simhavahini when riding her lion, Mahishasuramardini for killing the demon Mahishasura, Jagaddhatri as the mother of the universe, Kali when she killed the demon Raktavija, Tara when killing Shumba, etc. She assumes or incarnates in as many as 64 different forms, depending on her activities.

Dvapara-yuga--the third age which lasts 864,000 years.

*Dwaita*--dualism, the principle that the Absolute Truth consists of the infinite Supreme Being along with the infinitesimal, individual souls.

*Ekadasi*--a fast day on the eleventh day of the waxing and waning moon.

*Gandharvas*--the celestial angel-like beings who have beautiful forms and voices, and are expert in dance and music, capable of becoming invisible and can help souls on the earthly plane.

Ganesh--a son of Shiva, said to destroy obstacles (as Vinayaka) and offer good luck to those who petition him. It is generally accepted that the way Ganesh got the head of an elephant is that one time Parvati asked him to guard her residence. When Shiva wanted to enter, Ganesh stopped him, which made Shiva very angry. Not recognizing Ganesh, Shiva chopped off his head, which was then destroyed by one of Shiva's goblin associates. Parvati was so upset when she learned what had happened, Shiva, not being able to find Ganesh's original head, took the head of the first creature he saw, which was an elephant, and put it on the body of Ganesh and brought him back to life. The large mouse carrier of Ganesh symbolizes Ganesh's ability to destroy all obstacles, as rodents can gradually gnaw their way through most anything.

Ganges--the sacred and spiritual river which, according to the *Vedas*, runs throughout the universe, a portion of which is seen in India. The reason the river is considered holy is that it is said to be a drop of the Karana Ocean outside of the universe that leaked in when Lord Vishnu, in His incarnation as Vamanadeva, kicked a small hole in the universal shell with His toe. Thus, the water is spiritual as well as being purified by the touch of Lord Vishnu.

Garbhodakasayi Vishnu--the expansion of Lord Vishnu who enters into each universe.

Garuda--Lord Vishnu's bird carrier.

Gaudiya--a part of India sometimes called Aryavarta or land of the Aryans, located south of the Himalayas and north of the Vindhya Hills.

Gaudiya *sampradaya*--the school of Vaishnavism founded by Sri Caitanya.

*Gayatri*--the spiritual vibration or *mantra* from which the other *Vedas* were expanded and which is chanted by those who are initiated as *brahmanas* and given the spiritual understanding of Vedic philosophy.

*Ghat*--a bathing place along a river or lake with steps leading down to the water.

Goloka Vrindavana--the name of Lord Krishna's spiritual planet.

*Gosvami*--one who is master of the senses.

Govinda--a name of Krishna which means one who gives pleasure to the cows and senses.

Govindaraja--Krishna as Lord of the Cowherds.

*Grihastha*--the householder order of life. One of the four *ashramas* in spiritual life.

*Gunas*--the modes of material nature of which there is *sattva* (goodness), *rajas* (passion), and *tamas* (ignorance).

*Guru*--a spiritual master.

Hanuman--the popular monkey servant of Lord Rama.

Hare--the Lord's pleasure potency, Radharani, who is approached for accessibility to the Lord.

Hari--a name of Krishna as the one who takes away one's obstacles on the spiritual path.

*Haribol*--a word that means to chant the name of the Lord, Hari.

*Harinam*--refers to the name of the Lord, Hari.

*Hatha-yoga*--a part of the yoga system which stresses various sitting postures and exercises.

Hiranyagarbha--another name of Brahma who was born of Vishnu in the primordial waters within the egg of the universe.

Hiranyakashipu--the demon king who was killed by Lord Vishnu in His incarnation as Narasimha.

Impersonalism--the view that God has no personality or form, but is only an impersonal force (Brahman) which the individual souls merge back into when released from material existence.

Impersonalist--those who believe God has no personality or form.

Incarnation--the taking on of a body or form.

Indra--the King of heaven and controller of rain, who by his great

power conquers the forces of darkness.
ISKCON--International Society for Krishna Consciousness.
Jagannatha--Krishna as Lord of the Universe, especially as worshipped in Jagannatha Puri.
Jagat Kishora--name of Krishna.
*Jai* or *Jaya*--a term meaning victory, all glories.
Janardhana--name of Vishnu.
*Japa*--the chanting one performs, usually softly, for one's own meditation.
*Japa-mala*--the string of beads one uses for chanting.
*Jiva*--the individual soul or living being.
*Jivanmukta*--a liberated soul, though still in the material body and universe.
*Jiva-shakti*--the living force.
*Jnana*--knowledge which may be material or spiritual.
*Jnana-kanda*--the portion of the *Vedas* which stresses empirical speculation for understanding truth.
*Jnana-yoga*--the process of linking with the Supreme through empirical knowledge and mental speculation.
*Jnani*--one engaged in *jnana-yoga*, or the process of cultivating knowledge to understand the Absolute.
Jyestha--goddess Shakti.
*Kala*--eternal time, Yama.
Kali--the demigoddess who is the fierce form of the wife of Lord Shiva. The word *kali* comes from *kala*, the Sanskrit word for time: the power that dissolves or destroys everything.
Kali-yuga--the fourth and present age, the age of quarrel and confusion, which lasts 432,000 years and began 5,000 years ago.
Kalki--future incarnation of Lord Vishnu who appears at the end of Kali-yuga.
*Kalpa*--a day in the life of Lord Brahma which lasts a thousand cycles of the four *yugas*.
*Kama*--lust or inordinate desire.
*Kamanuga-bhakti*--That *raganuga sadhana* bhakti which is filled with intense longing and which follows after the *Kamarupa-ragatmika-bhakti* of the *siddha* bhaktas is called *kamanuga*

*bhakti*. There are two types: *sambhogeccha-mayi* and *tad-tad-bhavecchatma*. (BRS 1.2.297-298)

*Kamarupa-ragatmika-bhakti*--That type of bhakti with full absorption in the beloved which produces an intrinsic thirst for a conjugal relationship with the Lord. It is called bhakti because in that condition there is only eagerness for giving pleasure to Krishna. The other type of bhakti found in the inhabitants of Vraja is *sambandha-rupa-ragatmika-bhakti*.

Kapila--an incarnation of Lord Krishna who propagated the Sankhya philosophy.

Karanodakasayi Vishnu (Maha-Vishnu)--the expansion of Lord Krishna who created all the material universes.

*Karma*--material actions performed in regard to developing one's position or for future results which produce *karmic* reactions. It is also the reactions one endures from such fruitive activities.

*Karma-kanda*--the portion of the *Vedas* which primarily deals with recommended fruitive activities for various results.

*Karma-yoga*--system of yoga for using one's activities for spiritual advancement.

*Karmi*--the fruitive worker, one who accumulates more *karma*.

Karttikeya--son of Shiva and Parvati, also known as Skanda, Subramanya, Kumara, or son of the Pleiades (Krittika constellation).

Keshava--Krishna with long hair.

*Kirtana*--chanting or singing the glories of the Lord.

Krishna--the name of the original Supreme Personality of Godhead which means the most attractive and greatest pleasure. He is the source of all other incarnations, such as Vishnu, Rama, Narasimha, Narayana, Buddha, Parashurama, Vamanadeva, Kalki at the end of Kali-yuga, etc.

Krishnaloka--the spiritual planet where Lord Krishna resides.

*Kshatriya*--the second class of *varna* of society, or occupation of administrative or protective service, such as warrior or military personnel.

Ksirodakasayi Vishnu--the Supersoul expansion of the Lord who enters into each atom and the heart of each individual.

*Kumbha Mela*--the holy festival in which millions of pilgrims and sages gather to bathe in the holy and purifying rivers for liberation at particular auspicious times that are calculated astrologically. The Kumbha Mela festivals take place every three years alternating between Allahabad, Nasik, Ujjain, and Hardwar.

*Kuruksetra*--the place of battle 5,000 years ago between the Pandavas and the Kauravas ninety miles north of New Delhi, where Krishna spoke the *Bhagavad-gita*.

*Kurma*--incarnation of Vishnu as a tortoise.

*Lakshmi*--the goddess of fortune and wife of Lord Vishnu.

*Lila*--pastimes.

*Lilavataras*--the many incarnations of God who appear to display various spiritual pastimes to attract the conditioned souls in the material world.

*Linga*--the formless symbol of Lord Shiva, often represents universal space.

*Madana-mohana*--name of Krishna as one who fills the mind with love.

*Madhava*--Krishna.

*Mahabhagavata*--a great devotee of the Lord.

*Mahabharata*--the great epic of the Pandavas, which includes the *Bhagavad-gita*, by Vyasadeva.

*Mahabhava*--the supreme and ultimate domain of ecstatic experiences in the realm of loving Krishna; reserved solely for Radha and Her *sakhis*; the stage whereby *anuraga* attains the state of being perceived by itself, is revealed externally through *sattvika-bhavas*, takes shelter of the highest *raga*, and spreads its influence in all devotees. *Mahabhava* transforms the mind into *mahabhava*.

*Maha-mantra*--the best *mantra* for self-realization in this age, called the Hare Krishna *mantra*.

*Mahatma*--a great soul or devotee.

*Mahat-tattva*--the total material energy.

Maha-Vishnu or Karanodakasayi Vishnu--the Vishnu expansion of Lord Krishna from whom all the material universes emanate.

*Mandir*--a temple.

*Mantra*--a sound vibration which prepares the mind for spiritual realization and delivers the mind from material inclinations. In some cases a *mantra* is chanted for specific material benefits.

Martya-loka--the earth planet, the place of death.

*Maya*--illusion, or anything that appears to not be connected with the eternal Absolute Truth.

*Mayavadi*--the impersonalist or voidist who believes that the Supreme has no form, or that any form of God is but a product of *maya*.

Mitra--the deity controlling the sun, and who gives life to earth.

Mohini--Lord Vishnu's incarnation as the most beautiful woman.

*Moksha*--liberation from material existence.

Mukteshvara--Shiva as the giver of liberation.

Mukunda--Krishna as the giver of spiritual liberation.

*Murti*--a Deity of the Lord or an image of a demigod or spiritual master that is worshiped.

Murugan--means the divine child, the Tamil name for Subramaniya, one of the sons of Shiva and Parvati, especially worshiped in South India. It is said that he was born to destroy the demon Tarakasura. He was born in a forest of arrow-like grass and raised by the six divine mothers of the Krittika constellation (Pleiades). Thus, he is also called Kartikeya and Sanmatura, and he assumed six faces (and twelve arms) to suckle the milk of the six mothers. Being young and virile, he is also called Kumara or Sanatkumara. He is also called Skanda for being very forceful in war. His two consorts are Velli, the daughter of a humble chieftain of an agricultural tribe, and Devasena, the daughter of the demigod Indra.

Nanda--the foster father of Krishna.

Nandi--Shiva's bull carrier.

Narasimha--Lord Vishnu's incarnation as the half-man half-lion who killed the demon Hiranyakashipu.

Narayana--the four-handed form of the Supreme Lord.

Nataraja--King of Dance, usually referring to Shiva, but also Krishna.

*Nirguna*--without material qualities.

*Nirvana*--the state of no material miseries, usually the goal of the

Buddhists or voidists.

*Nistha*--Steadiness. Unshakable faith and steadiness in *sadhana* and *bhajana*.

Nityananda–the brother of Sri Chaitanya, and *avatara* of Lord Balarama.

*Om* or *Omkara*--*pranava*, the transcendental *om mantra*, generally referring to the attributeless or impersonal aspects of the Absolute.

*Paramahamsa*--the highest level of self-realized devotees of the Lord.

Paramatma--the Supersoul, or localized expansion of the Lord.

*Parampara*--the system of disciplic succession through which transcendental knowledge descends.

Parashurama--incarnation of Vishnu with an axe who cleansed the world of the deviant *kshatriya* warriors.

Parthasarathi--Krishna as Arjuna's chariot driver.

Parvati--Lord Shiva's spouse, daughter of Parvata. Parvata is the personification of the Himalayas. She is also called Gauri for her golden complexion, Candi, Bhairavi (as the wife of Bhairava, Shiva), Durga, Ambika, and Shakti.

Pashupati--Shiva as Lord of the animals.

Patanjali--the authority on the *astanga-yoga* system.

*Pradhana*--the total material energy in its unmanifest state.

*Prajapati*--deity presiding over procreation.

*Prakriti*--matter in its primordial state, the material nature.

*Prana*--the life air or cosmic energy.

*Pranayama*--control of the breathing process as in *astanga* or *raja-yoga*.

*Pranava*--same as *omkara*.

*Prasada*--food or other articles that have been offered to the Deity in the temple and then distributed amongst people as the blessings or mercy of the Deity.

*Prema*--Matured love for Krishna. Pure *rati* at the stage where only the Lord and nothing else is the subject, and is thus suitable for pastimes. When the relationship of love between the couple remains always without destruction even when there are causes for destroying it. When *bhava* become extremely condensed, it is called *prema*. It softens the heart completely and produces extreme possessiveness of the Lord in the experiencer. (BRS 1.4.1)

*Puja*--the worship offered to the Deity.

*Pujari*--the priest who performs worship, *puja*, to the Deity.

*Purusha* or *Purusham*--the supreme enjoyer.

Radha--Krishna's favorite devotee and the personification of His bliss potency.

*Raga*--Literally, attachment: an intense, irresistible, spontaneous absorption in, and attachment to, the object or person of one's attraction. A spontaneous deep thirst for the object of love. (BRS 1.2.272) The moods associated with this. More specifically, the stage of *prema* excelling *pranaya*, whereby suffering is removed by happiness in the heart on meeting Krishna. Or suffering becomes filled with happiness. The height of *raga* is when the height of suffering becomes filled with the height of enjoyment, meeting Krishna. When *anuraga* takes shelter of this "height of *raga*" it becomes *mahabhava*.

*Raganuga-bhakti*--That bhakti which follows after the *ragatmika bhakti* found distinctively in the residents of Vraja (BRS. 1.2.270) The person who is greedy for a *bhava* similar to that of the inhabitants of Vraja--who are fixed in *ragatmika bhakti*--is qualified for *raganuga* bhakti. (BRS 1.2.291)

*Ragatmika-bhakti*--Bhakti that is impelled exclusively by *raga* (deep spontaneous thirst for the object of love).

*Rajarsi*–a Raja or great *rishi* or sage.

*Raja-yoga*--the eightfold yoga system.

*Rajo-guna*--the material mode of passion.

Ramachandra--an incarnation of Krishna as He appeared as the greatest of kings.

Ramanuja--Vaishnava philosopher.

*Ramayana*--the great epic of the incarnation of Lord Ramachandra.

*Rasa*--an enjoyable taste or feeling, a relationship with God.

Ravana--demon king of the *Ramayana*.

*Rishi*--saintly person who knows the Vedic knowledge.

Sacrifice--in this book it in no way pertains to human sacrifice, as many people tend to think when this word is used. But it means to engage in an austerity of some kind for a higher, spiritual purpose.

*Sati*--Shiva's wife who killed herself by immolation in fire.

*Sac-cid-ananda-vigraha*--the transcendental form of the Lord or of the living entity which is eternal, full of knowledge and bliss.

*Sadhana*--a specific practice or discipline for attaining God realization.

*Sadhu*--Indian holy man or devotee.

*Saguna* Brahman--the aspect of the Absolute with form and qualities.

*Samadhi*--trance, the perfection of being absorbed in the Absolute.

*Sambandha*--Causes of a relationship. The excellence of the aggregate of noble family, beautiful form, bravery, good conduct, and other good qualities. A cause of *madhura-rati*, a love for the beloved.

*Sampatti-dasa*--The stage of accepting one's spiritual form in Krishna's unmanifest eternal pastimes.

*Samsara*--rounds of life; cycles of birth and death; reincarnation.

*Sanatana-dharma*--the eternal nature of the living being, to love and render service to the supreme lovable object, the Lord.

*Sangam*--the confluence of two or more rivers.

*Sankhya*--analytical understanding of material nature, the body, and the soul.

*Sankirtana-yajna*--the prescribed sacrifice for this age: congregational chanting of the holy names of God.

*Sannyasa*--the renounced order of life, the highest of the four *ashramas* on the spiritual path.

*Sarasvati*--the goddess of knowledge and intelligence.

*Sattva-guna*--the material mode of goodness.

Sati–the name of Durga after she sacrificed herself.

Satya-yuga--the first of the four ages which lasts 1,728,000 years.

*Shabda-brahma*--the original spiritual vibration or energy of which the *Vedas* are composed.

Shaivites--worshipers of Lord Shiva.

Shakti--energy, potency or power, the active principle in creation. Also the active power or wife of a deity, such as Shiva/Shakti.

*Shaktipeeth* or *shaktipith*–a great holy place, usually marked by a temple, where a part of the body of Sati or Durga fell to the earth.

*Shalagrama-shila*–the sacred stone that is accepted as a direct form of Lord Vishnu.

*Shastra*--the authentic revealed Vedic scripture.

Shiva--the benevolent one, the demigod who is in charge of the material mode of ignorance and the destruction of the universe. Part of the triad of Brahma, Vishnu, and Shiva who continually create, maintain, and destroy the universe. He is known as Rudra when displaying his destructive aspect.

*Siddha-deha*--The mentally conceived, perfect spiritual body, also known as *siddha-rupa* and *atma-svarupa*.

*Sikha*--a tuft of hair on the back of the head signifying that one is a Vaishnava.

Skanda--son of Shiva and Parvati, leader of the army of the gods; also known as Karttikeya and Subramanya or Murugan.

*Smaranam*--remembering the Lord.

*Smriti*--the traditional Vedic knowledge "that is remembered" from what was directly heard by or revealed to the *rishis*.

*Sneha*--Literally means "melting". *Prema* that ascends to its highest excellence, more fully illuminates the object of love, and liquefies the heart. When *sneha* arises, one can never be fully satisfied with seeing the Lord, nor can one tolerate even a moment's separation. (BRS 3.2.84).

*Sravanam*--hearing about the Lord.

Sri, Sridevi--Lakshmi, the goddess who embodies beauty and prosperity, wife of Lord Vishnu.

Sridhara--Lord Vishnu.

*Srimad-Bhagavatam*--the most ripened fruit of the tree of Vedic knowledge compiled by Vyasadeva.

*Sruti*--scriptures that were received directly from God and transmitted orally by *brahmanas* or *rishis* down through succeeding generations. Traditionally, it is considered the four primary *Vedas*.

*Sthayi-bhava*–the loving emotion, *rati*, evolves into this, it is the permanent and dominant emotional disposition and loving nature of the devotee.

*Stupa*–a Buddhist hemispherical or dome monument that often housed ashes or relics of great Buddhist teachers.

*Sudra*--the working class of society, the fourth of the *varnas*.

Surya--Sun or solar deity.

*Svabhava*--That *bhava* which does not depend on external causes but appears on its own, which is therefore causeless.

*Svami*--one who can control his mind and senses.

*Swayambhu* or *svayambhu*–a deity or image that is self-manifested, without being carved or produced by man.

*Tamo-guna*--the material mode of ignorance.

*Tapasya*--voluntary austerity for spiritual advancement.

*Tilok*--the clay markings that signify a person's body as a temple, and the sect or school of thought of the person.

*Tirtha*--a holy place of pilgrimage.

Treta-yuga--the second of the four ages which lasts 1,296,000 years.

*Trimurti*--triad of Vishnu, Brahma, and Shiva.

Trivikrama--Lord Vishnu as Vamadeva, the *brahmana* dwarf who covered the entire universe in three steps.

*Tulasi*--the small tree that grows where worship to Krishna is found. It is called the embodiment of devotion, and the incarnation of Vrinda-devi.

*Upanishads*--the portions of the *Vedas* which primarily explain philosophically the Absolute Truth. It is knowledge of Brahman which releases one from the world and allows one to attain self-realization when received from a qualified teacher. Except for the *Isa Upanishad*, which is the 40th chapter of the *Vajasaneyi Samhita* of the *Sukla (White) Yajur-veda*, the *Upanishads* are connected to the four primary *Vedas*, generally found in the *Brahmanas*.

*Vaikunthas*--the planets located in the spiritual sky.

Vaishnava--a worshiper of the Supreme Lord Vishnu or Krishna and His expansions or incarnations.

Vaishnava-*aparadha*--an offense against a Vaisnava or devotee, which can negate all of one's spiritual progress.

*Vaisya*--the third class of society engaged in business or farming.

Vamana--dwarf incarnation of Vishnu who covered the universe in

three steps.
*Vanaprastha*--the third of the four *ashramas* of spiritual life in which one retires from family life in preparation for the renounced order.

Varaha--Lord Vishnu's boar incarnation.

*Varna*--sometimes referred to as caste, a division of society, such as *brahmana* (a priestly intellectual), a *kshatriya* (ruler or manager), *vaisya* (a merchant, banker, or farmer), and *sudra* (common laborer).

*Varnashrama*--the system of four divisions of society and four orders of spiritual life.

Varuna--demigod of the oceans, guardian of the west.

*Vastu-siddhi*--The final spiritual body obtained by taking birth from a *nitya siddha gopi* an eternally perfect *gopi* in Krishna's earthly pastimes. The stage of identity transformation after *svarupa siddhi*, and before *sampatti siddhi*.

Vasudeva--Krishna.

Vayu--demigod of the air.

*Vedanta-sutras*--the philosophical conclusion of the four *Vedas*.

*Vedas*--generally means the four primary *samhitas;* Rig, Yajur, Sama, Atharva.

Venktateshvara--Vishnu as Lord of the Venkata Hills, worshiped in Tirumala.

*Vidya*--knowledge.

*Vikarma*--sinful activities performed without scriptural authority and which produce sinful reactions.

Virabhadra--vengeful form of Shiva.

Virajanadi or Viraja River--the space that separates the material creation from the spiritual sky.

Vishnu--the expansion of Lord Krishna who enters into the material energy to create and maintain the cosmic world.

Vishvanatha--Shiva as Lord of the universe, worshiped in Varanasi as a *linga*.

Vishvarupa--universal form of Lord Vishnu.

Vrindavana--the place where Lord Krishna displayed His village pastimes 5,000 years ago, and is considered to be part of the spiritual abode.

*Vyasadeva*--the incarnation of God who appeared as the greatest philosopher who compiled the main portions of the Vedic literature into written form.

*Yajna*--a ritual or austerity that is done as a sacrifice for spiritual merit, or ritual worship of a demigod for good *karmic* reactions.

*Yamaraja*--the demigod and lord of death who directs the living entities to various punishments according to their activities.

*Yamuna*--goddess personification of the Yamuna River.

*Yantra*--a machine, instrument, or mystical diagram used in ritual worship.

*Yashoda*--foster mother of Krishna.

*Yatra*–a spiritual pilgrimage to a holy site.

*Yatri*–a person who goes on a yatra.

*Yoga*--linking up with the Absolute.

*Yoga-siddhi*--mystic perfection.

*Yuga-avataras*--the incarnations of God who appear in each of the four *yugas* to explain the authorized system of self-realization in that age.

# REFERENCES

These are books that either directly contributed to the making of this present volume, or helped lay the philosophical foundation of this book.

*Agni Purana*, translated by N. Gangadharan, Motilal Banarsidass, Delhi, 1984

*Ananda Vrndavana Campu*, Srila Kavi-karnapura, Editor & Publisher Mahanidhi Swami, Vrindavana, 1999,

*Art of Sadhana: A Guide to Daily Devotion*, by Swami B. P. Puri Maharaja, Mandala Publishing Group, San Francisco, CA,

*Atharva-veda*, translated by Devi Chand, Munshiram Manoharlal, Delhi, 1980

*Bhagavad-gita As It Is*, translated by A. C. Bhaktivedanta Swami, Bhaktivedanta Book Trust, New York/Los Angeles, 1972

*Bhagavad-gita*, translated by Swami Chidbhavananda, Sri Ramakrishna Tapovanam, Tiruchirappalli, India, 1991

*The Song of God, Bhagavad-gita*, translated by Swami Prabhavananda and Christopher Isherwood, New America Library, New York, 1972,

*Bhagavad-gita*, translated by Winthrop Sargeant, State University of New York Press, Albany, 1984

*Bhakti-rasamrita-sindhu, (Nectar of Devotion)*, translated by A. C. Bhaktivedanta Swami, Bhaktivedanta Book Trust, New York/Los Angeles, 1970

*Bhakti Rasamarita Sindhu*, by Srila Rupa Gosvami, trans. By Bhanu Swami, Sri Vaikuntha Enterprises, Chennai, 2003

*Bhaktiratnakara*, Sri Narahari Cakravarti, translated by Kusakratha dasa, edited by Purnaprajna Dasa, Rasbihari Lal & Sons, Vrindavana, India, 2006.

*Bhakti-sandarbha sankhya*

*Bhavanasara Sangraha*, Sri Siddha Krsnadasa Tatapada, translated by Bhanu Swami, Editor Mahanidhi Swami, 2004.

*Bhavisya Purana,* by Srila Vyasadeva, translated by Bhumipati Dasa, published by Rasbikarilal & Sons, Vrindavana, India, 2007.

*Brahma Purana*, edited by J.L.Shastri, Motilal Banarsidass, Delhi 1985

*Brahmana & Vaishnava*, Srila Bhaktisiddhanta Sarasvati Thakur, trans. Bhumipati dasa, Vrajraj Press, Vrindavana, 1999

*Brahmanda Purana*, edited by J.L.Shastri, Motilal Banarsidass, 1983

*Brahma-samhita*, translated by Bhaktisiddhanta Sarasvati Gosvami Thakur, Bhaktivedanta Book Trust, New York/Los Angeles,

*Brahma-Sutras*, translated by Swami Vireswarananda and Adidevananda, Advaita Ashram, Calcutta, 1978.

*Brahma Sutras*, Baladeva Vidyabhusana, translated by H. H. Bhanu Swami, 2013.

*Brahma-Vaivarta Purana*, translated by Shanti Lal Nagar, edited by Acharya Ramesh Chaturvedi, Parimal Publications, Delhi, 2005.

*Brihad-vishnu Purana*

*Brihan-naradiya Purana*

*Brihadaranyaka Upanishad*

*Caitanya-caritamrta*, translated by A. C. Bhaktivedanta Swami, Bhaktivedanta Book Trust, Los Angeles, 1974

*Caitanya Upanisad*, translated by Kusakratha dasa, Bala Books, New York, 1970

*Chaitanya-chandramrita*,

*Chandogya Upanishad*,

*Dasa-mula-tattva*, Srila Bhaktivinode Thakura, Published by Rasbihari Lal & sons, Vrindavana, 2000

*Deity Worship and Vaishnava Vratas*, compiled by Bhumipati Dasa, Rasbihari Lal & Sons, Vrindavan, India, 2009.

*Experiences in Bhakti: The Science Celestial*, O.B.L.Kapoor, Sarasvati Jayasri Classics, Delhi, 1994

*Garbha Upanishad*

*Garga Samhita*, Sri Garga Muni, translated by Kusakratha dasa, edited by Purnaprajna Dasa, Rasbihari Lal & Sons, Vrindavana, India, 2006.

*Garuda Purana*, edited by J. L. Shastri, Motilal Barnasidass, Delhi, 1985

*Gaura-gana-svarupa-tattva-candrika: Light on the Identity of Gauranga's Associates*, Visvanatha Cakravarti, trans. by Demian Martins, Ph.D., Jiva Institute, Vrindavana, 2015

*Gaura Govindarena-smarana-paddhati*, by Dhyanacandra Goswami, translated by Haridhama dasa.

*Gautamiya Tantra*,

*Gitagovinda of Jayadeva*, Barbara Stoller Miller, Motilal Banarsidass, Delhi, 1977

*Gita Mahatmya of the Padma Purana and Srimad Bhagavata Mahatmya of the Skanda Purana*, by Krishna Dvaipayana Vyasa, Touchstone Media, Vrindavana, India, 2001

*Gopal-tapani Upanishad*, by Krsna Dvaipayana Vedavyasa, commentary by Visvanatha Cakravarti Thakura, translated by Bhumipati dasa, Ras Bihari Lal & Sons, Loi Bazaar, Vrindaban, UP, 281121, India, 2004

# References

*The Gosvamis of Vrindavana*, O.B.L.Kapoor, Sarasvati Jayasri Classics, Delhi, 1994
*Govinda Lilamrita*, by Krsnadasa Kaviraja, by Iskcon Media Vedic Library.
*Hari-bhakti-vilasa*,
*Hindu Samskaras*, by Dr. Raj Bali Pandey, Motilal Banarsidass, Delhi, 1969
*Hymns of the Rig-veda*, tr. by Griffith, Motilal Banarsidass, Delhi, 1973
*Jagannatha-vallabha-nataka*, Sri Ramananda Raya, translated by Kusakratha dasa, edited by Purnaprajna Dasa, Rasbihari Lal & Sons, Vrindavana, India, 2006.
*Jaiva Dharma*, Srila Thakur Bhakti Vinod, trans. By Bhakti Sadhaka Nishkinchana, Sree Gaudiya Math
*Jaiva Dharma, The Essential Function of the Soul*, Srila Bhaktivinoda Thakura, translated by Sarvabhavana dasa, Brihat Mrdanga Press, Vrindavana, India, 2004
*Kali-santarana Upanishad*,
*Kalki Purana*, by Sri Vyasadeva, translated by Bhumipati das, Jai Nitai Press, Mathura, India, 2006
*Katha Upanishad*
*Kaushitaki Upanishad*
*Krsna-karnamrta*, Sri Bilvamangala Thakura, translated by Kusakratha dasa, edited by Purnaprajna Dasa, Rasbihari Lal & Sons, Vrindavana, India, 2006.
*Krsnahnika Kaumudi*, by Srila Kavi-karnapura, Editor & Publisher, Mahanidhi Swami, Vrindavana, 2002.
*Krsna Sandarbha*, Jiva Gosvamai, translated by H. H. Bhanu Swami, Sri Vaikuntha Enterprises, Chennai, India, 2014.
*Kurma Purana*, edited by J. L. Shastri, Motilal Banarsidass, Delhi, 1981
*Laghu Bhagavatamrta*, Srila Rupa Gosvami, translated by Bhanu Swami, Sri Vaikuntha Enterprises, 2006.
*Laghu-bhagavatamrta*, Srila Rupa Gosvami, translated by Kusakratha dasa, Ras Bihari Lal & Sons, Loi Bazaar, Vrindaban, UP, 281121, India, 2007
*Madhurya Kadambini*, Srila Visvanatha Cakravarti Thakur, trans. By Dina Bandhu dasa, Vrinda Trust, Nandagram, 1993
*Madhurya Kadambini*, Srila Visvanatha Cakravarti Thakura, Sri Krsna Caitanya Shastra Mandira, Mathura, India, 2005
*Mahabharata*, translated by C. Rajagopalachari, Bharatiya Vidya Bhavan, New Delhi, 1972
*Mahabharata*, Kamala Subramaniam, Bharatiya Vidya Bhavan, Bombay, 1982

*Mahabharata*, Kesari Mohan Ganguli, Munshiram Manoharlal Publisher Pvt., Ltd., New Delhi, 1970

*Mahabharata, Sanskrit Text With English Translations*, by M. N. Dutt, Parimal Publications, Delhi, 2001

*The Manifestation and Realization of Your Eternal Identity*, by Uttamashloka dasa (Ron Marinelli), 2012.

*Mathura Meets Vrindavana*, Sri Srimad Gour Govinda Maharaja, Gopal Jui Publications, C/O Iskcon, National Highway No. 5., IRC Village, Bhubaneswar, Orissa, India 751015, 2004.

*Matsya Purana*,

*Minor Upanishads*, translated by Swami Madhavananda, Advaita Ashram, Calcutta, 1980; contains Paramahamsopanishad, Atmopanishad, Amritabindupanishad, Tejabindupanishad, Sarvopanishad, Brahmopanisad, Aruneyi Upanishad, Kaivalyopanishad.

*Mukunda-mala-stotra*

*Mundaka Upanishad*,

*Namamrta Samudra*, Sri Narahari Cakravarti Thakur, translated by Bhumipati dasa, Rasbihari Lal & Sons, Vrindavan, India, 2004.

*Narada-pancaratra*,

*Narada Pancharatram*, Swami Vijnananand, Parimal Publications, Delhi, 1993

*Narada Purana*, tr. by Ganesh Vasudeo Tagare, Banarsidass, Delhi, 1980

*Narada Sutras*, translated by Hari Prasad Shastri, Shanti Sadan, London, 1963

*Narada-Bhakti-Sutra*, A. C. Bhaktivedanta Swami, Bhaktivedanta Book Trust, Los Angeles, 1991

*Narasimha Purana*,

*Narottam-Vilas*, by Sri Narahari Cakravarti Thakur, translator unknown.

*Narottama Vilasa*, Sri Narahari Chakravarti Thakura, Edited by Purnaprajna Dasa, Rasbihari Lal & Sons, Vrindavan, India, 2005.

*The Nectar of Devotion, The Complete Science of Bhakti-yoga*, A. C. Bhaktivedanta Swami Prabhupada, The Bhaktivedanta Book Trust, Los Angeles, 1970.

*Padma Purana*, tr. by S. Venkitasubramonia Iyer, Banarsidass, Delhi, 1988

*Padmottara-khanda*

*Padyavali, Anthology of Devotional Poetry*, Srila Rupa Gosvami, translated by Kusakratha dasa, Ras Bihari Lal & Sons, Loi Bazaar, Vrindaban, UP, 281121, India, 2007

*Pancaratra Pradipa (Method of Deity Worship)*, Iskcon GBC Press, Mayapur, 1994

# References

*Prakrta Rasa Sata Dusani*, by Srila Bhaktisiddhanta Sarasvati Prabhupada, Gosai Publishers, 2008.
*Prameya-ratnavali*, Srila Baladeva Vidyabhusana,
*Prema-Vilas,* by Nityananda Das
*Prema Vivarta--Divine Transformations of Spiritual Love*, Srila Jagadananda Pandita, trans. by Sarvabhavana dasa, Harmonist Publications, Mumbai, 1991
*Priti Sandarbha*, Jiva Gosvamai, translated by H. H. Bhanu Swami, Sri Vaikuntha Enterprises, Chennai, India, 2014.
*Purana-vakya,*
*Radha Krishna Pastimes at Radha Kunda*, Mahanidhi Swami, 2014.
*Raga Vartma Candrika, A Moonbeam on the Path of Raganuga Bhakti*, Srila Visvanatha Cakravarti Thakura, Sri Krsna Caitanya Sastra Mandira, 1994.
*Raga Vartma Candrika, A Moonbeam on the Path of Raganuga Bhakti*, Srila Visvanatha Cakravarti Thakura, Commentary by Sri Narayana Maharaja, Gaudiya Vedanta Publications, Delhi, Vrindavana, 2015.
*Ramayana of Valmiki*, tr. by Makhan Lal Sen, Oriental Publishing Co., Calcutta
*Ramayana of Valmiki*, tr. by Makhan Lal Sen, Munshiram Manoharlal Publishers, New Delhi, 1976.
*Hymns of the Rig-veda*, tr. by Griffith, Motilal Banarsidass, Delhi, 1973
*Rig Veda, Krishna Upanishad*,
*Samnyasa Upanisads*, translated by Prof. A. A. Ramanathan, Adyar Library, Madras, India, 1978; contains Avadhutopanisad, Arunyupanisad, Katharudropanisad, Kundikopanisad, Jabalopanisad, Turiyatitopanisad, Narada-parivrajakopanisad, Nirvanopanisad, Parabrahmopanisad, Paramahamsa-parivrajakopanisad, Paramahamsopanisad, Brahmopanisad, Bhiksukopanisad, Maitreyopanisad, Yajnavalkyopanisad, Satyayaniyopanisad, and Samnyasopanisad.
*Sarartha Darsini*, Srila Visvanatha Cakravarti Thakura, translated by Bhanu Swami, Editor & Publisher Mahanidhi Swami, 2004.
*Shiva Purana*, edited by Professor J. L. Shastri, Banarsidass, Delhi, 1970
*Shri Chaitanya Mahaprabhu, His Life and Precepts*, Thakur Bhakti Vinode, Sree Gaudiya Math, Madras, 1991
*Siddhanta-darpana: The Mirror of Philosophical Conclusion*, Baladeva Vidyabhusana, trans. By Damian Martins, Ph.D., Jiva Institute, Faridabad, Haryana, India, 2014
*Siksastaka*, of Sri Caitanya Mahaprabhu.

*Sixty Upanisads of the Vedas*, by Paul Deussen, translated from German by V. M. Bedekar and G. B. Palsule, Motilal Banarsidass, Delhi, 1980; contains Upanisads of the Rigveda: Aitareya and Kausitaki. Upanisads of the Samaveda: Chandogya and Kena. Upanisads of the Black Yajurveda: Taittiriya, Mahanarayan, Kathaka, Svetasvatara, and Maitrayana. Upanisads of the White Yajurveda: Brihadaranyaka and Isa. Upanisads of the Atharvaveda: Mundaka, Prasna, Mandukya, Garbha, Pranagnihotra, Pinda, Atma, Sarva, Garuda; (Yoga Upanisads): Brahmavidya, Ksurika, Culik, Nadabindu, Brahma-bindu, Amrtabindu, Dhyanabindu, Tejobindu, Yoga-sikha, Yogatattva, Hamsa; (Samnyasa Upanisads): Brahma, Samnyasa, Aruneya, Kantha-sruti, Paramahamsa, Jabala, Asrama; (Shiva Upanisads): Atharvasira, Atharva-sikha, Nilarudra, Kalagnirudra, Kaivalya; (Vishnu Upanisads): Maha, Narayana, Atmabodha, Nrisimhapurvatapaniya, Nrisimhottara-tapaniya, Ramapurvatapaniya, Ramottaratapaniya. (Supplemental Upanisads): Purusasuktam, Tadeva, Shiva-samkalpa, Baskala, Chagaleya, Paingala, Mrtyu-langala, Arseya, Pranava, and Saunaka Upanisad.

*Skanda Purana*, by Srila Vyasadeva, Purnaprajna Dasa, Rasbihari Lal & Sons, Vrindavana, India, 2005.

*Sri Amnaya Sutra*, Srila Bhaktivinoda Thakura, translated by Kusakratha dasa, edited by Purnaprajna Dasa, Rasbihari Lal & Sons, Vrindavana, India, 2006.

*Sri Bhajana-rahasya*, Srila Bhaktivinoda Thakura, Published by Pundarika Vidyanidhi dasa, Vrindavana,

*Sri Bhakti-ratnakara*, by Sri Narahari Cakravarti Thakura.

*Sri Bhakti Sandarbha*, Srila Jiva Gosvami, translated by Dr. Satya Narayana Dasa, Edited by Bhrgu Natha Dasa, Jiva Institute, Vrindavana, India, 2005.

*Sri Brihad-Bhagavatamrita*, by Srila Sanatana Gosvami, trans. By Gopiparanadhana dasa, Bhaktivedanta Book Trust, Los Angeles, 2002.

*Sri Brihat Bhagavatamritam*, by Sri Srila Sanatana Gosvami, Sree Gaudiya Math, Madras, India, 1987

*Sri Caitanya Bhagavat,* by Sri Vrindavan dasa Thakura, 1538 AD.

*Sri Caitanya-Bhagavat,* by Sri Vrindavan dasa Thakura, trans. By Kusakratha dasa, Krsna Institute, Alachua, FL, 1994

*Sri Caitanya-carita-maha-kavya*, Srila Murari Gupta, translated by Swami Bhakti Vedanta Bhagavata Maharaja, edited by Purnaprajna Dasa, Rasbihari Lal & Sons, Vrindavana, India, 2006.

*Sri Caitanya Mangala*, Locana Dasa Thakura, trans. by Subhag Swami, published by Mahanidhi Swami, Vrindavana, 1994

# References

*Sri Caitanya Shikshamritam*, Thakura Bhakti Vinode, Sree Gaudiya Math, Madras, 1983

*Sri Caitanya-Siksamrta, The Nectarean Teachings of Sri Caitanya*, Srila Bhaktivinoda Thakura, translated by H. H. Bhanu Swami, Brihat Mrdanga Press, Vrindavana, India, 2004

*Sri Caitanya Upanishad*, from the Atharva-veda

*Sri Camatkara-candrika, A Moonbeam of Complete Astonishment*, by Srila Visvanatha Cakravarti Thakura, Gaudiya Vedanta Publications, 2006.

*Sri Gaura-ganoddesha dipika*, by Kavi Karnapura, translated by Bhumipati dasa, Ras Bihari Lal & Sons, Loi Bazaar, Vrindaban, UP, 281121, India, 2004

*Sri Gauranga-Mahima*, Sri Advaita Acarya & Sri Sarvabhauma Bhattacarya, trans. By Jaya Balarama dasa, Nectar Books, Culver City, CA, 1992

*Sri Gopal Sahasra Nama, One thousand names of Lord Gopala Krsna*, Spoken by Lord Shiva to Sri Parvati devi, translated by Bhumipati dasa, Ras Bihari Lal & Sons, Loi Bazaar, Vrindaban, UP, 281121, India, 2004

*Sri Gopala-Tapani Upanishad*, from the Atharva-Veda,

*Sri Govinda-Lilamrita (Nectarean Daily Pastimes of Lord Govinda)*, Srila Krishna dasa Kaviraja Gosvami.

*Sri Grantha Ratna Pancakam*, by Sri Visvanatha Cakravartipada, translated by Advaita dasa, Spanish Association of Vedic Culture Support.

*Sri Hari-bhakti-vilas*, Srila Sanatana Gosvami, translated by Bhumipati dasa, edited by Purnaprajna Dasa, Rasbihari Lal & Sons, Vrindavana, India, 2006.

*Sri Hari-bhakti-vilasa, Vilasas I & II*, Srila Sanatana Gosvami, and *Panca-samskara*, by Saccidananda Thakura Bhaktivinoda, Brihat Mrdanga Press, Vrindavana, India, 2005.

*Sri Hari-bhakti-vilasa*, by Srila Sanatana Gosvami, translated by Bhumipati Dasa, Rasbihari Lal & Sons, Vrindavan, India, 2005.

*Sri Harinam Cintamani*, Srila Bhaktivinoda Thakura, trans. Sarvabhavana dasa, Bhaktivedanta Books, Mumbai, 1990

*Sri Isopanisad*, translated by A. C. Bhaktivedanta Swami, Bhaktivedanta Book Trust, New York/Los Angeles, 1969

*Sri Jaiva Dharma*, Srila Bhaktivinoda Thakur, trans. Kusakratha dasa, Krsna Institute, Alachua, FL, 1993

*Sri Krsna Bhavanamrta Mahakavya*, by Srila Visvanatha Cakravarti Thakura, translated by Advaita dasa, Ras Bihari Lal & Sons, Loi Bazaar, Vrindaban, UP, 281121, India, 2000

*Sri Krishna Caitanya divya sahasra-nama, One thousand transcendental names of Sri Krsna Caitanya*, by Srila Rupa Gosvami, Translated by Bhumipati dasa, Ras Bihari Lal & Sons, Loi Bazaar, Vrindaban, UP, 281121, India, 2004.

*Sri Krishna Karnamritam & Chaitanya-chandramritam*, Lilasuka & Prabhodhananda, trans. Bhakti Sadhaka Nishkinchana, Sree Gaudiya Math, Madras

*Sri Krsna-samhita*, Srila Bhaktivinoda Thakur, trans. Bhumipati dasa, Vajraj Press, Vrindavana, 1998

*Sri Krsna Sandarbha*, Srila Jiva Gosvami, edited by Purnaprajna Dasa, Rasbihari Lal & Sons, Vrindavana, India, 2006.

*Srimad-Bhagavadgita*, Swami Ramsukhdas, translated by S. C. Vaishya, Sita Press, Gorakhpur, India.

*Srimad-Bhagavatam*, translated by A. C. Bhaktivedanta Swami, Bhaktivedanta Book trust, New York/Los Angeles, 1972

*Srimad-Bhagavatam*, translated by N. Raghunathan, Vighneswar Publishing House, Madras, 1976

*Srimad-Bhagavatam MahaPurana*, translated by C. L. Goswami, M. A., Sastri, Motilal Jalan at Gita Press, Gorkhapur, India, 1982

*Srimad Valmiki-Ramayana*, Gita Press, Gorakhpur, India, 1969

*Sri Madhava Mahotsava*, by Sri Jiva Gosvamipada, Bhanu Swami, published by Mahanidhi Swami, 2000.

*Sri Manah-Siksa*, Raghunatha dasa Gosvami, purports by Srila Bhaktivinoda Thakur, trans. Sarvabhavana dasa, Bhaktivedanta Books, Mumbai, 1989

*Sri Narada Pancharatram*,

*Sri Narada Pancaratra*, Vol. 1 & 2, Sri Krsna Dvaipayana Vyasa, translated by Bhumipati Dasa, Rasbihari Lal & Sons, Vrindavan, India, 2005.

*Sri Nityananda Caritamrite*, Srila Vrindavana dasa Thakur, trans. By Bhumipati dasa, Touchstone Media, Vrindavana, 2000

*Sri Nrsimha Sahasra-nama & Sri Nrsimha-Kavaca*, translated by Bhumipati dasa, Ras Bihari Lal & Sons, Loi Bazaar, Vrindaban, UP, 281121, India, 2006

*Sri Prema Bhakti-candrika, The Moonrays of Loving Devotion*, Narottama Dasa Thakur, commentary by Visvanatha Cakravarti Thakur, trans. Bhumipati dasa, Touchstone Media, Vrindavana, 1999

*Sri Priti Sandarbha*, Vols 1 & 2, Srila Jiva Gosvami, translated by Kusakratha Dasa, Ras Bihari Lal & Sons, Loi Bazaar, Vrindaban, UP, 281121, India, 2007.

# References

*Sri Radha-Krsna-Ganoddesa-Dipika*, A Lamp to See the Associates of Sri Sri Radha-Krisna, Srila Rupa Goswami, Trans. By Kusakratha dasa, 2009.

*Sri Radha-Krsna Ganoddesa Dipika*, Sri Rupa Gosvami, trans. By Bhumipati dasa, Rasbihari Lal & Sons, Vrindavana, 2004.

*Sri Radha-rasa-sudha-nidhi*, Prabodhananda Sarasvati, translated by Kusakratha dasa, India, 2011.

*Sri Rupa-cintamani, The Cintamani Jewel of Beauty*, Sri Visvanatha Cakravarti Thakur, translated by Kushakratha dasa, Rasbihari Lal & Sons, Vrindavana, 2014.

*Sri Rupa Gosvami's Upadesamrta: Illuminations by Srila B. R. Sridhara Deva Gosvami*, Gosai Publishers, Srirangapatna, Karnataka, India, 2009.

*Sri Sanatkumara-samhita*, from the Skanda Purana,

*Sri Sri Krishna Bhavanamrta Mahakavya*, Srila Visvanatha Chakravarti Thakura, completed in 1686

*Sri Sri Premadhama Deva Stotram*, Srila B. R. Sridhar Deva Gosvami, Sri Chaitanya Sarasvat Math, Nabavipa, 1983.

*Sri Sri Utkalika Vallari, A Vine of Eager Aspirations*, Srila Rupa Gosvami, Sri Krsna Caitanya Shastra Mandir, Mathura, India, 2005

*Sri Srimad Bhagavata-Arka Marichimala*, Thakura Bhakti Vinode, Sree Gaudiya Math, Madras, 1978

*Sri Suka-sari-stava*, by Srila Krishnadasa Kaviraja Gosvami, translated by Kushakratha Dasa, Ras Bihari Lal & Sons, Loi Bazaar, Vrindaban, UP, 281121, India, 2007

*Sri Uddhava-sandesha & Sri Hamsaduta*, Srila Rupa Gosvami, translated by Kusakratha dasa, edited by Purnaprajna Dasa, Rasbihari Lal & Sons, Vrindavana, India, 2006.

*Sri Ujjvala-Nilamani*, Srila Rupa Gosvami, translated by Kusakratha dasa, edited by Purnaprajna Dasa, Rasbihari Lal & Sons, Vrindavana, India, 2006.

*Sri Vidagdha-madhava*, Srila Rupa Gosvami, translated by Kusakratha dasa, edited by Purnaprajna Dasa, Rasbihari Lal & Sons, Vrindavana, India, 2006.

*Sri Vishnu Sahasra Naamam*, translated and Commentary by M. S. Parthasarathi, Bharatiya Vidya Bhavan, Mumbai, 1999

*Sri Visnu-sahasra-nama-stotra*, translated by Kusakratha dasa, edited by Purnaprajna Dasa, Rasbihari Lal & Sons, Vrindavana, India, 2006.

*Sri Vraja-riti-cintamani*, Srila Visvanatha Cakravarti Thakura, translated by Kusakratha dasa, edited by Purnaprajna Dasa, Rasbihari Lal & Sons, Vrindavana, India, 2006.

*Sri Vrindavana Mahimamrta: The Nectarean Glories of Sri Vrindavana*, Srila Prabodhananda Sarasvati, translated by Bhumipati Dasa, Rasbihari Lal & Sons, Vrindavan, India, 2002.

*Stava-mala*, Srila Rupa Gosvami, translated by Kusakratha dasa, Ras Bihari Lal & Sons, Loi Bazaar, Vrindaban, UP, 281121, India, 2007

*Story of Rasikananda*, Gopijanavallabha dasa, edited by Bhakti Vikas Swami, Mumbai, 1997

*Stotra-ratna*, Sri Yamunacarya,

*Svetasvatara Upanishad*,

*Tattva-Viveka, Tattva-Sutra, Amnaya Sutra*, Srila Bhaktivinode Thakur, Sree Gaudiya Math, Madras, 1979

*Twelve Essential Upanishads*, Tridandi Sri Bhakti Prajnan Yati, Sree Gaudiya Math, Madras, 1982. Includes the *Isha, Kena, Katha, Prashna, Mundaka, Mandukya, Taittiriya, Aitareya, Chandogya, Brihadaranyaka, Svetasvatara,* and *Gopalatapani Upanishad* of the Pippalada section of the *Atharva-veda*.

*Ujjval Nilmani*, by Srila Rupa Gosvami, translated and published by Puri Maharaja, Goudiya Vaishnava Association, Mayapur, Nadia, India, Feb. 24, 2000

*Upadesamrta (Nectar of Instruction)*, translated by A. C. Bhaktivedanta Swami, Bhaktivedanta Book Trust, New York/Los Angeles, 1975

*The Upanisads*, translated by F. Max Muller, Dover Publications; contains Chandogya, Kena, Aitareya, Kausitaki, Vajasaneyi (Isa), Katha, Mundaka, Taittiriya, Brihadaranyaka, Svetasvatara, Prasna, and Maitrayani Upanisads.

*The Upanishads*, translated by Swami Prabhavananda and Frederick Manchester, New American Library, New York, 1957; contains Katha, Isha, Kena, Prasna, Mundaka, Mandukya, Taittiriya, Aitareya, Chandogya, Brihadaranyaka, Kaivalya, and Svetasvatara Upanishads.

*Varaha Purana*, tr. by S.Venkitasubramonia Iyer, Banarsidass, Delhi, 1985

*Vayu Purana*, translated by G. V. Tagare, Banarsidass, Delhi, India, 1987

*Veda of the Black Yajus School: Taitiriya Sanhita*, translated by Arthur Keith, Motilal Banarsidass, Delhi, 1914

*Vedanta-Sutras of Badarayana with Commentary of Baladeva Vidyabhusana*, translated by Rai Bahadur Srisa Chandra Vasu, Munshiram Manoharlal, New Delhi, 1979

*Vishnu Purana*, translated by H. H. Wilson, Nag Publishers, Delhi

*Vishnu-smriti*,

# References

*Visnu Sarma, The Pancatantra*, trans. By Chandra Rajan, Penguin Books, New Delhi & New York, 1993

*White Yajurveda*, translated by Griffith, The Chowkhamba Sanskrit Series Office, Varanasi, 1976

*Yajurveda*, translated by Devi Chand, Munshiram Manoharlal, Delhi, 1980

**ABBREVIATIONS USED FOR MOST REFERENCES**
AOS = *Art of Sadhana*
Bg. = *Bhagavad-gita*
Bhag. = *Srimad-Bhagavatam* or *Bhagavata Purana*
BRS. = *Bhakti-rasamrita-sindhu*
Cc. = *Caitanya-caritamrita*
NOD = *Nectar of Devotion*
SCS = *Sri Caitanya-Siksamrta*
SHC = *Sri Harinam Cintamani*

# INDEX

Abhidheya............ 184
Absolute Truth
    three levels of
        understanding ... 269
Acharya
    meaning of ........ 144
    one who teaches by
        example......... 89
Acharyas
    who recommended
        bhakti-yoga...... 56
Ahimsa
    nonviolence........ 238
Ajamila
    the story of ........ 115
Anarthas.............. 63
Apana-dasa
    remembering Krishna's
        pastimes........ 139
Archa-vigraha
    the worshipful Deity . 253
Associating
    with devotees ....... 90
Astanga-yoga.......... 294
Avatars
    predicted in Vedic
        literature ....... 368
Bbhakti-yoga
    steps to develop topmost
        level........... 346
Bhagavad-gita
    essence of Upanishadic
        knowledge....... 88
    those who study it attain
        higher planets ... 361
Bhagavan.............. 14
    the Supreme Being .. 269
    understanding the
        personal aspect of
        God........... 201
Bhagavata Purana ...... 289
Bhaja Govindam
    by Adi Shankaracharya 24
Bhakti
    devotion draws attention
        of God......... 247
    in all religions ........ 9
    meaning of the word .. 57
Bhakti-lata-bija........ 322
    seed of devotional
        creeper.......... 65
bhakti-yoga
    advantages of......... 21
    affects mass
        consciousness of
        humanity....... 352
    an overview......... 51
    burns up subtle body .. 99
    can affect the whole
        world.......... 356
    can bring eternal life . 292
    changes ourselves ... 236
    dissolves our subtle body
        ................. 326
    easiest of all spiritual
        paths ........... 39
    encouraging others .. 358
    even best for

# Index

householders .... 232
every person's birthrite 40
feeling reciprocation
   from God....... 187
gives freedom from
   desires.......... 96
how it benefits others 352
how to be successful . 100
in the modes of material
   nature.......... 220
includes many activities
   ................. 226
its great benefits ..... 55
its purpose........... 8
its real goal ........ 46
its various stages of
   development ..... 57
makes Infinite submissive
   to infinitesimal ... 48
molding our life for
   progress......... 70
Nine primary ways ... 82
oneness with God ... 263
path to awaken pure love
   ................. 41
prepares us for the
   spiritual world... 327
rare opportunity to follow
   it ............. 54
regulative or spontaneous
   ................. 228
rising to pure bhakti . 231
samadhi in..... 261, 294
spiritualizes ourselves 291
stages of development. 63
starting with faith .... 60
steps beyond trance
   samadhi........ 296
steps to the highest level
   ................. 309
the main activities... 227
the most important
   principle in ..... 131
types of love for God 214
uniting with God through
   love ............ 11
what can ruin one's
   spiritual development
   ................. 100
why do it ........... 35
will spread around the
   world.......... 358
Bhakti-yoga
   getting a taste for our
      practice ........ 180
Bhava .............. 203
   symptoms of ....... 211
   when it is awakened . 102
Bhava-bhakti.......... 157
   loving ecstasy ....... 74
Bilvamangala Thakur 24, 323
Bliss
   in chanting holy names 18
   not described in early
      Vedic texts ..... 283
   reaching the spiritual joy 5
Bodily symptoms
   of deep spiritual love. 204
Brahman .......... 14, 269
   effulgent rays of the Lord
   ................. 318
   has a source........ 15
   spiritual sunshine ... 318
   what it is .......... 199

Caitanya Mahaprabhu 30, 364
  opposed impersonalistic philosophy...... 373
  personally start the religion for this age ............... 365
  predicted in Vedic literature ....... 368
  taught the world to chant Hare Krishna.... 125
  His life story ....... 366
  propagated chanting names of Krishna 107
Chanting of the holy name
  brings Krishna prema 136
  can bring Krishna's spiritual form.... 136
  the ten offenses..... 136
  brings bliss ........ 118
  no ordinary person who engages in ...... 117
  purifies the consciousness ................ 113
  how to reach pure chanting........ 138
  reaching pure chanting 138
Chanting the holy names
  brings prema ....... 122
  brings self realization 120
  how to do so ....... 132
  offers many benefits . 109
  recommended for Kali-yuga........... 104
Congregational chanting 364
Darkness of illusion
  can vanish.......... 98
Darshan........... 68, 182

Dashya rasa........... 216
Death
  remembering Krishna 320
Deity
  can reveal Himself .. 246
Deity of Krishna ........ 67
Devotee
  body becomes more spiritualized..... 324
  sees the Lord everywhere ................ 260
Devotees
  are best association... 91
  behavior of ........ 236
  brings whole family to spiritual destination ................ 355
  feels self-sufficient happiness....... 225
  how all differences become nullified . 282
  how we should treat them ................ 224
  purifies 21 generations of his family....... 355
  qualities of......... 240
  risk their lives to save others.......... 359
  second-class ....... 222
  the first-class....... 222
  the progress of...... 237
  third-class ......... 223
  three basic kinds .... 220
  two kinds of........ 228
  types of ........... 219
  who explain bhakti-yoga to others........ 360

# Index

Devotion
   gives direct experience of God .......... 233
   in the mood of separation ................. 308
   Nine primary ways ... 82
   process to realize Absolute Truth ... 48
Devotional activity
   two kinds .......... 228
Devotional creeper ..... 153
Devotional principles
   how to apply them to our lives ........... 84
Devotional service
   six characteristics ... 231
Devotional service
   gives results of other spiritual paths .... 46
   joyfully performed .. 192
   steps to reach topmost level .......... 346
   takes care of all obligations ...... 353
Devotional Yoga
   how it benefits others 352
Dhyana .............. 294
Diksha guru .......... 154
Disciple
   can acquire the qualities of a brahmana ... 169
   characteristics of .... 169
   duties of a ......... 168
   duty of the disciple .. 173
   if he rejects his guru . 176
Disciplic succession .... 162
Dvapara-yuga
   process of temple worship ........ 106
Ecstasy
   in spiritual development ................. 307
Ecstatic emotions ...... 281
Elevation to ecstasy ..... 210
Essence of religion ....... 9
Eternal
   three things that are ... 12
Food
   how it affects our consciousness .... 93
Four kinds of impious men ................... 220
Four types of pious men . 219
Gaudiya Vaishnava tradition ................... 88
Gayatri mantra .......... 88
Goal of life
   one is to see the Lord everywhere ..... 267
Goals of life ........... 203
God
   absorption in is goal of life ........... 266
   being absorbed in ... 259
   types of love for .... 214
God realization
   depends on intense longing ........ 248
Gokula ............... 340
Goloka Vrindavan ..... 153
Goloka Vrindavana . 319, 340
   activities there ...... 326
   descriptions ........ 338
   devotional service to

Radha Krishna... 296
   entering therein..... 299
   how to reach....... 186
   inhabitants of....... 300
   saturated with prema. 340
   supreme abode..... 333
   to qualify ourselves to enter........... 293
   the method to enter.. 346
Gopis
   how we need their help ................. 311
   their mood......... 309
   their service to Radha-Krishna........ 312
Guru
   different kinds...... 154
   meaning of........ 153
   must be spiritually realized........ 146
   must have strong connections with parampara...... 168
   qualifications of..... 89
   receiving blessings from ................. 167
   takes away karma... 168
   when he should be rejected........ 176
   who is qualified to be one ................. 145
Happiness
   how to attain......... 2
   reaching highest bliss 275
Hare Krishna.......... 104
   best spiritual process. 105
   getting a taste for our chanting....... 180
   best process of atonement ................. 109
Hare Krishna maha-mantra ............ 104, 301, 364
   can deliver all living beings......... 127
Hare Krishna mantra
   attaining samadhi... 120
   how to chant it...... 133
   most worshipable object ................. 129
   three stages of chanting ................. 135
   vanquishes bad karma 112
Hare Krishna mantra
   directs us to Radharani & Krishna......... 31
   is the same as Krishna 130
Haridasa Thakur....... 139
Harinama initiation...... 87
Hladini
   pleasure potency..... 30
   the bliss potency.... 287
Hladini-shakti.......... 276
   Krishna's pleasure potency........ 203
Holy names
   shows our spiritual form ................. 292
Household life
   not necessary to give it up ................. 86
Human body
   a fantastic vehicle..... 7
Human form
   attained only by great

# Index

fortune . . . . . . . . . . 55
   its purpose . . . . . . . . . . 38
Illusion . . . . . . . . . . . . . . . 1
Initiation . . . . . . . . . . . . . 165
   importance of . . . . . . 160
   takes away karma . . . 168
Japa . . . . . . . . . . . . . . . . . 104
   chanting Hare Krishna 126
Jiva soul
   its eternal function . . . 204
Kaladi . . . . . . . . . . . . . . . 25
Kali-yuga
   chanting the names of
      Krishna . . . . . . . . 106
   higher beings desire to
      take birth in . . . . . 107
   no liberation without
      devotional service . 49
Kanishtha-adhikaris . . . . 221
Kapila
   instructed His mother 323
Karana Ocean . . . . . . . . . 318
Karma
   how it affects us . . . . 326
   relieved by bhakti-yoga 44
   what it is . . . . . . . . . . . 44
Kathopanishad . . . . . . . . . 64
Koran
   turn to God . . . . . . . . . . 9
Krishna
   as the Supreme . . . . . . 15
   attracted to bhakti . . . 237
   beginning to understand
      . . . . . . . . . . . . . . . . 197
   can be understood
      through service . . 195
   can reveal Himself
      . . . . . . . . . . . . . 243, 257
   conquered by love . . . 250
   entering His pastimes 346
   entering His pastimes in
      another universe . 330
   has four kinds of friends
      . . . . . . . . . . . . . . . . 229
   His attractive qualities. 16
   His beauty captivates the
      mind . . . . . . . . . . 254
   His caring nature . . . . 188
   His two main purposes
      . . . . . . . . . . . . . . . . 364
   how to attain His mercy
      . . . . . . . . . . . . . . . . 322
   in the spiritual realm . 341
   is the Paramatma . . . . . 65
   meaning of the name. 204
   no truth superior . . . . . 15
   nothing more important
      . . . . . . . . . . . . . . . . 265
   protects His devotees 193
   realizing your
      relationship with . 291
   reciprocates one's love 214
   releases one from greatest
      danger . . . . . . . . . . 23
   reveals Himself . . . . . 292
   satisfied by our love . . 49
   seeing Him . . . . . . . . 252
   service generates ocean
      of happiness . . . . 277
   sometimes gives special
      attention . . . . . . . . 194
   Supreme Divinity . . . 285
   swift deliverer from birth
      and death . . . . . . . 317

the God of love ...... 38
the ways to attain Him 254
to be absorbed in Him 259
to fix our consciousness
   on Him .......... 39
understood only by
   devotional service 198
Krishna
   accepts our devotional
      intention ........ 85
   origin of Lord Vishnu . 82
Krishna consciousness
   removes darkness of
      ignorance........ 98
Krishna prema
   attained through chanting
   ............... 122
   how to attain it ..... 139
Krishna's name
   is blissful.......... 125
Krishnaloka....... 319, 340
   descriptions of...... 340
Krishna's pastimes
   eternally going on ... 331
Krishna's pleasure potency
   manifests in the devotee's
      heart........... 301
Krishna's spiritual form
   seen through chanting His
      name .......... 137
Liberation
   five kinds of ....... 231
   four kinds of liberation
      for devotees..... 317
   from material existence
   ............... 316
   how many persons have
      attained ........ 321
   into the Brahman.... 316
   into the Vaikuntha
      planets......... 317
Living being
   its loving nature...... 20
Lord
   accepts our intention .. 85
   reciprocates with us. . 249
   to see everything in
      relation to Him .. 260
Love
   is all that satisfies
      Krishna ......... 49
   is what we all look for. 36
Love for God
   how to attain it ..... 208
Love of God
   only real religion.... 211
   when it arises in the heart
   ............... 241
Madhura-rasa ......... 216
Madhurya-rasa..... 185, 310
Madhyama-adhikaris.... 221
Mantra-yoga .......... 104
Material association
   dangers of ......... 91
Material desires
   hinders spiritual
      advancement..... 99
Material desires
   rising above them .... 96
Material enjoyment
   keeps us bound to birth &
      death .......... 180
Material happiness
   like a temporary dream 280

Index

Material tribulations . . . . . 97
Materialistic person
    not feel much joy in
        bhakti. . . . . . . . . . 237
Moksha . . . . . . . . . 271, 316
Moksha, or liberation . . . 284
Mood of servitude . . . . . 183
Namabhasa . . . . . . . . . . . . 111
    second stage of chanting
        . . . . . . . . . . . . . . . . . 135
Namaparadha
    first stage of chanting 135
Nishta
    continual steadiness in
        one's faith in Krishna
        . . . . . . . . . . . . . . . . . . 63
Nitya-siddhas . . . . . . . . . 228
Nonviolence
    the principle of . . . . . 238
Oneness with God
    on path of bhakti . . . . 263
Padma Purana . . . . . . . . . . 82
Paramatma. . . . . . . . 14, 269
    understanding this form
        of God . . . . . . . . . 200
Parampara system
    disciplic succession. . 162
Prahlada Maharaja
    says devotees deliver his
        whole family . . . . 354
Prana-pratishta . . . . . . . . . 67
Prasada
    means Lord's mercy. . . 93
    spiritual food . . . . . . . . 92
Prasadam
    spiritual food . . . . . . . 353
Prayojana. . . . . . . . . . . . . 184

Prema . . . . . . . . . . . . 75, 217
    divine love for Radha and
        Krishna . . . . . . . . 102
    saturates Goloka . . . . 340
    supremely divine love 185
    two causes for it . . . . 303
    ultimate love for God 205
    what is it . . . . . . . . . . 211
Prema-bhakti. . . . . . . . . . 309
    divine love. . . . . . . . . . 74
Principles
    of bhakti-yoga . . . . . . . 78
Principles favorable for
    bhakti-yoga . . . . . . . 72
Pure bhakti
    the steps toward. . . . . 300
Pure devotee
    the good fortune of
        meeting one. . . . . 149
Pure devotee
    is the grace of God . . 159
    taking initiation . . . . . 160
    wants to increase
        devotees. . . . . . . . 358
Pure devotees
    protected by Krishna . 191
    stages of association . 155
Pure devotional service
    its definition . . . . . . . 207
Purusha Sukta . . . . . . . . . 284
Radharani . . . . . . . . . . . . . 26
    Descriptions of Her
        qualities. . . . . . . . . 31
    feminine potency of
        Krishna . . . . . . . . 275
Raga . . . . . . . . . . . . . . . . . 73
    attachment. . . . . . . . . 184

how to find it . . . . . . . 299
Raga-marga
   a taste for one's service to
      Krishna . . . . . . . . . 63
Raganuga. . . . . . . . . . . . . . 64
Raganuga bhakti . . . 294, 329
   brings the devotee to
      Krishna . . . . . . . . 306
   the ideal to reach Goloka
      . . . . . . . . . . . . . . . . . 299
   entering it . . . . . . . . . 301
   the steps to attain it . . 303
   what it means . . . . . . 298
Raja-yoga . . . . . . . . . . . . 294
Rasa
   a divine loving relation
      with Krishna . . . . 287
   relation of love . . . . . 181
   relationship . . . . . . . . 214
Reciprocation
   from God . . . . . . . . . 187
Regulated practices
   of bhakti-yoga . . . . . . . 64
Religion
   means to bring back or
      bind . . . . . . . . . . . . 10
   word comes from Latin
      religio . . . . . . . . . . 10
Ruchi. . . . . . . . . . . . . . . . . 63
Rupa Gosvami . . . . . . . . . 18
Sadhana-bhakta. . . . . . . . 300
Sadhana-bhakti . . . . . . 64, 74
   following regulative
      principles. . . . . . . . 64
   reaching higher levels of
      success. . . . . . . . . . 73
Sadhana-bhakti
   bhakti based on
      regulative principles 63
Sadhana-rupa. . . . . . . . . . 76
Sadhana-siddha
   perfected devotee by
      regulative principles
      . . . . . . . . . . . . . . . 296
Sadhana-siddhas . . . . . . 229
Sahajiyas . . . . . . . . . . . . 313
Sahkya-rasa. . . . . . . . . . 216
Sakshi-gopala . . . . . . . . 253
Samadhi
   in bhakti-yoga . . . . . 294
   through chanting . . . . 120
   trance in bhakti-yoga. 261
Sambandha . . . . . . . . . . 184
Sampradaya
   spiritual lineage. . . . . . 89
Samsara
   repeated birth and death
      . . . . . . . . . . . . . . . 316
Sandhini-shakti . . . . . . . 276
Sankirtana . . . . 108, 120, 364
Satya-yuga
   its spiritual process . . . 56
   process of meditation 106
Separation . . . . . . . . . . . 308
Shankaracharya
   advised everyone to
      worship Krishna . . 24
Shanta-rasa . . . . . . . . . . 215
Shiva
   always thinking of
      Krishna . . . . . . . . 257
Shraddha . . . . . . . . . . . . . 63
Shuddha nama
   reaching pure chanting 138

# Index

Shuddha-bhakti
   bhakti in pure goodness ................ 232
Shuddha-nama
   the pure name ...... 135
Shukadev Goswami .... 289
Siddha-deha ........... 347
Siddha-rupa ............ 76
Siddha-svarupa ........ 347
Siksha guru ........... 154
Soul
   nature is bliss ....... 275
   to love Supreme Soul 259
Spiritual body
   according to one's loving mood .......... 327
   how we attain it ..... 324
Spiritual development
   brings steady progress 242
Spiritual ecstasy ....... 307
Spiritual food
   best to eat .......... 92
Spiritual Identity
   realizing one's ...... 291
Spiritual knowledge
   the highest levels .... 268
Spiritual master
   gives knowledge of bhakti .......... 153
   is not different from Krishna ........ 147
   must we have one ... 150
   seek guidance from a .. 87
Spiritual master
   characteristics of .... 143
   duties of a ........ 167
   genuine is rare ...... 157
   gives Vedic knowledge ................ 178
   how he teaches ..... 170
   if disciple rejects him 175
   instructs those who will listen .......... 144
   knowing who is a ... 142
   must be cautious taking disciples ........ 169
   taking initiation ..... 160
   transmits spiritual sound ................ 157
   when he should be rejected ........ 176
Spiritual processes in various yugas ........... 56
Spiritual world
   entering it ......... 332
   how we enter ....... 323
Spiritual world
   how to reach it ...... 319
Spontaneous love ...... 214
   raganuga bhakti ..... 294
Srimad-Bhagavatam
   essence of all Vedas . xiii
   its potency ......... xiii
Supersoul ............. 269
   consultation with .... 247
   guides us from within 144
Supreme
   is both personal and impersonal ...... 285
Supreme Being
   beginning to understand the ............ 197
Svarupa-siddhi ........ 339
   one's eternal spiritual

form............139
Treta-yuga
    process of rituals ...106
Upanishads............286
Uttama-adhikaris........221
Vaidha-bhaktas..........63
Vaikuntha........229, 332
Vaikuntha planets......318
    descriptions of..332, 336
    no time exists......318
    residents are fully
        spiritual........319
    what activities go on
        there...........326
Vaikunthalokas.........332
Vastu-siddhi......339, 348
    one's form with Krishna
        ..................139
Vasudhaiva Kutumbakam
    the universe is one family
        ..................13
Vatsalya-rasa..........216

Vedanta
    highest levels of ....270
Vedanta Sutras .........58
Vedic Dharma
    for reaching our highest
        potential.........35
Vedic texts
    like a library.......283
    progressive ladder of
        spiritual education 288
Vegetarian food.........92
Viraja River............332
Vishnu
    mentioned in Vedic texts
        ..................283
Vrindavana-dham......342
Vyasadeva
    how he fixed his mind 257
Yoga
    means to link or unite . 10
Yuga-dharma..........105
Zoroastrianism
    worship God ........10

# ABOUT THE AUTHOR

Stephen Knapp grew up in a Christian family, during which time he seriously studied the Bible to understand its teachings. In his late teenage years, however, he sought answers to questions not easily explained in Christian theology. So he began to search through other religions and philosophies from around the world and started to find the answers for which he was looking. He also studied a variety of occult sciences, ancient mythology, mysticism, yoga, and the spiritual teachings of the East. After his first reading of the *Bhagavad-gita*, he felt he had found the last piece of the puzzle he had been putting together through all of his research. Therefore, he continued to study all of the major Vedic texts of India to gain a better understanding of the Vedic science.

It is known amongst all Eastern mystics that anyone, regardless of qualifications, academic or otherwise, who does not engage in the spiritual practices described in the Vedic texts cannot actually enter into understanding the depths of the Vedic spiritual science, nor acquire the realizations that should accompany it. So, rather than pursuing his research in an academic atmosphere at a university, Stephen directly engaged in the spiritual disciplines that have been recommended for hundreds of years. He continued his study of Vedic knowledge and spiritual practice under the guidance of a spiritual master. Through this process, and with the sanction of His Divine Grace A. C. Bhaktivedanta Swami Prabhupada, he became initiated into the genuine and authorized spiritual line of the Brahma-Madhava-Gaudiya *sampradaya*, which is a disciplic succession that descends back through Sri Caitanya Mahaprabhu and Sri Vyasadeva, the compiler of Vedic literature, and further back to Sri Krishna. At that time he was given the spiritual name of Sri Nandanandana dasa. In this way, he has been studying and practicing yoga since 1971, especially bhakti-yoga, and has attained many insights and realizations through this means. Besides being *brahminically* initiated, Stephen has also been to India more than 20 times and traveled extensively throughout the country, visiting most of the major holy places and gaining a wide variety of spiritual experiences that only such places can give. He has also spent nearly 40 years in the management of various Krishna temples.

Stephen has put the culmination of nearly 50 years of continuous research and travel experience into his books in an effort to share it with those who are also looking for spiritual understanding. More books are forthcoming, so stay in touch through his website to find out further developments.

More information about Stephen, his projects, books, free ebooks, and numerous articles and videos can be found on his website at: www.stephen-knapp.com or http://stephenknapp.info or his blog at http://stephenknapp.wordpress.com.

Stephen has continued to write books that include *The Eastern Answers to the Mysteries of Life* series:
1. *The Secret Teachings of the Vedas: The Eastern Answers to the Mysteries of Life*
2. *The Universal Path to Enlightenment*
3. *The Vedic Prophecies: A New Look into the Future*
4. *How the Universe was Created and Our Purpose In It*

He has also written:
5. *Toward World Peace: Seeing the Unity Between Us All*
6. *Facing Death: Welcoming the Afterlife*
7. *The Key to Real Happiness*
8. *Proof of Vedic Culture's Global Existence*
9. *The Heart of Hinduism: The Eastern Path to Freedom, Enlightenment and Illumination*
10. *The Power of the Dharma: An Introduction to Hinduism and Vedic Culture*
11. *Vedic Culture: The Difference it can Make in Your Life*
12. *Reincarnation & Karma: How They Really Affect Us*
13. *The Eleventh Commandment: The Next Step for Social Spiritual Development*
14. *Seeing Spiritual India: A Guide to Temples, Holy Sites, Festivals and Traditions*
15. *Crimes Against India: And the Need to Protect its Ancient Vedic Tradition*
16. *Yoga and Meditation: Their Real Purpose and How to Get Started*

17. *Avatars, Gods and Goddesses of Vedic Culture: Understanding the Characteristics, Powers and Positions of the Hindu Divinities*
18. *The Soul: Understanding Our Real Identity*
19. *Prayers, Mantras and Gayatris: A Collection for Insights, Protection, Spiritual Growth, and Many Other Blessings*
20. *Krishna Deities and Their Miracles: How the Images of Lord Krishna Interact with Their Devotees*
21. *Defending Vedic Dharma: Tackling the Issues to Make a Difference*
22. *Advancements of the Ancient Vedic Culture*
23. *Spreading Vedic Traditions Through Temples*
24. *The Bhakti-yoga Handbook*
25. *Lord Krishna and His Essential Teachings*
26. *Mysteries of the Ancient Vedic Empire*
27. *Casteism in India*
28. *Ancient History of Vedic Culture*
29. *A Complete Review of Vedic Literature*
30. *Destined for Infinity,* an exciting novel for those who prefer lighter reading, or learning spiritual knowledge in the context of an action oriented, spiritual adventure.

# THE BOOKS BY STEPHEN KNAPP

If you have enjoyed this book, or if you are serious about finding higher levels of real spiritual Truth, and learning more about the mysteries of India's Vedic culture, then you will also want to get other books written by Stephen Knapp, which include:

## *The Secret Teachings of the Vedas*
### The Eastern Answers to the Mysteries of Life

This book presents the essence of the ancient Eastern philosophy and summarizes some of the most elevated and important of all spiritual knowledge. This enlightening information is explained in a clear and concise way and is essential for all who want to increase their spiritual understanding, regardless of what their religious background may be. If you are looking for a book to give you an in-depth introduction to the Vedic spiritual knowledge, and to get you started in real spiritual understanding, this is the book!

The topics include: What is your real spiritual identity; the Vedic explanation of the soul; scientific evidence that consciousness is separate from but interacts with the body; the real unity between us all; how to attain the highest happiness and freedom from the cause of suffering; the law of karma and reincarnation; the karma of a nation; where you are really going in life; the real process of progressive evolution; life after death—heaven, hell, or beyond; a description of the spiritual realm; the nature of the Absolute Truth—personal God or impersonal force; recognizing the existence of the Supreme; the reason why we exist at all; and much more. This book provides the answers to questions not found in other religions or philosophies, and condenses information from a wide variety of sources that would take a person years to assemble. It also contains many quotations from the Vedic texts to let the texts speak for themselves, and to show the knowledge the Vedas have held for thousands of years. It also explains the history and origins of the Vedic literature. This book has been called one of the best reviews of Eastern philosophy available.

Trim size 6"x9", 320 pages, ISBN: 0-9617410-1-5, $14.95.

# *The Vedic Prophecies*
## A New Look into the Future

The Vedic prophecies take you to the end of time! This is the first book ever to present the unique predictions found in the ancient Vedic texts of India. These prophecies are like no others and will provide you with a very different view of the future and how things fit together in the plan for the universe.

Now you can discover the amazing secrets that are hidden in the oldest spiritual writings on the planet. Find out what they say about the distant future, and what the seers of long ago saw in their visions of the destiny of the world.

This book will reveal predictions of deteriorating social changes and how to avoid them; future droughts and famines; low-class rulers and evil governments; whether there will be another appearance (second coming) of God; and predictions of a new spiritual awareness and how it will spread around the world. You will also learn the answers to such questions as:

- Does the future get worse or better?
- Will there be future world wars or global disasters?
- What lies beyond the predictions of Nostradamus, the Mayan prophecies, or the Biblical apocalypse?
- Are we in the end times? How to recognize them if we are.
- Does the world come to an end? If so, when and how?

Now you can find out what the future holds. The Vedic Prophecies carry an important message and warning for all humanity, which needs to be understood now!

Trim size 6"x9", 325 pages, ISBN:0-9617410-4-X, $20.95.

# *How the Universe was Created And Our Purpose In It*

This book provides answers and details about the process of creation that are not available in any other traditions, religions, or areas of science. It offers the oldest rendition of the creation and presents insights into the spiritual purpose of it and what we are really meant to do here.

Every culture in the world and most religions have their own descriptions of the creation, and ideas about from where we came and what we should do. Unfortunately, these are often short and generalized versions that lack details. Thus, they are often given no better regard than myths. However, there are descriptions that give more elaborate explanations of how the cosmic creation fully manifested which are found in the ancient Vedic *Puranas* of India, some of the oldest spiritual writings on the planet. These descriptions provide the details and answers that other versions leave out. Furthermore, these Vedic descriptions often agree, and sometimes disagree, with the modern scientific theories of creation, and offer some factors that science has yet to consider.

Now, with this book, we can get a clearer understanding of how this universe appears, what is its real purpose, from where we really came, how we fit into the plan for the universe, and if there is a way out of here. Some of the many topics included are:

- Comparisons between other creation legends.
- Detailed descriptions of the dawn of creation and how the material energy developed and caused the formation of the cosmos.
- What is the primary source of the material and spiritual elements.
- Insights into the primal questions of, "Who am I? Why am I here? Where have I come from? What is the purpose of this universe and my life?"
- An alternative description of the evolutionary development of the various forms of life.
- Seeing beyond the temporary nature of the material worlds, and more.

This book will provide some of the most profound insights into these questions and topics. It will also give any theist more information and understanding about how the universe is indeed a creation of God.

This book is 6" x 9" trim size, $19.95, 308 pages, ISBN: 1456460455.

# *Proof of Vedic Culture's Global Existence*

This book provides evidence which makes it clear that the ancient Vedic culture was once a global society. Even today we can see its influence in any part of the world. Thus, it becomes obvious that before the world became full of distinct and separate cultures, religions and countries, it was once united in a common brotherhood of Vedic culture, with common standards, principles, and representations of God.

No matter what we may consider our present religion, society or country, we are all descendants of this ancient global civilization. Thus, the Vedic culture is the parent of all humanity and the original ancestor of all religions. In this way, we all share a common heritage.

This book is an attempt to allow humanity to see more clearly its universal roots. This book provides a look into:
- How Vedic knowledge was given to humanity by the Supreme.
- The history and traditional source of the Vedas and Vedic Aryan society.
- Who were the original Vedic Aryans. How Vedic society was a global influence and what shattered this world-wide society. How Sanskrit faded from being a global language.
- Many scientific discoveries over the past several centuries are only rediscoveries of what the Vedic literature already knew.
- How the origins of world literature are found in India and Sanskrit.
- The links between the Vedic and other ancient cultures, such as the Sumerians, Persians, Egyptians, Romans, Greeks, and others.
- Links between the Vedic tradition and Judaism, Christianity, Islam, and Buddhism.
- How many of the western holy sites, churches, and mosques were once the sites of Vedic holy places and sacred shrines.
- The Vedic influence presently found in such countries as Britain, France, Russia, Greece, Israel, Arabia, China, Japan, and in areas of Scandinavia, the Middle East, Africa, the South Pacific, and the Americas.
- Uncovering the truth of India's history: Powerful evidence that shows how many mosques and Muslim buildings were once opulent Vedic temples, including the Taj Mahal, Delhi's Jama Masjid, Kutab Minar, as well as buildings in many other cities, such as Agra, Ahmedabad, Bijapur, etc.
- How there is presently a need to plan for the survival of Vedic culture.

This book is sure to provide some amazing facts and evidence about the truth of world history and the ancient, global Vedic Culture. This book has enough startling information and historical evidence to cause a major shift in the way we view religious history and the basis of world traditions.

This book is 6"x9" trim size, 431 pages, ISBN: 978-1-4392-4648-1, $20.99.

# *Toward World Peace: Seeing the Unity Between Us All*

This book points out the essential reasons why peace in the world and cooperation amongst people, communities, and nations have been so difficult to establish. It also advises the only way real peace and harmony amongst humanity can be achieved.

In order for peace and unity to exist we must first realize what barriers and divisions keep us apart. Only then can we break through those barriers to see the unity that naturally exists between us all. Then, rather than focus on our differences, it is easier to recognize our similarities and common goals. With a common goal established, all of humanity can work together to help each other reach that destiny.

This book is short and to the point. It is a thought provoking book and will provide inspiration for anyone. It is especially useful for those working in politics, religion, interfaith, race relations, the media, the United Nations, teaching, or who have a position of leadership in any capacity. It is also for those of us who simply want to spread the insights needed for bringing greater levels of peace, acceptance, unity, and equality between friends, neighbours, and communities. Such insights include:
- The factors that keep us apart.
- Breaking down cultural distinctions.
- Breaking down the religious differences.
- Seeing through bodily distinctions.
- We are all working to attain the same things.
- Our real identity: The basis for common ground.
- Seeing the Divinity within each of us.
- What we can do to bring unity between everyone we meet.

This book carries an important message and plan of action that we must incorporate into our lives and plans for the future if we intend to ever bring peace and unity between us.

This book is $6.95, 90 pages, 6" x 9" trim size, ISBN: 1452813744.

# *Facing Death*
## *Welcoming the Afterlife*

Many people are afraid of death, or do not know how to prepare for it nor what to expect. So this book is provided to relieve anyone of the fear that often accompanies the thought of death, and to supply a means to more clearly understand the purpose of it and how we can use it to our advantage. It will also help the survivors of the departed souls to better understand what has happened and how to cope with it. Furthermore, it shows that death is not a tragedy, but a natural course of events meant to help us reach our destiny.

This book is easy to read, with soothing and comforting wisdom, along with stories of people who have been with departing souls and what they have experienced. It is written especially for those who have given death little thought beforehand, but now would like to have some preparedness for what may need to be done regarding the many levels of the experience and what might take place during this transition.

To assist you in preparing for your own death, or that of a loved one, you will find guidelines for making one's final days as peaceful and as smooth as possible, both physically and spiritually. Preparing for death can transform your whole outlook in a positive way, if understood properly. Some of the topics in the book include:

- The fear of death and learning to let go.
- The opportunity of death: The portal into the next life.
- This earth and this body are no one's real home, so death is natural.
- Being practical and dealing with the final responsibilities.
- Forgiving yourself and others before you go.
- Being the assistant of one leaving this life.
- Connecting with the person inside the disease.
- Surviving the death of a loved one.
- Stories of being with dying, and an amazing near-death-experience.
- Connecting to the spiritual side of death.
- What happens while leaving the body.
- What difference the consciousness makes during death, and how to attain the best level of awareness to carry you through it, or what death will be like and how to prepare for it, this book will help you. Retail Price, $13.95, 135 pages, 6"x9" trim size, .

# *The Key to Real Happiness*

This book is actually a guide to one of the prime purposes of life. Naturally everyone wants to be happy. Why else do we keep living and working? Now you can find greater levels of happiness and fulfillment. Using this knowledge from the East, you can get clear advice on the path for reaching an independent and uninterrupted feeling of well-being. This information is sure to open your eyes to higher possibilities. It can awaken you to the natural joy that always exists within your higher Self.

Many people consider happiness as something found with the increase of pleasure and comforts. Others look for position, or ease of living, thrills, or more money and what it can buy. However, by using knowledge from the East and taking an alternative look at what is advised herein, we get guidance on our true position and the means necessary for reaching the happiness for which we always hanker. Some of the topics include:

- What keeps us from being truly happy.
- How all suffering exists only within the illusion.
- Your spiritual Self is beyond all material limitations.
- How to uplift your consciousness.
- How your thoughts and consciousness create your future and determines your state of happiness and outlook on life.
- How to defend yourself from negativity.
- How real independent and self-sufficient happiness is already within you, and how to unveil it.
- How to enjoy that ever-existing pleasure within.
- This book and its easy to understand information will show you how to experience real happiness and joy, and reach the spiritual level, the platform of the soul, beyond the temporary nature of the mind and body.

Retail Price: $6.95, 95 pages, trim size 5 1/2" x 8 1/2", ISBN: 1-930627-04-1.

# *Destined for Infinity*

Deep within the mystical and spiritual practices of India are doors that lead to various levels of both higher and lower planes of existence. Few people from the outside are ever able to enter into the depths of these practices to experience such levels of reality.

This is the story of the mystical adventure of a man, Roman West, who entered deep into the secrets of India where few other Westerners have been able to penetrate. While living with a master in the Himalayan foothills and traveling the mystical path that leads to the Infinite, he witnesses the amazing powers the mystics can achieve and undergoes some of the most unusual experiences of his life. Under the guidance of a master that he meets in the mountains, he gradually develops mystic abilities of his own and attains the sacred vision of the enlightened sages and enters the unfathomable realm of Infinity. However, his peaceful life in the hills comes to an abrupt end when he is unexpectedly forced to confront the powerful forces of darkness that have been unleashed by an evil Tantric priest to kill both Roman and his master. His only chance to defeat the intense forces of darkness depends on whatever spiritual strength he has been able to develop.

This story includes traditions and legends that have existed for hundreds and thousands of years. All of the philosophy, rituals, mystic powers, forms of meditation, and descriptions of the Absolute are authentic and taken from narrations found in many of the sacred books of the East, or gathered by the author from his own experiences in India and information from various sages themselves.

This book will prepare you to perceive the multi-dimensional realities that exist all around us, outside our sense perception. This is a book that will give you many insights into the broad possibilities of our life and purpose in this world.

Published by iUniverse.com, 255 pages, 6" x 9" trim size, $16.95, ISBN: 0-595-33959-X.

# *Reincarnation and Karma: How They Really Affect Us*

Everyone may know a little about reincarnation, but few understand the complexities and how it actually works. Now you can find out how reincarnation and karma really affect us. Herein all of the details are provided on how a person is implicated for better or worse by their own actions. You will understand why particular situations in life happen, and how to make improvements for one's future. You will see why it appears that bad things happen to good people, or even why good things happen to bad people, and what can be done about it.

Other topics include:
- Reincarnation recognized throughout the world
- The most ancient teachings on reincarnation
- Reincarnation in Christianity
- How we transmigrate from one body to another
- Life between lives
- Going to heaven or hell
- The reason for reincarnation
- Free will and choice
- Karma of the nation
- How we determine our own destiny
- What our next life may be like
- Becoming free from all karma and how to prepare to make our next life the best possible.

Combine this with modern research into past life memories and experiences and you will have a complete view of how reincarnation and karma really operate.

Retail Price, $13.95, 135 pages, 6" x 9" trim size.

# Vedic Culture
## The Difference It Can Make In Your Life

The Vedic culture of India is rooted in Sanatana-dharma, the eternal and universal truths that are beneficial to everyone. It includes many avenues of self-development that an increasing number of people from the West are starting to investigate and use, including:
- Yoga
- Meditation and spiritual practice
- Vedic astrology
- Ayurveda
- Vedic gemology
- Vastu or home arrangement
- Environmental awareness
- Vegetarianism
- Social cooperation and arrangement
- The means for global peace
- And much more

*Vedic Culture: The Difference It Can Make In Your Life* shows the advantages of the Vedic paths of improvement and self-discovery that you can use in your life to attain higher personal awareness, happiness, and fulfillment. It also provides a new view of what these avenues have to offer from some of the most prominent writers on Vedic culture in the West, who discovered how it has affected and benefited their own lives. They write about what it has done for them and then explain how their particular area of interest can assist others. The noted authors include, David Frawley, Subhash Kak, Chakrapani Ullal, Michael Cremo, Jeffrey Armstrong, Robert Talyor, Howard Beckman, Andy Fraenkel, George Vutetakis, Pratichi Mathur, Dhan Rousse, Arun Naik, Parama Karuna Devi, and Stephen Knapp, all of whom have numerous authored books or articles of their own.

For the benefit of individuals and social progress, the Vedic system is as relevant today as it was in ancient times. Discover why there is a growing renaissance in what the Vedic tradition has to offer in *Vedic Culture*.

Published by iUniverse.com, 300 pages, 6"x 9" trim size, $22.95, ISBN: 0-595-37120-5.

# The Power of the Dharma
## An Introduction to Hinduism and Vedic Culture

*The Power of the Dharma* offers you a concise and easy-to-understand overview of the essential principles and customs of Hinduism and the reasons for them. It provides many insights into the depth and value of the timeless wisdom of Vedic spirituality and why the Dharmic path has survived for so many hundreds of years. It reveals why the Dharma is presently enjoying a renaissance of an increasing number of interested people who are exploring its teachings and seeing what its many techniques of Self-discovery have to offer.

Herein you will find:
- Quotes by noteworthy people on the unique qualities of Hinduism
- Essential principles of the Vedic spiritual path
- Particular traits and customs of Hindu worship and explanations of them
- Descriptions of the main Yoga systems
- The significance and legends of the colorful Hindu festivals
- Benefits of Ayurveda, Vastu, Vedic astrology and gemology,
- Important insights of Dharmic life and how to begin.

The Dharmic path can provide you the means for attaining your own spiritual realizations and experiences. In this way it is as relevant today as it was thousands of years ago. This is the power of the Dharma since its universal teachings have something to offer anyone.

Published by iUniverse.com, 170 pages, 6" x 9" trim size, $16.95, ISBN: 0-595-39352-7.

# Seeing Spiritual India
## A Guide to Temples, Holy Sites, Festivals and Traditions

This book is for anyone who wants to know of the many holy sites that you can visit while traveling within India, how to reach them, and what is the history and significance of these most spiritual of sacred sites, temples, and festivals. It also provides a deeper understanding of the mysteries and spiritual traditions of India.

This book includes:
- Descriptions of the temples and their architecture, and what you will see at each place.
- Explanations of holy places of Hindus, Buddhists, Sikhs, Jains, Parsis, and Muslims.
- The spiritual benefits a person acquires by visiting them.
- Convenient itineraries to take to see the most of each area of India, which is divided into East, Central, South, North, West, the Far Northeast, and Nepal.
- Packing list suggestions and how to prepare for your trip, and problems to avoid.
- How to get the best experience you can from your visit to India.
- How the spiritual side of India can positively change you forever.

This book goes beyond the usual descriptions of the typical tourist attractions and opens up the spiritual venue waiting to be revealed for a far deeper experience on every level.

Published by iUniverse.com, 592 pages, $33.95, ISBN: 978-0-595-50291-2.

# Crimes Against India:
## And the Need to Protect its Ancient Vedic Traditions

### 1000 Years of Attacks Against Hinduism and What to Do about It

India has one of the oldest and most dynamic cultures of the world. Yet, many people do not know of the many attacks, wars, atrocities and sacrifices that Indian people have had to undergo to protect and preserve their country and spiritual tradition over the centuries. Many people also do not know of the many ways in which this profound heritage is being attacked and threatened today, and what we can do about it.

Therefore, some of the topics included are:
- How there is a war against Hinduism and its yoga culture.
- The weaknesses of India that allowed invaders to conquer her.
- Lessons from India's real history that should not be forgotten.
- The atrocities committed by the Muslim invaders, and how they tried to destroy Vedic culture and its many temples, and slaughtered thousands of Indian Hindus.
- How the British viciously exploited India and its people for its resources.
- How the cruelest of all Christian Inquisitions in Goa tortured and killed thousands of Hindus.
- Action plans for preserving and strengthening Vedic India.
- How all Hindus must stand up and be strong for Sanatana-dharma, and promote the cooperation and unity for a Global Vedic Community.

India is a most resilient country, and is presently becoming a great economic power in the world. It also has one of the oldest and dynamic cultures the world has ever known, but few people seem to understand the many trials and difficulties that the country has faced, or the present problems India is still forced to deal with in preserving the culture of the majority Hindus who live in the country. This is described in the real history of the country, which a decreasing number of people seem to recall.

Therefore, this book is to honor the efforts that have been shown by those in the past who fought and worked to protect India and its culture, and to help preserve India as the homeland of a living and dynamic Vedic tradition of Sanatana-dharma (the eternal path of duty and wisdom).

Available. 370 pages, $24.95, ISBN: 978-1-4401-1158-7.

# *Yoga and Meditation Their Real Purpose and How to Get Started*

Yoga is a nonsectarian spiritual science that has been practiced and developed over thousands of years. The benefits of yoga are numerous. On the mental level it strengthens concentration, determination, and builds a stronger character that can more easily sustain various tensions in our lives for peace of mind. The assortment of *asanas* or postures also provide stronger health and keeps various diseases in check. They improve physical strength, endurance and flexibility. These are some of the goals of yoga.

Its ultimate purpose is to raise our consciousness to directly perceive the spiritual dimension. Then we can have our own spiritual experiences. The point is that the more spiritual we become, the more we can perceive that which is spiritual. As we develop and grow in this way through yoga, the questions about spiritual life are no longer a mystery to solve, but become a reality to experience. It becomes a practical part of our lives. This book will show you how to do that. Some of the topics include:

- Benefits of yoga
- The real purpose of yoga
- The types of yoga, such as Hatha yoga, Karma yoga, Raja and Astanga yogas, Kundalini yoga, Bhakti yoga, Mudra yoga, Mantra yoga, and others.
- The Chakras and Koshas
- Asanas and postures, and the Surya Namaskar
- Pranayama and breathing techniques for inner changes
- Deep meditation and how to proceed
- The methods for using mantras
- Attaining spiritual enlightenment, and much more

This book is 6"x9" trim size, $17.95, 240 pages, 32 illustration, ISBN: 1451553269.

# *Avatars, Gods and Goddesses of Vedic Culture*

## The Characteristics, Powers and Positions of the Hindu Divinities

Understanding the assorted Divinities or gods and goddesses of the Vedic or Hindu pantheon is not so difficult as some people may think when it is presented simply and effectively. And that is what you will find in this book. This will open you to many of the possibilities and potentials of the Vedic tradition, and show how it has been able to cater to and fulfill the spiritual needs and development of so many people since time immemorial. Here you will find there is something for everyone.

This takes you into the heart of the deep, Vedic spiritual knowledge of how to perceive the Absolute Truth, the Supreme and the various powers and agents of the universal creation. This explains the characteristics and nature of the Vedic Divinities and their purposes, powers, and the ways they influence and affect the natural energies of the universe. It also shows how they can assist us and that blessings from them can help our own spiritual and material development and potentialities, depending on what we need.

Some of the Vedic Divinities that will be explained include Lord Krishna, Vishnu, Their main avatars and expansions, along with Brahma, Shiva, Ganesh, Murugan, Surya, Hanuman, as well as the goddesses of Sri Radha, Durga, Sarasvati, Lakshmi, and others. This also presents explanations of their names, attributes, dress, weapons, instruments, the meaning of the Shiva lingam, and some of the legends and stories that are connected with them. This will certainly give you a new insight into the expansive nature of the Vedic tradition.

This book is: $17.95 retail, 230 pages, 11 black & white photos, ISBN: 1453613765, EAN: 9781453613764.

# *The Soul*
# Understanding Our Real Identity
## The Key to Spiritual Awakening

This book provides a summarization of the most essential spiritual knowledge that will give you the key to spiritual awakening. The descriptions will give you greater insights and a new look at who and what you really are as a spiritual being.

The idea that we are more than merely these material bodies is pervasive. It is established in every religion and spiritual path in this world. However, many religions only hint at the details of this knowledge, but if we look around we will find that practically the deepest and clearest descriptions of the soul and its characteristics are found in the ancient Vedic texts of India.

Herein you will find some of the most insightful spiritual knowledge and wisdom known to mankind. Some of the topics include:

- How you are more than your body
- The purpose of life
- Spiritual ignorance of the soul is the basis of illusion and suffering
- The path of spiritual realization
- How the soul is eternal
- The unbounded nature of the soul
- What is the Supersoul
- Attaining direct spiritual perception and experience of our real identity

This book will give you a deeper look into the ancient wisdom of India's Vedic, spiritual culture, and the means to recognize your real identity.

This book is 5 1/2"x8 1/2" trim size, 130 pages, $7.95, ISBN: 1453733833.

# *Prayers, Mantras and Gayatris*
## A Collection for Insights, Spiritual Growth, Protection, and Many Other Blessings

Using mantras or prayers can help us do many things, depending on our intention. First of all, it is an ancient method that has been used successfully to raise our consciousness, our attitude, aim of life, and outlook, and prepare ourselves for perceiving higher states of being.

The Sanskrit mantras within this volume offer such things as the knowledge and insights for spiritual progress, including higher perceptions and understandings of the Absolute or God, as well as the sound vibrations for awakening our higher awareness, invoking the positive energies to help us overcome obstacles and oppositions, or to assist in healing our minds and bodies from disease or negativity. They can provide the means for requesting protection on our spiritual path, or from enemies, ghosts, demons, or for receiving many other benefits. In this way, they offer a process for acquiring blessings of all kinds, both material and spiritual. There is something for every need. Some of what you will find includes:

- The most highly recommended mantras for spiritual realization in this age.
- A variety of prayers and gayatris to Krishna, Vishnu and other avatars, Goddess Lakshmi for financial well-being, Shiva, Durga, Ganesh, Devi, Indra, Sarasvati, etc., and Surya the Sun-god, the planets, and for all the days of the week.
- Powerful prayers of spiritual insight in Shiva's Song, along with the Bhaja Govindam by Sri Adi Shankaracharya, the Purusha Sukta, Brahma-samhita, Isha Upanishad, Narayana Suktam, and Hanuman Chalisa.
- Prayers and mantras to Sri Chaitanya and Nityananda.
- Strong prayers for protection from Lord Narasimha. The protective shield from Lord Narayana.
- Lists of the 108 names of Lord Krishna, Radhika, Goddess Devi, Shiva, and Sri Rama.
- The Vishnu-Sahasranama or thousand names of Vishnu, Balarama, Gopala, Radharani, and additional lists of the sacred names of the Vedic Divinities;
- And many other prayers, mantras and stotras for an assortment of blessings and benefits.

This book is 6"x9" trim size, 760 pages, ISBN:1456545906, $31.95.

# *Krishna Deities and Their Miracles*
## How the Images of Lord Krishna Interact with Their Devotees

This book helps reveal how the Deities of Krishna in the temple are but another channel through which the Divine can be better understood and perceived. In fact, the Deities Themselves can exhibit what some would call miracles in the way They reveal how the Divine accepts the Deity form. These miracles between the Deities of Krishna and His devotees happen in many different ways, and all the time. This is one process through which Krishna, or the Supreme Being, reveals Himself and the reality of His existence. Stories of such miracles or occurrences extend through the ages up to modern times, and all around the world. This book relates an assortment of these events to show how the images in the temples have manifested Their personality and character in various ways in Their pastimes with Their devotees, whether it be for developing their devotion, instructing them, or simply giving them His kindness, mercy or inspiration.

This book helps show that the Supreme Reality is a person who plays and exhibits His pastimes in any manner He likes. This is also why worship of the Deity in the temple has been and remains a primary means of increasing one's devotion and connection with the Supreme Being.

Besides presenting stories of the reciprocation that can exist between Krishna in His Deity form and the ordinary living beings, other topics include:

- The antiquity of devotion to the Deity in the Vedic tradition.
- Historical sites of ancient Deity worship.
- Scriptural instructions and references to Deity veneration.
- The difference between idols and Deities.
- What is darshan and the significance of Deities.
- Why God would even take the initiative to reveal Himself to His devotees and accept the position of being a Deity.

This book will give deeper insight into the unlimited personality and causeless benevolence of the Supreme, especially to those who become devoted to Him.

This book is 6"x9" trim size, 210 pages, $14.95, ISBN: 1463734298.

# *Advancements of Ancient India's Vedic Culture*
## The Planet's Earliest Civilization and How it Influenced the World

This book shows how the planet's earliest civilization lead the world in both material and spiritual progress. From the Vedic culture of ancient India thousands of years ago, we find for example the origins of mathematics, especially algebra and geometry, as well as early astronomy and planetary observations, many instances of which can be read in the historical Vedic texts. Medicine in Ayurveda was the first to prescribe herbs for the remedy of disease, surgical instruments for operations, and more.

Other developments that were far superior and ahead of the rest of the world included:
- Writing and language, especially the development of sophisticated Sanskrit;
- Metallurgy and making the best known steel at the time;
- Ship building and global maritime trade;
- Textiles and the dying of fabric for which India was known all over the world;
- Agricultural and botanical achievements;
- Precise Vedic arts in painting, dance and music;
- The educational systems and the most famous of the early universities, like Nalanda and Takshashila;
- The source of individual freedom and fair government, and the character and actions of rulers;
- Military and the earliest of martial arts;
- Along with some of the most intricate, deep and profound of all philosophies and spiritual paths, which became the basis of many religions that followed later around the world.

These and more are the developments that came from India, much of which has been forgotten, but should again be recognized as the heritage of the ancient Indian Vedic tradition that continues to inspire humanity.

This book is 6"x9" trim size, 350 pages, $20.95, ISBN: 1477607897.

# *The Bhakti-yoga Handbook*
## A Guide for Beginning the Essentials of Devotional Yoga

This book is a guide for anyone who wants to begin the practice of bhakti-yoga in a practical and effective way. This supplies the information, the principles, the regular activities or *sadhana*, and how to have the right attitude in applying ourselves to attain success on the path of bhakti-yoga, which is uniting with God through love and devotion.

This outlines a general schedule for our daily spiritual activities and a typical morning program as found in most Krishna temples that are centered around devotional yoga. In this way, you will find the explanations on how to begin our day and set our mind, what meditations to do, which spiritual texts are best to study, and how we can make most everything we do as part of bhakti-yoga. All of these can be adjusted in a way that can be practiced and applied by anyone by anyone regardless of whether you are in a temple ashrama or in your own home or apartment.

Such topics include:
- The secret of bhakti-yoga and its potency in this day and age,
- The essential morning practice, the best time for meditation,
- The standard songs and mantras that we can use, as applied in most Krishna temples,
- Understanding the basics of the Vedic spiritual philosophy, such as karma, reincarnation, the Vedic description of the soul, etc.,
- How Vedic culture is still as relevant today as ever,
- Who is Sri Krishna,
- How to chant the Hare Krishna mantra,
- Standards for temple etiquette,
- The nine processes of bhakti-yoga, a variety of activities from which anyone can utilize,
- How to make our career a part of the yoga process,
- How to turn our cooking into bhakti-yoga,
- How to set up a home altar or temple room, depending on what standard you wish to establish,
- How to take care of deities in our home, if we have Them,
- How to perform the basic ceremonies like arati,
- How to take care of the Tulasi plant if you have one,
- And the spiritual results you can expect to attain through this yoga.

All of the basics and effective applications to get started and continue with your practice of bhakti-yoga is supplied so you can progress in a steady way, from beginner to advanced.

This is 278 pages, $14.95, ISBN: 149030228X.

# Lord Krishna and His Essential Teachings
## If God Were to Tell You the Truth About Life, This Is It

If God were to tell you the truth about life, this is it, or as close to it as you are going to find. Often times we go through life and occasionally find ourselves confused about why are we here, or what we are supposed to do. That is normal when we do not have proper knowledge or guidance. But such insight is available if we know where to look for it.

Some of the most plentiful, prominent and clearly defined spiritual teachings of all are found in the Vedic tradition, especially those that have been given to us by Lord Sri Krishna Himself. He has provided some of the most elaborate, detailed and direct of all spiritual knowledge that can be acquired by anyone. Therefore, this book uses numerous verses of Lord Krishna's directions as found in the various Vedic texts, all divided according to topic. So here is the heart or essential spiritual message of what Lord Krishna has given for the benefit of all mankind so we can progress onward and upward from whatever position we may find ourselves in this material world.

Some of the topics include:
- Who is Krishna, evidence from the ancient texts
- The most secret of all knowledge about life
- The rarity of human birth
- The real purpose of this creation
- How to perceive our spiritual identity
- How to practice mystic yoga
- Description of the Supersoul
- The way to meditate
- How to be a spiritual person in this material world
- The highest levels of spiritual enlightenment
- How to follow the process of bhakti or devotional yoga
- How bhakti frees us from past karma
- The importance of *Bhagavad-gita* in this day and age, and much more.

The instructions of Lord Krishna are like the comforting nectar that can warm the heart and soothe the soul.

This is 290 pages, $18.95, ISBN: 1499655878

# Mysteries of the Ancient Vedic Empire
Recognizing Vedic Contributions to Other Cultures Around the World

The Vedic culture is accepted by numerous scholars as one of the most sophisticated civilizations to appear after the last glacial period of 12,000 years ago. It developed in ancient India, and as the people populated the region, they also expanded and spread into other parts of the planet, taking much of their culture with them.

This book takes us on a journey through history and across many countries as we point out similarities and remnants of the Vedic tradition that remain there to this day. These include forms of art, philosophy, religion, architecture, temples, ways of living, and so on. Such countries include: Nepal, Burma, Cambodia, Thailand, Vietnam, Korea, Malaysia, Indonesia, Sri Lanka, Egypt, Africa, the Middle East, Iraq, Afghanistan, Syria, Central Asia, Greece, Italy, Germany, Russia, Ireland, Scandinavia, the Americas, and more.

This book also explains:
- How many religions in the world have features that clearly descended from the oldest form of spiritual knowledge and truth as found in Vedic Dharma.
- How Vedic Dharma is still relevant today and can help establish peace through its timeless spiritual wisdom.
- It also helps unravel and reveal the true nature of the Vedic civilization, and how and why it infiltrated and contributed to so many areas and cultures of the world.
- It also shows a mysterious side of history that few others have recognized.

This book will help anyone understand how the advanced nature of the Vedic civilization and its universal spiritual principles fit into the development of so many other cultures and still contributes to the upliftment of society today.

This book is the follow-up of a previous volume called Proof of Vedic Culture's Global Existence, but with completely different information and resources, as well as updates, written in a more academic style, using hundreds of references, quotes and notes to verify all the information that is used.

This book is 460 pages, 6" x 9" trim size, $22.95, ISBN - 10: 1514394855, ISBN - 13: 978-1514394854.

# A Complete Review of Vedic Literature
## India's Ancient Library of Spiritual Knowledge

The Vedic texts of India provide some of the highest levels of spiritual knowledge known to man. But it is not just one book, it is a complete library that offers explanations of many aspects of spiritual development, and of the Absolute Truth, or God. These also describe the processes by which a person can directly perceive and attain the Supreme and enter the spiritual realm.

This book shows how these many texts fit together, their divisions, the supplements, what information they contain, and their philosophical conclusions. The contents of this book include:
Understanding the Spiritual Truths in Vedic Literature;
If You are New to the Study of Vedic Culture;
The Four Primary Vedas;
The Brahmanas and Aranyakas;
The Upanishads;
The Upa-Vedas and Vedangas;
The Sutras and Supplements;
The Smritis;
The Vedanta and Vedanta-Sutras;
The Itihasas;
A Review of the Puranas;
The Srimad-Bhagavatam;
The Preeminent Nature of the Srimad-Bhagavatam;
Different Paths in the Vedic literature;
The Ultimate Path to the Absolute.

This book is 106 pages, 5 ½"x8 ½", Paperback $5.99, and Kindle Ebook $1.99. ISBN-10: 1547278862.

# www.Stephen-Knapp.com
# http://stephenknapp.info
# http://stephenknapp.wordpress.com

Be sure to visit Stephen's web site. It provides lots of information on many spiritual aspects of Vedic and spiritual philosophy, and Indian culture for both beginners and the scholarly. You will find:

- All the descriptions and contents of Stephen's books, how to order them, and keep up with any new books or articles that he has written.
- Reviews and unsolicited letters from readers who have expressed their appreciation for his books, as well as his website.
- Free online booklets are also available for your use or distribution on meditation, why be a Hindu, how to start yoga, meditation, etc.
- Helpful prayers, mantras, gayatris, and devotional songs.
- Over two hundred enlightening articles that can help answer many questions about life, the process of spiritual development, the basics of the Vedic path, or how to broaden our spiritual awareness. Many of these are emailed among friends or posted on other web sites.
- Over 150 color photos taken by Stephen during his travels through India. There are also descriptions and 40 photos of the huge and amazing Kumbha Mela festival.
- Photographic exhibit of the Vedic influence in the Taj Mahal, questioning whether it was built by Shah Jahan or a pre-existing Vedic building.
- A large list of links to additional websites to help you continue your exploration of Eastern philosophy, or provide more information and news about India, Hinduism, ancient Vedic culture, Vaishnavism, Hare Krishna sites, travel, visas, catalogs for books and paraphernalia, holy places, etc.
- A large resource for vegetarian recipes, information on its benefits, how to get started, ethnic stores, or non-meat ingredients and supplies.
- A large "Krishna Darshan Art Gallery" of photos and prints of Krishna and Vedic divinities. You can also find a large collection of previously unpublished photos of His Divine Grace A. C. Bhaktivedanta Swami.

This site is made as a practical resource for your use and is continually being updated and expanded with more articles, resources, and information. Be sure to check it out.